The Experts Praise *The Catalog Strategist's Toolkit*

The best investment you'll make for your catalog all year. Guaranteed. Nobody knows more about successful catalog marketing than Katie Muldoon. This "must have" compendium is chock full of everything that you need to organize your catalog operation so it runs as smoothly and profitably as possible. I was floored to see page after page of step-by-step forms, handy charts and easy-to-use checklists for outsmarting your competition, developing a sure-fire strategic plan, creating a dynamic merchandising strategy, streamlining your creative and production operations, building a successful customer acquisition plan, designing analytical tools that help you and more, It's thirty years of Katie's expertise—the culmination of in-the-trenches successes and learning experiences—all wrapped in one. Buy one. Buy two. Buy ten. Just make sure you BUY this book.

AMY AFRICA
CEO
Creative Results

Finally, a comprehensive g[...]ires! Another great one from one of the Gr[...]or the new-to-the-industry and the seasoned [...]ther book like this one . . . absolutely everyth[...]ome another well-honed tool in your shed o[...]

JILL EASTMAN VIDAL
Director, Third Party Mar[...]
1-800-FLOWERS.COM

Success in direct marketin[...]l of the science of mathematics with the crea[...]relationship, Katie Muldoon has continued to [...]s right and add the magic. Our direct marketi[...]profitable segment of our multi-channel sales [...]reference guide on the desk of every member [...]ing our well-worn copies of Katie's original b[...]g.

MARSHA EVERTON
President & CEO
The Pfaltzgraff Co.

OK, so you're serious about launching a new catalog. . . . Stop right there. . . . Before you do anything read Katie's step-by-step, super practical guide to getting it done. You'll save yourself headaches, time and most importantly, money!

MICHAEL GOTFREDSON
CFO & Chief Runner
Road Runner Sports Catalog

If you're a catalog marketer who thinks you've read everything worth reading, you haven't gotten hold of Katie Muldoon's latest book. Drawing on 30 years of proven experience and industry leadership, Muldoon provides a wide range of blueprints and checklists that effectively guide readers in the successful development and enhancement of catalogs. This information is fresh, practical, and highly relevant in this time of tremendous change in the catalog industry.

JOHN A. GRECO, JR.
President & CEO
Direct Marketing Association

Katie is the best! Nobody knows more.

TODD HATOFF
President
Allen Brothers
The Great Steakhouse Steaks

The best of the best puts it all down for the rest of us to understand in simple terms. Katie Muldoon is to catalog marketing what Stan Fenvessey was to fulfillment. She gives us the roadmap to success.

TIMOTHY J. HOLODY
COO
Seta Corporation

Why didn't someone think of this sooner? Here are all the answers for planning and producing a catalog in an E-Z read, E-Z reference format

Perfect for the busy catalog exec! Quick and easy solutions for any question or problem . . . from strategic planning to merchandising and pagination.

Katie knows what works, and shares it to save you the time and effort of trial and error. Instead of rehashing rote formulas, she gives you both a methodology and a contextual education for thinking about catalog marketing so you can be structured and consistent while still gaining fresh insights with every use.

LIZ KIZLIK
President
Liz Kislik Associates LLC

Only a seasoned catalog expert like Katie could develop so many helpful forms, charts, and checklists to simplify any catalog task.

JIM KOBS
President
Kobs Strategic Consulting

Katie Muldoon is a creative genius; her knowledge of direct marketing, from catalogs to e-commerce is superlative; her contacts with other experts are extensive; her wisdom is invaluable. Best of all, she has been able to translate her verbal expertise to the written word, time and again. Her books are "must reads" for anyone who wants to succeed in direct marketing.

DWIGHT MORRIS
President
Carrot-top Industries, Inc.

Katie Muldoon is the Strategic Catalog Marketing Sensei. She synthesizes art, science and basic human behavior in her methodology designed to maximize the brand building and profit-making potential of any catalog program. Her step-by-step approach makes perfect sense and it really works. And the best part is that it's fun!

KERRY A. NICOLICH
Communications Planning Specialist
Mercedes-Benz USA, LLC

"Katie's direct marketing knowledge and experience are unmatched, if my company could implement half of what she has forgotten we would be twice our size. Buy this book. Read it. Implement what it says. And watch your business grow. It's that easy.

ADAM PRESS
CEO
The St. John Companies, Inc

The most difficult part of most strategic projects is getting started . . . This book goes a long way toward solving that problem for the most critical aspects of the catalog business.

STEVE ROWLEY
President & CEO
Paragon Gifts, Inc.

Katie Muldoon has already written one indispensable book for catalog marketers. Now she has written another one. *The Toolkit* is a virtual blueprint of how to succeed in the catalog business, and how to master its processes.

RAY SCHULTZ
Editorial Director
DIRECT

Katie Muldoon's book offers a smart, knowledgeable and comprehensive guide to catalog marketing. Her strategies and techniques are practical, creative, and very helpful.

LILLIAN VERNON
Founder
Lillian Vernon Corporation

Katie has provided all the in-depth tools for managers, business owners and entrepreneurs, regardless of experience, to pick up critical information to succeed.

CRAIG WINER
Vice President
Garrett Wade Company

The Catalog Strategist's Toolkit

Rules, Tools, Forms and Lists
for Both Printed and Electronic Catalogs

KATIE MULDOON

Evanston, Illinois

© Copyright 2006 Racom Communications

Published by
Racom Communications
1604 Chicago Avenue, Suite 6
Evanston, IL 60202
www.racombooks.com

and

The Direct Marketing Association
1120 Avenue of the Americas
New York, NY 10036-6700
www.the-dma.org

All rights reserved. No part of this book may be reproduced,
stored, in a retrieval system or transmitted in any form or by an means,
electric, electronic, mechanical, photocopying, recording, or
otherwise, without the prior written permission of the Publisher.

Catalog-in-Publication data available from the Library of Congress.

Printed in the United States of America.

ISBN: 0-9704515-9-8

For the two loves of my life:
 Jacob Robert Baer, my husband, Renaissance man, and life's sparkle.
 Patrick James Muldoon, my son, inspiration and pure pleasure.

Contents

Chapter 1 Introduction 1
    How the Tools Came to Be 1
    What Are the Tools? 1
    How to Adapt the Tools 2
    How to Successfully Use the Tools. 3
    Why It Is Worth the Time and Effort to Use These Tools 3
    Who Are the Tools Meant For? 3

Chapter 2 What Is a Catalog? 5
    Printed Catalogs 5
    Electronic Catalogs 6
    Catalog Definition 7
    Catalog Types 7
    Types of Consumer Catalogs 10
    What Is the #1 Reason for Your Catalog to Be? 11
    An Overview of the Process... 12

Chapter 3 Getting Started 17
    Key Needs for the Success of Start-Ups, Add-Ons and/or Updates 17
        Sufficient Financial Backing..................................... 18
        Distinctive, Lasting Positioning 18
        Sufficient Resources in Personnel and Time 19
        Adaptable, Disposable, Seasonally Expandable Product Mix 19
        Appropriate Mindset 20
            SERVICE 20
            CONTROLLED GROWTH 20
            ANALYSIS 21
        Ample, Relatively Readily Accessible Customer Universe 21
        Research: A Real Understanding of Your Customer's Wants and Needs ... 21
    Process Flow 22
    Joint Ventures/Alliances/Affiliates 24

Chapter 4 Researching Your Competition 30
    Determine Who Your Competitors Are 30
    Create a Competitive Grid.. 33

Chapter 5 Researching Your Market 53
Six Simple Research Rules 54
Be Clear About the Goal of the Research 55
Keep the Meaning of the Questions Simple, Direct, Reasonably Short and Clear 55
Always Understand Where the Question You Wish to Ask Will Lead You . 55
Remember That Research Is Only a Guide 56
Use Benchmarking 56
Understand Statistical Validity 56
Printed Research Forms 57
Internet Research Forms 66
Telephone Surveys 70
What a Focus Group Is . . . and Isn't 73

Chapter 6 Scheduling 83
Scheduling the Catalog 83
Feasibility Study 83
Business Review 103

Chapter 7 Launching Your Catalog 108
Launch Catalog Preparation and Implementation 108
The Catalog Plan of Action 109
The Numbers 120

Chapter 8 Organizing for Success 138
Catalog Staff 138
Starting on a Small Scale 139
Expanding the Organization 141
Job Descriptions for Exhibit 8.5 147

Chapter 9 Developing Your Strategy: Brainstorming and Positioning .. 156
Brainstorming/Planning Sessions 156
Positioning Statement 167

Chapter 10 Merchandising 174
Product Strategy 174
Merchandise Criteria 181
The Difference Between a Buyer and a Merchandiser 184
Vendor Contracts 187
Final Selection and Pagination 188

Merchandise Information Forms 194
Pick-Up and Pagination Considerations. 199
Tools for Staying Organized and On Track 201
Managing Merchandise Across Channels 204

Chapter 11 Creative and Production 205
Overview of the Process. 205
Creative Strategy 210
 Customer Profiles. 212
 Brand Statement 213
Pre-Consulting with the Printer 215
The Hand-Off Meeting 217
Writing Great Copy 219
Sizzling and Smart Layouts 221
Making Sure Everything Is Accurate 223
Style Guides = Professional Consistency 227
Photography Types and Techniques, Preparation, Forms, and Legalities 233
 Techniques. 233
 Preparation 234
 Re-shoots 239
 Locations 242
 Forms and Legalities 244
Using an Outside Agency. 248
Pre-Press and DAM (Digital Asset Management). 259
Printing Types and Selection Guidelines. 264
 Paper Primer 266
 Bindery Overview 268
Web Design 269

Chapter 12 Customer Acquisition and Leveraging. 274
Customer Acquisition 275
 List Rental 275
 Circulation Plan. 277
 Pull Marketing 287
 Public Relations. 290
 Media Planning 293
Leveraging 307
 House List Hygiene 307
 Real Contact Strategy 307
 Offers. 311

Contents

Reactivation 311
Your List as a Profit Center 312
E-Mail Marketing 313
Loyalty Programs 314
Package Inserts 318
Code Tracking 319

Chapter 13 Operations as a Marketing Tool 320
Forecasting 322
Response Curves 327
Timely Reports 329
Customer Service Policies 331
Back Orders 335
FTC Mail Order Rule 336
Returns 337
Delivery Costs 341
Packaging 343
Inserts 344
Gift-Wrap, Cards, and Certificates 344

Chapter 14 Basic Analysis 346
Data Capture 346
Merchandise 349
Circulation 359
Seasonality 365
Lifetime Value (LTV) 365
Offer Testing 368
Web Site Analysis 370
Other Forms of Analysis 371
RFM 372
CHAID 372
Regression and Scoring 372
Marketing/Merchandising to the Highest Value House File Segment 373
Prospect Analysis 373

Glossary 374
Index 382
About the Author 387

List of Exhibits

Chapter 2 What Is a Catalog?
    2.1 Biggest Difference Between Consumer and Business Catalogs............. 8

Chapter 3 Getting Started
    3.1 Front-End Process Flow Chart 23
    3.2 Back-End Process Flow Chart 24
    3.3 Checklist: Joint Venture/Alliance................................... 26
    3.4 Checklist: Affiliate Program 28

Chapter 4 Researching Your Competition
    4.1 Competitive Grid Outline 34
    4.2 Competitive Grid Explanations..................................... 36
    4.3 Competitive Grid Example (Core Target Market)...................... 42

Chapter 5 Researching Your Market
    5.1 Research Flow Chart 54
    5.2 Printed Market Research Survey Outline 58
    5.3 Printed Market Research Survey Example 59
    5.4 Internet Market Research Survey Categories......................... 67
    5.5 Internet Market Research Survey Example 68
    5.6 Telephone Survey Flow Chart 72
    5.7 Focus Group Construction Example 73
    5.8 Focus Group Plan Outline... 75
    5.9 Focus Group Plan Example.. 78

Chapter 6 Scheduling
    6.1 Schedule for Start-Up Catalog 84
    6.2 Schedule for Ongoing Catalog 86
    6.3 Feasibility Study/Business Plan Outline.............................. 96
    6.4 Feasibility Study/Business Plan Explanation 100
    6.5 Business Review Materials Needed 104
    6.6 Outline of Common Report Areas for Company Evaluation 106

Chapter 7 Launching Your Catalog
    7.1 Launch Catalog Plan of Action 110

7.2	Financial Plan Development	114
7.3	Start-Up Venture Checklist	119
7.4	Catalog Sales Plan Form	120
7.5	Catalog Sales Plan	123
7.6	Financial Plan Outline	126
7.7	Financial Plan Including Revenue, Cost, Cash Flow, Net Income (Loss)	131

Chapter 8 Organizing for Success

8.1	Job/Functions Chart	138
8.2	Typical Job Descriptions for a Three-Person Staff	139
8.3	Job Descriptions as Catalog Grows	142
8.4	Organization Chart for Exhibit 8.3	145
8.5	Expanded, Internal Organization Chart	146

Chapter 9 Developing Your Strategy: Brainstorming and Positioning

9.1	Strategic Planning Diagram	157
9.2	Strategic Planning/Brainstorming Outline (Form Only)	158
9.3	Strategic Planning/Brainstorming Outline (Example of an Adapted and Completed Form)	162
9.4	Rules Checklist	166
9.5	Positioning Statement Outline	167
9.6	Positioning Statement Explanation	168
9.7	Positioning Statement Example, Consumer	170
9.8	Positioning Statement Example, Business-to-Business	172

Chapter 10 Merchandising

10.1	Product Strategy Form for One Issue	175
10.2	Product Strategy Form One Issue Example	177
10.3	Merchandise Initial Selection Criteria Checklist	181
10.4	Smart Merchandiser's Four Part To Do List	184
10.5	Contract Considerations Checklist	187
10.6	Product Review and Pagination Plan Outline	189
10.7	Final Selection Merchandise Criteria Form	192
10.8	Final Merchandise Criteria Form Example	193
10.9	Merchandise Information Form, Long Version	194
10.10	Merchandise Information Form Explanation	197
10.11	Merchandise Information Form, Short Version	198
10.12	Pick-Up Checklist	199
10.13	Pagination Pointers Checklist	200
10.14	Spread Record Sheet	202
10.15	Spread Record Sheet Example	202
10.16	Initial Pagination Histogram	203

10.17 Optimal Price Range Histogram 204

Chapter 11 Creative and Production

11.1 Basic Creative/Production Work Flow. 206
11.2 Basic Creative/Production Explanation 207
11.3 Creative Strategy Outline 210
11.4 Customer Profile Example. 212
11.5 Creative Model Example. 213
11.6 Printer Checklist and Explanation. 215
11.7 Client Turn-In Checklist 217
11.8 Client Turn-In Checklist Explanation 218
11.9 Best Selling Copy Checklist. 219
11.10 Checklist of What an Artist Needs from You 221
11.11 Checklist of What You Need from an Artist. 222
11.12 Layout Review Checklist (Ambrosi) 224
11.13 Art & Copy Review Checklist (Ambrosi) 224
11.14 Change Form 225
11.15 Final Proof Review Checklist (Ambrosi) 226
11.16 Style Guide Checklist 227
11.17 Photography Preparation Checklist. 235
11.18 Shooting Schedule Checklist 236
11.19 Prop Background Checklist. 237
11.20 Pre-Production Meeting Checklist. 238
11.21 Re-Shoot/New Photo Request Form 240
11.22 Digital Photography Checklist. 241
11.23 Location Photography Checklist 243
11.24 Photography Release Form 245
11.25 Model Release Form 246
11.26 Location Release Form 247
11.27 RFP for Creative Agency Outline 248
11.28 RFP for Creative Agency Example 250
11.29 Pointers on the RFP 257
11.30 Creative Agency Evaluation Form. 258
11.31 Catalog Agency Evaluation Form Completed 259
11.32 Digital File Information Checklist (DFIC). 260
11.33 DFIC Explanation. 262
11.34 DAM Potential Features Checklist 263
11.35 Selecting a Printer Checklist 265
11.36 Paper Checklist. 267
11.37 Basic Bindery Checklist. 268
11.38 Internet Catalog Critique Form. 270

Chapter 12 Customer Acquisition and Leveraging

- 12.1 Influence of Circulation on Other Functions 274
- 12.2 List Rental Card Checklist of Terms and Their Explanation 275
- 12.3 Circulation Plan Form 278
- 12.4 Circulation Plan Explanation 280
- 12.5 Circulation Plan Example 282
- 12.6 Circulation Plan Summary Form 284
- 12.7 Circulation Plan Summary Example 284
- 12.8 Reverse Timeline Form (Estee Marketing Group, Inc.) 285
- 12.9 Reverse Timeline Example (Estee Marketing Group, Inc.) 286
- 12.10 Pull Marketing, Checklist of Potential Avenues 287
- 12.11 PR Game Plan 291
- 12.12 Printed Press Release Outline 292
- 12.13 Online Press Release Outline 292
- 12.14 Press Release Copy Checklist 293
- 12.15 Media Plan Overview Checklist 294
- 12.16 Printed Media Plan Form 295
- 12.17 Printed Media Plan Example 296
- 12.18 Internet Marketing Deal Evaluation Checklist 298
- 12.19 Internet Marketing Deal Evaluation Explanation 299
- 12.20 Internet Marketing Deal Evaluation Example 303
- 12.21 Customer Contact Strategy Overview Form 308
- 12.22 Customer Contact Strategy Overview Example 309
- 12.23 House List Rental Checklist 312
- 12.24 E-Mail Marketing Checklist 313
- 12.25 Loyalty Club Plan Checklist 315
- 12.26 Loyalty Club Plan Example 316
- 12.27 Package Insert Pointers 318

Chapter 13 Operations as a Marketing Tool

- 13.1 Operations Flowchart 321
- 13.2 Forecasting Influencers 322
- 13.3 Forecasting Criteria Checklist 324
- 13.4 Forecasting Spreadsheet Form 325
- 13.5 Forecasting Spreadsheet Example 325
- 13.6 Forecasting Spreadsheet Explanation 326
- 13.7 Weekly Response Curve Example (Individual Weeks) 328
- 13.8 Cumulative Response Curve Example (Cumulative Weeks) 328
- 13.9 Daily Sales Report Form 329

13.10 Daily Sales Report Example ... 329
13.11 Weekly Sales Report Form ... 330
13.12 Weekly Sales Report Example ... 330
13.13 Customer Policies Checklist ... 332
13.14 Customer Phone and E-mail Representative Checklist ... 333
13.15 Back Orders ... 336
13.16 Return Form Checklist ... 338
13.17 Returns by Vendor Form ... 339
13.18 Returns by Vendor Examples ... 340
13.19 Shipping Costs vs. Revenue Form ... 342
13.20 Shipping Costs vs. Revenue Example ... 342
13.21 Packaging Checklist ... 343
13.22 Gift-Wrap, Cards, and Certificates Checklist ... 345

Chapter 14 Basic Analysis

14.1 Data Capture Checklist ... 347
14.2 Data Capture Explanation ... 348
14.3 Item Level Square Inch Analysis Form ... 351
14.4 Item Level Square Inch Analysis Example ... 351
14.5 Item Level Square Inch Analysis Explanation ... 352
14.6 Category Level Square Inch Analysis Form ... 353
14.7 Category Level Square Inch Analysis Example ... 353
14.8 Square Inch Price Point Analysis Form ... 355
14.9 Square Inch Price Point Analysis Example ... 355
14.10 Categories versus Price Form ... 356
14.11 Categories versus Price Example ... 357
14.12 Basic List Segment Analysis Form ... 359
14.13 Basic List Segment Analysis Example ... 360
14.14 Basic List Segment Analysis Explanation ... 361
14.15 List Segment Analysis with Costs and Marketing Margin Form ... 362
14.16 List Segment Analysis with Costs and Marketing Margin Explanation ... 363
14.17 List Segment Analysis with Costs and Marketing Margin Example ... 364
14.18 LTV Form ... 366
14.19 LTV Explanation ... 366
14.20 LTV Example ... 367
14.21 Offer Testing Form ... 368
14.22 Offer Testing Example ... 369
14.23 Web Site Analysis Checklist ... 370

Acknowledgements

No one writes a book alone. I owe many, many wise folks who over the years have taught and inspired me. In particular, I would like to thank: my husband, Jack R. Baer, for being a loving, comfortable support . . . and having unfathomable knowledge in such critical areas as analysis and business planning; Jan Baiden, for being witty , wise and for keeping me current in data management; Geoffrey Batrounney of Estee Marketing, for limitless knowledge on circulation and all it entails; Liz Kislik, savvy lady on all that matters in customer satisfaction (and much, much more); Bob Hovan of R. R. Donnelley, endless, knowledgeable resource of all that concerns printing, paper and pre-press; Alan Rimm-Kaufamnn, smart, savvy, new breed of electronic direct marketer, Dennis Worth, deeply knowledgeable of creative/production, Steve Rowley, a wizard at many things, most especially (for this book) operations, Ambrosi, for current and totally useful forms in the real-life adventure of catalog creative; Craig Roeller of Banta, for state-of-the-art production assistance; Iris Shokolf of Iris Shokoff for her review of the print media section and, most especially, my editor magnficanté, Rich Hagle, as well as his eagle-eyed compatriots Margaret Maloney and Cheryl Wilson. Plus a very big thank you to so many of you who have shared your invaluable knowledge over many decades.

1 Introduction

How the Tools Came to Be

In 1979, with almost a decade's worth of direct marketing and advertising experience already under my belt, I started a little one "man" direct marketing agency devoted to cataloging. Having only pennies to my name wasn't as big a problem as you might suspect because friends stepped up and made anything they had available. One even lent me a New York City office in his advertising agency in exchange for passing whatever creative business I could find on to him, an arrangement that worked perfectly for a mutually satisfying two years. Then growth meant finding new lodgings but, thankfully, not new friends.

Almost 10 years to the first day of business in my borrowed space I was able to sell what had become a 40-person, thriving independent direct marketing agency on its own floor on Park Avenue South. Young & Rubicam, Dentsu and Havas, all giant agencies in their parts of the world, had joined together to create a direct division; we became one of the first acquired in that venture.

During the decade spent building and running The Muldoon Agency, as well as another 14 years spent consulting after leaving the agency, I have had the excitement, challenge and just plain enjoyment of working with hundreds of companies, from teeny tiny newborns to long established mega institutions.

It has been my observation that no matter what the level of experience in catalog marketing, clients find tools that provide concrete, organized guidance extraordinarily helpful. Whatever the task to be done or problem to be solved, it goes more efficiently with a guideline to follow.

What Are the Tools?

The Tools in this book act as simple step-by-step forms and charts that not only walk you through the process, but also provide simple examples* and explanations of how the process actually works. In order to give you a better idea of the range of possibilities, a wide variety of company types are used in the examples. In addition, there are checklists that assist in helping you to be certain that all the elements necessary for a particular project, assignment or event have been considered. Blank forms are included so that you can copy or adapt them without the verbiage used in the examples and explanations.

When someone asks you to create something, the hardest part, it is said, is putting something down on a blank sheet of paper. With *The Catalog Strategist's Toolkit*, there are no blank pieces of paper.

The guides, checklists and forms are based on over 30 years experience and knowledge of over 350 different companies' needs. They take elements from all that input and construct Tools that act as an adaptable base for your own unique business.

The Tools are specifically designed for the printed catalog business, as this is generally considered the base of any direct marketing catalog. However, elements have been included that address the Internet and some store traffic considerations.

How to Adapt the Tools

Every document created using *The Catalog Strategist's Toolkit* should be considered a living thing. No one form, checklist, chart or outline is absolutely perfect for a particular company's needs. Try using the guide as it is, then start adding important-to-your business elements and cutting away at less than relevant features. If you have any other similar documents, match them up and take the best parts of both to make one unique to your needs.

All of the forms are based on a combination of Business-to-Consumer (B2C) and Business-to-Business (B2B) experience; however, more forms lean to consumer catalogs than the business types. In some cases simple substitutions will do (e.g., end-user for consumer as the target audience), in others you may need to add or subtract data. In some cases, we have noted specific differences as relate to B2C versus B2B in order to help you make appropriate changes.

How to Successfully Use the Tools

As efficient and helpful as these tools can be, sometimes they do not provide all the benefits they could. Why? Because the results of the tools are meant to be shared and built upon. Once you have created a document that influences your business, share it with team members.

Given a concrete written statement, the team will better understand the thinking and direction the writer feels is important to the overall success of the business. Because the team has become more educated about the writer's understanding of particular issues, they can provide more meaningful contributions and legitimate support.

Update all such documents regularly. Merchandise checklists, financial plan checklists, focus group outlines—whatever they are, the content you derive from using the outlines and checklists ages. Do not fall into the trap of directing your company based on plans that have outlived their real value.

Why It Is Worth the Time and Effort to Use These Tools

Yeats said "Think like a wise man but communicate in the language of the people." The right Tools first help you to unearth and gather wisdom by making you think about areas in a clear, organized fashion. By taking the time to work through each exercise, it is not unusual to see fresher, more insightful directions for the particular project on which you are working.

Additionally, as some of the Tools are constructed specifically to be done with others, the direction that evolves is one based upon a cohesive team's effort. This has two immediate benefits: 1) clear understanding by each member of the team as to exactly what the plan and preferred outcome will be and 2) support of all involved.

Who Are the Tools Meant For?

Catalog owners, managers, consultants, agencies, art directors, writers, analysts, merchandisers, photographers, database managers, circulation planners, fulfillment supervisors—all will find forms that help improve their businesses.

The thrust of the book is written with those responsible for planning, but each chapter in the book will have Tools that are particularly applicable to individual disciplines in catalog marketing. Just as important, *The Catalog Strategist's Toolkit* allows those who are not specifically in strategy and planning, to better understand the parts of catalog marketing with which they are less familiar.

Written primarily for those with some catalog experience, there is a helpful glossary that should be of assistance to those not as familiar with the "lingo."

Company examples have been used with the permission of their organizations. In instances where confidentiality considerations were a concern, fictitious companies have been used in place of actual ones.

2 What Is a Catalog?

Printed Catalogs

They say that Benjamin Franklin actually started it all in 1744 when he created what is believed to be the first printed catalog of scientific and academic books. Not content to be a mere cataloger, scientist, inventor, and all-around Renaissance man, Franklin went on to become the original postmaster general of the United States.

In 1872, Aaron Montgomery Ward began the renowned, Chicago-based company that would live, in one form or another, until 2000. As most of us think of Montgomery Ward as the origin of the truly big, telephone-book-sized catalog, it is interesting to realize that the first effort was just an 8″ × 12″ single-page, complete with what must have seemed very necessary at the time: instructions on how to order. Montgomery Ward has another notable claim to fame: In 1939 Robert L. May, a Ward copywriter, devised Rudolf the Red-Nosed Reindeer for a holiday promotion.

Next was Sears, which debuted in 1894 and billed itself as "Book of Bargains: A Money Saver for Everyone," and the "Cheapest Supply House on Earth." Originally free, in 1896, Sears moved to charging a whopping 25 cents (refunded if you spent 10 dollars or more). Color was added the following year, and the next year brought the onset of specialty books. In 1903, the founder, Richard Sears, added the now-famous industry standard: the open-ended money-back guarantee. While Sears is still operating, you are more likely to find an electronic version of the catalog than a printed one.

In 1912 along came L.L. Bean with his four-page flyer advertising, among other things, the Bean Boot. Business grew, and, in 1925, the first full-size catalog hit the mails. But Bean was always more than just sporting products; he helped establish a basic way of doing business that is still honored by catalogers today. Leon Leonwood Bean's stated his Golden Rule: "Sell good merchandise at a reasonable profit, treat your customers like human beings, and they will always come back for more."

The next two individuals to have the greatest impact on catalog marketing—and for very different reasons—were Lillian Vernon and Roger Horchow.

Through Lillian Vernon's unique and often personalized offerings, consumers could find highly affordable and desirable goodies that made their neighbors both thrilled and a little envious. Using space advertisements to sell a variety of personalized goods, Vernon started her business literally off her kitchen table. She became known for shopping the world (long before that was a relatively easy task) to find the most unusual and best. Begun in the early 1950s, Lillian Vernon today has a stable of different titles and is a name familiar to more than 47 million Americans.

Twenty years later, Roger Horchow was the first to teach the public that they, too, could reflect impeccably good taste—all they had to do was buy from his catalog. While other catalogs offered a potpourri of items, Horchow, in 1971, began a catalog that was a collection of only the finest luxuries, elegant for sure, but not necessarily expensive. Horchow pre-selected for the customer, assuring that the customer's product choices would be admired and respected. Most consider this the first boutique catalog and the style precursor to the majority of catalogs today. Horchow is now a division of the Neiman-Marcus Group.

Electronic Catalogs

Electronic Catalogs are another matter altogether. Their history is, to say the least, blurred. The general belief is that the web itself started in the early 1960s. The purpose at that time was, as now, the sharing of information, but it was limited to the military and scientific communities. The Internet, which came along in 1969, was designed to be a method of communication that could, should the need ever arise, withstand attack. And, no, Al Gore did not invent the Internet, but he did, as an influential elected official, strongly support it.

Library catalogs, which debuted in 1990, and were the first catalogs on the Internet. To view a "selling" type of catalog, complete with pretty pictures, you needed a graphics-type browser. Microsoft Internet Explorer solved that in the early 1990s around the same time Delphi first offered a commercial online service, complete with e-mail capability. AOL, and now-defunct others, came aboard in 1995. The growth of the Internet and, in particular, Internet shopping is happening so quickly any numbers written are almost immediately extinct. As high-speed access becomes even more available, there is no doubt that virtually everyone with access to a computer will be shopping via the Internet, especially if a printed catalogs alerts as to what can be found there.

When catalogs first went on the Internet, there was a tendency to simply clone the printed version. This proved too "flat" and did not take advantage of the interactive, dimensional nature of the web. It was soon clear that this new selling medium deserved a new design and interaction palette, one that is being constantly updated and improved upon.

Catalog Definition

Since the 1970s a catalog has been a printed advertising vehicle. A general industry consensus determined that, in order to be considered a catalog and not just a flyer, the advertising vehicle had to consist of 16 pages or more. How big those pages have to be is anybody's guess, but the size you will see most often is a variation of an 8⅜" × 10⅞".

Internet catalogs are still being defined, but tend to come in two major categories:

1. A web site that offers a variety of products for sale on its home page and elsewhere in the catalog; this is really just a normal web site selling stuff, but many refer to it as a catalog.

2. An electronic catalog with a "page-turning" feature that mimics a printed catalog from the same company. As you click at the bottom of the page, the sound and visual let you know that you have "turned" an electronic page. This latter type of catalog is found on the seller's web site. For instance, on Patagonia's web site you can choose to shop by category, searching for an item or opening their online catalog where you can, according to Patagonia, "Browse a digitized version of the print catalog(s) and add products from its pages to your shopping cart with a few clicks."

Catalog Types

Whether printed or electronic, catalogs tend to fall into two major categories:

1. Business-to-Business (B2B).
2. Business-to-Consumer (B2C).

Naturally, there are hybrids that can go to both markets. For example, the office supplies industry is one that can easily appeal to business as well as the home.

B2B catalogs tend to be targeted to particular industries. Because those industries can be diverse in product line and sales size, many B2B catalogers will create separate catalogs per industry. These catalogs can be entirely different per business, or, more likely, just have certain sections that change based on the needs of the industry being mailed to. In addition, some business-to-business catalogs are used both as a selling piece sent directly to the end-user and as a selling tool by a sales rep. In the latter case, it is probable that the catalog would have a separately printed price sheet, thus allowing the sales rep to have flexibility in pricing.

Just some examples of the industries served by B2B catalogs:

Archival	Photography
Auto	Premium/Incentive
Dry-cleaning	Printing
Educational	Prison supplies
Hardware	Religion
Human resources	Restaurant/Food
Industrial	Roofing
Legal	Safely
Lists	Scientific
Medical	Service
Office	Software
Paper products	Uniforms
Patriotic	

Exhibit 2.1 Biggest Differences Between Consumer and Business Catalogs

---

⇨ Mailing Strategy

- While most consumer catalogs mail very frequently, business catalogs historically tend to have one big reference-type book mailed once a year and then augmented by smaller mailings.

⇨ Copy Detail

- Because products in B2B can be more complicated than in B2C, copy must be certain to provide the level of detailed copy essential to high level decision making.

⇨ Layout by Category Rather Than by Theme

- Generally used as a reference tool rather than an impulse purchase vehicle, B2B catalogs are designed for the quick and easy location of items.

⇨ Back Covers Need to Address Routing Information

- Because business catalogers must get through the "gatekeeper" (mailroom, assistant), the back cover frequently contains more than the intended recipient's name; it may also show other appropriate titles in order to help the catalog get to the right person even if that person is no longer at the company or in that office.

⇨ Want Number of Pages Enough to Have a Spine

- One of the major intents of a B2B catalog is to be retained. A spine, complete with company name and contact information, implies that this is a catalog that belongs on a shelf or in a file.

⇨ More Charge Options

- The use of purchase orders is common; in addition, some special offers will provide long term financing options.

⇨ Lack of Seasonality

- Though there are exceptions, such as the educational market, B2B tends to be less seasonal than the often fourth-quarter dependent consumer market.

⇨ More Demanding Customer Service

- Business marketers must have highly trained, knowledge reps familiar and conversant with every aspect of the product line and service policies.

⇨ Incentives

- Some types of business cataloging are highly reliant on incentives to purchase; this is especially true in such commodity areas as office products.

Types of Consumer Catalogs

The types of B2C catalogs are virtually limitless but here are the most common categories:

- Incentive
    - Merchandise that can be purchased for points or is awarded based on the achievement of certain sales goals. An example the former would be the American Express Membership Awards; the latter type would likely be more relevant as a B2B catalog used as an incentive for a sales force.
- Manufacturer
    - Company sponsored, this type of catalog advertises only the item offered by the business, such as The Pfaltzgraff Company, behind the catalog.
- Nonprofit
    - Revenue and image-generators for nonprofit institutions that help support such diverse areas as museums, wild life, ethnic groups, environmental issues and children around the world.
- Retail
    - Catalogs associated with a brick-and-mortar presence; can be used to sell directly off the page, generate traffic and/or enhance image.
- Showroom
    - Discount retailers sometime employ these as advertising vehicles that help consumers realize the extent of product and/or unearth categories they may not have known existed before; mostly traffic generators, not intended for off-page sales.
- Syndicated
    - A noncatalog company that, for a fee or percentage of sales, puts together and manages key elements such as merchandising, creative and production in order to create a catalog for a company that either does not have a catalog or does not have one of this particular consistency.
- Unaffiliated
    - An independent catalog without a brick and mortar presence, nor is it backed by a specific manufacturer.

What is the #1 Reason for Your Catalog to Be?

First and foremost, you need to decide what the major goal of your catalog is. No one can create an effective plan of action without knowing exactly what constitutes success. As an agency, we have often heard "we have two goals; we want the catalog to be a really slick-looking image maker and make tons of money, too." Both reasonable desires, but if you give them equal importance, neither will be given the full attention it deserves with the result being that neither will be as good as it could be. Yes, you can have both—but not in equal weight.

Once you fully commit to the criteria for success, you can begin to plot the strategy (see Chapter 9, Developing Your Strategy). Success comes in many forms; the three chosen most often are:

- Bottom line sales
  While image can certainly help improves sales, it can also be expensive in both creative costs and space allocation, two considerations which negatively affect the bottom line

- Traffic generation—store and or web site
  Sometimes viewed as a cross between a catalog looking for bottom line sales and image, most effective when the message clearly directs the reader to the store or web site

- Image
  Often seen at holiday times, these catalogs tend to be stunningly pictorial with minimal verbiage

    —If sponsored by a retail store, can easily double as traffic generation

    —Can be produced by a manufacturer who chooses not to include minimal contact information in lieu of the overall image impact

As mentioned earlier, big catalogs with a huge selection, such as Montgomery Ward, no longer appear to be the way that consumers wish to shop. Yet as a cataloger gets more and more successful, the natural inclination is to increase the product line so that existing customers have fresh choices and prospects find new items that appeal to them. Before long, catalogers can fall into the trap of creating a catalog that has become so diverse that it has diluted the strength of its initial, successful image.

What to do? The solution is not to just keep adding to the old catalog but to create a *new* catalog that leverages such existing equities as the catalog's database of responsive names. But be alert. Not only should the new venture be even surer that this catalog has a distinctive reason to be, but it also needs to be certain that the new venture augments the existing business without detrimentally splitting sales.

To further answer "why does this catalog exist?" a strategy is needed that not only defines objectives but also details how to achieve them (Exhibit 9.2). Then you must stay on top of it. Even the greatest game plan has a wear-out factor if not regularly revitalized. Use yearly Brainstorming Sessions (Exhibit 9.3) to keep your catalog at the top of its game.

An Overview of the Process

Cataloging is almost always broken into two main areas: Front End and Back End. Front End covers the strategy, marketing, merchandising, creative and production part of the catalog process. Back End is the term for the operations/service part of cataloging.

Exhibits 3.1 and 3.2 in Chapter 3 show each stop of the Front-End and Back-End processes. Chapter 13, Exhibit 13.1, gives another picture of operations (basically the back-end process). But how does it all look together? Let's skip the charts for now and give a top-line outline of the process, complete with mini explanations that point to chapters that match areas of interest.

I. The FRONT END

    A. Planning

1. Business plan—The written strategy that details the plan by which a company intends reach certain goals, including but not limited to financial projections.
2. Financial plan—Concentrates on financial operations, overall sales goals and how they will be achieved.
3. Funding—Determines where, and when, the money is coming from to support the effort.
4. Board presentation—Assuming that the catalog venture is funded by a company with a board, this meeting would review the feasibility of the plan; the desired outcome would be approval to proceed with the plan as presented.
5. Market research/competitive data compilation—Underlying information that confirms the assumptions about the market and its attitudes.
6. Strategic planning session—Also called a brainstorming session, this is where the overall goals and tactics to achieve those goals are discussed and solutions for success determined.

7. Press release—A coordinated effort is developed and the plan for implementation is finalized.
8. Positioning statement, initial or update—What makes this catalog different and appealing to the target audience is defined and/or refined.

B. Merchandising
1. Review merchandise sales—The results of overall sales and number of units (demand, actual shipped, net and gross) in conjunction with analysis of space allocated to items and categories.
2. Merchandise strategy—The overall game plan for what will be run, and at what prices, in which catalogs; can be per catalog and/or for the year.
3. Merchandise sourcing and development—Products that are found and/or designed/manufactured based on the direction given by the merchandise strategy.
4. Merchandise samples—The physical collection of potential products for the catalog.
5. Merchandise selection and pagination—Determination of what items will be rerun and what items will be new; finalization of what items will go on what pages.
6. Copy information collected—Merchandise information collected from vendors/manufacturers by the catalog merchandiser/buyer to allow the creative team to have sufficient knowledge to write copy that sells.
7. Forecasting—Quantities per item needed for predetermined time periods are established and purchase orders are written.

C. Circulation
1. Lists results reviewed—House database, rentals, coop databases tests and successes from past issues are checked in order to help decide an appropriate circulation plan; availability of those lists of interest is determined.
2. Circulation and contact plans—Determination is made of who will be mailed when and what.

3. Offer testing strategy—What incentives, if any, will be offered to whom and for what length of time.
4. Lists selected and ordered—After having given consideration to past results and new potential lists and databases, appropriate quantities are ordered from the proper vendors.
5. Merge/purge—All lists, minus address duplicates, are combined into one major list per mailing.
6. Lists at bindery—Lists are electronically sent to the bindery that will be using them to apply addresses and their codes to each catalog.

D. Creative/Production

1. Pre-press planning meeting—As creative must live with the rules of a printing press, the time to understand what those limitations—or opportunities—might be is prior to beginning the design; additionally, knowing who will be handling what in the production cycle helps determine a realistic schedule.
2. Creative concept meeting—Used when a new creative direction is required; requires tools such as verbal discussion and a positioning statement to help the creative team understand the new goals; needs to be coordinated with the web design team.
3. Concept design—The review of initial creative concepts devised based on the concept meeting.
4. Creative hand-off—The physical release of all elements, such as copy information, product sheets, actual product samples, needed by the creative team to develop the catalog.
5. Initial copy—First draft of the selling text as well as any editorial verbiage.
6. Initial layouts—The first look at the graphic design per spread in the catalog; often shows pick-up photography, may include digitized new product photos.
7. Pre-plan photograph meeting—A meeting of the artist and the photographer to plan props, backgrounds, locations and so on prior to shooting the photography.
8. Revised layouts—A second look at the spreads, this one reflecting any changes that have been made to this point by the catalog team.

9. Revised copy—A second look at the text, this one reflecting any changes that have been made to this point by the catalog team.
10. Photography—The actual shooting of products; if a company is using digital photography, this can be concurrent with each phase of layout design.
11. Photo selection re-shoots—Redos of photos that are not deemed acceptable.
12. Final copy—Last chance to catch any text errors before the catalog is released to pre-press.
13. Final layouts—Last chance to catch any graphic errors before the catalog is released to pre-press.
14. Pre-press/Digital Asset Management—May or may not involve separating the layouts into film; most companies are now using direct from computer-to-printing technology.
15. Postage estimate and check—Determination of the potential postage cost; making certain that the check arrives at the printer or post office in time for the catalog to go in the mail when planned.
16. Printing—The actual printing of the catalog and, if used and separate from the body of the book, its order form.
17. Binding—Putting the catalog together with saddle stitching or perfect binding, addressing it and inserting any order forms or other inserts.
18. Mailing (also called In-Mail)—The time period from the catalog leaving the bindery to being received by the consumer in their home or office.
19. Delivery/In-Home—The actual expected delivery date of the catalog by the recipient.

II. The BACK END

   A. Operations

      20. Orders

         a. Input what was received by mail, phone, Internet.
         b. Verify orders, credit card info.
         c. Inventory checked.

21. Packages—Sort for least cost shipping.
22. Credit cards—Charge when items are shipped.
23. Back orders—Send necessary FTC notices.
    a) Items shipped when in stock
24. Returns handling—Checked to be returned to stock, returned to vendor or liquidated.
25. Inventory updated.

B. Analysis

26. Determination of winners and losers for the following:
    a. Merchandise
    b. Circulation
    c. Offers

3 Getting Started

The words "Getting Started" might lead you to believe that this chapter is devoted to start-up catalogs alone. Not so. Many thriving catalog companies choose to add new titles to their existing mix of brands while other experienced catalogers may wish to freshen a particular catalog's look, feel, and merchandise mix. Still others may look to Alliance, Affiliate, or Joint Venture programs to augment and enhance their existing efforts. So whether you are:

- Starting a catalog from scratch
- Adding a new title to an up and running catalog group
- Updating an existing equity, or
- Exploring a new venture

there is a logical, time-saving, efficient manner in which to approach these tasks.

Key Needs for the Success of Start-Ups, Add-Ons and/or Updates

Several elements are key to every successful catalog. They include:

- Sufficient financial backing.
- Distinctive, lasting positioning.
- Sufficient resources in personnel and time.
- Adaptable, disposable, seasonally expandable product mix.
- Appropriate mindset.
- Ample, relatively readily accessible customer universe.
- A real understanding of your customer's wants and needs.

Alliances, joint ventures, and affiliate partnerships have an additional set of criteria, addressed later in this chapter.

Sufficient Financial Backing

There are two areas that newcomers to cataloging, as well as those with some experience under their belt, always underestimate: Costs and time. Almost without exception, the days of making a million dollars off your kitchen table are gone. The exception, of course, is a web-based catalog. But even these can be more expensive than you might anticipate. And like most growing businesses, the more successful you become, the more that cash flow becomes a problem, necessitating a greater infusion of money than anticipated.

So, the first and most important need for success is a realistic business and financial plan (see outline, Chapter 6. When I owned a direct marketing agency in New York City and a client balked at writing a financial plan, I used to suggest that we simply take whatever money he had accumulated for this catalog launch and just throw it out the window of our many-storied building. The reasoning: Tossing the money to the wind would be a lot less trouble and have about the same result as trying to construct a catalog business without the "blueprint" of a sound financial plan. A well-thought-out, realistic financial plan—one that doesn't just inflate numbers in order to accumulate funding—is the most important element to catalog success.

The actual amount of money you will need can be highly flexible. A start-up, for example, might choose one of three possible ways to launch their catalog business:

1. Rent other catalogers' names (see Chapter 12). This generally has the highest financial risk but the fastest return.

2. Launch only with a web site and evolve to a printed catalog. This can have minimal financial risk, but a slower return.

3. Employ space advertisements with or without a small web site, and evolve to a catalog. This usually has the least financial risk, but the slowest in return.

Note: Unless you have a totally unique concept, such as eBay, the industry has found that printed catalogs still are needed to drive business to the web; hence, all options above have a printed catalog as the cornerstone of the business.

Distinctive, Lasting Positioning

Be aware of trends and beware of fads. While the style-of-the-moment may look like the road to riches, consumers can be a fickle lot, heading off to the next fad and leaving you wondering were all the customers went.

Your product line may not be unique, but it must look like it is. Positioning your catalog so that it is distinctive and memorable means creating an entity that is not just products, but a comfortable, entertaining, enriching and exciting environment to which the consumer returns again and again.

For instance, while many catalogs offer T-shirts, a consumer might choose Patagonia for its environmental-friendly connection, A&F for its on-the-edge attitude, or L. L. Bean for its long-time trustworthiness. (See Chapter 9 for detailed guidance on positioning.)

Additionally, your creative approach should be individual enough that a customer would recognize it even if they didn't see the catalog cover. We'll cover how to do this in Chapter 9. Just remember, even the most earth-shattering creative, just like your product offering, will need refreshing over time.

Sufficient Resources in Personnel and Time

Let's say that you already have an established, successful business that just doesn't happen to be in cataloging. So you can tap those smart people already on your staff, creating just a little extra work for them and a new business for the company, right? Wrong.

Take a look at Exhibit 3.1, which addresses the "front end" of catalog marketing. While this just outlines the initial steps that go into the making of a profitable catalog business, it will give you a necessary overview of the resources that will be needed for success. Doing something right takes planning and commitment, and that takes time. Be sure to allow enough of it.

Adaptable, Disposable, Seasonally Expandable Product Mix

Being in the right place at the right time with the right offer is the dream of most business professionals. Creating a product mix based on research and a complete understanding of what your targeted audience wants is the ideal way to start. But that product mix must also be such that it can rapidly adapt to changing times.

During a speech at a direct marketing industry event during the 1990s, Richard Thalheimer, Founder, Chairman and Chief Executive Officer of Sharper Image, announced to a most attentive audience that he felt he had neglected to keep up with his audience's product needs, resulting in down sales for more years than would make any of us happy. Taking corrective action put the company back on its traditionally strong growth pattern . . . and taught Richard that not taking customers' merchandise choices for granted was such a valuable lesson that he was willing to share it with hundreds of fellow catalogers.

Why is apparel the top selling category in direct sales? One of the major reasons is because it is disposable. Not only does it wear out, but, more important, we get tired of it, making it psychologically disposable. Obviously, a product line that needs regular replacement or updating raises your odds of increased frequency of purchase, a key component to growth.

There once was a catalog containing only Christmas products. It was quite a lovely book and, since Christmas is such a big holiday, such a catalog seemed like a reasonable idea. There was just one, big problem. You only need to buy from the catalog once a year. While many catalogers, due largely to gift giving, experience heavier sales in the fourth quarter, we are able to adapt our product mix to appeal to consumers throughout the rest of the year as well. Through analysis of their sales, the business owners adapted their product mix and their Christmas catalog is now a year-round gift catalog.

Appropriate Mindset

Service

You'll hear a lot of talk about how important service is in "catalogland." Some will even boast that the superior service offered by catalogs is largely responsible for converting retail shoppers into direct shoppers. Maybe. The reality is that too many catalogers believe their service is sufficient, but don't really know if the customer shares this belief. Top-notch service has a price; be certain that you know what the personnel and equipment needed for superior service really costs and evaluate those costs against lost customers.

Just as important, employees listen to the bosses' directives but they emulate the bosses' attitude. Road Runner Sports, Country Curtains . . . these are just two very different catalogs with one big thing in common: their phone personnel convey friendly professionalism and a willingness, even a desire, to go the extra step to see that the customer is totally satisfied. For more on empowering phone personnel, see Chapter 13.

Service doesn't stop at phone reps. It includes everything from speed of product delivery to how you handle returns, to how explanatory your copy is, and how accurate your photography. For a smart approach to estimating what services are important, first become your own customer. Then add to your observations with ongoing customer research (See Chapter 5) that lets you hear firsthand what customers feel is important to them.

Controlled Growth

Impossible though it may seem when you are writing your business plan, rapid growth can be a bad thing. The biggest problem with unanticipated demand is lack of inventory and the inability to quickly service customers. Not getting the product they desired in a timely manner almost always has a lasting, negative effect on a relationship, changing a new customer's attitude from positive to vengeful, not only losing you an expensively acquired customer, but also being the cause of bad word of mouth.

Analysis

Virtually every cataloger now analyzes data to run their businesses efficiently. One of the blessings of the catalog business is the ability to track who bought what, when, from what list, at what price point, in what month, based on what offer, and so on. Cataloging is a lovely combination of creativity and science.

Just remember to use the analysis as a guide, not a directive. Don't overwhelm yourself with more reports than you need and be certain that each report contains the information that is necessary to the person who will be using it the most. See Chapter 14 for help in this area.

Ample, Relatively Readily Accessible Customer Universe

A catalog targeted to only blue-eyed Scandinavians probably wouldn't be a good idea even in northern Europe, but it wouldn't surprise me if someone thought its very uniqueness would make it an ideal choice for a new business here in the US.

In cataloging, two areas need constant updating: buyers and merchandise. First, the target audience must be large enough to acquire a base of customers of sufficient size to support a business designed specifically for their needs and desires. Second, as you will experience customer attrition, that same target audience must be replenished, meaning that you will constantly need to find more of the same good folks who bought from you in the first place just to maintain your current customer base, let alone grow it.

Several past clients have had the good misfortune to have an aging customer base. While "good misfortune" may sound like an oxymoron, it really isn't. The good thing is that older audiences tend to be more loyal than younger ones. The bad thing is that "older" means a shorter life expectancy. Many catalogers who market to the 60+ consumer find that, due to that customer-replacement need, they are required to adapt enough to appeal to a younger group (say 45+) without turning off their core, older customer.

Research: A Real Understanding of Your Customer's Wants and Needs

"Why do we need to do research? We know who our customer is and what they want." Wrong. As your needs have changed over the years, so have your customers' needs. While, from my experience, catalogers who think they know their customer are usually 80 percent correct, that means they are also 20 percent wrong, resulting in missing those delicious low-fruit opportunities.

Research takes many forms (see Chapters 4 and 5), but it should not be approached in a helter-skelter manner. Find a budget for a yearly game plan, even if it's as small as regularly planned package inserts or web questionnaires. Listen in on phone calls from your customers to your phone reps. Read a sampling of complaints and compliments from customers. Design your research so you don't just talk *to* customers; listen as well. Get in touch with:

- Ex-customers: Why did they leave?
- Requestors who didn't convert: Why did they request a catalog and then not order?
- Competitors' customers: What does the competition do better than you do?

When it comes to customers' needs and desires, don't assume. Know.

Process Flow

It is an understatement to say that no two companies function the same. However, there is a pattern of preparation and implementation. As noted in Chapter 2, the creation of catalogs is traditionally divided into two processes: The Front-End Process and the Back-End Process. The front-end process covers everything from Strategy and Marketing to Merchandising to Creative and Production. The back-end process generally covers Operations and Analysis.

Based on these processes, I have created two flow charts for a generic version of the front end of a catalog (Exhibit 3.1) and the back end of a catalog (Exhibit 3.2). Some of the back-end functions, such as analysis, are shown in Exhibit 3.1, as they are tools directly used by those in the front end. For a more detailed explanation of the back-end process, see a Back-End Process in Chapter 13. To get an even better grasp of Exhibit 3.1, use it in combination with the Exhibit 6.1 in Chapter 6.

Exhibit 3.1 Front-End Process Flow Chart

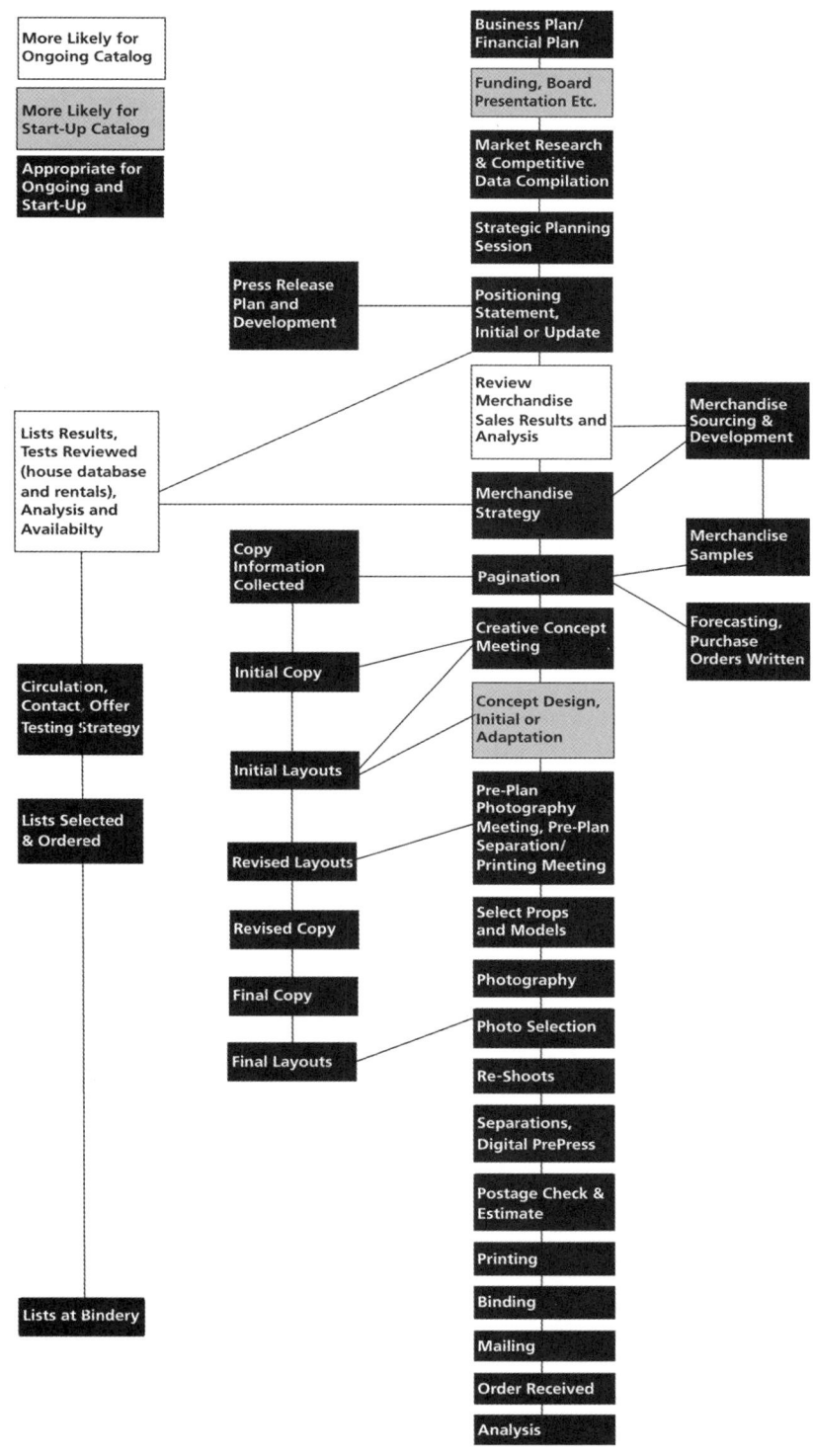

Exhibit 3.2 Back-End Process Flow Chart

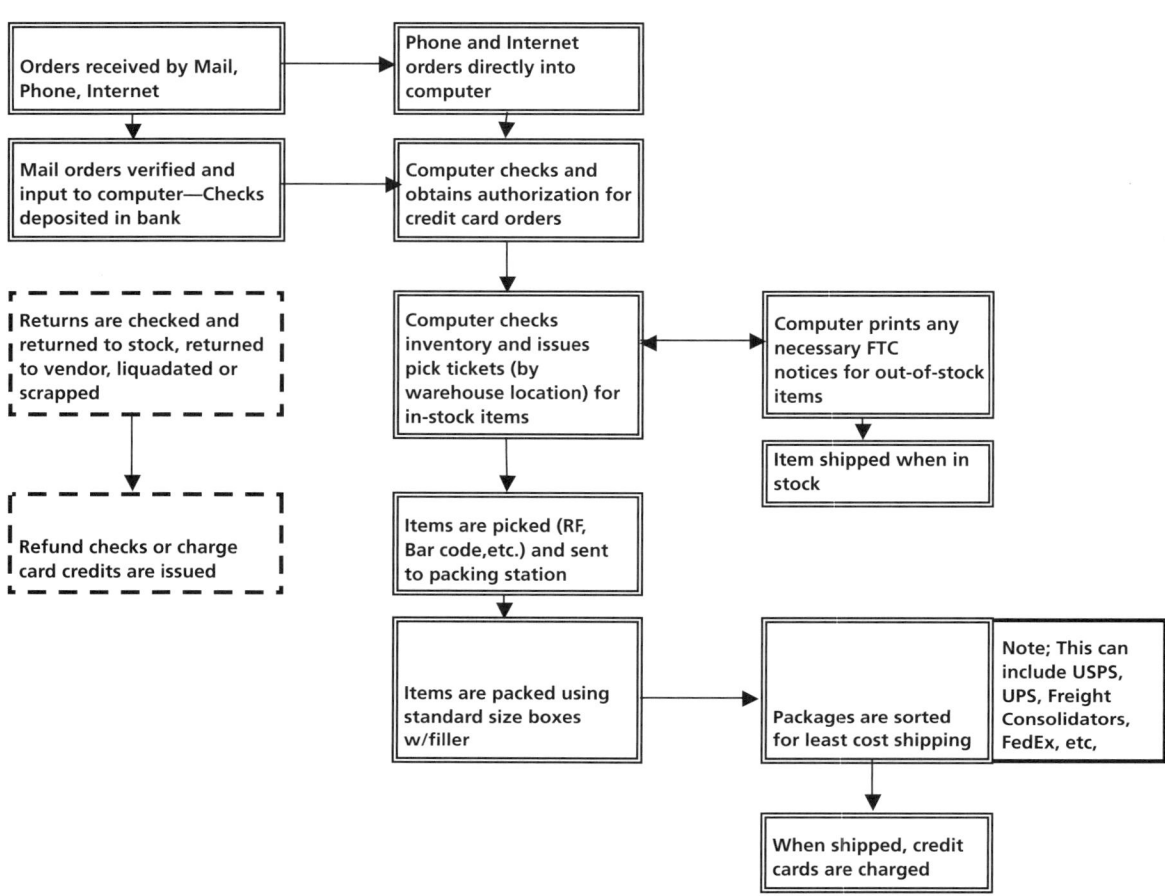

Joint Ventures/Alliances/Affiliates

Put two or more companies together and, voila, you suddenly have a much bigger, stronger, more economically efficient company. In addition, maybe one partner can bring beneficial name recognition or a new customer base to the venture. At least that's the theory. In real life, such ventures are fraught with potential pitfalls.

When asked to characterize the success of their joint ventures, a minority of CEOs in a recent Conference Board survey responded, "Very successful."

However, when well thought out, we have seen excellent results.

To make this approach to business growth even more daunting, joint ventures, alliances, and affiliates are words that are often, sometimes incorrectly, used interchangeably.

Let's look at what dictionary.com has to say about these three relationships:

- **Joint Venture:** A partnership or conglomerate, formed often to share risk or expertise.

- **Alliance:** A close association of groups, formed to advance common interests or causes. A formal agreement establishing such an association. Really a partnership.

- **Affiliate Programs:** A person, organization, or establishment associated with another as a subordinate, subsidiary, or member. We most often think of an affiliate as part of another company's Internet site; they can provide an implied endorsement and, often, access to a new market.

There is plenty of room for interpretation, but from our experience a joint venture tends to be a looser, often shorter-term agreement than either an alliance or an affiliate program. Here are two examples: One photo-developing client temporarily fused with a children's wear catalog to offer free film with children's wear order. The children's wear cataloger increased response; the film company tapped a natural audience and gained new customers. Two other catalog company clients, both of whom sold dinnerware, could have thought of themselves exclusively as competitors. But being disciplined, forward thinkers, they found a way for one entity to offer products manufactured by the other company, broadening the product line for one partner and increasing product sales for the other.

An alliance, while closer to a joint venture than an affiliate relationship, most often has deeper roots and longer-term ramifications. Probably one of the best known alliances is that of HP (Hewlett-Packard) and Apple, which came together to deliver an HP-branded digital music player based on Apple's iPod™. This is a win-win, as Apple gets greater distribution and HP gets to ride on the success of Apple.

In cataloging, a perfect example of an alliance is what Seta Corporation offers. Seta, whose clients include such companies as Spiegel and Redcats USA, provides a customized jewelry insert that is incorporated into the cataloger's own catalog, thus expanding the cataloger's product line with no financial risk, since Seta pays for the cost of the creative, production, and incremental postage and even handles the fulfillment and customer service. In exchange, Seta pays the cataloger a mutually agreed upon percentage of sales.

In an affiliate program, one company is in a subordinate position to the other partners. Companies participating in joint ventures and alliances tend to be more on equal footing than those in affiiations.

These days an affiliate program almost always refers to an Internet-based "associate" program in which members sign up to promote the company offering the affiliate membership. Amazon is generally credited with being one of the first, if not the first, to offer programs that pay referral fees to those who drive traffic to its site. Amazon pays "up to 10%" based on performance and link types used, e.g., a direct link, which connects directly to an item, will earn a higher fee than an indirect link, which is a non-title spacific page, such as a home page. Links are made readily and simply available; quarterly reports state how much you have earned, how many items have shipped, and what has been returned.

All such arrangements, however, have one thing in common: Both sides must understand the rules governing the relationship. The checklists in Exhibits 3.3 and 3.4 outline some of the major areas of a venture you should evaluate. Joint ventures and alliances are covered in Exhibit 3.3. While Affiliates can also benefit from this checklist, I have added an additional group of criteria (Exhibit 3.4) that apply specifically to affiliates. Start-up ventures are covered in Exhibit 7.3.

Exhibit 3.3 Checklist: Joint Venture/Alliance

☐ *Expansion*

___ Will it help you to expand sales to a new trading area, bringing new customers not as easily acquired through your normal methods?

___ Does it allow you to learn about another type of business, effectively eliminating a learning curve for your entry into that business?

___ If this combination of entities creates a wholly new product/program, what is the likelihood that this shared-revenue venture will some day threaten your base business?

___ Does it allow you to add breadth and depth to your product line without cannibalizing your core business?

___ Is the image that your partner brings to the table one that enhances your company's reputation and selling power? Will it give you stronger brand recognition?

☐ *Money*

___ Do you and the potential partner have the same long-term and short-term goals? What happens if one partner achieves their goal before the other?

___ Does it minimize your investment, either in "bricks and mortar" or human resources?

___ Is it going to improve your sales closing rate or give you a shorter sales cycle time?

___ Are both partners absolutely clear and in agreement with what constitutes success? And how will it be measured?

___ Have you determined exactly what, and how often, reports are needed to monitor the key elements (not just financial, but other elements, such as service, that affect the finances)?

___ Is there a solid business plan that provides you with enough financial incentive for the time it takes to negotiate and implement such an arrangement?

___ Who owns the names generated from this venture and how will they be used?

☐ *Personalities*

___ Do your partner's ethics meet yours?

___ Are both heads of companies totally behind the venture? And is their attitude reinforced throughout the management structure?

___ Do you find that communication is easy and direct or that misunderstanding or confusion has already occurred? Do the styles of the people involved mesh or conflict? Do you have a written communication plan?

___ Do both parties honestly feel that they are being fairly compensated?

___ Do both parties have the same viewpoint—either entrepreneurial or corporate?

☐ *Control*

___ Will both companies have equal responsibilities? Or in appropriate percentage to investment?

___ Will both companies have equal input? Or in appropriate percentage to investment?

___ What happens if a key player leaves?

___ Are you clear on exactly who is going to be responsible for what? Do you have an organization chart, complete with job descriptions, or something equivalent in writing?

___ Who has creative and production control (makes the final decisions)? Who makes the marketing decisions? Who sources and/or selects the merchandise? Who determines the service level?

☐ *Confidences*

___ Is your partner equally willing to share data . . . or is this going to be too much of a one-way street?

☐ *Customer Care*

___ Will your partner treat your current and/or shared customers with the same attitude and service standard that you would or do?

___ Is your customer going to see a benefit in areas such as quicker response or higher satisfaction?

☐ *The Details*

___ Are you both either union or non-union shops?

___ Can your computers talk to each other?

___ Do you have compatible technologies and systems overall?

Exhibit 3.4 Checklist: Affiliate Program

☐ Determine major goal

☐ Requirements

___ Complementary, non-competitive product line that appeals to target market

☐ If large corporation, competitive concerns could be overcome if project is assigned to non-competitive branch of main business

___ Meets majority of criteria (Checklist 3.3)

___ Has dedicated personnel, both parties

___ Acceptable profit and loss (P&L) for three-year time period

___ Willingness to back-test

___ Agreed to time frame of key elements, such as launch date and/or go/no-go decision date

☐ Steps

___ Assign in-house person whose major responsibility is acquisition of appropriate potential affiliates

___ Determine who will be contacted within the target companies

___ Develop and finalize offer to be made to target companies

___ Determine cost allocation per company (yours versus theirs)

___ Determine fee/commission structure

___ Determine/finalize communication method

___ Prepare and send/deliver materials to affiliate prospects

___ Evaluate level of interest of targeted affiliate partners

___ Adapt plan as needed

How important is it to review the criteria in the checklists in Exhibits 3.3 and 3.4? Here's an example:

> I had firsthand knowledge of a partnership that was doomed to fail. The partner I was associated with had relatively deep pockets, but a somewhat low-end image. It wanted a prestigious partner and, regrettably, found one. That partner wanted a catalog that enhanced its elegant image and, to put it kindly, profits were not a top priority.
>
> Just one of the very poorly thought-out agreements was that the prestigious partner was allowed to source and select all merchandise offered in the catalog. The low-end image, silent partner agreed, even though they had no input into product selection, to "eat" any merchandise that did not sell. Naturally, there was very little impetuous for the high-end partner to be terribly concerned about whether or not items actually sold, as long as the catalog looked good. The bottom line: a smashing looking, money-losing catalog.

4 Researching Your Competition

Never has there been a more brilliant idea for a new catalog than the one that you and your team have. Something just tells you that this is the unbeatable one. Maybe your idea is based on observations of consumer trends. Maybe it's based on a merchandising opportunity you spotted in an existing catalog. Whatever the inspiration, you believe you have discovered a hole in the universe and you intend to fill it.

Just try to be sure that somebody else isn't already aiming for that same hole! Worse yet, they may have not only the same idea, but they may be a stronger player with deeper pockets or teams of more experienced catalogers ready to take on the challenge of a new venture.

Maybe the potential competition we're talking about isn't even a new catalog venture, but a catalog that has been in existence for some time, one whose management feels its owners/managers already have a pretty firm handle on what any existing competition is doing and how to combat it.

Foolish, foolish. No one instinctively knows a competitor's strengths and weaknesses for the simple reason that businesses are never static. So, never assume. Know. Prepare quarterly reports for the core competitors and yearly reports for the peripheral ones.

There are two major methods of knowing your competition:

1. Primary data: New information that is collected specifically for the cataloger.

2. Secondary data: Existing information that is compiled specifically for the cataloger.

Let's address secondary data first. (Primary data will be discussed in Chapter 5.)

Determine Who Your Competitors Are

The first step in using secondary data for competitive analysis is to determine who your competitors are and then divide them into two groups: 1) core and 2) peripheral. The *core competitors* are the ones that may be currently eating your lunch or showing signs that they could. They also include companies that sell basically the same stuff you do to the same market. The *peripheral group* indicates the direction you would like to go if you could expand your business into a tangential market. Some examples: a cataloger of children's clothing moving into a market that sells products for moms or a company going after a market that merely expands its age range appeal.

Fortunately, creating a list of competitors has never been easier. The simplest method is to hire a firm that specializes in unearthing competitors. Some of these firms, most of which can be found quickly with a web search, concentrate their services exclusively on web entities; others look at a host of competitor elements.

Electronic methods can, with some browsers, help you get a head start on creating a list of competitors. Although not all browsers allow this type of electronic "shopping"—and the Internet is an ever-changing equity, it's still worth a try. Go to the web sites of competitors you already know about and go to "Show Related Links" (under Tools on the pull-down menu at the top of your computer screen). This can often direct you to new competitive companies. One example:

When its web site was requested to Show Related Links, Patagonia the outdoor sports apparel company, listed:

- Merrel
- Lowe Alpine
- Mountain Safety Research
- REI
- Marmot
- Walrus Gear
- Kestrel Wind/Weather Instruments
- Cartom Outdoor Travel & Photography
- Mount Sopris Unlimited
- Outdoors Plus More

Not all of these might be considered competitive, but they are informative: They open up potential market avenues you may not have considered.

For another way to use competitors' web sites for competitive information, check out "Source" under the View menu at the top of your computer screen; this will reveal the source coding used to create the particular page you are viewing. OK, we are getting into code writing, which is some pretty technical stuff. Show a copy of this page to your tech guy or gal, and they will let you know what keywords are in the code that can identify what this company believes are important to search engines. Don't be disappointed if you or your tech person cannot pull up the source code; some companies will have this information blocked.

Patagonia's web site lists these keywords:

Outdoor	Fishing	Sweaters
Clothing	Biking	Gloves
Gear	Running	Underwear
Discount	Outdoor sport	Sportswear
Clothes	Company	Men's
Camping	Catalog	Women's
Climbing	Apparel	Kid's
Hiking	Outerwear	Children's
Travel	Fleece	Patagonia
Survival	Jackets	Padagonia
Skiing	Pullovers	Pategonia
Snowboarding	Pants	

OK, no competitive names, but plenty of ideas for areas in which you may not have looked for competitors, e.g., snowboarding.

It's easier to get information on publicly held companies, but even private ones have information available on such web sites as Hoovers (www.hoovers.com), which, not incorrectly, bills itself as the Business Information Authority. Hoovers can show leads on competitors. For instance, a review of IBM Hardware noted three competitors if you were not a paid subscriber to Hoovers, and 18 more if you were a Hoovers' subscriber.

Other reference avenues:

- Relevant trade associations (e.g., The Direct Marketing Association http://www.dma.org) as they provide member directories, often by industry.

- Yellow Pages (e.g., http://yp.lycos.com).

- Dun & Bradstreet (http://www.dnb.com), which offers a variety of databases by competition, revenue, etc.

- Government web sites such as:
    —U.S. Securities and Exchange Commission (http://www.sec.gov/edgar.shtml). As this web site states: All companies, foreign and domestic, are required to file registration statements, periodic reports, and other forms electronically through EDGAR (the Electronic Data Gathering, Analysis, and Retrieval system). Anyone can access and download this information for free. Here you'll find links to

a complete list of filings available through EDGAR and instructions for searching the EDGAR database.

- Annual reports; either peruse them online or buy some stock and get on the mailing list for regular updates.

- List usage on list data cards
    — List Data Cards, which are the printed data or electronic document containing all information about a list, can show basic information, such as the number of customers, about a company. In addition, list brokers can provide some usage. For instance, if a particular list, The Who Knows Company, works for your catalog, find out who else rents this list. If you are new to the business, determine which lists you assume to be competitors and ask your list broker to provide, where possible, the lists that those competitors use. Again, this is a suggestion only, but can give you very sound clues to competitors you may not have naturally thought of.

Create a Competitive Grid

After you have determined who your competitors are, your next step is to start gathering data in an organized, easy-to-use format. Competitive grids can vary depending upon the need of the company employing them and the particular areas of concentration. For a start-up catalog, you would want detailed information about the competitive companies themselves (see Exhibit 4.1). For an ongoing catalog business, you might want to concentrate on a particular area of competition, such as merchandising, web site, or customer service.

While noting all the specific information per area per company, the absolutely essential part of this grid is the last column: *Point of Difference*.

From our experience, this is what counts. This column must answer questions such as "Why are we better?," "Why are they better?," and "What can we do to stand out?"

The column labeled *Reason or Type of Competition* will help team members who read these findings to understand inclusion choices.

For illustration purposes, we have kept our examples to four companies indicated in Exhibit 4.1, in the row labeled *Competitor*. However, it is probable that you would review more than four competitors, but, in order to keep the report from becoming information-heavy, we recommend that you have no more than eight competitors for core and five for peripheral.

For explanations of each field in the Competitive Grid Outline, see Exhibit 4.2.

Exhibit 4.1 Competitive Grid Outline

CATALOG NAME	REASON OR TYPE OF COMPETITION

COMPETITOR	Made for Missies Catalog	Secret Weapon Catalog	The One & Only Catalog	My Favorite Collection	POINT OF DIFFERENCE
BUSINESS OVERVIEW					
Catalog Issue Reviewed					
Ownership/# of Years in Catalog Business					
Sales/Average Order $/ Buys Per Year/Rate of Growth					
Circulation/List Information					
% of Business Overall (if owned by a parent)					
Percentage of Business by Selling Avenue					
Health of Business Overall and by Selling Avenue					
Stated Customer Profile					
Product Offerings (% by category)					
Percentage of Exclusive Products					
Product Category Approximate Price Range/Average Retail					
Merchandise Positioning					
Stated Catalog Positioning/ Tag Line					
Impressions of Positioning Based on Review of Catalog					
How Creative Execution Creates the Positioning Impression					
Average Product Density Per Spread					

COMPETITOR	Made for Missies Catalog	Secret Weapon Catalog	The One & Only Catalog	My Favorite Collection	POINT OF DIFFERENCE
SERVICE OVERVIEW (services offered in catalog)					
24-Hour Ordering					
Toll-Free Ordering					
Internet Address					
Toll-Free Fax #					
Toll-Free Customer Service Number					
Gift-Wrap					
Gift Certificate					
Stated Standard Delivery Time and Shipping Charges					
Proprietary Charge Card					
VIP/Loyalty Program					
Personal Shopping Service					
Letter from Company					
Socially-Conscious Program (including privacy)					
Volume Discount					
Strength of Internet Tie-in to Printed Catalog or Retail Stores					
Guarantee Parameters					
Other Services					
CREATIVE OVERVIEW (printed catalog)					
Size					
Folio Count					
Type					
Paper and Printing Quality					
# of Photo Images					
Style of Photography					
Copy Tone, Amount					
Model Types					
Additional Decorative Elements					

Exhibit 4.2 Competitive Grid Explanations

BUSINESS OVERVIEW	
Catalog Issue Reviewed	• The ideal situation is to review every competitor in the same time frame every year. • As it is usually not feasible to review every issue of a catalog during the year, most catalogers select what they believe to be the most important issue out of the year. You can usually tell this from your own sales; e.g., monitor the competitors' catalogs received in November if that is the best sales time for you. • If a competitor does not mail as frequently as you do, and therefore does not have a catalog in the exact same month as your best sales occur, choose either the equivalent quarter (e.g., if you knew that November was best for you, monitor your competitor's catalogs in the fourth quarter) or a catalog mailed as close to possible in the same time frame (e.g., if there is no competitor November edition, check out their December or October issue). • If you have no sales history, go with what your secondary research tells you and adjust the issue reviewed as needed as you obtain real data.
Ownership/# of Years in Catalog Business	• Is this catalog private, part of a conglomerate or a single, publicly held unit? • The good news is that, if a catalog is publicly held, information is easier to obtain. The bad news is that publicly held companies tend to own a variety of catalogs. One example is Williams-Sonoma which owns, to name just a few of their stable of eight, Pottery Barn, Hold Everything, and PB Teen. You must carefully separate data that is relevant only to your area of competition from the data for the whole company. • The number of years in business can help you get a grasp on at least a part of the mindset of this business. A new entry might have greater financial concerns than a more established opponent. One thing this could mean, when taken in conjunction with the other information you are compiling, is that you might find the new entry a weaker opponent—hence a better target to go after—than a more established one. • Sometimes older companies have hit plateaus and don't appear to be able to move off them. Such an opponent might also be a less problematic competitive target than another.
Sales/Average Order $/Buys Per Year/Rate of Growth	• What are the overall sales for each company? These can be found at some of the sources already listed in this chapter as well as by searching on business web sites, such as the *Wall Street Journal* (http://online.wsj.com/public/us) and industry web sites, such as *Catalog Age* (http://cj.pbsub.com). • Determining the average order (the amount a customer spends on average per purchase) is as simple as referring to a List Card (see Chapter 12). • Buys Per Year refers to how frequently customers purchase from the catalog. This information is difficult to obtain, although checking List Cards for the number of multi buyers versus single buyers will give you a relatively reliable assumption. • Rate of growth can be viewed in two ways: overall sales or growth of customer files. Both should be watched vigilantly. Sales, naturally, show whether this is a thriving or stagnant business, but sluggish customer growth is also a telling sign of a company that's in a poor market category, risk averse or just poorly managed.

BUSINESS OVERVIEW	
Circulation/List Information	• Once again, turn to List Cards for tons of information, including target profiles and most of the data listed in this section. More on this in Chapter 12. • What is the universe of customers per catalog competitor? How many are recent customers (ordered in the last six months) and what is the quantity breakout of the older customers by time period since they have ordered? • How did each competitor acquire their customers—via catalog mailings, Internet, space ads, and so on? • Circulation is harder to come by because what you really want in this case is how many catalogs are mailed per drop date (the day the catalog goes in the mail) per competitor. The exhibit illustrates a competitive grid explanation. You should be looking for circulation quantities for every drop date for the entire year. Another competitive grid might look at circulation only for a particular time period. • Search business sites such as *Catalog Age*, as some catalogers will actually report these numbers to the press, allowing you to find the information you need in an article. • Annual reports, too, can verbalize why circulation was increased or decreased to accomplish a particular goal. • Printers, who know the quantity printed, and list brokers, who know the lists mailed, are sometimes willing to share these numbers.
% of Business Overall (if owned by a parent)	• If you can't get the actual dollar sales breakout, go for the percentage and construct your own guesstimate.
Percentage of Business by Selling Avenue	• Another valuable piece of info that you can often unearth from annual reports is how sales are generated, e.g., what percentage of sales comes from retail stores, wholesale distribution, web sites, and so on. • Use these statistics in conjunction with the other pieces you are collecting to start to get a more insightful overview.
Health of Business Overall and by Selling Avenue	• This is the part where you take the numbers and secondary research you have acquired and write up what you think it all means.
Stated Customer Profile	• Most often found on the List Card, the customer profile also can be located in any number of the sources previously listed. • If your competitor has stores, go there in person and see who is frequenting the stores and observe who is actually buying and not just shopping from them.
Product Offerings (% by category)	• Set up categories of products of your competitors that match your own categories as much as possible. Then count (literally) the number of items per category and overall in the issue reviewed, doing the math necessary to come up with category percentages of the overall. • Do not count every SKU (stock keeping unit); rely more on photo depictions. In other words, do not count every size or color of a sheet offered. But do include the blanket, coverlet, dust ruffle, etc., that might be shown in the same photo.

BUSINESS OVERVIEW	
Percentage of Exclusive Products	• Most catalogers note an exclusive with an exclusive icon. Count exclusives up and determine the percentage of the overall product offering. • Being the only resource for an item can be a huge competitive advantage. Your analysis (Chapter 14) can help you determine if this is true for your business.
Product Category Approximate Price Range/Average Retail	• Ideally you would record every price of every product per category of every competitor. Most of us do not have this luxury of time. • Eyeball the price ranges per product categories. If some categories are more important to you than others, check real figures (attained by actually determining exactly how many items are offered per price range) against what you have eyeballed. This accomplishes two purposes: You see how good you are at guessing price ranges and you get the real price ranges for vital categories.
Merchandise Positioning	• Frequently, a letter in the catalog (often found on page 2) will address why the merchandise has been chosen for this particular edition or the catalog's overall merchandising philosophy. Alternately, some catalogs will announce their merchandising intent on the cover, e.g., "head to the beach." • If the merchandising plan for the issue reviewed has not been made so obvious, it is time for you to review the catalog and solve this mystery through your own observations. Helpful hints can sometimes be contained in the body copy (the copy that is used to describe the products themselves).
Stated Catalog Positioning/Tag Line	• Most catalogs proudly display their tag lines on the cover. Simply include that information here.
Impressions of Positioning Based on Review of Catalog	• OK, you have pulled together what you think your competitors' stated positioning is. Now look at their catalog again. Do you believe that they are stating and reinforcing their positioning through the three major elements: merchandising, creative, and services?
How Creative Execution Creates the Positioning Impression	• Here you will need to evaluate how much you feel that the creative contributes to the positioning impression. • This is beyond the previous statement in that it is asking you to determine how much the creative alone is responsible for strengthening the positioning.
Average Product Density Per Spread	• As creative execution is very much influenced by how many items the artist is compelled to show on a page, this area helps illuminate one of the reasons the creative works as well as it does or doesn't. • Density also can provide insight into whether or not this catalog may be used solely for traffic generation. Very low-density catalogs (1 to 2 items per page) generally do not offer enough merchandise to provide sufficient income for the catalog to be profitable. • Conversely, extremely high-density catalogs (10 items or more per page) may, due to the sheer amount of merchandise offered, generate significant income for their owners but also tend to convey a value positioning.

SERVICE OVERVIEW (services offered in catalog)	
24-Hour Ordering	• Is the catalog store open every hour of the day? Surprisingly, some catalogs are not.
Toll-Free Ordering	• Does the customer have to pay a charge to place an order with this company?
Internet Address	• How often is this displayed? How well? • How well does the way the address is shown or talked about make you want to visit the site? • How well does it reinforce the positioning overall?
Toll-Free Fax #	• Yes, some people still prefer to fax their orders. Is this number easily visible and as free as ordering via phone or the Internet?
Toll-Free Customer Service Number and Overall Service Information	• Must the customer pay to ask questions or inquire about an order? • How well and often is this number displayed? • How complete and easy to understand is the customer service information? Is it easy to find and read or is it in tiny print somewhere hidden in the catalog? If the latter, why?
Gift-Wrap	• Is gift-wrap offered? • How well/often is it displayed? What is the charge for it?
Gift Certificate	• Gift certificates are increasing in popularity. Do your competitors take advantage of this trend? • How well/often is this service shown?
Stated Standard Delivery Time and Shipping Charges	• While most catalogers offer expedited delivery, many don't help the customer to understand what the normal shipping time is. Do your competitors? • What are the charges for shipping, normal and expedited? • Are there any beyond-the-norm charges, such as extra shipping for heavy items?
Proprietary Charge Card	• Do your competitors offer their own credit cards, e.g., L.L. Bean has a L. L. Bean credit card. • This can encourage loyalty and additional spending as well as provide further reasons for contacting the customer with offers.
VIP/Loyalty Program	• Loyalty plans are excellent ideas for some types of businesses and lousy ones for others. Which appears to be the case in your competitive arena? See Chapter 12 for Loyalty Club Plan Checklist.
Personal Shopping Service	• Personal Shopping goes beyond just helpful customer service phone or Internet reps. • A shopping service assists with product selection and may also provide a special occasion reminder service to help customers with gift giving.
Letter from Company	• Does the catalog highlight a personal letter from the company, usually from the president or owner? • Does the content of the letter add to the catalog's impact or just waste space?
Socially-Conscious Program (including privacy)	• Some companies add depth to their positioning via alliances with socially-conscious programs; others use a social agenda as their main reason to be (see Exhibit 9.6 in Chapter 9). • As privacy can be a hot button with consumers, stating a cataloger's policy regarding renting their customers' names has become both logical and ethically sound.

SERVICE OVERVIEW *(services offered in catalog)*	
Volume Discount	• Volume discounts most often apply to business-to-business catalogs as they are generally marketing to companies that buy in quantity. • However, many consumer catalogs will also offer such incentives as two-fers (buy two at a cheaper price than one), bundles (buy these items together and get them for less than if you purchased them separately), same address discounts (buy multiples of the same item, often holiday gifts, shipped to the same address for a discount). • As these "deals" are often hidden in fine print or body copy, check carefully to unearth them.
Strength of Internet Tie-in to Printed Catalog or Retail Stores	• Just listing the Internet address is less than ideal marketing. How effectively, in your judgment, do your competitors leverage the synergies available via multiple selling avenues?
Guarantee Parameters	• Do your competitors offer open-ended guarantees? If there are no limitations stated, the guarantee is considered open-ended. • Is the guarantee stated consistently throughout, or is the elaboration found only on the ordering info page? • Is the message overall a positive one? Is this effectively restated throughout the catalog?
Other Services	• Check throughout the catalog and Internet site to see if there is something special, in terms of service, about these competitors.
CREATIVE OVERVIEW *(printed catalog)*	
Size	• What does the catalog measure in size?
Folio Count	• How many pages long is it? Some catalogs have inserts that have different numbers, so be certain that you do not just look at the last page in the catalog and assume that that is the number (plus the back cover) of the pages in the entire catalog. • When counting pages, count the front cover as page one and the back cover as the highest number in the folio count. • Unless products are sold on the order form, do not count the order form as part of the folio count.
Type	• If you know the actual typefaces used, include that information but that is not the main purpose of this info collection. • The main purpose is to determine the style and feeling of the type used. Is it flowery, conservative, heavy-handed, feathery, confusing (too many different typefaces used together), well organized, distinctive? Does it complement the photography or takes away from it? These are examples of what you are looking for. Construct your own list of attributes that are right for your competitive group.
Paper and Printing Quality	• How does the paper feel to you? Low end? Upscale? Slick? Glossy? Suede-like? Does it smear or tear? Can you, due to bleed through, see products on one side of the paper through to the other side, thus interfering with a product's presentation? • It is not as important to have the details of the paper used as it is to understand the image it is attempting to convey. • Are the colors bright and in register? Is everything sharp and clear?
# of Photo Images	• Determine how many photos on average appear per page. This relates to the density issue discussed earlier in the grid under "Business Overview."

CREATIVE OVERVIEW (printed catalog)	
Style of Photography	• Lighting and tone are the primary issues here. • Flat lighting (less natural, a more even lighting look overall that can actually make products look flatter rather than three-dimensional) is more downscale. However, this simple style lighting may be totally appropriate for utilitarian products such as computers, even if they are upscale. • More contemporary, upscale lighting tends to make the items look like they are in a room setting, complete with such influences as shadows that appear to be caused by sunlight streaming through the window. Has a warmer feeling with more depth of tone. • Does your competition go for unusual photo techniques, like purposely-blurred model activity, odd angled stills, models cropped so tightly that only the bottom half of the face is shown? • New trends in photography are one way to sharpen older creative, so be especially alert to this area.
Copy Tone, Amount	• Light and fluffy, educational, confidentially personal tone or all business: What is the feeling you get from both the headlines (if they are used) and the body copy? • Does each product have long sentences to describe it or is the copy sparse and minimal? If the latter, is there enough information provided? Is too much copy wasting space that could have allowed larger photos? • What about editorial? Is it used at all and, if so, is it effective? • Are customer testimonials used?
Model Types	• Young, older, ethnic mix, interaction with each other, males or females as props, activity level, expression (smiling, more runway-style serious), these are just examples from which you will need to create your own list of observations. • Determine percentages shown per your categorized observations.
Additional Decorative Elements	• Headlines, illustrations, captions, borders, tabs—there are many possibilities of additional elements, so be on the lookout for graphic touches that make the catalog you are reviewing standout.

Exhibit 4.3 Competitive Grid Example (Core Target Market)

Example would be same for Peripheral Market, but each grid should indicate if it is Core or Peripheral.

This example is for a start-up catalog offering women's clothing in sizes 14 to 6X. The only dissimilarity would be in the Point of Difference column.

CATALOG NAME	REASON OR TYPE OF COMPETITION
Made for Missies Catalog	Appropriate size range.
Secret Weapon Catalog	Clothing similar to potential product addition (undergarments).
The One & Only Catalog	Has very comparable product, but also offers accessories. Also has retail stores.
My Favorite Catalog	Appears to be related product, but for younger audience than we currently target. Has retail stores.

COMPETITOR	Made for Missies Catalog	Secret Weapon Catalog	The One & Only Catalog	My Favorite Catalog	POINT OF DIFFERENCE
BUSINESS OVERVIEW					
Catalog Issue Reviewed	September	October	October	October	
Ownership/# of Years in Catalog Business	Private 4 under current owner	Public 4	Public 6	Public 12	• All competitors have greater experience and actual sales history.
Sales/Average Order $/ Buys Per Year/Rate of Growth	$65 1.8 buys per year Sales $14.7MM (based on 0–12 month, so is a minimum sales #) 8% growth per year	$59 1.2 buys per year Sales 2.1MM 4% growth	$85 $23MM direct 15% growth rate	$60 direct $100 retail Sales $38.2MM 15% growth for 5 years	• The catalog (The One & Only) that offers broader product range appears to have a higher average order.
Circulation/List Information	143,000 12 month buyers	30,000 12 month buyers	9MM circulation	Does not rent their list. Circulation is 3.9MM.	• Our initial mailing will be 3 million.
% of Business Overall (if owned by a parent)	24%	100% catalog and Internet	NA	NA	• NA

COMPETITOR	Made for Missies Catalog	Secret Weapon Catalog	The One & Only Catalog	My Favorite Catalog	POINT OF DIFFERENCE
BUSINESS OVERVIEW					
Percentage of Business by Selling Avenue	NA	Growth is low	60% retail 40% direct	74% retail 26% direct	• Estimated to be 60% retail, 15% Internet, 15% catalog
Health of Business Overall and by Selling Avenue	Adequate, but not a star.	Growth is low; business is under-funded.	Strong direct store sales have not grown in 2 years.	Retail and direct growing Strong competition.	• Well-funded, can be strong.
Stated Customer Profile	Offers sizes XL to 6X, casual lifestyle, yet professional women.	Large size women who desire sexy undergarments as well as those that are practical, ages 25–55, HHI (Household Income) $50,000+, presence of children or grandchildren.	Female, 25–65, 80% college educated, 75% own homes, 55% own luxury car, active charitable donors.	Young women, 18–35, middle to high income, college-educated, presence of children, sizes 12 to 3X.	• We will extend our age range to cover both young (18) and young at heart (65). Our price ranges will start lower than the competition in order to allow for penetration in lower income households.
Product Offerings (% by category)	Blouses Cruisewear Dresses Jackets Loungewear Outerwear Skirts Slack sets Slacks Sweaters Swimwear/ Tops	Body liners/wraps Bras, active Bras, minimize Bras, sexy Camisoles Girdles Hosiery Loungewear Nightgowns & Sleep sets Pajamas Panties Slips T-shirts, oversize	Accessories, other Blouses Dresses Jackets Jewelry Loungewear Outerwear Shoes Skirts Slack sets Slacks Sweaters Tops	Blouses Dresses Jackets Outerwear Skirts Slack sets Slacks Sweaters Tops	• We will include casual wear (no business attire), accessories, including jewelry and shoes and undergarments. • We will have special issues per time of year, e.g., winter cruisewear. • We will include more up-to-the minute trends such as ethnic wear and retro wear.

COMPETITOR	Made for Missies Catalog	Secret Weapon Catalog	The One & Only Catalog	My Favorite Catalog	POINT OF DIFFERENCE
BUSINESS OVERVIEW					
Percentage of Exclusive Products	20%	10%	80%	40%	• Many of our clothes will be our own, original designs.
Product Category Approximate Price Range/ Average Retail	$15–130 price range $70 average retail	$20–110 price range $55 average retail	$30–150 price range $87 average retail	$40–100 price range $49 average retail	• $35–175 price range • $80 average retail
Merchandise Positioning	Traditional clothing but updated, mostly casualwear, but some appropriate for work.	Support garments that add to larger women's sexy look and feel.	Clothing designed to make a larger woman look good and feel good about herself; accessories in correct proportions for larger women.	Youthful look for larger women.	• Today's fun & fanciful looks at affordable prices.
Stated Catalog Positioning/Tag line	Clever Classics Made Fun	Sexy & Savvy!	Sensational Styles that Fit & Flatter	Super Finds You Won't Find Anywhere Else	• Made for Fun! Made for You Alone! • Sub-tag: serving you any way you want: retail, phone, or online.
Impressions of Positioning Based on Review of Catalog	Items are classic but not fun, too staid and somewhat dated.	Very sexy. The photography, type, models and merchandise selection live up to the tag line.	Very wide range of products; gives the feeling that there is everything the larger woman needs in this catalog.	Clothes don't really look all that different from the competition, though styles featured do tend to be for a younger audience.	• We will have large assortment like The One and Only Catalog, but our products will be trendier. • We will incorporate some of the sexy attitude of Secret Weapon Catalog, but not make it our main thrust.

COMPETITOR	Made for Missies Catalog	Secret Weapon Catalog	The One & Only Catalog	My Favorite Catalog	POINT OF DIFFERENCE
BUSINESS OVERVIEW					
How Creative Execution Creates the Positioning Impression	Location photography and models look just like every other catalog.	Moody lighting really helps some products feel sexy. Smart to include male models as it intimates that wearing these garments attracts men.	Pretty crowded look, but helps to give the impression that this catalog contains a lot of product. Traditional creative a bit boring.	Lively presentation with mostly younger models of many ethnic groups.	• Our catalog will have great diversity of models in ethnicity and age. We will include some male models as props. Most of the products will not be shot on location for a more modern look.
Average Product Density Per Spread	6	6	7	6	• 5 products per spread; we will be using the catalog to strongly promote our stores and web site so do not feel that we need as high density as some of our competitors.
SERVICE OVERVIEW (services offered in catalog)					
24-Hour Ordering	Yes	Yes	Yes	Yes	• Yes. We have no distinctive edge here.
Toll-Free Ordering	Yes Also included number for international orders.	Yes	Yes	Yes	• Yes. We have no distinctive edge here.
Internet Address	No	Yes Pushed web site address for international orders.	Yes, promotes store finder.	Yes	• We will promote the address for ordering, but also for exciting info on upcoming fashions and style tips. • We will use web site address for international orders.

COMPETITOR	Made for Missies Catalog	Secret Weapon Catalog	The One & Only Catalog	My Favorite Catalog	POINT OF DIFFERENCE
SERVICE OVERVIEW (services offered in catalog)					
Toll-Free Fax #	No	No	Yes	Yes	• We will offer and promote this service.
Toll-Free Customer Service Number	No	Yes	No	Yes	• We will offer and promote this service.
Gift-Wrap	Yes, simple white box with silver tie, FREE.	Yes, flat fee of $4.95. No photo or description of gift-wrap.	No	Yes, $6.00 photo of blue box with white satin ribbon plus disclaimers about what can and cannot be gift wrapped.	• Yes, silver paper with black satin tie at a flat cost of $5.00. • Will also indicate what cannot be wrapped.
Gift Certificate	Yes, in $10, $20, $25, $50 values.	Yes, in, $20, $25, $50, $75 values.	Yes, in, $20, $25, $50, $75, $100 values.	Yes, in $10, $20, $25, $50 values.	• Yes, in, $20, $25, $50, $75, $100 values. • Beyond just offering the gift certificate, we will provide elegant paper "wallet" for presentation to gift recipient. • This will be photographed and advertised in the catalog.
Stated Standard Delivery Time and Shipping Charges	No	Yes, all in stock orders within one business day of receipt or order.	Yes, will be in customer's home within 3–4 days of receipt of order.	No	• We will ship all in-stock orders the day they are received and promote that in the catalog. • This should mean that customers will receive their orders in 2–3 days.

COMPETITOR	Made for Missies Catalog	Secret Weapon Catalog	The One & Only Catalog	My Favorite Catalog	POINT OF DIFFERENCE
SERVICE OVERVIEW *(services offered in catalog)*					
Proprietary Charge Card	No	No	Yes	Yes	• We cannot offer a Proprietary Charge Card at this time. • We will investigate this option for Year Two of our catalog launch and tie-in with our stores.
VIP/Loyalty Program	Yes, 10% discount. $25 fee refundable if you do not save that much in one year.	No	Yes, 5% discount on all purchases, free shipping, birthday gifts, exclusive savings offers and other invitations. No charge to join.	Not really a club, but points with use of Propriety Charge Card.	• We cannot offer a Loyalty Club at this time. • We will investigate this option for Year Two of our catalog launch and tie-in with our stores.
Personal Shopping Service	No	Yes, concentrates on helping customers get the right size undergarments, has a reminder service for basic items such as hosiery.	No	No	• We cannot offer this service at this time, but will we have well-trained phone personnel to offer assistance with questions.

COMPETITOR	Made for Missies Catalog	Secret Weapon Catalog	The One & Only Catalog	My Favorite Catalog	POINT OF DIFFERENCE
SERVICE OVERVIEW (services offered in catalog)					
Letter from Company	Yes, addresses how buyers find the items offered in the catalog. Is on page 2.	Yes, talks about the excitement of owning sensual clothing. Is on page 2.	No	No	• Yes, will change from issue to issue, addressing what is special in that particular issue.
Socially-Conscious Program (including privacy)	No	No	No	No	• Yes, will donate a portion of sales to breast cancer research.
Volume Discount	No	No	No	No	• No • We do not feel this is appropriate for our sales category. • We will most likely add discounts when we introduce our Proprietary Credit Card.
Strength of Internet Tie-in to Printed Catalog or Retail Stores	No Internet option.	Web site editorial in a few places in the catalog tells how the web can help the customer get the right fit/size for foundation items.	Promotes stores on order form by giving web site where customer can find local store. Is on almost every page and shown with the 800# but does not provide reason to go the web site.	Shows with 800# on every other spread; no editorial coverage about web site.	• Web site will be promoted as the place to be for all the great new fashions for large size women. • "We speak your language" approach. • Will appear in editorial about every 5 spreads. • Site address and toll-free numbers for service and fax will be shown together on every spread.

COMPETITOR	Made for Missies Catalog	Secret Weapon Catalog	The One & Only Catalog	My Favorite Catalog	POINT OF DIFFERENCE
SERVICE OVERVIEW (services offered in catalog)					
Guarantee Parameters	Unlimited	90 days	30 days	Unlimited	• Unlimited. • To increase the strength of our guarantee, we may test paying for return postage on exchanges for some product categories or even overall. • Normally, we will include a return label that deducts the cost of returning the item from the credit due to the customer.
Other Services	$25 off coupon	Payment Plan, no interest until January,	Offered measurement chart, but type and drawing too small to read easily.	No	• We will have a service called "By Appointment" that will allow customers to have personal consultation by appointment. • Can be over the phone (they can send digital photo) or come into one of our stores.

COMPETITOR	Made for Missies Catalog	Secret Weapon Catalog	The One & Only Catalog	My Favorite Catalog	POINT OF DIFFERENCE
CREATIVE OVERVIEW (printed catalog)					
Size	7½″ x 10″	7½″ x 10″	7½″ x 10″	7½″ x 10″	• Our catalog will be the same as our competitors for this issue. • We need to investigate the size of other issues as we wish to have some different sizes based on special issues, such as a square format swimwear issue mailed in late spring.
Folio Count	56	56	62	62	• 64—no point of difference.
Type	Old-fashioned serif typeface. Headlines are different from body copy and in color that distracts from the photography. Prices also in color, but so light that they are hard to read.	Sans serif, flowery, light and feminine, easy-to-read, no headlines. Prices same color and size as body copy.	Sans serif, italic lead-ins to each body copy paragraph, no headlines, price same color and size as body copy, but SKU number is in bold. Feels very professional, contemporary, but not fun.	Sans serif body copy and headlines, but trite headlines waste space; overall very contemporary, light feeling. Uses bold for prices, which seems to indicate that this catalog believes it has a value statement.	• Sans serif, contemporary, prices in dark gray so stand out, but do not look like sale prices. • Use different type for headlines than for body copy; headlines will also be in dark gray. • Editorial copy will be italic version of body copy.

COMPETITOR	Made for Missies Catalog	Secret Weapon Catalog	The One & Only Catalog	My Favorite Catalog	POINT OF DIFFERENCE
CREATIVE OVERVIEW (printed catalog)					
Paper and Printing Quality	Glossy, very lightweight, has some show through, feels a little rough to the touch. Good printing, but paper does not allow for real depth of color.	Glossy, heavy stock, feels expensive and makes you think the products might be expensive, too. Printing very rich.	Glossy, light weight, some color shows through the pages, feels thin, not high quality. Printing sharp.	Shiny, lightweight, paper tends to stick together, but holds color well. Very good printing shows product detail well even on lightweight paper.	• Suede finish paper, lower weight, but not lowest weight, which will stand out against all the shiny, glossy papers. • Printing will be top caliber
# of Photo Images	6	6	7	6	• 5
Style of Photography	Location, natural lighting, very posed looking.	Mostly indoor locations, darkly lighted for sexy feel, but lighted so well that product detail can still be seen.	Very old-fashioned, flat lighting, some location. but mostly simple set up on seamless backgrounds.	Combination of location and silhouettes, excellent texture detail and depth of field.	• Few major photos on location for mood setting. • Most of photography silhouetted on white background. • Crisp, clean contemporary feel.
Copy Tone, Amount	Simply states the facts, very little romancing. Minimal copy.	Minimal, but with sexy undertones. Specific about fit.	Sparse, but efficient. Friendly.	Tries to have fun with some copy being light-hearted. More copy than other competitors.	• Will keep copy to a minimum, but try to incorporate real personality of fun and some humor. • Since we have so many exclusives, may create names for the items that are funny or tongue-in-check.

COMPETITOR	Made for Missies Catalog	Secret Weapon Catalog	The One & Only Catalog	My Favorite Catalog	POINT OF DIFFERENCE
CREATIVE OVERVIEW (printed catalog)					
Model Types	Blond, primarily Caucasian, mostly late 20's, early 30's, traditional, but bland.	Middle 20's to a few in the early 50's. Broad mixture of ethnic groups.	Mostly under 30, some ethnic, but largely Caucasian.	Young, high concentration of ethnic models.	• From young (teen) to mature (65). • Mixture of ethnic groups, leaning toward more exotic looks. • Occasional male as prop.
Additional Decorative Elements	Terrific swatching, easy to find and understand, consistent location.	No	Uses little colored tabs to divide the catalog by product category.	No	• We will use some illustrations to reinforce an activity, e.g., bicycle drawing with sports clothes.

5 Researching Your Market

There are two basic types of research, both with options. We will address each area in detail individually, but first let's look at an overview of the types of research preferred by the majority of catalogers:

1. Quantitative: Precise, deals with numbers, percentages and other such quantifiable data and tends to deal with large samples (100+ contacts). The types that catalogers most use are market research questionnaires:

    - In mail.

    - In outgoing packages.

    - Via the Internet.

    - Telephone surveys.

2. Qualitative: Esoteric, deals with options and attitudes and works with small samples, generally under 25. The forms most used by catalogers are focus groups and, occasionally, one-on-one-depth interviews:

    - One-on-one-depth interviewing consists of a facilitator who interviews one person at a time.
      Due to expense, this is used less often than groups. Exhibit 5.1 would be applicable to a one-on-one interview as well as a more traditional focus group of 10 to 20 people.

    - Groups consists of a variety of interviewees, all controlled by one facilitator; though a group size can go up to 20, for better control and input we prefer groups of no more than 15 people.

Exhibit 5.1 Research Flow Chart

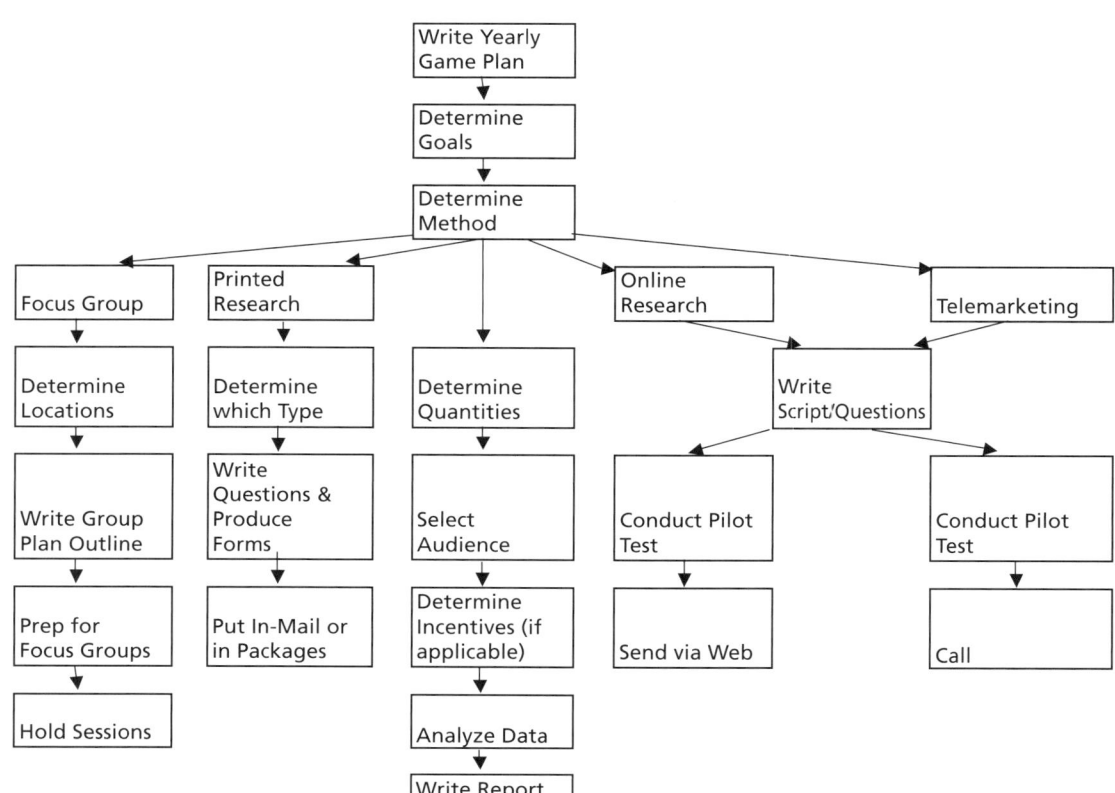

Six Simple Research Rules

Research can be wildly complex, but the profitable use of research comes down to six simple, practical rules:

⇨ Be clear about the goal of the research.

⇨ Keep the meaning of questions simple, direct, reasonably short and clear.

⇨ Always understand where the question you wish to ask will lead you.

⇨ Remember that research is only a guide.

⇨ Use benchmarking.

⇨ Understand statistical validity.

Be Clear About the Goal of the Research

Understand exactly what you are measuring and be certain that all team members agree on the expected outcome. See Exhibit 5.8, Focus Group Plan Outline, which notes Key Take-Aways as part of the document.

Keep the Meaning of Questions Simple, Direct, Reasonably Short and Clear

Tell the person answering the research up front how long the process is going to take and that all information will be kept confidential. Exhibit 5.2 shows a printed example of a survey. For a phone survey, interviewers should, as the questions progress, make a reassuring statement such as "We are almost finished" or "Just a few more questions now."

Internet or online surveys often show a chart that indicates how much progress you have made, e.g., 45 percent completed. This is effective if the survey isn't too long. If the survey is going to take more than 10 to 15 minutes to complete, consider not using a gauge that shows how much more time will be needed to complete all the questions.

Don't allow questions to be too broad. "How would you rate our service?" isn't detailed enough. Rather, make the question precise, e.g., "How would you rate the level of service you experienced on your recent telephone contact with us?"

Before finalizing your questions, run them by someone not familiar with the company or project (allow for confidentiality concerns). Without providing an explanation, do they understand exactly what you are trying to learn from the questions? If not, rewrite. While the length of the survey does affect the response rate, it is even more important to make sure the questions are easy and comfortable to answer.

Always Understand Where the Question You Wish to Ask Will Lead You

Too often we have seen companies ask interviewees questions that lead to answers that the company cannot act on. For instance, do not explore doubling the page count of your catalog per issue. It is unlikely that an immediate move to a much larger catalog would be financially viable.

Word questions so that you achieve actionable direction. In the case of the page count increase, a viable question might be: "Would you be more inclined to order from our holiday catalog, usually received in your home in late November, if it contained more pages of products? How many more pages do you think would be the correct number?"

Remember That Research Is Only a Guide

You are talking to a small sampling of your customer or prospect base. Yes, you will strive for statistical validity (see below), but, unless you talk to each and every person in your database, research results are for direction only.

If most of the attendees of a focus group like the idea of 20 percent off, this, rather than the other promotional ideas you have been considering, will make an excellent first test. But it should not become an absolute way of doing business.

Use Benchmarking

Repeat your research year to year using basically the same set of questions to the same group (not the same people within the group, but different ones). This way you can see if you have made progress in the areas in which you have surveyed customers. Regular, consistent research allows you, with input from your customers, to set a baseline against which you can judge your company's performance.

Understand Statistical Validity

Statistical validity concerns itself with the reproducibility of results. This means that if you obtain a certain result from research, how likely is it that the result is real and not just a random effect?

Three factors are involved in understanding statistical validity:

1. Population: For example, if you are trying to find information on your 0–12 month buyers, the total number of 0–12 month buyers is the population.

2. Sample size: The number of people who respond to the survey or answer the phone questions.

3. Response rate: The percentage of response that gives a particular answer to a question.

The formulas (found in basic statistics books) relate these quantities to a level of confidence in the reproducibility of results (the non-randomness), which generally is 90 percent, 95 percent, or 99 percent. The higher the confidence level, the more you can rely on the data you have obtained. If you start with a desired level of confidence, the equations can be used to show the spread in the response percentage or the needed sample size (but not both).

Printed Research Forms

Some pointers:

1. In the past we avoided open-ended questions due to cost and time to review, tabulate, and digest. However, Automated Text Analysis software can use a combination of predicative and manual techniques to categorize responses to open-ended questions, thus making the use of open-ended questions more approachable.

2. Make the type large enough to read easily, especially if you are going to an older audience.

3. Tell the reader up front how long the process will take.

4. Tell the reader in a friendly manner why you want the information.

5. Thank the reader at the end of the form.

6. Ask for confidential info (such as salaries) at the end of the research form.

7. It usually is not necessary to offer incentives to customers other than postage-paid return envelope, but response can be increased with gift certificates. Always enclose the incentive with the research form.

8. Incentives may be needed for non-customer research. The most common incentive is an enclosed dollar bill.

9. For ease of readership, design the survey so that that it is airy, with plenty of space between lines.

10. Consider adapting the basic survey so that it is specific for a customer and a non-customer version.

Exhibit 5.2 Printed Market Research Survey Outline

A. Letter introducing the research survey, explaining the time required of and benefit to the person who is being asked to answer the questions.

   1. Print on company letterhead.

   2. May wish to include picture of the catalog for reinforcement and clarification.

B. Questions that will support the fact that the survey is going to the group you had planned to receive it.

C. Questions that provide overall input as to the attitudes and feeling about the catalog.

D. Questions that are specific to a particular area, such as merchandise, creative or service.

E. A section of questions that tends to be more open-ended or that gathers competitive information. Put this in the latter part of the document because it is more difficult for the respondents to answer and can be intimidating if positioned at the beginning of the research survey.

F. Confidential information about the responder.

G. Closing "Thank You."

H. Postage-paid envelope for returning the survey.

A survey like the one shown in Exhibit 5.3 should be mailed specifically to those customers the cataloger believes have purchased gifts from the catalog. Question #3 helps to clarify if the assumption that these are gift givers is correct. Include a picture and description of the catalog to help recipients remember what the Catherine M catalog looks like and what it contains.

If the survey were to be a bounceback (which are put into outgoing packages), it would have considerably fewer questions. Because opening the package distracts a customer, bounceback questionnaires generally have a lower response rate than in-mail questionnaires. To help increase response, bounceback questionnaires should contain no more than ten questions.

Exhibit 5.3 Printed Market Research Survey Example

(Date)

Dear Catherine M. Customer,

We really value your opinion!

It is always our desire to make your gift purchasing more pleasurable. Your attention to our questions today will help assure that we are offering you what you want and in the way you want it.

Answering the questions will most likely take no more than 10 minutes. Though it is only a token, in appreciation we have enclosed a $10 gift certificate redeemable on your next purchase with Catherine M.

Be assured that all information will be kept strictly confidential and used only to help us better serve you.

My sincerest thanks,

Catherine M.

CATHERINE M. CUSTOMER SURVEY

1. When did you last receive your Catherine M. catalog? Within:
    ( ) the past month   ( ) 3–6 months   ( ) 1–2 years
    ( ) 1–2 months   ( ) 7–12 months   ( ) over 2 years
    ( ) never (if never, please skip to question 35)

2. Have you purchased from Catherine M. in the last 12 months?
    ( ) Yes   ( ) No (if no, please skip to question 35)

3. Was the item you bought:
    ( ) a gift   ( ) for yourself   ( ) both

Overall

Rank the importance of the following statements. Circle the number that indicates whether you **disagree strongly, agree, or agree strongly.**

		Disagree Strongly				Agree				Agree Strongly	
4.	An important reason to purchase Catherine M. products is because they are made by craftsmen.	1	2	3	4	5	6	7	8	9	10
5.	Catherine M. provides an excellent value for my money.	1	2	3	4	5	6	7	8	9	10
6.	I feel that Catherine M. provides me with a risk-free gift (one that I am very sure the recipient will like).	1	2	3	4	5	6	7	8	9	10
7.	I feel that the items in Catherine M. are truly unique.	1	2	3	4	5	6	7	8	9	10
8.	A major reason I have chosen to purchase is that Catherine M. gives a portion of their profits to charity.	1	2	3	4	5	6	7	8	9	10
9.	I don't shop from Catherine M. often because there is not enough product selection.	1	2	3	4	5	6	7	8	9	10
10.	Catherine M. sometimes has so many choices I have trouble making up my mind.	1	2	3	4	5	6	7	8	9	10
11.	I just don't give very many gifts anymore.	1	2	3	4	5	6	7	8	9	10

	Disagree Strongly				Agree				Agree Strongly	

12. The catalog gives me the feeling, whether I have actually used Catherine M. service or not, that Catherine M. has excellent service.
1 2 3 4 5 6 7 8 9 10

13. The unlimited guarantee is very important to me.
1 2 3 4 5 6 7 8 9 10

14. I tend to choose gifts from companies that offer me dollars or percentages off the base price.
1 2 3 4 5 6 7 8 9 10

15. In comparison to other catalogs, Catherine M.'s prices are fair.
1 2 3 4 5 6 7 8 9 10

16. The gift-wrap is one of the reasons I buy gifts from Catherine M.
1 2 3 4 5 6 7 8 9 10

17. All gift catalogs pretty much offer the same products; Catherine M. is no different.
1 2 3 4 5 6 7 8 9 10

18. I prefer to shop over the Internet for gifts now.
1 2 3 4 5 6 7 8 9 10

19. No extra charge for 2nd day air shipment would be a deciding factor in choosing Catherine M.
1 2 3 4 5 6 7 8 9 10

20. I prefer to shop from Catherine M's web site rather than from the printed catalog.
1 2 3 4 5 6 7 8 9 10

Shopping from the Catalog

Rank the importance of the following statements. Circle the number that indicates whether you **disagree strongly, agree, or agree strongly**.

		Disagree Strongly				Agree				Agree Strongly	
21.	I feel that Catherine M. catalogs arrive at my home when I need them.	1	2	3	4	5	6	7	8	9	10
22.	I wish I received the catalog more often.	1	2	3	4	5	6	7	8	9	10
23.	I get ideas from the catalog, but prefer to shop at retail outlets.	1	2	3	4	5	6	7	8	9	10
24.	The main reason I shop from the catalog is variety.	1	2	3	4	5	6	7	8	9	10
25.	There are too many choices, so I put off purchasing and then forget.	1	2	3	4	5	6	7	8	9	10
26.	The copy information clearly explains why I should choose Catherine M. products over another brand.	1	2	3	4	5	6	7	8	9	10
27.	I like the way the products are photographed.	1	2	3	4	5	6	7	8	9	10
28.	The detail shown in the photographs is sufficient for me to make a purchase decision.	1	2	3	4	5	6	7	8	9	10
29.	It's hard to find the service information I need.	1	2	3	4	5	6	7	8	9	10
30.	The products are easier to find online than in the catalog.	1	2	3	4	5	6	7	8	9	10

	Disagree Strongly				Agree				Agree Strongly	
31. The typeface used for the copy in the catalog isn't always easy to read.	1	2	3	4	5	6	7	8	9	10
32. Catherine M.'s return policy affects my decision to purchase.	1	2	3	4	5	6	7	8	9	10
33. The catalog is organized in a way that it helps me find and purchase the items I want.	1	2	3	4	5	6	7	8	9	10
33. I have a certain budget in mind and look for products in that price range.	1	2	3	4	5	6	7	8	9	10
34. I like to buy the same gifts year after year.	1	2	3	4	5	6	7	8	9	10

Just a Few More Questions
(Reminder: All information is strictly confidential.)

35. Please name your favorite gift catalog _____
_____

36. What is your prime source for the purchase of gifts? (Please check one that most closely applies.)
    - ( ) catalog
    - ( ) Internet site
    - ( ) boutique store
    - ( ) discount store
    - ( ) department store
    - ( ) other (please specify)_____

37. Approximately how many times do you give gifts per year?
    - ( ) less than 1
    - ( ) 1–2
    - ( ) 3–4
    - ( ) more than 5

38. Please rank the following reasons why you would choose to order from a catalog of high-quality crafts products:

	Disagree Strongly				Agree				Agree Strongly	
38a. reasonable prices	1	2	3	4	5	6	7	8	9	10
38b. good selection	1	2	3	4	5	6	7	8	9	10
38c. reputable company	1	2	3	4	5	6	7	8	9	10
38d. incentives with purchase	1	2	3	4	5	6	7	8	9	10
38e. good customer service	1	2	3	4	5	6	7	8	9	10

38f. other (please specify) _____

_____

39. What would be the single most important incentive in influencing you to purchase? _____

_____

40. Please place a check in the space that best describes your level of education.
    ( ) attended high school
    ( ) completed high school
    ( ) attended some college
    ( ) completed college (4 years)
    ( ) attended or completed graduate studies

41. What is your current employment status? (Please check one.)
    ( ) Entrepreneur
    ( ) Health Care Professional
    ( ) Educational Professional
    ( ) Legal Professional
    ( ) Arts Professional
    ( ) Science Professional
    ( ) Technical Professional (computer, air control, technician other than health)
    ( ) Sales Professional

( ) Administrative Support
( ) Personal Service Industry Professional
( ) Maintenance Professional
( ) Protective Service Professional
( ) Farming, Forestry, Fishing Professional
( ) Executive, Administrator, Manager
( ) Laborer
( ) Homemaker
( ) Retired
( ) Student
( ) Other (please specify) _____

42. Please indicate your current marital status.
    ( ) single   ( ) divorced   ( ) widowed
    ( ) married   ( ) separated

43. Please indicate in the appropriate box the category in which your age falls.
    ( ) under 18   ( ) 35–39   ( ) 55–59
    ( ) 18–24   ( ) 40–44   ( ) 60–64
    ( ) 25–29   ( ) 45–49   ( ) 65–70
    ( ) 30–34   ( ) 50–54   ( ) 71+

44. Please check the space that best describes your total annual family income before taxes.
    ( ) under $10,000   ( ) $60,000–$69,999
    ( ) $10,000–$19,999   ( ) $70,000–$79,999
    ( ) $20,000–$29,999   ( ) $80,000–$89,999
    ( ) $30,000–$39,999   ( ) $90,000–$99,999
    ( ) $40,000–$49,999   ( ) $100,000–$125,000
    ( ) $50,000–$59,999   ( ) $125,001 or more

Not Essential, But Would Appreciate It

Name _____

Address _____

City/State/Zip _____

Home Phone _____ Business Phone _____

E-mail Address _____

THANK YOU SO MUCH! Please return your completed survey in the postage paid envelope provided.

Internet Research Forms

Even faster than telephone surveys, online research gets you data quickly. While this is a new method and the overall effect on your customers is still unknown, responses to these surveys tend to be higher than to a printed survey. Either way, be sure to track customer performance of those who have been sent research forms versus those who have not.

You have two main choices when deciding to do online research. Do you want to hire a professional to handle everything or do it yourself? There are many options and advantages for both choices.

An experienced research company has been conducting research for decades and has had experience with hundreds of businesses. Experience translates into knowing what questions to ask and how to read the results. These companies often have a database with over a million people, helping assure representative samples of virtually any target market.

In addition, some such companies generally have the software and technology to conduct online focus groups. One more point: When you work with a research firm, you can share the expense of incentives with others, a key factor in getting response. Copy on the web site page of one such company, Greenfield Online, illustrates this fact: "Sharing your opinions online is easy and always confidential. Join now and be entered to win our $2,000 cash giveaway as well as hundreds of other prizes."

On the other hand, a growing number of web sites offer survey software that allows you to create custom, professional surveys and gives you the tools you need to analyze the results. You can use a web-based service where all you need is the software and a browser. Send the surveys out by e-mail to your own list or, with some survey web sites, tap into their lists. The options in survey services available are growing rapidly; a quick search on the Internet will give you a wide range of choices and pricing structures.

Include a photo of your catalog for easy identification. Questions are basically the same as are found in printed research (Exhibit 5.3), though there are some differences:

- Ask for the e-mail address of the respondent (if using web-delivery).
- Keep it short and simple.
- Include an incentive to help avoid the unfilled out return of your survey.

Subjects that can be researched are almost unlimited. For an excellent guide to some possibilities see http://www/surveyconsole.com.

Exhibit 5.4 is a partial list from the survey console web site (the numbers in brackets equal the number of surveys available in that category):

Exhibit 5.4 Internet Market Research Survey Categories

    Satisfaction
        Customer satisfaction (15)
        Product surveys (25)
        Service evaluation (19)
    Marketing
        New product/concept testing (20)
        Focus group recruitment
        Web site
        Conference feedback
        Hardware/software
    Services
        Hotels/restaurant (6)
        Retail (16)
        Health care (10)
        B2B (8)
        Travel (4)

As with printed research surveys, an online survey would lead off with the reason you wish the information, an incentive to complete the research, and conclude with a thank you.

Exhibit 5.5 Internet Market Research Survey Example

Below is a Service Evaluation from the Free Survey Template Library of surveyconsole.com.

Have you ever ordered (PRODUCT) from (COMPANY)?
- ☐ Yes
- ☐ No

Overall, how would you rate (COMPANY)?
- ☐ Excellent
- ☐ Good
- ☐ Average
- ☐ Poor
- ☐ Terrible
- ☐ Not sure

How satisfied are you with your service from (COMPANY)?
- ☐ Extremely satisfied
- ☐ Very satisfied
- ☐ Neutral
- ☐ Very dissatisfied
- ☐ Extremely dissatisfied

Would you recommend (COMPANY) to a friend?
- ☐ Yes
- ☐ No
- ☐ Not sure

If no, why not?

For your next (PRODUCT) purchase, how likely are you to purchase from (COMPANY)?
- ☐ Definitely would buy
- ☐ Probably would buy
- ☐ Might or might not buy
- ☐ Probably would not buy
- ☐ Definitely would not buy
- ☐ N/A

Which of the following modes did you use to place the order for (PRODUCT)?
- ☐ Mail order
- ☐ Internet
- ☐ Over the phone
- ☐ Fax
- ☐ Other _____

What are the **THREE** main reasons you didn't purchase [PRODUCT] from [OTHER COMPANY]?

What would you change about the process of purchasing (PRODUCT)?
(i.e., placing the order, mode of payment, delivery, etc.) from [COMPANY]?

Are there any other comments you have for [COMPANY]?

Here is a checklist of questions to ask when interviewing online research resources:

1. How much does it cost? Be certain exactly what is and isn't covered, and what software level you are buying. For instance, you want to pay only for incoming responses, not outgoing questions.

2. How personal, professional, and effective is the customer service? There should be a real person to talk to, as well as e-mail support.

3. Do you love the references? If not, find someone else.

4. How private is data really? Make privacy a #1 concern, and make sure the vendor adheres to CASRO's Code of Standards and Ethics for Survey Research (www.casro.org).

5. How fast is the software? It should be robust enough to handle several thousand outbound e-mails and incoming responses in a matter of hours.

6. Can the technology deal with bounce and unsubscribe messages? This is a must-have.

7. How good is online reporting? You generally get what you pay for.

8. How much survey design guidance are you getting? Either hire somebody who makes the survey stimulating and detailed enough to get the kind of responses you want, or make certain the software you choose offers survey and response type templates that help achieve your business objectives.

9. How long has the vendor has been in this business? You want someone with online research expertise, not just research experience.

10. How good is the quality of the data? Remember, you want actionable information.

Telephone Surveys

Telephone Marketing Surveys, of course, can be more detailed than Exhibit 5.6. Nevertheless, typically about 10 minutes, they most often are one of the shortest in length of all of the types of research formats addressed in this chapter.

The intent of the telephone survey illustrated in Exhibit 5.6 is to get a snapshot of how well the catalog is being remembered and, generally, how well the customer service is perceived. In addition, this company wants to delete the names of those individuals who show no interest in receiving the catalog. Note, however, that the company does not delete the names from the customers who have ordered, even though some of these customers indicate that it is "Very Unlikely" that they will order again. The reasoning is that these customers have ordered before and may be tempted by future merchandise offers. Those who do indicate "Very Unlikely" could be tagged in the database and deleted in the future if they don't, indeed, order again.

The phone survey would most likely have a preamble in which the surveyor asked the person being surveyed if they could ask them a few questions: "Hi! I'm from the John Jones Market Research firm. We are doing some research for the ABC Catalog Company. May I have five minutes of your time to ask you just a few questions?"

Exhibit 5.6 tracks how the surveyor would walk the customer through the process. Some of the questions require a straight "yes" or "no" answer; others are open-ended. The person conducting the survey would have a list of potential answers to check against as well as space to indicate answers that are not on that list. One example of this would be the question, "What is the reason you chose not to order?" A list of possible responses to this question, as well as instructions on how the surveyor should respond per customer, are included in the table below.

Reasons Not to Order and Possible Responses

Customer Response	Surveyor Response
• No merchandise/products I liked.	
• Prices too high.	
• Had a bad experience previously.	Ask customer to describe.
• Didn't have time.	
• Plan to later.	Skip the question, "How likely is it that you will place another order in the future" is this is the reason.
• Other.	Get specific information.

72 The Catalog Strategist's Toolkit

Exhibit 5.6 Telephone Survey Flow Chart

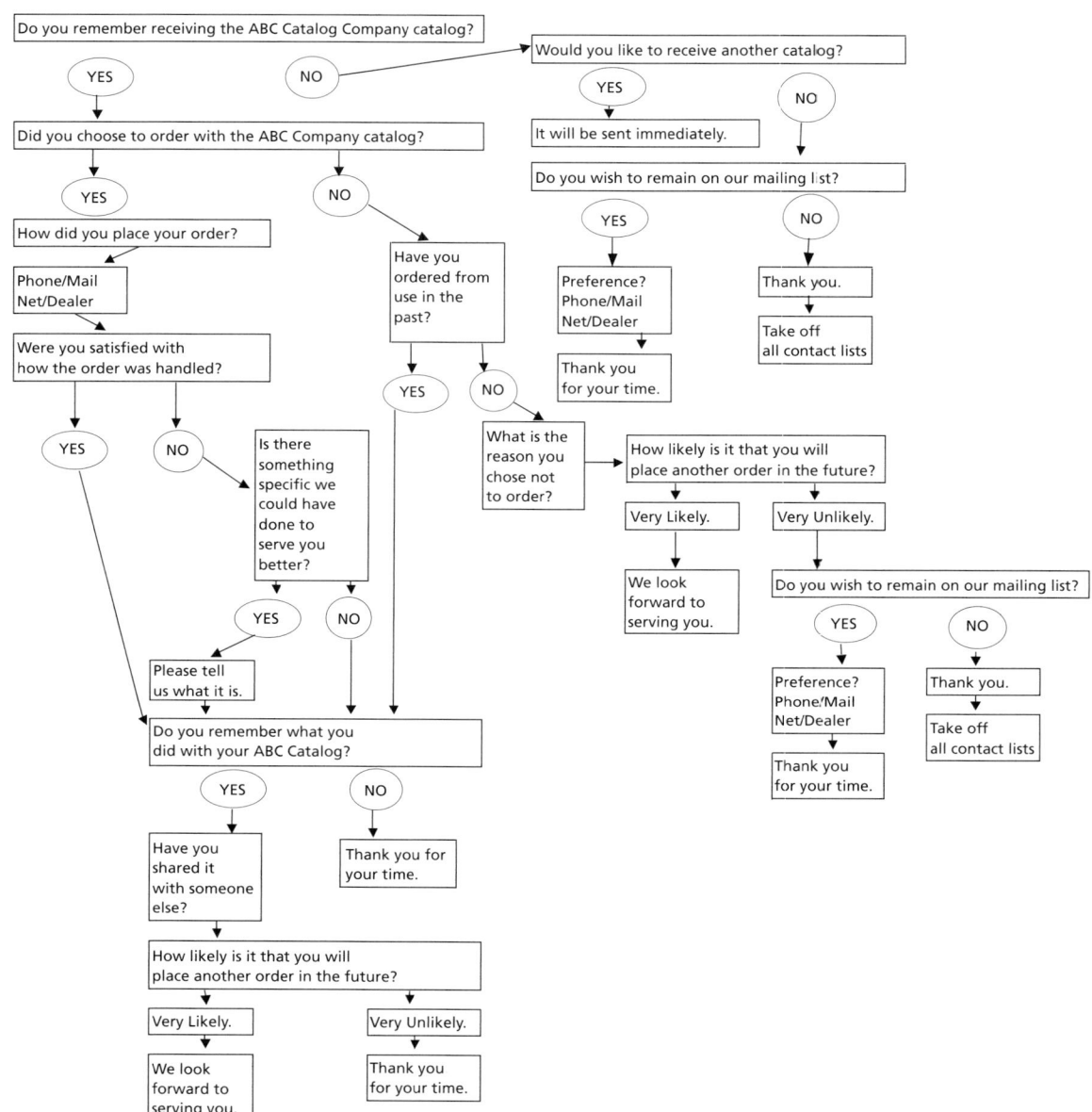

What a Focus Group Is . . . and Isn't

For this type of research, individuals sit around a table that can be viewed from behind a two-way mirror. Guided by a facilitator with a script (Exhibit 5.9), the attendees discuss the merits of your catalog.

The ideal structure for focus groups is:

- Four groups selected from the list of likely segments below.

- Three sessions each in three or four cities. (This is so results are not geographically skewed and provide a balanced picture of the entire United States. If this is not possible, select one or two cities that best represent your target market.)

Some likely segments:

- Recent (zero-six month) customers who have purchased.

- 12-month customers who purchased once (or twice) and then never purchased again.

- Requestors who have never converted.

- Males only.

- Females only.

- Purchasers of competitive products.

Exhibit 5.7 Focus Group Construction Example

CITY	GROUP #1	GROUP #2	GROUP #3
Cincinnati	Zero-six month customers, males only.	Zero-six month customers, females only.	Customers who have not purchased in over a year, male and female.
Austin	Customers who have not purchased in over a year, male only.	Zero-six month customers, males only.	Zero-six month customers, females only.
Oklahoma City	Purchasers of competitive products.	Six month customers, females only.	Customers who have not purchased in over a year, male and female.

Exhibit 5.7 is totally dependent on your overall mix of customers. For instance, if the catalog had a 90 percent female customer base, you would have no male only or male and female segments. Locations would be based on the availability of customers in particular areas. Attempt to get a broad mix that reflects both your current customers and your target market.

Always include sales-resistant consumers, such as those who have stopped purchasing and those that requested a catalog but did not order. If you talk only to customers, you will only hear the good stuff. You want to know what you did wrong, not just what you did right.

We prefer to structure groups, if at all possible within a budget, with either all females or all males. Groups of the same sex tend to have less interaction with one another, resulting in less power-mongering and more honest answers.

Information obtained during a focus group is viewed by you (behind two-way mirrors), taped (audio and/or video) and transcribed by the facilitator who records what he or she believed was learned. If several people from your company attend, have them take notes as well, as we all hear things differently. If you get written input from a variety of sources, you will have a better overall understanding of what the attendees really meant.

It's up to the facilitator, working with the facility in which the focus groups are held, to find and qualify the attendees. Always bring catalogs and gift certificates to the focus group. Attendees, after talking about your catalog for over an hour, are very receptive to purchase.

Remember, focus groups are a great source of information, but they are not definitive. Use their input with other research and your own common sense.

Exhibit 5.8, the Focus Group Plan Outline, should be given to the group facilitator days or weeks before the focus group session in order to provide him or her with direction. This will allow the facilitator to fully understand what the cataloger desires from this focus group session.

Recommended times to be spent on each area to be addressed are in brackets. The cataloger and the facilitator should discuss the viability of these times for the amount of information that is hoped to be gained. This particular outline covers more than could be addressed comfortably in a focus group within a normal time frame of one hour to 90 minutes, but it can be edited easily to your particular needs.

You will note the occasional use of handouts. Handouts provided prior to the discussion of a subject allow individual attendees to record their feelings before they are influenced by the feelings of others. The process is:

- Handouts are given out. (See Exhibits 5.8 and 5.9 for examples.)
- Attendees are asked to complete the handouts.
- The facilitator collects the completed handouts.
- Discussion is conducted so each person can explain why they wrote what he or she did.

Exhibit 5.8 Focus Group Plan Outline

This outline would most likely be used for a start-up catalog, although all areas would apply to an existing catalog that was considering changing in some way.

I. Introductions. (10 minutes)

II. Basic concept of the catalog. (Summary) (5 minutes)

III. Primarily areas to be explored.

    A. General direct marketing shopping habits. (10 minutes)

    B. Merchandise. (25 minutes)

        1. A handout listing products under consideration for inclusion in the catalog will be provided for grading before discussion by the focus group participants.

        2. Photos of the products will also be displayed on the walls of the focus group room. These mounted photos will be kept under cover until all focus group attendees have been seated and the facilitator has covered details leading up to this phase.

        3. Photos will not be the exact products but will be representative of product categories.

        4. The facilitator will ask attendees what they think the key products are worth. This could be a handout that would show up to ten products representing different categories. Attendees should be asked to write what they would pay for each product on the handout.

            a) Discussion will begin after the handouts are completed by the attendees and collected by facilitator.

    C. Creative. (25 minutes)

        1. Mounted layout designs representing four different creative approaches.

            a. More than four concepts can overwhelm and confuse participants.

            b. Concepts usually consist of:

                (1) Cover.

                (2) Two spreads that accompany the cover.

c. Concepts are numbered on the back for easy reference, e.g., "Do you prefer concept one over two?" It is not unusual for attendees to want to mix the concepts: "I like cover one better with the inside pages of concept two." It is important that attendees understand that they have the freedom to do this. Occasionally you need to have an example of an actual catalog in order to make this clear.

d. As attendees are only seeing a couple pages of a catalog, they sometimes think that this is the number of pages the actual catalog will be. It is important not to assume that they understand that these few pages will evolve into a catalog of many pages. Explain this in detail before they begin to discuss the layouts.

e. Sometimes actual mock-ups of the concept pages are given to the interviewees. This would mean that those being asked their opinion are holding a six-page catalog on much heavier paper (concept paper) than that on which the actual catalog would be printed.

  (1) While it is convenient for all attendees to have catalog concepts that they can hold in their hands, we do not recommend this. We believe that better interaction, less confusion, and more valid input comes from allowing the attendees to get up out of their seats and walk up to the layouts that are on the walls.

D. Competition. (10 minutes)

1. Verbal exploration of attendees' views on who they consider to be the competition.
    a. No initial prompting. Allow attendees to determine who they believe the competition to be based on the merchandise and creative they have seen.
    b. If the group gets bogged down on only a few competitors, have your competitors' catalogs handy to show for stimulation.
    c. Actually handing them out can aid input, but it will also lengthen the time needed for this section, so keep that in mind if you feel that reminding the attendees of competitors' catalogs' content is important.

2. Exploration of why.
   a. Encourage the facilitator to dig deeply into why the attendees believe the catalogs, retailers or Internet sites would be competition.
   b. In this plan, there is not enough time to ask the attendees what the new catalog might do to beat the competition, but this question could be asked if some of the other areas were assigned less time.

E. Promotion. (15 minutes)
   1. Explore how audience feels about the promotion in context with this brand.
   2. Explore what the primary motivations might be. (Handout will be provided for grading before discussion).
      a. In this case, you would prepare a handout that would list some of the promotions you are considering and ask the attendees to rank their favorites in order from one to ten. Promotions you might wish them to rank could be:
         (1) 10 percent off, no purchase minimum.
         (2) 20 percent off with order of $50 or more.
         (3) Free shipping and handling, no purchase minimum.
         (4) Free upgrade on basic shipping and handling charge (you pay shipping and handling but can overnight at no extra cost).
         (5) Free gift with purchase.
         (6) Buy now, pay later.
         (7) Buy now, interest-free monthly bills for a year.
         (8) $5 off, no purchase minimum.
         (9) $10 off with order of $50 or more.
         (10) All orders automatically shipped overnight.

IV. Key Take-Aways. (These are the most important points that you want to gather from the research.)

   A. Identify similarities/differences between customer/non-customer segments.
   B. Have clear direction on creative approach.
   C. Have clear direction on merchandise approach.
   D. Have understanding of promotional motivations.

Exhibit 5.9 Focus Group Plan Example

Slight adaptations have been made to Exhibit 5.8 to create Exhibit 5.9 in order to show how easily the form can be adapted to fit different situations. The focus group in Exhibit 5.9 is designed to determine the viability of a potential new catalog entry.

KING VIDEO Focus Group Plan
Currently scheduled for January 12, 2006

I. Facilitator introduces herself and invites attendees to tell the group a little about themselves. (10 minutes)

II. Basic concept of the catalog. (10 minutes)

   A. A mail order catalog that:

      1. Sells audio, video, and entertainment-related products that are:

         a. Exclusive or preemptive.

            (1) Some products are unique and not available in retail or through other mail order catalog, TV commercials, or Internet sites.
            (2) Other products have been adapted to provide unique benefits, such as directors' cuts.
            (3) Other products have been teamed with such collectibles as signed posters.
            (4) All are new or new versions of classics.
            (5) Some products will be themed to important events.

         b. Product offerings are limited in selection, as each product is individually chosen from the vast collection available from the top entertainment producers in the world.

III. Primarily areas to be explored.

   A. General direct marketing shopping habits. (10 minutes)

      1. How do you prefer to shop?
      2. Do you shop by catalog often? What about by Internet?
      3. What is better about paper catalogs than an Internet site and vice versa?

4. Do you have favorite companies that you shop from in each area (paper and Internet)?
5. What's the best and the worst thing about shopping by mail?

B. Merchandise (40 minutes)—Potential product categories and themes include, but are not limited to:
  1. Theatre.
     a. Stage.
        (1) Broadway.
            - Unique combinations of show tunes.
            - Hard-to-find or special edition videos of shows.
            - Collectible posters.
            - T-shirts printed with images related to old shows.
            - Film productions of the making of new Broadway shows.
        (2) Dance.
        (3) Opera.
        (4) Music.
            - Great composers' series.
  2. Documentaries.
     a. History.
     b. Limited edition books of postal stamps that depict key events.
     c. Directors' cuts.
     d. Old posters.
  3. Nature.
     a. Combination sets of videos and books on the National Parks.
     b. Combination sets of videos and books on traveling for the physically challenged.
     c. Books and calendars on the National Parks.
  4. Educational.
     a. Art.
        (1) Videos on art appreciation.
        (2) Videos on stories about famous artists.
     b. Religion.
        (1) Videos and book combination that traces the path of Jesus.

(2) Videos that explain creation.

(3) Videos that explore non-traditional religions.

c. Travel.

(1) Videos that explore honeymoon destinations.

(2) Videos that explore spa destinations.

(3) Videos that explore historical trips, such as following the path of Lewis & Clark.

d. Pets.

(1) Exclusive video series from the ASPCA that explains how to care for dogs and cats.

(2) Videos on caring for exotic animals.

e. Home decorating

(1) How to decorate with sheets video.

(2) Extreme makeover video.

5. Radio

a. Retro.

(1) Special edition of old radio programs.

(2) Unique combinations of the hits of the 40's, 50's, 60's, 70's.

(3) Exclusive combination of Motown's greatest hits.

6. Video award winners.

a. Classics.

(1) The making of *Mary Poppins*.

(2) Director's cuts of *The Muppets*.

(3) Original posters.

(4) Videos of all or the best of the Academy Award presentations.

7. TV.

a. Retro.

(1) Exclusive Rocky & Bullwinkle videos.

(2) Cliffhanger series.

(3) Outtakes from Star Trek.

8. Hot & new.

a. Music.

(1) Fantasy camps that let you become a rock & roll star.

b. Electronic games.

(1) Exclusive T-shirts and posters of favorite electronic game characters.

c. Electronics.
   (1) Two or three of the newest video equipment available before it is in retail.
9. Children's.
   a. Some items previously listed under other categories.
   b. Puzzles.
   c. Books.
10. Personalities.
    a. Famous artists.
       (1) Elvis limited editions.
11. Storage.
    a. Music and video.
       (1) Specially designed storage units for collectors.

C. Concept versions. (10 minutes)

1. Customer has easy access to lesser known entities through editorial assistance that offers educated, intelligent guidance.
   a. Product reviews.
   b. Product history.
   c. Specially developed products.
   d. Toll-free and Internet in-depth info regarding particular selections.
   e. Look-up service for hard-to-find music and video titles.

2. Catalog consists of collectibles only.
   a. Limited editions.
   b. Signed editions.
   c. Directors' cuts.
   d. Hard-to-find product combinations.

D. Promotion. (5 minutes)

1. Individual bonus gifts tied to some products.

2. Unlimited guarantee.

3. Two-day delivery at no extra charge over basic delivery charge.

4. Gift cards.

5. Free UPS pick up. (Items cannot be returned to the stores.)

6. Sell catalog for $2 at store, but comes with $5 certificate redeemable in catalog or store.

E. Name and Tag Lines. (10 minutes)

1. Sights & Sounds by King Video.
    a. Your source for owning unusual and exciting VCRs, CDs, and other entertainment options.

2. Explorations by King Video.
    a. Your access to new, exciting, and different entertainment products.

3. Sights & Sounds exclusively from King Video
    a. The smart way to own new, exciting, and unusual entertainment products.
    b. (Alternate) The smart way to collect new, exciting, and unusual entertainment products.

4. Access exclusively from King Video.
    a. Your access to unusual entertainment products you'll be proud to own and give.

5. Access from King Video.
    a. Your authoritative source for exciting, reliable entertainment options.
    b. (Alternate) Your source for the newest twist on offbeat classics.

IV. Key Take-Aways.

A. Understand if the catalog concept is a viable and, if so, which concept is the most desirable.

B. Have clear direction on merchandise approach.

C. Have understanding of promotional motivations.

D. Determine name and tag line for catalog.

6 Scheduling

Scheduling the Catalog

Proper groundwork is foremost for a healthy business, whether it is a new business or an established business trying to improve. For newcomers, the most underestimated area of a catalog business is the time it takes to correctly launch a solid business. Schedules, which can also be called "Work Action Timelines," vary by the number of pages, percentage of new photos versus pick-up photos, the number of people assigned to the task, and the number of catalogs the company sends out per year.

Exhibit 6.1 provides an example of a start-up catalog. The column labeled "Explanation of Activity" would not be a part of the schedule. It is shown here in order to clarify the terms used in the "Activity" column. "Status" is not indicated, but this column would indicate what was complete and what was still to be done.

Actual names would be used under the "Responsibility" column. Titles have been shown to clarify who would most likely handle each particular task. In some cases, more than one person would be listed in this column. In such cases, the person with the final responsibility should be at the top of the list. For this schedule, we have indicated that only one person is responsible. For an explanation of titles, see "Job Descriptions" in Chapter 8.

The schedule for an ongoing catalog can be much simpler because the cataloger is experienced in each phase and does not have the burden of creating a business plan and strategies per catalog issue. However, strategies and business plans should be updated yearly. In these cases, of course, this schedule would be slightly more complicated. Exhibit 6.2 is an example of how a schedule might look for an ongoing catalog of approximately 64 pages in length, with about 50 percent pick-up.

Feasibility Study

Some companies, prior to embarking on a catalog launch, will develop a *Feasibility Study Plan*, sometimes incorrectly called a *Business Plan*. The purpose of Feasibility Study Plan is to review the positive and negative potential of this new enterprise. The report should indicate advice on whether or not it is wise to precede.

Exhibit 6.1 Schedule for Start-Up Catalog

	Activity Name	Start Date	Finish Date	Duration	Responsibility	Comments	Feb '06 12	19	26
1	New Product Development and Selection								
2	Find new products for 10 new pages	Fri 2/17/06	Thurs 4/27/06	50.00	Cataloger		◇		
3	Decide on number of pages for upcoming	Fri 2/3/06	Fri 2/3/06	1.00	Cataloger				
4	New product selection	Fri 4/28/06	Mon 6/5/06	27.00	Cataloger	New items to be incorporated with old			
5	New product presentation	Fri 5/5/06	Fri 5/5/06	1.00	Cataloger	Need to explain benefits to agency			
6	Creative/Productioin								
7	Cover concepts, initial receipt through	Mon 5/8/06	Mon 5/15/06	6.00	Creative Agency	Will use best of new products			
8	New copy and page spread sheets to artist	Mon 5/8/06	Wed 5/17/06	8.00	Cataloger				
9	Call Center receives and approves layout for item numbers	Tues 5/9/06	Tues 5/30/06	16.00	Cataloger				
10	Page layouts for all 48 pages complete	Tues 5/30/06	Tues 6/13/06	11.00	Agency				
11	Final prices from finance to artist	Fri 6/2/06	Fri 6/2/06	1.00	Cataloger	Reminder: they usually need to be nagged			
12	New item numbers and prices into computer	Fri 6/2/06	Fri 6/2/06	1.00	Cataloger	Really takes one day? Need to double check this			
13	1st round revisions	Fri 6/9/06	Thurs 6/15/06	5.00	Creative Agency				
14	Photography	Fri 6/9/06	Thurs 6/15/06	5.00	Creative Agency	Need to determine which will be supplier photos			
15	1st round page proofing	Fri 6/16/06	Tues 6/20/06	3.00	Cataloger				
16	2nd round page proofing	Fri 6/16/06	Mon 6/19/06	2.00	Cataloger				
17	2nd round page revisions	Mon 6/19/06	Tues 6/20/06	2.00	Creative Agency				
18	Appropriate info and materials to Internet staff	Mon 4/25/05	Mon 4/25/05	1.00	Creative Agency				
19	Art to pre-press	Mon 6/26/06	Mon 6/26/06	1.00	Creative Agency				
20	Proofs to Printer	Wed 7/5/06	Wed 7/5/06	1.00	ABC Resource				
21	Final edit to pre-press	Tues 7/11/06	Tues 7/11/06	1.00	Cataloger				
22	Press date/run	Thurs 7/13/06	Mon 7/17/06	3.00	Printer	Check to be sure this time includes binding			
23	Bindery	Tues 7/18/06	Wed 7/19/06	2.00	Printer				
24	Circulation								
25	List order to List Broker	Mon 6/12/06	Mon 6/12/06	1.00	Cataloger				
26	Tapes to lettershop	Mon 7/10/06	Wed 7/12/06	3.00	Cataloger	Phone to make sure tapes arrived OK			
27	Mail Date	Thurs 7/20/06	Mon 7/24/06	3.00	Printer				
28	In home	Mon 7/31/06	Fri 8/4/06	5.00	Printer	This is late; we may need to redo the schedule			
							12	19	26

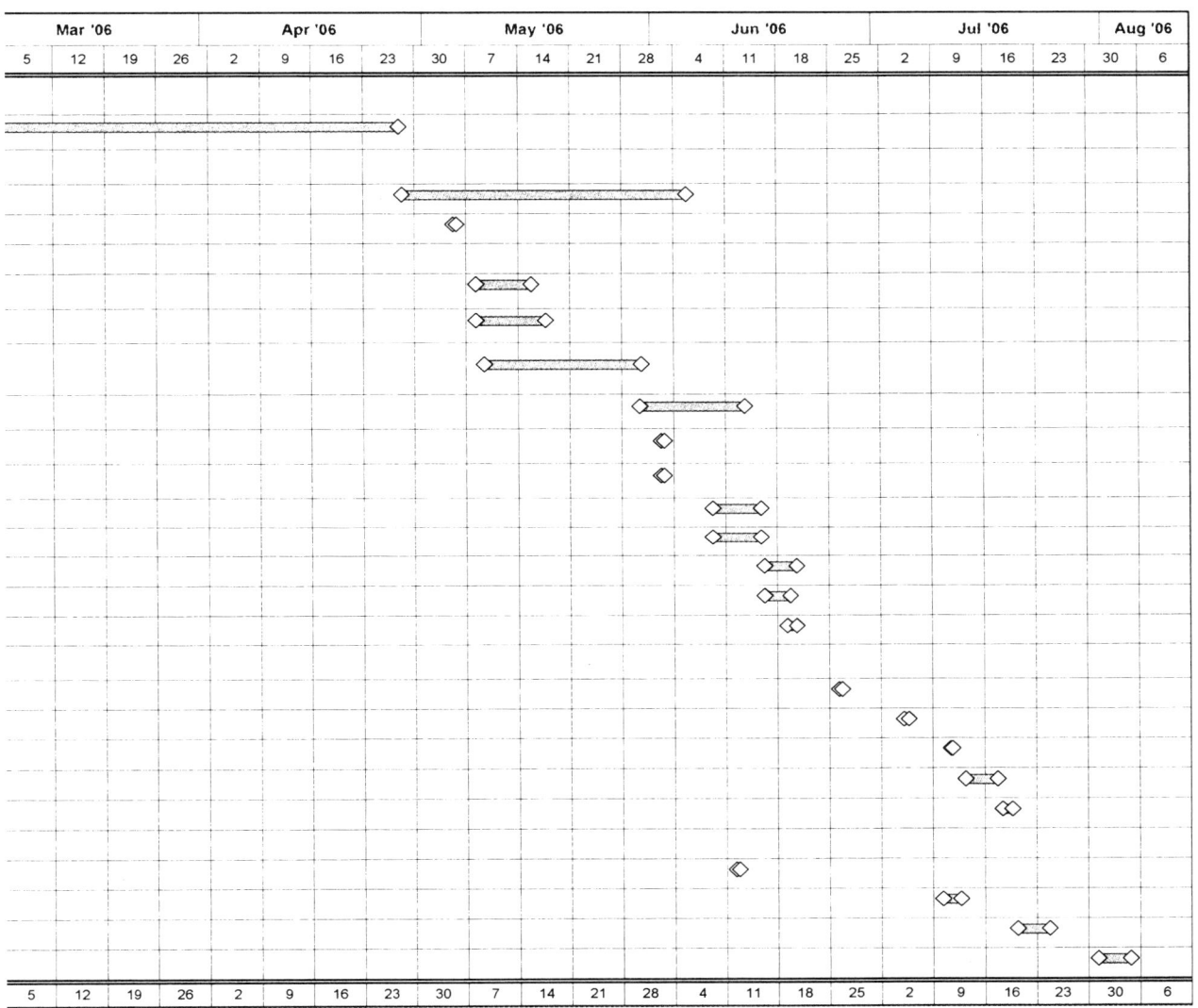

Exhibit 6.2 Schedule for an ongoing Catalog

	Activity Name	Explanation of Activity	Start Date	Finish Date	Duration (Work Days)	Responsibility	Status
1	Write an Overall Business Plan, including Business, Financial Plans and Cash Flow	See Exhibits 7.4 and 7.6	Wed 1/4/06	Tues 3/7/06	45.00	President	
2		Need to understand what inside and outside resources will be utilized for costing purposes	Mon 2/6/06	Fri 2/17/06	10.00	All Directors	
3	Merchandise Planning		Thurs 3/9/06	Thurs 4/20/06	31.00		
4	review and create written merchandise strategy, including criteria for pick-up, price point and category direction	See Chapter 10	Thurs 3/9/06	Fri 3/17/06	7.00	Director, Merchandising	
5	obtain input and approval of team		Fri 3/17/06	Fri 3/17/06	1.00	Director, Merchandising	
6	begin initial sourcing of product	Start process; will be adapted after focus groups	Fri 3/17/06	Fri 4/14/06	21.00	Merchandise Buyer	
7	provide vendors with Merchandise Information Forms and initial order quantities	See Chapter 10 for form	Fri 3/17/06	Thurs 4/20/06	25.00	Merchandise Buyer	
8	create semi-final strategy document (will be adapted after Focus Group input)	Merch strategy will be further edited after research	Mon 3/20/06	Tues 3/21/06	2.00	Director, Merchandising	
9	Database Analysis/Mailing Strategy		Thurs 3/2/06	Thurs 6/15/06	76.00		
10	enlist service bureau for database build	Take all house lists and put into one database	Fri 3/3/06	Fri 3/31/06	21.00	Director, Operations	
11	obtain any other relevant corporate data on tapes	Include this info in the one database	Thurs 3/2/06	Thurs 3/9/06	6.00	Manager, Systems	
12	determine available information and missing data		Mon 3/13/06	Mon 5/1/06	36.00	Service Bureau	
13	determine optimum mailing plan/frequency for requester/single buyers	Choose when and how many times to mail segments	Fri 4/14/06	Mon 5/1/06	12.00	Director, Circulation	
					2,771.00		

	Activity Name	Explanation of Activity	Start Date	Finish Date	Duration (Work Days)	Responsibility	Status	2005	2006
14	perform basic calculation of LTV to determine non-catalog buyers vs. retention/conversion of catalog buyers	See Chapter 14	Fri 4/14/06	Thurs 6/15/06	45.00	Circulation Analyst			
15	review house file segment analysis and create strategic plan	This is long term planning	Thurs 3/2/06	Thurs 6/15/06	76.00	Director, Circulation			
16	Initial Database Modeling		Tues 4/18/06	Wed 7/19/06	67.00				
17	develop scoring models; to include recency, frequency, monetary and/or regression models	See Chapter 14	Tues 4/18/06	Tues 5/30/06	31.00	Circulation Analyst			
18	use models to pull correct names for mailing	Models will give highest scoring segments; mail heavily	Fri 6/30/06	Wed 7/19/06	14.00	Circulation Analyst			
19	clearly define target audience and establish methods for reaching		Thurs 3/2/06	Thurs 6/15/06	76.00	Director, Circulation			
20	Fulfillment		Tues 2/7/06	Mon 1/1/07	235.00				
21	determine customer service policies		Tues 2/7/06	Thurs 2/9/06	3.00	Operations VP			
22	determine contenders for fulfillment and write RFP	Choose outside resource and ask for proposal	Mon 2/13/06	Tues 2/14/06	2.00	Director, Operations			
23	create list of reports/data requirements needed		Thurs 2/23/06	Fri 2/24/06	2.00	VP, Marketing			
24	write and send RFP	The Request for Proposal goes to chosen resources	Tues 2/14/06	Wed 2/15/06	2.00	Director, Operations			
25	RFP's returned	Filled out forms returned to Director, Operations	Mon 2/27/06	Wed 3/1/06	3.00	Service Bureaus			
26	review RFQ's (request for quote)		Wed 3/1/06	Fri 3/3/06	3.00	Director, Operations			
27	interview vendor group	Either by phone or vendor visits you	Fri 3/3/06	Wed 3/8/06	4.00	Director, Operations			
28	determine who moves forward and visits applicable warehouse	Keep this to a minimum, but essential to see in person	Wed 3/8/06	Mon 3/20/06	9.00	Director, Operations			
29	select fulfillment vendor		Tues 4/4/06	Tues 4/4/06	1.00	VP, Marketing			
					2,771.00				

Exhibit 6.2 Schedule for an ongoing Catalog continued

	Activity Name	Explanation of Activity	Start Date	Finish Date	Duration (Work Days)	Responsibility	Status	2005 1st 2nd 3rd 4th	2006 1st 2nd 3rd 4th
30	integrate vendor and catalog systems/personnel/ communications/reports	Involves all directors for best results	Thurs 4/6/06	Mon 6/5/06	43.00	All Directors			
31	continue review/upgrade of vendor	An ongoing job to assure top quality	Tues 6/6/06	Mon 1/1/07	150.00	Director, Operations			
32	Financial Plan Review/Update		Tues 4/4/06	Mon 6/12/06	50.00				
33	review/update catalog plan including response rates, average orders by segment, revenues, and detailed costs	This should be done after each mailing	Tues 4/4/06	Mon 5/1/06	20.00	Director, Finance			
34	budget parameters	The allowable costs to obtain desired results	Tues 4/4/06	Mon 4/17/06	10.00	Director, Finance			
35	ROI metrics/P&L	Measure Return on Income, update the P&L	Tues 5/2/06	Mon 6/12/06	30.00	Director, Finance			
36	Creative Review		Thurs 3/2/06	Tues 5/16/06	54.00				
37	recommend/review contenders	Create a list of agencies that might do the creative	Thurs 3/2/06	Fri 3/3/06	2.00	VP, Marketing			
38	determine contenders	Select up to 4 to compete for the business	Fri 3/3/06	Fri 3/3/06	1.00	Director, Creative			
39	create draft RFQ for agencies; includes requirements identified	Write a Request for Proposal (see Chapter 11)	Thurs 3/2/06	Fri 3/3/06	2.00	Director, Creative			
40	creative strategy for creative direction, positioning statement	Write a creative strategy (see Chapter 11)	Thurs 3/2/06	Thurs 3/16/06	11.00	Director, Creative			
41	brief reviewed and discussed by team	Team comes to agreement on materials for agencies	Thurs 3/16/06	Fri 3/17/06	2.00	Director, Creative			
42	final RFQ written and sent out		Fri 3/17/06	Tues 3/21/06	3.00	Director, Creative			
43	completed form filled out and received from agencies (form only, no concepts)	Agencies return information requested by catalog	Tues 3/21/06	Thurs 3/30/06	8.00	Agencies			
44	initial agency selection	Agencies chosen to compete	Thurs 3/30/06	Mon 4/3/06	3.00	Director, Creative			
					2,771.00			1st 2nd 3rd 4th	1st 2nd 3rd 4th

	Activity Name	Explanation of Activity	Start Date	Finish Date	Duration (Work Days)	Responsibility	Status	2005 1st 2nd 3rd 4th	2006 1st 2nd 3rd 4th
45	information determined for concept and merchandise development	Team agrees on what goes to agency and focus group	Tues 3/28/06	Mon 4/3/06	5.00	Director, Creative			◇
46	agencies (up to 2 for round two) given direction	See Chapter 11	Tues 4/4/06	Tues 4/4/06	1.00	Director, Creative			◇
47	agencies prepare layouts for focus groups	See Chapter 11	Tues 4/4/06	Mon 4/17/06	10.00	Agencies			◇
48	determination of agency of record (after Focus Groups)		Tues 5/16/06	Tues 5/16/06	1.00	Director, Creative			◇
49	Marketing includes Research, Service as Marketing Tool, Customer Prospect/Leveraging		Tues 3/14/06	Thurs 3/30/06	13.00				
50	write initial positioning statement	See Chapter 9	Tues 3/14/06	Fri 3/17/06	4.00	VP, Marketing			◇
51	input from team		Fri 3/17/06	Mon 3/27/06	7.00	All Directors			◇
52	final compiled and written		Tues 3/28/06	Thurs 3/30/06	3.00	VP, Marketing			◇◇
53	Research (Focus Groups)	See Chapter 5	Wed 3/1/06	Wed 5/17/06	56.00				◆
54	write strategy outline		Fri 4/7/06	Tues 4/11/06	3.00	VP Marketing			◇
55	determine group content and locations		Fri 4/7/06	Mon 4/10/06	2.00	VP Marketing			◇
56	find and hire facilitator		Wed 3/15/06	Fri 4/7/06	18.00	Asst. to VP			◇◇
57	send materials re: project to facilitator		Fri 4/7/06	Mon 4/10/06	2.00	Asst. to VP			◇
58	write screener and discussion guide and receive input		Fri 3/10/06	Tues 3/14/06	3.00	VP Marketing			◇
59	revisions made to discussion guide		Tues 4/11/06	Wed 4/12/06	2.00	VP Marketing			◇
60	focus groups held		Thurs 4/27/06	Wed 5/3/06	5.00	Focus Groups			◇
61	report written and reviewed by team		Wed 5/3/06	Fri 5/12/06	8.00	Facilitator			◇
					2,771.00			1st 2nd 3rd 4th	1st 2nd 3rd 4th

Exhibit 6.2 Schedule for an ongoing Catalog continued

	Activity Name	Explanation of Activity	Start Date	Finish Date	Duration (Work Days)	Responsibility	Status	2005	2006
62	concept approval direction made based on group input		Tues 5/16/06	Wed 5/17/06	2.00	VP Marketing			
63	Service as Marketing Tool		Thurs 4/27/06	Wed 5/24/06	20.00				
64	write list of competitors and receive agreement from team		Mon 5/22/06	Wed 5/24/06	3.00	VP Marketing			
65	compile service policies of competitors		Thurs 4/27/06	Wed 5/10/06	10.00	Asst. to VP			
66	determine competitive edge	Write what makes your catalog better service-wise	Wed 5/10/06	Tues 5/16/06	5.00	VP Marketing			
67	Customer/prospect Leveraging		Thurs 6/1/06	Mon 6/26/06	18.00				
68	determine other methods of leverage, such as bouncebacks, e-mail programs	Create separate programs P&L's for alternate media	Thurs 6/1/06	Wed 6/7/06	5.00	VP Marketing			
69	determine sales facilitators such as percentage off, free shipping and handling	Determine what to test for sales leveraging	Wed 6/7/06	Tues 6/13/06	5.00	VP Marketing			
70	create testing grid for Fall/Holiday and Spring	Plan a test for each catalog	Tues 6/13/06	Mon 6/26/06	10.00	VP Marketing			
71	Merchandise Selection/Inventory		Tues 4/4/06	Tues 10/24/06	146.00				
72	edit merchandise strategy based on Focus Group input		Tues 5/16/06	Mon 5/22/06	5.00	Director, Merchandise			
73	determine what products/price to be sourced/developed (using analysis first, then adapting after focus groups)	This helps direct the merchant in finding product	Tues 4/4/06	Tues 5/30/06	41.00	Director, Merchandise			
74	continue sourcing and producing product; provide vendors with Merchandise Information forms, terms, contracts, potential quantities	Merchandisers never really stop looking for product	Fri 4/14/06	Tues 5/23/06	28.00	Buyers			
75	all samples due for pagination		Tues 5/30/06	Tues 5/30/06	1.00	Buyers			
					2,771.00				

#	Activity Name	Explanation of Activity	Start Date	Finish Date	Duration (Work Days)	Responsibility	Status	2005 1st 2nd 3rd 4th	2006 1st 2nd 3rd 4th
76	determination of what goes on what pages	Price points are also determined at this time	Thurs 6/1/06	Thurs 6/1/06	1.00	Director, Merchandise			◊
77	reevaluate pagination and make recommendations for additional/different product	This catalog has two paginations; there is usually one	Fri 6/2/06	Fri 6/2/06	1.00	Director, Merchandise			◊
78	source additional product	Product is found to fill the weaknesses	Fri 6/2/06	Wed 6/21/06	14.00	Buyers			◊
79	final pagination including creation of bundles/cross references	Final product determination including any offers	Wed 6/21/06	Wed 6/21/06	1.00	Director, Merchandise			◊
80	collect all copy and info for agency	Getting everything together for the copy and layout	Wed 6/21/06	Tues 6/27/06	5.00	Buyers			◊
81	hand-off to agency	All details given to external or internal agency	Tues 6/27/06	Tues 6/27/06	1.00	Director, Merchandise			◊
82	determine initial projections and place initial orders		Thurs 6/29/06	Fri 6/30/06	2.00	Merchandise Analyst			◊
83	create prediction/response curve table and adjust orders	Predicts what to order overall based on initial orders	Tues 10/17/06	Tues 10/24/06	6.00	Merchandise Analyst			◊
84	Creative/Production Supervision		Tues 5/16/06	Tues 12/5/06	146.00				◆
85	concept adaptation based on Focus Group input	Adjust layouts based on what research has said	Tues 5/16/06	Mon 5/29/06	10.00	Sr. Art Director			◊
86	select models, stylist, photographer, locations	Determine correct model look, right stylists, locations	Tues 5/23/06	Mon 6/5/06	10.00	Director, Creative			◊
87	agency hand-off, agency receives all materials	The day that all final info is given to the creative team	Tues 6/27/06	Tues 6/27/06	1.00	Creative/Marketing			◊
88	initial layouts (first wave, not entire catalog) with pick-up photos in place and copy space allocated	Work in waves so that you can easily make changes	Tues 6/27/06	Wed 7/5/06	7.00	Sr. Art Director			◊
89	initial copy (first wave) separate, not part of layouts	Some include copy in layout; this company doesn't	Tues 6/27/06	Wed 7/5/06	7.00	Sr. Writer			◊
					2,771.00			1st 2nd 3rd 4th	1st 2nd 3rd 4th

Exhibit 6.2 Schedule for an ongoing Catalog continued

	Activity Name	Explanation of Activity	Start Date	Finish Date	Duration (Work Days)	Responsibility	Status	2005 1st 2nd 3rd 4th	2006 1st 2nd 3rd 4th
90	review copy and layouts and get back to agency with recommendations	Cataloger makes changes and returns to copy writer	Fri 7/7/06	Wed 7/12/06	4.00	All Directors			◇
91	review 2nd wave layouts (revisions and new)	Revisions are made as have been instructed	Fri 7/7/06	Mon 7/17/06	7.00	Artist			◇
92	review 2nd wave copy (revisions and new)	Revisions are made as have been instructed	Tues 7/11/06	Wed 7/19/06	7.00	Writer			◇
93	make sure all photo samples are at the photographer	Late sample jeopardize the whole schedule	Fri 7/14/06	Fri 7/14/06	1.00	Traffic Controller			◇
94	agency makes final corrections, catalog reviews layouts with copy, pick-up photos and initial revisions in place	Agency can be external or internal; new products will not have photos	Thurs 7/20/06	Wed 8/2/06	10.00	Artist			◇
95	review cover concepts	Covers are done separately as there are often many versions	Mon 6/12/06	Wed 6/14/06	3.00	Director, Creative			◇
96	adapt cover concepts and resubmit for approval, review and approve		Fri 7/14/06	Mon 7/24/06	7.00	Sr. Art Director			◇
97	determine order form tactics	To be decided: on page, separate insert, use at all	Thurs 7/6/06	Thurs 7/6/06	1.00	Director, Marketing			◇
98	prepare and review order form layout		Fri 7/7/06	Mon 7/17/06	7.00	Sr. Art Director			◇
99	review revised order form layout		Tues 7/18/06	Mon 7/24/06	5.00	Artist			◇
100	pre-photography meeting to determine sets, locations, models, etc.		Tues 7/18/06	Tues 7/18/06	1.00	Sr. Art Director			◇
101	photography	Sr. Art Director and someone from Merchandise will also attend	Tues 7/18/06	Mon 8/7/06	15.00	Photographer			◇
102	photo presentation and OK by catalog	All photos are reviewed by catalog and final selections made	Tues 8/8/06	Tues 8/8/06	1.00	Sr. Art Director			◇
103	re-shoots	If some photos are not good, they will be redone	Wed 8/9/06	Wed 8/9/06	1.00	Photographer			◇
104	review layouts with all changes and new photos in place	In conjunction with Directors, Creative and Merchandising	Tues 8/8/06	Wed 8/9/06	2.00	Director, Marketing			◇
105	layouts to separater (if using separations)	Currently, most layouts still go to film, but can be direct digital to printer	Wed 8/9/06	Mon 8/21/06	9.00	Mgr., Print Production			◇
					2,771.00			1st 2nd 3rd 4th	1st 2nd 3rd 4th

	Activity Name	Explanation of Activity	Start Date	Finish Date	Duration (Work Days)	Responsibility	Status	2005	2006
								1st 2nd 3rd 4th	1st 2nd 3rd 4th
106	review separations and indicate what corrections are to be made		Thurs 8/31/06	Fri 9/1/06	2.00	Mgr., Print Production			◇
107	review final separations and release to printer		Fri 9/1/06	Mon 9/4/06	2.00	Mgr., Print Production			◇
108	paper samples requested and reviewed	Some companies buy their own paper in order to save money	Fri 9/29/06	Tues 10/3/06	3.00	Mgr., Print Production			◇
109	determination of potential cost savings based on paper choices	Sometimes printers have excellent costs for paper so compare	Tues 9/5/06	Thurs 9/7/06	3.00	Mgr., Print Production			◇
110	paper selection	Choose paper no matter what the source	Wed 5/17/06	Tues 5/30/06	10.00	Mgr., Print Production			◇
111	paper purchase and delivery for printer testing		Tues 6/6/06	Fri 6/9/06	4.00	Mgr., Print Production			◇
112	printer tests separations and paper	If purchased from other than the printer, have it tested for strength	Thurs 9/7/06	Fri 9/8/06	2.00	Printer			◇
113	postage check at printer	No credit with the post office; this MUST be ready on time	Thurs 9/7/06	Thurs 9/7/06	1.00	Mgr., Print Production			◇
114	printing	A supervisor should go on press with the job	Wed 9/13/06	Thurs 9/14/06	2.00	Mgr., Print Production			◇
115	bindery	A supervisor should also check items being bound in and ink jetting	Fri 9/29/06	Mon 10/2/06	2.00	Mgr., Print Production			◇
116	first drop and in-home date	Date in the mail and anticipated in-home	Fri 9/15/06	Fri 9/22/06	6.00				◇
117	second drop and in-home date	This catalog will mail to different segments over different months	Mon 10/9/06	Wed 10/18/06	8.00				◇
118	third drop and in-home date	See Chapter 12 for Contact Strategy	Mon 10/23/06	Tues 12/5/06	32.00				◆
119	Lists/Database		Mon 2/6/06	Thurs 8/24/06	144.00				◆
120	write circulation plan for the year	See Chapter 12	Mon 2/6/06	Thurs 2/23/06	14.00	Director, Circulation			◇
121	interview and determine what list brokers will be used	Brokers make presentation of recommendations	Thurs 6/15/06	Fri 6/23/06	7.00	Director, Circulation			◇
122	provide selected brokers with positioning statement, creative overview and merchandise strategy	Sometimes brokers are given this data prior to presentation	Fri 6/23/06	Fri 6/23/06	1.00	Director, Marketing			◇
					2,771.00			1st 2nd 3rd 4th	1st 2nd 3rd 4th

Exhibit 6.2 Schedule for an ongoing Catalog continued

	Activity Name	Explanation of Activity	Start Date	Finish Date	Duration (Work Days)	Responsibility	Status	2005 1st 2nd 3rd 4th	2006 1st 2nd 3rd 4th
123	determine what house file segments will be used	Who will be mailed from the catalog's file of buyers and requesters	Tues 6/20/06	Tues 7/11/06	16.00	Circulation Analyst			◇
124	brokers make initial recommendations		Fri 7/14/06	Fri 7/14/06	1.00	Brokers			◇
125	determine what rented names will be used	Also determine which brokers will be used	Tues 7/18/06	Wed 7/26/06	7.00	Director, Circulation			◇
126	rental names are reviewed in conjunction with house file segments and overall circulation plan	Look at all the information to adapt in one cohesive plan	Wed 7/26/06	Fri 7/28/06	3.00	Director, Circulation			◇
127	release tape or post net output to service bureau's web site for merge/purge	One main tape is sent to Service Bureau to eliminate duplicate names	Tues 8/1/06	Wed 8/2/06	2.00	Circulation Analyst			◇
128	merge/purge, include instructions to service bureau and obtain security password for posting on printer's web site	This can be two processes, one to house, one with rental & house	Thurs 8/3/06	Wed 8/16/06	10.00	Circulation Analyst			◇
129	tape or post to printer's website to printer from service bureau		Fri 7/21/06	Tues 7/25/06	3.00	Circulation Analyst			◇
130	printer performs quality check on data	Make sure that there are no glitches with the list data at the bindery	Wed 8/23/06	Thurs 8/24/06	2.00	Printer			◇
131	Telemarketing, inbound and outbound		Tues 1/10/06	Thurs 8/24/06	163.00				
132	determine overall strategy including segments to be contacted	Decide if there will be an outbound program and to whom	Tues 1/10/06	Mon 2/6/06	20.00			◇	
133	determine upsell technique	Create offers to make additional sales while customer on inbound call	Fri 5/19/06	Tues 6/20/06	23.00				◇
134	determine FAQ's and provide script to telemarketing	Plan for questions that customers will ask phone reps about products	Tues 6/20/06	Mon 7/10/06	15.00				◇
135	train inbound telemarketers	Train on how to properly handle customers	Mon 7/10/06	Fri 8/18/06	30.00				◇
136	create and test outbound program	Write a script and test to targeted audience	Fri 7/14/06	Thurs 8/24/06	30.00				◇
					2,771.00			1st 2nd 3rd 4th	1st 2nd 3rd 4th

	Activity Name	Explanation of Activity	Start Date	Finish Date	Duration (Work Days)	Responsibility	Status	2005 1st 2nd 3rd 4th	2006 1st 2nd 3rd 4th
137	Internet		Tues 3/7/06	Mon 6/26/06	80.00				
138	create e-commerce integration strategy	Determine how the catalog will work with the existing web site	Tues 3/7/06	Mon 4/17/06	30.00				
139	create outbound e-mail program	Plan and write an ongoing strategy for e-mail sales	Mon 4/24/06	Fri 6/23/06	45.00				
140	Customer Acquisition (other than existing database and list rental)		Thurs 6/1/06	Mon 7/10/06	28.00				
141	determine how to use PR, resource, prepare plan, implement and track results	Create a written of strategy of what will be added when	Thurs 6/1/06	Wed 6/14/06	10.00	Director, Marketing			
142	determine method of cost effectively utilizing space advertising	Look into the viability of advertising in publications	Wed 6/14/06	Tues 6/27/06	10.00	Director, Creative			
143	determine any other method inherent in company organization	Determine what other ways there might be to reach the customer	Tues 6/27/06	Mon 7/10/06	10.00	Director, Marketing			
					2,771.00			1st 2nd 3rd 4th	1st 2nd 3rd 4th

Exhibit 6.3 Feasibility Study/Business Plan Outline

    I. Executive Summary
- A. Background.
- B. Concept.
- C. Business objective.
- D. Management.
- E. Direct-marketing environment.
- F. Marketing strategy.
- G. Trademark equity.
- H. Multi-channel opportunities.
- I. Inter-channel consideration/constraints.
- J. Finance.
- K. Conclusion.

    II. The Company
- A. Tax considerations, corporate structure, location.
- B. Products and services.
- C. Price structure.
- D. Customers.
- E. Distribution.
- F. Management.

    III. Objectives
- A. Primary objectives.
- B. Driving forces.
- C. Rationale.
- D. Financial objectives.
- E. Position for growth.

    IV. Management and Organization
- A. Organizational philosophy.
- B. Year One allocation of responsibilities.
- C. Additions/changes for Year Two.
- D. Organization charts.
- E. Responsibilities.
- F. People/talent required.

    G. Government regulations.
    H. Work action timelines.
V. Marketing Plan and Sales Strategy
    A. Comprehensive plan.
    B. Product strategy.
    C. Marketing positioning.
    D. International market.
    E. Competitive environment.
VI. Business Relationships
    A. Existing relationships.
    B. Joint marketing agreements.
    C. Third-party supplier agreements.
    D. Joint development efforts.
    E. Resources.
VII. Pricing Philosophy
    A. Influences.
    B. Perceived value.
    C. Mark-up.
    D. Elasticity.
    E. Seasonality.
VIII. Product/Service Description
    A. Competitive differences.
    B. Product/service development.
    C. Proprietary technology.
    D. Payback from customer perspective.
    E. Testing.
    F. Product/service life cycle.
    G. Planned products/services.
    H. Products' service characteristics.
        1. Product mix and price range.
        2. Services by year.
IX. Market Opportunity
    A. Catalog industry overview.
    B. Market definitions.
    C. Competition.

D. Relevant catalog industry issues and how they relate.
   E. Trends, buying patterns, and shopping patterns.
X. Focus Group Research
XI. The Competition
   A. Market drivers.
   B. Market evolution.
   C. Product.
   D. Target.
   E. Market outlook.
   F. Channel dynamics.
   G. Customer acquisition.
   H. Systems.
   I. Conclusions.
   J. Entry challengers.
   K. Entry requirement.
   L. Competitive grid.
   M. Competitive position.
XII. Reaching the Target Market
   A. Advertising and promotion objectives.
      1. Media objectives.
      2. Media strategy.
      3. Preliminary media budget allocation.
   B. Alliances.
   C. Sales facilitation approach and potential tests.
   D. Initial contact strategy.
   E. The catalog.
   F. Other media to be used.
   G. Public relations objectives.
      1. Strategies.
      2. Company background.
      3. Press releases.
      4. Budget.
XIII. Catalog Operations
   A. Administration.
   B. Fulfillment.

C. Merchandising.

D. Marketing.

XIV. Financial Summary Data and Assumptions

A. Pro formas and assumptions.

B. Optimistic, pessimistic and most likely.

XV. Financial Strategy

A. Goals and finances.

B. Funding sources and allocations.

C. Actions/commitments.

D. Possible business scenarios and investment returns.

XVI. Long Term Development, Exit Strategy

A. Diversifications.

B. Exit options.

XVII. Exhibits

A. Cost of operation.

1. Functional analysis.
2. Organization structure and headcount.
3. Review and cost of alternative methods of distribution.

B. Five-Year (Three-Year Detail) financial projections (worst, best, most likely).

1. Revenue summary.
2. Expense summary.
3. Profit and loss statement.
4. Balance sheet, cash flow, and investment timing.
5. Return on Sales (ROS) and Return on Investment (ROI) analysis.
6. Sensitivity analysis.
7. Notes to financial projections.

XVIII. Addenda

A. Job descriptions.

B. Resumes.

C. Work action timeline.

D. Potential lists.

E. Product development timeline.

F. Future contact strategy.

G. Media projected responses.

Exhibit 6.4 Feasibility/Business Plan Explanation

The following questions provide examples of what needs to be known for a catalog program to be initiated. The answers to many of these questions are found throughout this book, e.g., organizational considerations are covered in Chapter 8.

I. Executive Summary
   - This should be a succinct, bulleted summation of what appears in your report. It should state the market knowledge, research, and financial considerations about the potential program. Is it a "go" or "no go" and why?

II. The Company
   - This is a summation of the parts that create the whole company. Each area will be elaborated on in the feasibility document.
   - What are the benefits of this organization? How will it add to its parent company or what makes it strong enough to stand profitably on its own?
   - What are the tax considerations? If it is part of a large corporation, where will it be physically located? How will its corporate structure work with the parent company? If independent, location and corporate structure still must be addressed.
   - What will be its products and services? Does this work with the parent or, if independent, bring an unusual strength or advantage to the business?
   - How will the price structure compare to the competition? Will promotional pricing be used?
   - Are there current customers? If not, how will they be acquired?
   - How will the catalogs by distributed: Mail, stores, other? How will any synergies be leveraged?
   - What is the anticipated management structure? How will this interact with any parent or outside resources?

III. Objectives
   - What are the primary objectives of this program? What are the dominant driving forces?
   - State your reasons why this catalog will or will not succeed. State the overall financial objectives. What must be accomplished for the catalog to be positioned for ongoing growth?

IV. Management and Organization

- What is your organizational philosophy? Define the first year's allocation of responsibilities. State what changes or additions would be made in Year Two. Illustrate with an organizational chart.
- Indicate the responsibilities per individual. What talent is required? Where will this talent be found?
- State any government regulations.
- Include a Work Action Timeline (such as Exhibit 6.1).

V. Marketing Plan and Sales Strategy

- What is the comprehensive plan? What is the product strategy? Why are these better than what now exists elsewhere?
- What is the market positioning? What synergies are possible between the different sales avenues, e.g., printed and the web?
- Are there any international implications?

VI. Business Relationships

- Do any existing supplier relationships affect this business? Do any existing joint marketing agreements or alliances exist? If not, are there plans for some?
- Will there be any joint marketing developments? Who will be responsible for the business relationships?

VII. Pricing Philosophy

- What influences went into establishing prices? Do the prices support the perceived value? What will the mark-up be? Is there any elasticity or seasonality?

VIII. Product/Service Description

- What are the competitive differences? Will product be sourced or developed? If both, in what combination?
- What percentage will employ proprietary technology? What is the payback from the customer's perspective? Will there be any price testing? What is the product life cycle?
- What plans are there for new product and service development? What are the major characteristics that make this product appealing and different?
- What is the product mix and price range? What is the rationale for the categories being offered? Be specific per category.

- What services will be offered in Year One? Why have these particular services been chosen? How will these be expanded in Year Two?
- How will the target market evolve as it affects product and services? In other words, what markets will be targets with what products in Year One and in Year Two?

IX. Market Opportunity

- What is the overall catalog industry environment? How does this environment look in the particular sectors that are being targeted? Specifically define targeted markets.
- What is the competition in these markets? What is the market share of competitors?
- What are relevant catalog industry issues as they relate to this catalog? Some examples might be privacy issues, sales tax concerns, shrinking universe of names, availability of skilled personnel.
- What are the relevant trends, buying behaviors and shopping patterns?

X. Focus Group Research

- What is the primary purpose? What is the group make-up? What are key discussion points? What are the study findings?

XI. The Competition

- Who are the major competitors by category? What are the entry requirements—in essence, what must the catalog do better to beat the competition?

XII. Reaching the Target Market

- What are the advertising and promotion objectives? Specifically, what are the media objectives and strategy? Indicate example of media schedule and budget.
- What is the advertising campaign advantage? How do alliances play into the media plan? What is the sales facilitation approach and test strategy?
- What is the initial contact strategy? What will the catalog physically look like? How will the web interact with the printed catalog? What are the public relations objectives and strategies? Show a company background press release example for print and the Internet. Show a budget for PR.

XIII. Catalog Operations
- What are the staffing needs for operations in Year One and Year Two? If outsourced, what, if any, is the timetable for bringing in-house?

XIV. Financial Summary Data and Assumptions
- Explain how the numbers were arrived at. Provide three different possibilities from best to worst case.

XV. Financial Strategy
- What is the catalog doing for positional differentiation? What will be the areas of differentiation? What are the growth factors? Be specific as to how these factors can achieve the financial goals.

XVI. Long-Term Development, Exit Strategy
- Discuss the potential for diversification, spin-offs, international expansion, and other relevant methods of growth.
- Specify the "go"/"no go" time frame. Indicate when the catalog is expected to be profitable.

XVII. Exhibits

XVIII. Addenda
- Most of the above are illustrated throughout this book.

Business Review

If a catalog is up for sale or simply wants to be sure that it is operating as expediently as possible, a *Business Review* is in order.

In most cases, if the catalog is for sale, the potential buyer will hire an outside, objective resource to evaluate the profitability and functionality statements that the catalog seller is making. Whether the review is for a company that is for sale or just wishing to do a better job, the business review almost always makes recommendations as to how the business could be improved as well as stating the areas in which the business excels.

To begin a business review, a great deal of information needs to be made available. To make certain that all involved are clear about who is doing what, indicate a specific person responsible in the areas marked "Add person responsible."

Exhibit 6.5 Business Review Materials Needed

The information generally covers the last two years. Not all of the information listed below is always available, but the more information, the better the review.

I. Market Position
   A. Positioning statement and/or charter and mission.
   B. Size of overall current market.
   C. Current share of market.
   D. Major competitors, samples of their catalogs (if available), and their approximate market shares.

II. Economics
   A. Detailed profit and loss (P/L) statement.
   B. Net sales per product, category, and medium.
      1. Ranked by highest sales (dollar per thousand ($ per M) or per book).
      2. Top 20 best sellers, top 20 worst sellers (for most recent year and for one specific book, preferably from best season).
      3. Marked-up book corresponding to best sellers list.
      4. By price point (percent offered versus percent sold).
      5. By category (percent offered versus percent sold).
      6. Square-inch analysis by category and product.

III. Circulation/ Lifetime Value (LTV)
   A. Circulation plan, gross demand, and net sales per segment. Include breakout of mailing lists rented and which portions of the house file were utilized and any other media response, including the Web, and conversion data.
      1. Separate all media data by type: List, web, e-mail campaign, space ads, other.
      2. Test data per medium should be separate from sales.
      3. If top performing rental lists are not yet known, provide list cards for basic information about the lists used.
      4. Rank media results with best $/M or per mailing or e-mail date for each solicitation.
      5. Responses, requests, and conversions per media (in other words, break out by how the name was acquired).
      6. For each mailing, e-mail, web site sale, or space ad, note the percentage of prospects versus customers versus requesters acquired per medium.

7. Cross tabs such as frequency of purchase versus date of last purchase (see Chapter 14, "Basic Analysis," for example) per method name acquired.
8. Multi-buyer ratio (what percentage of purchasers have bought again) by media.
9. For multi-buyers, average time between purchases (this helps determine the buying cycle) by media.
10. Any lifetime value analysis or any scoring with results (see Chapter 14, "Basic Analysis").

B. Contact schedules, quantities, and circulation with samples and results (What offers, if any testing was done, went to which segments and with what results?) by media (mailing versus e-mail).

C. House file growth, including breakout of single versus multi-buyer (What percentage increase is there in the house file for each single or multi-buyer segment?) by media acquired.

D. Segmentation of customers by category (market and product, if possible).

E. Response rates and average order amounts by segment acquired.

IV. Creative
   A. Any creative specifications/requirements/guidelines.
   B. Creative costs.
   C. Production costs.

V. Merchandise
   A. Unit prices, average.
   B. Gross margins.
   C. Proprietary, patented or exclusive products, if any.
   D. Number of units per order, average.

VI. Operations
   A. Rate of returns, based on category.
   B. Rate of cancellations resulting in back orders.
   C. Percentage of sales per phone, fax, Internet, mail.
   D. Order/payment types and credit policies.
   E. Percentage of sales per payment type.
   F. Estimated degree of cross-sell/up-sell.
   G. Any significant policies that might have an impact on customer relations and/or customer service.

H. Fulfillment costs, which could cover:
  1. Inbound telemarketing and fulfillment costs per order.
  2. Outbound costs and response/conversion data.
  3. Labor rates.
  4. MIS hardware and software description.
  5. Telemarketing hardware and software description.
  6. Describe physical fulfillment process.
  7. Describe telemarketing setup and warehouse, such as how many phone stations, how many pallets high, etc.
  8. How are warehouse locations allocated?
  9. Is least cost shipping or consolidator used?
  10. First and final fill ratios.

VII. Management
  A. Company organization chart.

After all the materials have been gathered together and reviewed by experts, a report is written. Though the content of reports can vary, the content will most likely address the issues listed in Exhibit 6.6.

Exhibit 6.6 Outline of Common Report Areas for Company Evaluation

---

I. Creative Review and Adjustments
  A. Written review of the catalog.
  B. Positioning.
  C. Clarity of message.
  D. Design and layout.
  E. Copy and tone.
  F. Phone meeting to review recommendations.
  G. Work with artists to implement recommendations.

II. Database Review and Adjustments
   A. Review of past results (included in information collection).
   B. Determine peripheral market.
   C. Work with catalog's existing brokers (or recommended brokers) to determine peripheral market accessibility/availability.
   D. Work with brokers to create test plan.
   E. Determine offer tests for expanded market(s).
III. Merchandise Review and Adjustments
   A. Review of past sales analysis, circulation analysis (included in information collection).
   B. Determine capabilities of staff in sourcing/development.
   C. Write merchandise strategy, including price point philosophy, categories to be expanded (and time frame).
   D. If needed, make recommendations for freelance buyers to assist in sourcing/development.
   E. Review materials sourced and advise on progress.
   F. Review presentation of products, from merchandising viewpoint, in catalog.
IV. Expansion Planning
   A. Versioning/segments. (This refers to whether or not different versions of the catalog are used, e.g., a changed cover but the same interior mailed to virtually the same audience, but at a different time than the original catalog.)
   B. Reporting structure/analysis.
   C. Mail and Internet plan/how quickly to expand.
   D. Merchandise expansion plans.
   E. Creative expansion plans.
   F. Service expansion plans.
V. Summation
   A. Requirements for success.
   B. Summary of top strategic recommendations.

7 Launching Your Catalog

As you can see, much preparation goes into determining the viability of a new catalog entry or even just making certain that an existing entity is functioning fully. A full-fledged launch, however, means even more work must be done.

Let's assume that the feasibility study showed that this new catalog business had potential for success. What are the next steps? There is some overlap with a Business Review (Exhibits 6.1 through 6.6), but a launch is not the same as a review. There are even more steps in a launch.

Exhibit 7.1 is an example of many of the areas that new companies traditionally need to explore prior to entering the catalog market. Exhibit 7.2 takes the process one step further and shows not only the top-line steps, but details that must also be addressed.

Launch Catalog Preparation and Implemetation
TO DO LIST

A catalog launch most often follows this typical path:

Phase One—Pre-Planning.

1. Information Gathering.
   - Determination of Core and Peripheral Markets.
   - Preparation of Competitive Data.
   - Positioning including Product and Services Strategies.
   - Evaluation of Positioning by Focus Groups.
   - Financial Plan Development.
   - Additional Information Gathering as Needed.
2. Plan Preparation.

Phase Two—Implementation.

- Analysis and Recommendation of Fulfillment and Customer Service Policies/Facilities.
- Contact Strategy.
- Merchandising and Pagination.
- Creative Team Review, Recommendations and Supervision.
- Database Review and/or Development.
- Ongoing Analysis of Effectiveness of Program.

The Catalog Plan of Action

The first step in the catalog launch is developing the plan of action. Note that virtually all of the following areas are elaborated on within this book.

    A. Background Information Gathering. (Part of Exhibit 7.1).

    B. Information Gathering/Definition Meeting.

Upon initiation of the program, the cataloger needs to provide specific background information regarding the overall program parameters to all members of the team, both internal and external.

Exhibit 7.1 Launch Catalog Plan of Action

Information	Provided by
1. The corporate culture and its goals.	Add name of person who is responsible.
2. The corporate financial goals.	Add name of person who is responsible.
3. Corporate philosophy and policy related to customer sales and service, by customer segment.	Add name of person who is responsible.
4. Management, operational and support resources available for the program and for the development of marketing and financial plans.	Add name of person who is responsible.
5. Profiles of primary target customer, by segment, as well as immediate and secondary peripheral targets.	Add name of person who is responsible.
6. Merchandise availability, development cycles, future product plans, sourcing and development strengths and weaknesses.	Add name of person who is responsible.
7. Current and anticipated margin structure.	Add name of person who is responsible.
8. Inventory availability and policy, both for the program and any inter-channel constraints.	Add name of person who is responsible.
9. Input on any desires regarding catalog creative concept, general approach, including any corporate limitations.	Add name of person who is responsible.
10. Policy and operational considerations involving internal versus external fulfillment/telemarketing within the plan's time frame.	Add name of person who is responsible.
11. Review of any past marketing surveys or other research that may relate to this project.	Add name of person who is responsible.

Information Gathering

⇨ Determination of Both Core and Peripheral Markets.

Requires:

- Refinement of the target audience, including:
  - Understanding of availability of primary and secondary targets.
  - Understanding of attitudes of primary and secondary targets.
  - Incorporation of target into positioning statement.
  - Refinement of the targeting and contact strategy.
- Specifically:
  - Specify methods of determining the variable most affecting customer/prospect performance. (In other words, is the most important element in a customer's performance how recently they ordered, how much they ordered, or one of several other possibilities?)
  - Specify analyses to rank and score customers and file segment.
  - Establish "universes" of ranged prospects based on the analysis.

⇨ Database.

This is an evaluation and recommendation of the internal database and any applicable outside lists in order to insure proper match of known customer, plus determination of tests required for expansion into fringe customer areas. A budget must be determined and allocated based upon assumed return per medium. Requires a media plan incorporating variety of appropriate media. Will necessitate research. A preliminary media plan would recommend potential test areas, size of insertions, basic approach, and budget costs.

Requires:

- Targeted, mixed media approach which includes such test areas as:
  - Lists and their segments.
  - Space advertising.
  - Electronic e-mail campaigns and web site.

⇨ Competitive Evaluation.

Requires:

- Research of marketplace to select the competition to be studied, including the collection of printed and Internet samples.
- Compilation of information based on Competitive Grid, with an emphasis on merchandising and positioning.
- Summation of entry challenges, requirements and strength of competitive position.

⇨ Positioning including Product and Service Strategies.

Positioning Statement

Requires:

- Clear-cut understanding of the power of the program and its benefits as they apply to the target audience.
- Writing of a document clearly outlining the product and service positioning for use by the marketing and creative team.
- Each team member fills out independently. Discussion creates one cohesive document.

Product and Service Strategies

Requires:

- Determination of pricing philosophy appropriate for the target market.
    - —Influences.
    - —Perceived value.
    - —Mark-up, margin requirements.
    - —Elasticity.
    - —Seasonality.
- Approach that will establish and leverage:
    - —Any competitive differences, as well as similarities.
    - —Any proprietary technology.
- Determination of product mix, price range and any necessary support services for development/sourcing of those products.

⇨ Evaluation of Positioning by Focus Groups.

Requires:

- Creation of clear objectives for the focus groups, assumed, at this time, to be:

    —Feasibility of program.

    —Feasibility of merchandise approach.

    —Feasibility of positioning/creative approach, including name.

    —Need for particular service offers.

- Determination of market representation in focus groups.
- Planning and coordination of all elements, including:

    —Timing.

    —Materials selection and format.

    —Writing of leading questions.

    —Recommending of and negotiating with Focus Group Facilitator and, through the Facilitator, the Facility.

    —Determination of appropriate cities in which the focus groups will be held.

    —Preparing Facilitator.

    —Attending groups and making adjustments to script as necessary.

    —Analyzing results.

Exhibit 7.2. Financial Plan Development *(Additional Information Gathering)*

Information	Provided by
1. Report formats, fiscal year, depreciation, and amortization policy.	Add name of person who is responsible.
2. Overhead allocations.	Add name of person who is responsible.

Plan Preparation

Requires:

- Establishment of acceptable financial goals.
- Preparation of a three- to five-year financial business plan*. (*Three years in detail.)
- Establishment of guideline parameters for success.
- Revision of the plan once pagination, product mix and prices are determined.

Such a plan should include the following elements and should be used to create benchmarks for success:

- Response rates.
- Order amounts.
- Profit & loss.

The Financial Plan should cover the following; responsibility for collecting information can be divided as follows:

Information	Provided by
1. Mailing schedules and quantities.	Add name of person who is responsible.
2. Anticipated buyer file growth from program inception.	Add name of person who is responsible.
3. Anticipated response rates and average order amounts.	Add name of person who is responsible.
4. Book specifications (number of pages, paper type/weight, etc.).	Add name of person who is responsible.

5. Anticipated creative costs. — Add name of person who is responsible.

6. Anticipated production costs. — Add name of person who is responsible.

7. Anticipated web site costs. — Add name of person who is responsible.

8. Anticipated postage costs, including presort quantities, if any. — Add name of person who is responsible.

9. Anticipated inventory needs. — Add person's name who is responsible

10. Anticipated rate of returns, overall. — Add name of person who is responsible.

11. Anticipated rate of cancels resulting from back orders. — Add name of person who is responsible.

12. Unit prices, average. — Add name of person who is responsible.

13. Anticipated number of units per order, average. — Add name of person who is responsible.

14. Shipping costs, with best shipping resource determined. — Add name of person who is responsible.

15. Overnight shipping costs and percentages. — Add name of person who is responsible.

16. Anticipated telemarketing and fulfillment costs. — Add name of person who is responsible.

17. Overhead costs. — Add name of person who is responsible.

18. Anticipated credit card processing costs. — Add name of person who is responsible.

19. Inflation rate used for financials. — Add name of person who is responsible.

20. Anticipated order entry and processing costs. — Add name of person who is responsible.

21. Order/payment types and credit policies. — Add name of person who is responsible.

22. Allowance for alternate customer acquisition programs. — Add name of person who is responsible.

Data Provided and Plan Review Process

Data:

- Data should be provided on a Catalog Financial Model that is adaptable to alternative scenarios. Scenarios should be provided for Best Case, Worst Case, and Most Likely Case.
- Beyond the customized Catalog Financial Model, the cataloger will also need a Contact Strategy, the intent of which is to leverage the primary mailings for increased frequency of contact with certain list segments, thus increasing overall profitability.

Review Process:

- Initial review of Most Likely Case.
- Input incorporated into Most Likely Case document.
- Adjustment based on input incorporated into other two scenarios.
- Further adjustments can be made before final, formal document.

The development of the plan is a fluid process. Therefore, interim meetings and/or phone conferences among involved parties are likely to be necessary.

⇨ Analyze and Recommend Fulfillment and Customer Service Operations (see Chapter 13).

Requires:

- Determination of desired fulfillment abilities, policies, standards.
- Description of hardware/software recommended to be used in fulfillment process.
- Establishment of performance and customer satisfaction standards.
- An understanding of current resources and their ability to be incorporated into the program at some future date.

Specifically:

- Establish fulfillment policies, standards, costs, customer satisfaction.
- Assess competitive environment for customer service.
- Establish short- and long-term goals for using fulfillment to improve customer satisfaction. Coordinate implementation of what is currently needed and determine schedule of long range improvements.

- Create a report set for ability to measure performance improvements.
- Set up system parameters for order cycle management.

⇨ Contact Strategy.

Requires:

- Segmentation of customer/prospect by anticipated value.
- Regular, inexpensive, memorable contact to those segments that appear to offer the most value.
- Cohesive look and approach for each contact.
- Tests for offer, frequency of approach.

This can be incorporated into the Business Plan; however, it is sometimes approached as a separate entity, incorporating additional points of contact beyond those originally shown in the base plan.

Determination is made of:

- Number of mailings/e-mail contacts, type, and message to prospects.
- Number of mailings/e-mail contacts, type, and message to one-time users, by product dollars spent and frequency of usage.
- Number of mailings/e-mail contacts, type, and message to two-time users, by product, dollars spent and frequency of usage.
- Number of mailings/e-mail contacts, type, and message to non-users.
- Number of mailings/e-mail contacts, type, and message to inactives.
- Potential inclusion of bouncebacks.

⇨ Merchandising and Pagination.

Requires:

- Based on input from Focus Groups and needs of the Financial Plan, refine definition of product mix, price range, and any necessary support services for those products.
- If needed, review and determine appropriate buyer(s) to source merchandise and negotiate with vendors; can be internal or external.
- Pagination of product (may require a second and even third pagination) to determine what products go on what pages at what prices.
- Make inventory projections.

⇨ Creative Team Review, Selection and Supervision.

Requires:

- Determination of needs for the program.
- Preparation of Request for Proposal (RFP) (also called a Request for Quote or RFQ) if choosing to use outside resources.
- Create initial round list of freelance/agency teams to approach.
- Review first group of potential artists/writers.
- Make final selection.
- Supervise internal or agency creative team, input for appropriate direct marketing catalog techniques.

⇨ Database Review and/or Development.

Plan for database development and segmentation in conjunction with internal MIS department or external service bureau and also in conjunction with ongoing programs.

Requires understanding of capabilities and usage data for:

- Determination of file structure, format and information flow in order to create a useful database.
- Design file specifications, design flow chart and report set level to allow segmentation and tracking efficacy.
- Specify analytical/modeling techniques to allow superior response rates and contribution.
- Prepare for the coordination of analytical results to improve and project mail plan performance in the future.

⇨ Ongoing Analysis of Effectiveness of Program.

Requires:

- Segment by segment response and projected lifetime value calculations.
- Analysis of the effectiveness of promotional elements in increasing response and program returns.
- Use of calculated data to provide extrapolated overall program effectiveness for future mailing cycles.

Specifically:

- Define (to flow chart level) the integration of ongoing analyses into the database/order tracking system. Can cover:
  —Customer/prospect performance.

—Effectiveness of promotional elements for both sales and contribution.

—Product/product category performance on absolute and relative efficiency scales.

—Establish the computer links and report set needed by marketing and operation personnel and management to monitor program progress on a timely basis.

Exhibit 7.3 Start-Up Venture Checklist

Putting all the details aside for a moment, what are the key areas that you should look at before deciding to start a catalog? No company has all of the following, but the more you have the better are your chances for continued success.

- ☐ Reason for existence.

    ___ The product line has attributes that can be better explained or shown in a catalog than in a store or on the Internet. Alternatively, there are areas of the product line that will shine better in a catalog that is complementary to your store or Internet business.

    ___ No other company adequately serves this particular consumer need at this time.

    ___ The target market is large enough to be profitable now and there are strong expansion possibilities in the future.

    ___ The market is relatively easy to reach.

    ___ The product line has the potential for diversification.

    ___ The product line is not seriously affected by seasonality.

- ☐ Finances.

    ___ Enough capital is available to sustain the venture over a reasonable start-up period (up to three years).

    ___ The product line will provide a satisfactory return on investment.

    ___ Sales will not be greatly affected by the loss of any one supplier.

    ___ Frequency of purchase will be higher than the norm.

    ___ The necessary facilities (warehouse, office space, and so on) are available at a reasonable cost.

☐ Management.

    ___ Key people have previous mail order experience, preferably in printed catalog and the Internet.

    ___ Key people also have previous experience in running a business, preferably more than one type of business so that they have diversified experiences.

    ___ Management is knowledgeable about strategy and long-range planning.

The Numbers

Most catalogers customize their sales plans and profit and loss statements so that they are, literally, tailor-made. However, the next two outlines and two forms will provide you with enough details to create your all-important fiscally responsible approach.

Exhibit 7.4 Catalog Sales Plan Form

Catalog Issue								
Month								
Drop Date								
Circulation								
Buyers								
Catalog								
Web								
Store								
Total Buyers								
Requestors								
Catalog								
Web								
Store								
Total Requestors								
Prospects								
Multis								
Lifestyle Database #1								
Lifestyle Database #2								
Rentals								
Total Prospects								
Other/Bulk								
Total								

Orders								
Buyers								
Catalog								
Web								
Store								
Total Buyers								
Requestors								
Catalog								
Web								
Store								
Total Requestors								
Prospects								
Multis								
Lifestyle Database #1								
Lifestyle Database #2								
Rentals								
Total Prospects								
Other/Bulk								
Total Orders								
Response Rate								
Buyers								
Catalog								
Web								
Store								
Total House File								
Requestors								
Catalog								
Web								
Store								
Total Requestors								
Prospects								
Multis								
Lifestyle Database #1								
Lifestyle Database #2								
Rentals								
Total Prospects								
Other/Bulk								
Total Response Rates								
Average Order								
Buyers								
Catalog								
Web								
Store								
Total Buyers								
Requestors								
Catalog								
Web								
Store								
Total Requestors								
Prospects								
Multis								
Lifestyle Database #1								
Lifestyle Database #2								
Rentals								
Total Prospects								
Other/Bulk								
Total Average Orders								

Demand									
Buyers									
Catalog									
Web									
Store									
Total House File									
Requestors									
Catalog									
Web									
Store									
Total Requestors									
Prospects									
Multis									
Lifestyle Database #1									
Lifestyle Database #2									
Rentals									
Total Prospects									
Other/Bulk									
Total = Gross Sales									
$ Per Catalog									
Buyers									
Catalog									
Web									
Store									
Total Buyers									
Requestors									
Catalog									
Web									
Store									
Total Requestors									
Prospects									
Multis									
Lifestyle Database #1									
Lifestyle Database #2									
Rentals									
Total Prospects									
Other/Bulk									
Total $ Per Catalog									

This is a basic form used to plan out every catalog issue for one year. Each issue will have indications of its circulation by segment and how that segment is expected to perform. See Exhibit 7.5 for details.

Exhibit 7.5 Catalog Sales Plan

(All figures are estimated and subject to change) (add date) (add plan version)

Catalog Issue	Spring 1	Spring 2	Spring 3	Fall 1	Fall 2	Fall 3	Hol 1
Month	February	April	May	July	August	September	October
Drop Date	2/27	4/10	5/22	7/22	8/15	9/19	10/10
Circulation							
Buyers							
Catalog	65,120	66,396	47,421	60,000	80,000	60,000	84,358
Web	20,764	8,551	5,000	10,000	25,000	10,000	25,000
Store	72,792	10,441	19,712	10,000	80,000	20,000	46,500
Total Buyers	**158,676**	**85,388**	**72,133**	**80,000**	**185,000**	**90,000**	**155,858**
Requestors							
Catalog	5,565	4,342	1,477	-	6,000	3,000	6,500
Web	9,770	6,330		-	5,000	3,000	5,500
Store	-			-			
Total Requestors	**15,335**	**10,672**	**1,477**	**-**	**11,000**	**6,000**	**12,000**
Prospects							
Multis	8,397	5,301	27,216	-	15,000	65,000	35,000
Lifestyle Database #1	-		44,301	-	200,000	-	250,000
Lifestyle Database #2	54,867		26,544	-	50,000	-	50,000
Rentals	263,938		71,423	-	365,000	-	300,000
Total Prospects	**327,202**	**5,301**	**169,484**	**-**	**630,000**	**65,000**	**635,000**
Other/Bulk	53,530	4,240	8,477	11,000	11,000	10,500	11,000
Total	**554,743**	**105,601**	**251,571**	**91,000**	**837,000**	**171,500**	**813,858**
Orders							
Buyers							
Catalog	1,589	1,208	887	1,684	1,674	1,290	2,190
Web	490	137		271	460	184	461
Store	408	77	201	64	681	235	483
Total Buyers	**2,487**	**1,422**	**1,088**	**2,019**	**2,815**	**1,709**	**3,134**
Requestors							
Catalog	85	60	25		95	48	150
Web	146	92			83	50	76
Store							
Total Requestors	**231**	**152**	**25**		**179**	**98**	**226**
Prospects							
Multis	85	41	223		123	533	459
Lifestyle Database #1			452		2,040		3,326
Lifestyle Database #2	510		276		465		585
Rentals	2,798		743		3,869		3,193
Total Prospects	**3,393**	**41**	**1,694**		**6,497**	**533**	**7,564**
Other/Bulk	209	41	36	49	49	47	152
Total Orders	**6,319**	**1,615**	**2,843**	**2,069**	**9,540**	**2,387**	**11,076**
Response Rate							
Buyers							
Catalog	2.44%	1.82%	1.87%	2.81%	2.09%	2.15%	2.60%
Web	2.36%	1.60%		2.71%	1.84%	1.84%	1.85%
Store	0.56%	0.74%	1.02%	0.64%	0.85%	1.17%	1.04%
Total House File	**1.57%**	**1.67%**	**1.51%**	**2.52%**	**1.52%**	**1.90%**	**2.01%**
Requestors							
Catalog	1.53%	1.38%	1.69%		1.59%	1.59%	2.31%
Web	1.49%	1.45%			1.67%	1.67%	1.38%
Store							
Total Requestors	**1.50%**	**1.42%**	**1.69%**		**1.62%**	**1.63%**	**1.88%**

Prospects								
Multis		1.0%	0.8%	0.8%		0.8%	0.8%	1.3%
Lifestyle Database #1								
Lifestyle Database #2		0.9%		1.0%		0.9%		1.2%
Rentals		1.1%		1.0%		1.1%		1.1%
Total Prospects		**1.0%**	**0.8%**	**1.0%**		**1.0%**	**0.8%**	**1.2%**
Other/Bulk		0.4%	1.0%	0.4%	0.4%	0.4%	0.4%	1.4%
Total Response Rates		**1.1%**	**1.5%**	**1.1%**	**2.3%**	**1.1%**	**1.4%**	**1.4%**
Average Order								
Buyers								
Catalog		$114	$110	$106	$114	$114	$114	$119
Web		$105	$106	$110	$105	$105	$105	$109
Store		$134	$156	$90	$134	$134	$134	$140
Total Buyers		**$116**	**$112**	**$103**	**$114**	**$118**	**$116**	**$121**
Requestors								
Catalog		$115	$97	$85		$115	$115	$120
Web		$93	$105			$93	$93	$96
Store								
Total Requestors		**$101**	**$102**	**$85**		**$105**	**$104**	**$112**
Prospects								
Multis		$81	$89	$121		$81	$81	$84
Lifestyle Database #1				$90		$95		$99
Lifestyle Database #2		$134		$116		$134		$139
Rentals		$105		$97		$105		$109
Total Prospects		**$109**	**$89**	**$102**		**$104**	**$81**	**$106**
Other/Bulk		$133	$0	$98	$133	$133	$133	$138
Total Average Orders		**$112**	**$111**	**$102**	**$114**	**$108**	**$108**	**$110**
Demand								
Buyers								
Catalog		$181,535	$132,889	$93,758	$192,351	$191,300	$147,417	$260,171
Web		$51,419	$14,554	$7,150	$28,478	$48,268	$19,307	$50,356
Store		$54,754	$12,036	$18,106	$8,650	$91,445	$31,511	$67,442
Total House File		**$287,707**	**$159,479**	**$111,864**	**$229,480**	**$331,013**	**$198,235**	**$377,969**
Requestors								
Catalog		$9,812	$5,789	$2,114		$10,973	$5,487	$17,977
Web		$13,471	$9,629			$7,716	$4,629	$7,329
Store								
Total Requestors		**$23,283**	**$15,419**	**$2,114**		**$18,689**	**$10,116**	**$25,306**
Prospects								
Multis		$6,868	$3,617	$27,048		$9,961	$43,162	$38,652
Lifestyle Database #1				$40,632		$193,800	$0	$328,625
Lifestyle Database #2		$68,442		$32,086		$62,370	$0	$81,661
Rentals		$294,155		$72,208		$406,787	$0	$349,154
Total Prospects		**$369,464**	**$3,617**	**$171,974**		**$672,918**	**$43,162**	**$798,093**
Other/Bulk		$27,662	$0	$3,571	$6,537	$6,537	$6,240	$20,965
Total = Gross Sales		**$708,117**	**$178,515**	**$289,523**	**$236,016**	**$1,029,156**	**$257,753**	**$1,222,333**

$ Per Catalog								
Buyers								
Catalog		$2.79	$2.00	$1.98	$3.21	$2.39	$2.46	$3.08
Web		$2.48	$1.70	$1.43	$2.85	$1.93	$1.93	$2.01
Store		$0.75	$1.15	$0.92	$0.87	$1.14	$1.58	$1.45
Total Buyers		**$1.81**	**$1.87**	**$1.55**	**$2.87**	**$1.79**	**$2.20**	**$2.43**
Requestors								
Catalog		$1.76	$1.33	$1.43		$1.83	$1.83	$2.77
Web		$1.38	$1.52			$1.54	$1.54	$1.33
Store								
Total Requestors		**$1.52**	**$1.44**	**$1.43**		**$1.70**	**$1.69**	**$2.11**
Prospects								
Multis		$0.82	$0.68	$0.99		$0.66	$0.66	$1.10
Lifestyle Database #1				$0.92		$0.97	$0.00	$1.31
Lifestyle Database #2		$1.25		$1.21		$1.25	$0.00	$1.63
Rentals		$1.11		$1.01		$1.11	$0.00	$1.16
Total Prospects		**$1.13**	**$0.68**	**$1.01**		**$1.07**	**$0.66**	**$1.26**
Other/Bulk		$0.52		$0.42	$0.59	$0.59	$0.59	$1.91
Total $ Per Catalog		**$1.28**	**$1.75**	**$1.17**	**$2.59**	**$1.23**	**$1.50**	**$1.50**

This plan indicates the expected sales for a particular catalog over one year. The document would be dated and would include which version of the plan it was, as sometimes there are many versions.

The *Drop Date* shows the date that the catalog actually goes in the mail. The *Circulation* is broken out by the different segments that will be mailed; note that these quantities will differ per mailing. This is so not all of the segments always get every catalog. The frequency the catalog is received by particular segments depends on historical data performance. *Other Bulk* generally refers to printed catalogs that do not go into the mail stream, e.g., catalogs that are given to a catalog company's retail stores.

Orders show the number of orders that are expected from each of the segments. *Response Rates* and *Average Orders* are based on historical data or input from experts. *Demand* is a combination of the average order times the percentage response, times the circulation.

Most catalogs look for the critical *Dollars Generated Per Book* (or per thousand circulated), as this number is the summation of all the elements (circulation, average order, percentage response) that go into the actual demand.

Exhibit 7.6 Financial Plan Outline

Basically a profit and loss statement that itemizes expense details and shows the cash flow for an entire year.

Cash on Hand At End of Prior Fiscal Year	Cash at Start of Month (allow for 12 columns, one per month)	Cash at End of Fiscal Year TOTAL
	_____	_____

Revenue
Consumer Catalog Sales _____ _____
Corporate Sales _____ _____
Internet Sales _____ _____
Other Sales _____ _____

Total Merchandise Sales _____ _____

Shipping & Handling
Shipping & Handling—Consumer _____ _____
Shipping & Handling—Corporate _____ _____
Shipping & Handling—Internet _____ _____
Shipping & Handling—Other _____ _____

Total Shipping & Handling _____ _____

GROSS SALES _____ _____

Sales Discounts
Goodwill _____ _____
Gift Certificates Expense _____ _____
Public Relations Discounts _____ _____
Sales Discounts—Consumer _____ _____
Sales Discounts—Corporate _____ _____
Sales Discounts—Internet _____ _____
Test Shipments _____ _____
Over/Short _____ _____

Total Discounts _____ _____

Returns & Allowances

Merchandise Exchange (not restockable)	_____	_____
Customer Write-Offs	_____	_____
Returns & Allowances—Consumer	_____	_____
Returns & Allowances—Corporate	_____	_____
Returns & Allowances—Internet	_____	_____
Returns & Allowances—Other	_____	_____
Total Returns & Allowances	_____	_____
NET SALES	_____	_____

Cost of Goods Sold

Merchandise Purchases	_____	_____
Freight In	_____	_____
Change in Inventory	_____	_____
Total Cost of Goods Sold	_____	_____

Gross Profit

List Rental Income	_____	_____
GROSS OPERATING INCOME	_____	_____

Direct Costs Marketing

	_____	_____
Incentives	_____	_____

Catalog

List Maintenance	_____	_____
List Rental	_____	_____
Merchandise Samples	_____	_____
Order Form	_____	_____
Postage—Catalog	_____	_____
Printing—Catalog	_____	_____
Production—Catalog	_____	_____
Public Relations	_____	_____
Total Catalog	_____	_____

Strategic Partnerships & Promotions
Campaign Expenses _____ _____
Commissions _____ _____
Employee Benefits _____ _____
Payroll Taxes _____ _____
Salaries _____ _____
Telephone _____ _____

Total Str. Ptrs. & Promos. _____ _____

Internet
Amortization—Outside Contract _____ _____
Employee Benefits _____ _____
Outside Service _____ _____
Payroll Taxes _____ _____
Retirement Savings Plan Expense _____ _____
Salaries _____ _____
Transaction Fees _____ _____
Web Page Design _____ _____

Total Internet _____ _____

Total Marketing _____ _____

Freight Expenses
Freight Out—Consumer _____ _____
Freight Out—Corporate _____ _____
Freight Out—Internet _____ _____
Freight Out—Other _____ _____

Total Freight Expenses _____ _____

Order Processing & Fulfillment
Call Centers
Auto & Travel _____ _____
Call Center Fees _____ _____
Communications Link _____ _____
Commissions—Outbound _____ _____
Commissions—Corporate _____ _____
Contract Labor _____ _____
Employee Benefits _____ _____
Payroll Tax _____ _____
Recruiting _____ _____
Retirement Savings Plan Expense _____ _____

Salaries _____ _____
Supplies & Repairs _____ _____
Telephone _____ _____
Training & Supervision _____ _____
Travel _____ _____

Total Call Centers _____ _____

Order Processing
Auto & Travel _____ _____
Credit Card Fees _____ _____
Employee Benefits _____ _____
Drop Ship Expense _____ _____
Outside Services— _____ _____
   Order Fulfillment
Payroll Tax _____ _____
Retirement Savings Plan Expense _____ _____
Salaries _____ _____
Supplies & Repairs _____ _____

Total Order Processing _____ _____

Miscellaneous
Distribution Center _____ _____
Packaging Supplies & Expenses _____ _____
Warehouse _____ _____

Total Miscellaneous _____ _____

Total Order Proc. & Fulfillment _____ _____

Total Direct Costs _____ _____

OPERATING INCOME _____ _____

General and Administrative
Compensation _____ _____
Salaries _____ _____
Payroll Taxes _____ _____

Total Compensation _____ _____

Accounting _____ _____
Auto & Travel _____ _____
Bank Charges _____ _____
Computer Hardware _____ _____
   Maintenance

Computer Software Maintenance _____   _____
Consulting _____   _____
Continuing Education _____   _____
Dues & Subscriptions _____   _____
Employee Benefits _____   _____
Entertainment _____   _____
Equipment Operating Lease _____   _____
Equipment Rental _____   _____
Insurance _____   _____
Legal _____   _____
Licenses & Fees _____   _____
Maintenance & Repairs _____   _____
Office Supplies _____   _____
Outside Services _____   _____
Postage _____   _____
Recruiting _____   _____
Rent _____   _____
Supplies _____   _____
Taxes, Miscellaneous _____   _____
Telephone _____   _____

Total General and Administrative _____   _____

Other Income/Expenses _____   _____
Interest Income _____   _____
Other Income (Loss) _____   _____
Disposal of Equipment (Gain/Loss) _____   _____

Total Other Income/Expenses _____   _____

EBITDA (Earnings before interest, taxes, depreciation and amortization) _____   _____

Depreciation & Amortization _____   _____

EBIT (Earnings before interest and income taxes) _____   _____

Interest Expense _____   _____
Income Tax _____   _____

Net Income (Loss) _____   _____

Exhibit 7.7 Financial Plan Including Revenue, Cost, Cash Flow, Net Income (Loss)

	Cash at Start of Month													Cash at End of Fiscal Year
Cash on Hand At End of Prior Fiscal Year	$550,000	$388,036	$137,097	-$13,740	-$275,531	-$394,169	$343,409	-$139,095	-$486,359	-$606,184	-$699,406	-$341,970		-$470,859
$550,000	July	August	September	October	November	December	January	February	March	April	May	June		Total
Revenue														
Consumer Catalog Sales	$603,022	$540,093	$587,936	$574,527	$1,220,735	$4,886,242	$912,264	$1,246,958	$1,262,649	$1,138,772	$5,081,580	$760,574		$18,815,353
Corporate Sales	$47,358	$41,891	$54,728	$71,713	$115,607	$395,477	$81,447	$83,856	$105,910	$166,600	$156,800	$79,000		$1,400,386
Internet Sales	$10,834	$11,859	$11,287	$16,470	$23,519	$116,233	$36,227	$84,542	$31,474	$24,505	$109,347	$16,366		$492,663
Other Sales	$3,158	$1,566	$1,455	$1,554	$1,222	$9,705	$892	$1,657	$0	$0	$0	$0		$21,208
Total Merchandise Sales	$664,372	$595,408	$655,406	$664,264	$1,361,083	$5,407,657	$1,030,830	$1,417,013	$1,400,033	$1,329,877	$5,347,727	$855,940		$20,729,609
Shipping & Handling														
Shipping & Handling - Consumer	$57,137	$52,910	$64,722	$66,423	$126,662	$541,111	$93,353	$141,933	$175,892	$150,080	$634,804	$93,267		$2,198,294
Shipping & Handling - Corporate	$4,787	$3,706	$5,094	$6,280	$11,618	$46,386	$6,277	$9,929	$12,433	$20,471	$19,014	$9,223		$155,217
Shipping & Handling - Internet	$0	$0	$1,580	$2,449	$2,893	$12,397	$4,266	$10,915	$3,695	$3,011	$13,259	$1,911		$56,376
Shipping & Handling - Other	$600	$342	$333	$259	$332	$2,015	$235	$298	$0	$0	$0	$0		$4,414
Total Shipping & Handling	$62,524	$56,958	$71,729	$75,411	$141,505	$601,908	$104,131	$163,075	$192,020	$173,562	$667,077	$104,401		$2,414,300
Gross Sales	$726,895	$652,366	$727,134	$739,676	$1,502,588	$6,009,565	$1,134,961	$1,580,088	$1,592,053	$1,503,439	$6,014,804	$960,341		$23,143,910
Sales Discounts														
Goodwill	$1,316	$886	$415	$356	$728	$11,605	$1,553	$969	$0	$0	$0	$0		$17,827
Gift Certificates Expense	$249	-$3	$492	$51	$1,326	$2,549	$1,974	-$5,785	$0	$0	$0	$0		$853
Public Relations Discounts	$987	$420	$1,089	$227	$2,058	$982	$2,692	$1,399	$0	$0	$0	$0		$9,853
Sales Discounts - Consumer	$207	$172	$4,875	$3,086	$8,417	$28,902	$372	$793	$8,181	$6,980	$29,526	$4,338		$95,849
Sales Discounts - Corporate	$255	$273	$847	-$661	$740	-$744	$181	$438	$578	$952	$884	$429		$4,172
Sales Discounts - Internet	$0	$0	$20	$0	$103	$0	$0	$0	$172	$140	$617	$89		$1,141
Test Shipments	$2,974	$2,855	$2,774	$5,288	$1,579	$10,005	$2,187	$284	$0	$0	$0	$0		$27,947
Over/Short	$7,095	-$3,892	$3,977	$4,512	$1,912	-$11,475	$8,087	$12,030	$500	$500	$500	$500		$24,245
Total Discounts	$13,083	$711	$14,487	$12,858	$16,863	$41,825	$17,047	$10,127	$9,431	$8,572	$31,527	$5,356		$181,887
Returns & Allowances														
Merchandise Exchange (not restockable)	$8,769	$6,706	$5,840	$5,024	$7,208	$34,124	$17,737	$16,010	$12,400	$6,317	$32,086	$8,131		$160,352
Customer Write-Offs	$4,371	$2,074	$2,475	$466	$2,213	$1,513	$1,800	$3,052	$0	$0	$0	$0		$17,964
Returns & Allowances - Consumer	$26,261	$12,790	$17,520	$14,038	$15,787	$103,505	$59,745	$49,676	$25,936	$29,195	$140,787	$14,358		$509,598
Returns & Allowances - Corporate	$0	$0	$0	$0	$0	$0	$0	$0	$3,247	$5,346	$4,966	$2,409		$15,968
Returns & Allowances - Internet	$0	$629	$0	$0	$0	$0	$0	$0	$0	$0	$0	$0		$629
Returns & Allowances - Other	$0	$0	$0	$0	$0	$0	$0	$0	$965	$786	$3,463	$499		$5,713
Total Returns & Allowances	$39,402	$22,199	$25,835	$19,528	$25,208	$139,142	$79,282	$68,738	$42,548	$41,644	$181,302	$25,397		$710,223
Net Sales	$674,411	$629,457	$686,812	$707,290	$1,460,517	$5,828,598	$1,038,632	$1,501,222	$1,540,074	$1,453,223	$5,801,975	$929,588		$22,251,799

	Cash on Hand At End of Prior Fiscal Year	Cash at Start of Month												Cash at End of Fiscal Year
	$550,000	$550,000	$388,036	$137,097	-$13,740	-$275,531	-$394,169	$343,409	-$139,095	-$486,359	-$606,184	-$699,406	-$341,970	-$470,859
		July	August	September	October	November	December	January	February	March	April	May	June	Total
Cost of Goods Sold														
Merchandise Purchases		$265,749	$238,163	$262,162	$265,706	$544,433	$2,163,063	$412,332	$566,805	$560,013	$531,951	$2,139,091	$342,376	$8,291,844
Freight In		$5,621	$8,587	$6,590	$9,070	$11,927	$17,503	$15,285	$10,693	$0	$0	$0	$0	$85,276
Change in Inventory		$0	$0	$0	$0	$0	$0	-$23,452	$81,797	$0	$0	$0	$0	$58,345
Total Cost of Goods Sold		$271,370	$246,750	$268,752	$274,775	$556,360	$2,180,566	$404,165	$659,295	$560,013	$531,951	$2,139,091	$342,376	$8,435,464
Gross Profit		$403,041	$382,707	$418,060	$432,514	$904,158	$3,648,032	$634,467	$841,928	$980,061	$921,272	$3,662,884	$587,212	$13,816,335
List Rental Income		$68,466	$86,166	$43,560	$18,264	$33,695	$28,996	-$3,271	$13,952	$17,400	$14,080	$700	$44,950	$366,957
Gross Operating Income		$471,507	$468,873	$461,620	$450,778	$937,852	$3,677,028	$631,197	$855,879	$997,461	$935,352	$3,663,584	$632,162	$14,183,292
Direct Costs														
Marketing														
Incentives		$0	$0	$0	$0	$0	$0	$0	$2,012	$0	$0	$0	$0	$2,012
Catalog														
List Maintenance		$4,735	$1,151	$1,017	$2,497	$12,734	$32,058	$11,684	$8,522	$4,587	$3,965	$18,474	$2,886	$104,311
List Rental		$12,745	$11,478	$6,868	$6,642	$55,632	$191,882	$47,346	$48,890	$40,048	$34,615	$161,285	$25,201	$642,632
Merchandise Samples		$37	$42	$192	$193	$370	$1,275	$480	$185	$203	$176	$818	$128	$4,098
Order Form		$2,413	$2,198	$5,131	$6,024	$7,935	$41,291	$14,945	$8,378	$9,871	$8,532	$39,754	$6,212	$152,684
Postage - Catalog		$97,188	$10,288	$12,420	$17,157	$171,651	$522,871	$157,227	$158,886	$122,611	$105,979	$493,794	$77,157	$1,947,231
Printing - Catalog		$26,948	$152,609	$75,238	$76,815	$104,600	$521,725	$169,017	$207,236	$131,355	$113,536	$529,012	$82,660	$2,190,750
Production - Catalog		$1,774	$1,664	$7,609	$15,464	$13,771	$46,998	$21,321	$24,323	$8,927	$7,716	$35,954	$5,618	$191,139
Public Relations		$654	$444	$678	$2,884	$2,007	$10,016	$2,741	$3,945	$8,138	$7,738	$15,631	$6,661	$61,536
Total Catalog		$146,494	$179,873	$109,154	$127,676	$368,699	$1,368,117	$424,760	$460,366	$325,740	$282,257	$1,294,722	$206,523	$5,294,381
Strategic Partnerships & Promotions														
Campaign Expenses		$31	$0	$59	$431	$3,753	$2,020	$3,417	$35,172	$4,332	$10,497	$19,237	$4,024	$84,474
Commissions		$0	$0	$1,110	$0	$20	$50	$0	$0	$0	$0	$0	$0	$1,179
Employee Benefits		-$15	$0	$0	$0	$0	$0	$0	$0	$169	$169	$169	$169	$659
Payroll Taxes		$192	$0	$0	$0	$464	$458	$444	$332	$149	$149	$149	$149	$2,486
Salaries		$405	$0	$0	$0	$4,144	$3,457	$4,419	$4,006	$1,810	$1,810	$1,810	$1,810	$23,671
Telephone		$0	$0	$0	$0	$0	$0	$0	$0	-$22	$445	$1,107	$0	$1,530
Total Str. Ptrs. & Promos.		$613	$0	$1,168	$431	$8,381	$6,884	$8,280	$39,511	$6,438	$13,070	$22,472	$6,752	$113,999

Exhibit 7.7 Financial Plan Including Revenue, Cost, Cash Flow, Net Income (Loss) continued

Cash on Hand At End of Prior Fiscal Year	Cash at Start of Month												Cash at End of Fiscal Year
$550,000	$550,000	$388,036	$137,097	-$13,740	-$275,531	-$394,169	$343,409	-$139,095	-$486,359	-$606,184	-$699,406	-$341,970	-$470,859
	July	August	September	October	November	December	January	February	March	April	May	June	Total
Internet													
Amortization - Outside Contract	$333	$333	$333	$333	$333	$333	$333	$333	$333	$333	$333	$333	$3,999
Employee Benefits	$0	$0	$0	$0	$0	$0	$0	$0	$238	$238	$238	$238	$952
Outside Service	$0	$0	$0	$0	$105	$0	$0	$0	$0	$0	$0	$0	$105
Payroll Taxes	$0	$0	$0	$0	$246	$676	$622	$379	$481	$481	$481	$481	$3,847
Retirement Savings Plan Expense	$0	$0	$0	$0	$0	$0	$0	$48	$0	$0	$0	$0	$48
Salaries	$0	$0	$0	$0	$2,233	$6,228	$6,266	$5,689	$5,833	$5,833	$5,833	$5,833	$43,747
Transaction Fees	$1,512	-$133	$0	$5,129	$1,575	$7,941	$7,220	$2,558	$2,178	$1,766	$8,706	$1,259	$39,711
Web Page Design	$0	$0	$0	$0	$0	$140	$0	$6,927	$0	$0	$0	$0	$7,067
Total Internet	$1,845	$200	$333	$5,462	$4,493	$15,318	$14,441	$15,934	$9,063	$8,651	$15,591	$8,144	$99,476
Total Marketing	$148,953	$180,074	$110,656	$133,570	$381,572	$1,390,319	$447,481	$517,823	$341,240	$303,977	$1,332,784	$221,418	$5,509,868
Freight Expenses													
Freight Out - Consumer	$92,269	$121,099	$121,997	$116,605	$192,843	$637,490	$187,646	$211,505	$246,983	$97,442	$953,017	$137,666	$3,116,560
Freight Out - Corporate	$10,325	$9,455	$6,886	$10,909	$18,115	$55,074	$4,024	$18,015	$17,884	$14,256	$29,407	$14,299	$208,648
Freight Out - Internet	$2,363	$2,404	$1,626	$2,552	$4,045	$14,417	$1,352	$6,280	$5,315	$2,097	$20,507	$2,962	$65,919
Freight Out - Other	$1,765	$876	$666	$684	$490	$1,415	$162	$2,162	$0	$0	$0	$0	$8,221
Total Freight Expenses	$106,721	$133,833	$131,175	$130,750	$215,493	$708,396	$193,183	$237,962	$270,182	$113,795	$1,002,931	$154,927	$3,399,348
Order Processing & Fulfillment													
Call Centers													
Auto & Travel	$195	$3,078	$1,884	$246	$0	$1,008	$1,476	$3,125	$0	$0	$0	$0	$11,012
Call Center Fees	$30,486	$2,326	$44,438	$21,000	$42,188	$128,561	$3,053	-$92	$48,624	$111,148	$207,436	$43,026	$682,193
Communications Link	$3,714	$5,435	$0	$3,909	$0	$3,964	$8,467	$0	$0	$0	$0	$0	$25,489
Commissions - Outbound	$232	$120	$173	$0	$0	$0	$0	$0	$0	$0	$0	$0	$525
Commissions - Corporate	$1,831	$2,472	$0	$0	$0	$0	$0	$5,538	$0	$0	$0	$0	$9,841
Contract Labor	$25,699	$26,403	$20,140	$63,624	$74,135	$94,792	$83,570	$92,626	$67,950	$96,261	$109,002	$0	$754,202
Employee Benefits	$1,438	$1,164	$1,379	$1,507	$1,356	$1,377	$1,377	$1,112	$2,034	$2,034	$2,034	$2,034	$18,846
Payroll Tax	$4,051	$3,158	$2,987	$2,926	$3,019	$3,418	$6,732	$4,908	$6,348	$8,095	$6,377	$6,348	$58,367
Recruiting	$0	$0	$0	$0	$0	$0	$0	$0	$0	$0	$0	$0	$40
Retirement Savings Plan Expense	$0	$0	$0	$0	$0	$0	$0	$136	$0	$0	$0	$0	$136
Salaries	$37,967	$38,596	$38,304	$40,761	$47,838	$49,164	$59,932	$51,093	$71,880	$91,303	$72,202	$71,881	$670,921
Supplies & Repairs	$1,857	$1,446	$657	$4,213	$1,288	$929	$445	$345	$1,400	$2,100	$2,200	$600	$17,481
Telephone	$5,995	$29,769	-$5,223	$27,687	$24,084	$65,351	$20,046	$11,956	$15,052	$13,140	$51,107	$8,172	$267,135
Training & Supervision	$0	$0	$0	$237	$1,128	$0	$0	$0	$500	$0	$500	$0	$2,365
Travel	-$186	$0	$931	$1,926	$226	-$8	$1,137	$0	$0	$0	$0	$0	$4,026

	Cash on Hand At End of Prior Fiscal Year	Cash at Start of Month											Cash at End of Fiscal Year
	$550,000	$550,000	$388,036	$137,097	-$13,740	-$275,531	-$394,169	$343,409	-$139,095	-$486,359	-$606,184	-$699,406	-$341,970	-$470,859
		July	August	September	October	November	December	January	February	March	April	May	June	Total
Total Call Centers		$113,279	$113,967	$105,669	$168,036	$195,261	$348,597	$186,235	$170,748	$213,788	$324,081	$450,858	$132,061	$2,522,579
Order Processing														
Auto & Travel		$0	$0	$0	$0	$0	$0	$749	$0	$0	$0	$0	$0	$749
Credit Card Fees		$14,202	$13,456	$14,651	$15,362	$32,584	$129,470	$26,338	$33,630	$38,390	$20,354	$141,401	$22,174	$502,012
Employee Benefits		$202	$143	$180	$306	$328	$321	$194	$165	$213	$213	$213	$213	$2,690
Drop Ship Expense		$2,175	$1,758	$3,925	$6,460	$1,994	$2,409	$2,430	$5,165	$1,913	$1,729	$6,645	$1,040	$37,645
Outside Services - Order Fulfillment									$493					$493
Payroll Tax		$540	$428	$364	$457	$414	$625	$694	$616	$664	$664	$664	$664	$6,795
Retirement Savings Plan Expense		$0	$0	$0	$0	$0	$0	$0	$18	$0	$0	$0	$0	$18
Salaries		$4,001	$5,646	$5,027	$6,188	$5,989	$7,765	$6,209	$6,068	$7,383	$7,383	$7,383	$7,383	$76,425
Supplies & Repairs		$516	$903	$195	$533	$535	$550	$1,221	$371	$0	$0	$0	$0	$4,825
Total Order Processing		$21,635	$22,335	$24,342	$29,308	$41,845	$141,140	$37,835	$46,527	$48,563	$30,343	$156,306	$31,474	$631,652
Miscellaneous														
Distribution Center		$0	$0	$0	$0	$0	$574	$0	$0	$0	$0	$3,000	$0	$3,574
Packaging Supplies & Expenses		$2,994	$15,190	$18,591	$14,989	$17,457	$57,399	$33,776	$21,252	$20,495	$18,525	$71,201	$11,143	$303,012
Warehouse		$8,359	$26,229	$10,010	$8,498	$13,147	$57,909	$9,095	$20,946	$9,920	$18,430	$62,199	$11,629	$256,371
Total Miscellaneous		$11,353	$41,419	$28,601	$23,487	$30,604	$115,881	$42,871	$42,198	$30,415	$36,955	$136,400	$22,772	$562,957
Total Order Proc. & Fulfillment		$146,267	$177,720	$158,613	$220,831	$267,710	$605,618	$266,942	$259,473	$292,766	$391,379	$743,564	$186,307	$3,717,188
Total Direct Costs		$401,940	$491,627	$400,443	$485,150	$864,775	$2,704,333	$907,606	$1,015,258	$904,188	$809,151	$3,079,279	$562,652	$12,626,403
Operating Income		$69,566	-$22,754	$61,177	-$34,372	$73,077	$972,695	-$276,410	-$159,378	$93,273	$126,201	$584,305	$69,510	$1,556,889
General and Administrative														
Compensation														
Salaries		$76,524	$78,861	$78,648	$79,303	$90,271	$84,116	$98,382	$89,847	$94,735	$94,862	$94,967	$94,970	$1,055,487
Payroll Taxes		$4,298	$4,850	$4,917	$4,056	$4,366	$4,203	$11,824	$7,292	$7,843	$7,853	$7,861	$7,861	$77,223
Total Compensation		$80,822	$83,711	$83,565	$83,359	$94,637	$88,319	$110,206	$97,139	$102,578	$102,715	$102,828	$102,831	$1,132,710
Accounting		$2,918	$2,918	$2,918	$2,750	$2,918	$5,684	$2,917	$3,297	$2,917	$2,917	$2,917	$2,917	$37,986
Auto & Travel		$714	$7,133	$1,430	$5,237	$1,013	$2,639	$63	$4,831	$7,500	$7,500	$7,500	$7,500	$53,062
Bank Charges		$240	$7,333	$0	-$578	$1,087	$0	$30	$215	$0	$0	$0	$0	$8,327
Computer Hardware Maintenance		$8,058	$5,070	$1,778	$445	$13,632	$3,643	$4,538	$5,941	$1,962	$2,487	$1,962	$1,962	$51,477
Computer Software Maintenance		$10,068	$18,220	$4,087	$4,700	$6,472	$2,597	$9,024	$1,611	$7,553	$7,870	$6,120	$6,120	$84,442
Consulting		$23,091	$11,011	$23,146	$18,989	$41,174	$33,110	$2,669	-$11,650	$12,600	$12,600	$12,600	$12,600	$191,940
Continuing Education		$695	$0	$0	$200	$495	$0	$0	$1,350	$666	$666	$666	$666	$5,404
Dues & Subscriptions		$78	$2,550	$0	$1,055	$175	$1,608	$270	$104	$150	$150	$150	$150	$6,440
Employee Benefits		$2,733	$1,712	$3,058	$5,899	$1,301	$2,337	$3,930	$8,682	$2,808	$2,808	$2,808	$2,808	$40,883

Exhibit 7.7 Financial Plan Including Revenue, Cost, Cash Flow, Net Income (Loss) continued

	Cash at Start of Month													Cash at End of Fiscal Year
Cash on Hand At End of Prior Fiscal Year	$550,000	$388,036	$137,097	-$13,740	-$275,531	-$394,169	$343,409	-$139,095	-$486,359	-$606,184	-$699,406	-$341,970		-$470,859
$550,000	July	August	September	October	November	December	January	February	March	April	May	June		Total
Equipment Rental	$0	$1,790	$0	$0	$0	$0	$0	$0	$0	$0	$0	$0		$1,790
Insurance	$1,656	$1,656	$1,683	-$733	$1,656	$1,900	$1,514	$0	$1,900	$0	$1,900	$1,900		$16,930
Legal	$411	$206	$2,844	$1,727	$1,633	$447	$0	$357	$2,000	$2,000	$2,000	$2,000		$15,624
Licenses & Fees	$0	$0	$0	$638	$149	$245	$125	$0	$100	$0	$10	$0		$1,267
Maintenance & Repairs	$224	$224	$224	$309	$0	$41	$254	$121	$500	$500	$500	$500		$3,397
Office Supplies	$1,389	$1,823	$2,048	$2,586	$1,918	$6,810	$2,190	$886	$1,667	$1,667	$1,667	$1,667		$26,318
Outside Services	$9,185	$9,132	$4,388	$17,470	$7,339	$2,746	$3,366	$7,640	$595	$595	$595	$595		$63,647
Postage	$556	$128	$2,296	$1,155	$643	$1,979	$1,324	$1,367	$1,000	$1,000	$1,000	$1,000		$13,447
Recruiting	$0	$0	$0	$0	$0	$0	$0	$44,190	$0	$0	$0	$0		$44,190
Rent	$72,670	$72,670	$72,670	$72,670	$72,670	$72,670	$62,724	$46,553	$72,669	$72,669	$72,669	$72,669		$835,972
Supplies	$7	$17	$0	$0	$0	$0	$317	$0	$0	$0	$0	$0		$341
Taxes, Miscellaneous	$15,361	$0	$2,954	$240	$0	$6	$200	$11,967	$250	$250	$250	$250		$31,227
Telephone	$4,398	$1,790	$6,158	$4,595	$5,849	$6,538	$4,349	$3,587	$4,350	$4,350	$5,850	$4,350		$56,664
Total General and Administrative	$167,941 $248,763	$162,998 $246,709	$145,125 $228,690	$154,817 $238,175	$175,332 $269,968	$160,069 $248,388	$114,872 $225,078	$147,192 $244,330	$136,124 $238,702	$137,116 $239,831	$135,851 $238,679	$134,591 $237,422		$1,772,026 $2,904,736
Other Income/Expenses														
Interest Income	$24,501	$22,044	$16,677	$14,999	$11,337	$16,560	$22,194	$17,518	$28,578	$23,302	$14,622	$41,753		$254,085
Other Income (Loss)	$0	$0	$0	$0	$70,206	$0	$0	$43,683	$0	$0	$0	$0		$113,889
Disposal of Equipment (Gain/Loss)	$0	$0	$0	$0	$0	$0	$0	-$1,626	$0	$0	$0	$0		-$1,626
Total Other Income/Expenses	$24,501	$22,044	$16,677	$14,999	$81,542	$16,560	$22,194	$59,575	$28,578	$23,302	$14,622	$41,753		$366,348
EBITDA(Earnings before interest, taxes, depreciation and amortization	-$154,696	-$247,419	-$150,837	-$257,548	-$115,349	$740,867	-$479,294	-$344,134	-$116,851	-$90,328	$360,248	-$126,159		-$981,500
Depreciation & Amortization	$31,420	$33,586	$34,073	$34,005	$38,387	$38,041	$41,662	$51,500	$38,167	$38,391	$38,433	$38,475		$456,140
EBIT(Earnings before interest and income taxes)	-$186,117	-$281,005	-$184,910	-$291,553	-$153,736	$702,826	-$520,956	-$395,633	-$155,018	-$128,719	$321,815	-$164,633		-$1,437,639
Interest Expense	$7,268	$3,520	$0	$3,444	$3,289	$3,288	$3,210	$3,131	$2,974	$2,894	$2,812	$2,731		$38,560
Income Tax	$0	$0	$0	$800	$0	$0	$0	$0	$0	$0	$0	$0		$800
Net Income (Loss)	-$193,384	-$284,525	-$184,910	-$295,797	-$157,024	$699,537	-$524,166	-$398,764	-$157,992	-$131,613	$319,003	-$167,364		-$1,476,999

Some notes about this exhibit:

- All *Sales* are taken in the month of mailing.
- The sales order curve is specific to this catalog; you must adjust it based on your own sales.
- *Other Sales* should include revenues from outside ventures, such as affiliations, alliances, partnerships, and joint ventures.
- *Shipping & Handling* revenue is taken at the same time as *Sales*. In this example shipping & handling is considered a part of sales; others may take it into account as a part of operations.
- *Goodwill* can refer to discounts taken in exchange for goods or services.
- *Gift Certificates* will not apply to all catalogs.
- *Over/Short* mainly concerns customers' checks that have been miscalculated.
- *Merchandise Exchange* is primarily merchandise returned with defects from manufacture or shipping.
- *Customer Write-Offs* would include bad debt from checks and/or credit cards.
- All *Returns & Allowances* would include costs of receiving, restocking, and new order shipping.
- *Net Sales* are gross sales less returns, discount, and allowances.
- *List Maintenance* should include cleaning, updates, and modeling.
- *Production—Catalog* includes creative, separations (if any), cost of freelancers, i.e., basically all costs associated with creative and production of the catalog.
- *Amortization* sometimes should be considered only if the Internet program is a separate cost center, otherwise the costs can be taken in operations or *General and Administration* (G&A) as required.
- *Freight-Out* is the actual freight costs and should not include handling costs.
- If *Order Processing & Fulfillment Call Centers* are internal, then all the costs would go here; if third party phones are used, replace headings with those on the phone center invoices.

- Under *Outside Services—Order Fulfillment*, use only if the order processing is done externally.

- *Distribution Center* is used for rent and other expense associated with internal fulfillment.

- Under *Warehouse* include the cost of insurance for the warehouse.

- *General and Administration* (G&A) may be taken as costs prior to calculating operating income.

8 Organizing for Success

Catalog Staff

Catalogs can have staffs of just about any size. The number of employees doesn't depend just on the size of business; it is also reflected by how much work is done internally versus externally. First, let's look at the general job functions and potential outside resources (Exhibit 8.1).

Exhibit 8.1 Job/Functions Chart

JOB/FUNCTION	OUTSIDE SERVICE EQUIVALENT
Merchandise manager, Buyer, Product developer	Buying service or freelance buyer
Creative director, Copywriter, Artist Production manager, Webmaster	Direct marketing or catalog creative agency Web design and/or management Freelance professionals
List manager	List broker/manager
Statistician (analyst)	Computer service bureau List broker/manager (for circulation needs)
Marketing manager	Direct marketing consultant Direct marketing agency
Order processor	Fulfillment service
Telephone order taker, Telephone order manager	Fulfillment service or phone service bureau
Data entry personnel Office manager (data processing manager) Picker/packer, Receiving/shipping clerk Warehouse manager	Fulfillment service
Web site manager	Web site freelance or agency
Customer service personnel Customer service manager Operations vice president	Fulfillment service
Bookkeeper, Accounting manager/vice president	Accountant, Fulfillment/computer service bureau
Finance vice president Human resources manager/vice president	Outside accountant
Attorney	Outside attorney
Owner/president	
Administrative assistant/receptionist	

Starting on a Small Scale

Many companies choose to start with minimal internal personnel, using experienced outside resources to help them get safely to a sales level that allows internalization of resources bit by bit. Exhibit 8.2 shows such an example. This set up could work for either a privately held business or one with a parent.

Exhibit 8.3 shows how the organization might grow over the next year or two. This version also has a devoted liaison to the parent company. This position would, of course, not be necessary if this catalog was independent.

Exhibit 8.2 Typical Job Descriptions for a Three-Person Staff

CATALOG MANAGER/ COORDINATOR	ANALYSIS/OPERATIONS MANAGER/COORDINATOR	MERCHANDISER
Most Important: Planning, Coordination with All Team Members and Outside Resources, Budget and Schedule Control	*Most Important:* Providing Understandable Statistical Information to Team and Staying in Control of Operations	*Most Important:* Product Development and Timely Updates on Any Product Problems that Might Affect Sales
Budgets: Keeps creative and production on budget and up to quality standards	Budgets: Reviews and negotiates invoices and contract with fulfillment and analytical service bureaus	Controls: All aspects of each product's quality and price controls, from prototype to warehouse samples
Coordinates: All elements, is the hub of the project	Coordinates: With service bureaus to direct and obtain analytical reports	Coordinates: Makes team aware of any quality or delivery problems which may affect the re-running of a product or any other relevant happenings
Coordinates: Acts as internal liaison for any needed approvals	Coordinates: Is liaison between internal resources and appropriate service bureaus	Coordinates: Traffics all paper work
Coordinates: Is key contact with marketing consultants	Coordinates: Is the catalog's representative to any database operation	Coordinates: Writes all purchase orders and follows up on outstanding information needed for creative and/or fulfillment center
Coordinates: Keeps all team members informed of key elements, such as mailing plan, sales results, research	Coordinates: Makes certain that all printed materials which will be used by the fulfillment house (such as order forms) are reviewed by the fulfillment house prior to mailing	Develops: Finds applicable resources for the production of the products

CATALOG MANAGER/ COORDINATOR	ANALYSIS/OPERATIONS MANAGER/COORDINATOR	MERCHANDISER
Directs: Oversees catalog creative and production, both print and Internet	Coordinates: Minimum of weekly contact with warehouse for review of any outstanding issues	Negotiates: Terms for all aspects of merchandise, including returns, allowances, COG, delivery terms, etc.
Directs: Digital content system for archiving creative	Coordinates: Provides inventory status information to Catalog Manager/Coordinator and Merchandise Manager/Coordinator	Negotiates: Works with all merchandise vendors for initial and subsequent price negotiations and quality control
Organizes: Creates product pagination, both print and Internet	Plans and Coordinates: Working in conjunction with the Merchandiser, develops inventory projections and monitors warehouse inventory levels	Organizes: Creates all Merchandise Information Forms (Chapter 10) in order to provide sufficient information for product selection and for copy writing purposes
Organizes: Prepares, with materials provided by Merchandiser, complete folders for Agency hand-off meeting	Plans and Coordinates: Works with warehouse and Merchandiser in determining and maintaining product quality levels	Organizes: Has acceptable, timely samples for pagination and merchandise photography
Plans: Coordinates and directs all research	Plans: Directs and oversees warehouse operations and recommendations for policies	Other: Handles corporate needs for merchandise
Plans: Creates an acquisition plan for the gathering of more potential buyers	Plans: Implements and oversees all analysis	Plans: Arranges for back-up merchandise and initial delivery terms
Plans: Determines and writes long-term plans for the catalog	Plans: Proactive involvement with service bureau on the development and maintenance of the database	Plans: Creates bundles and cross references
Plans: Determines types and frequency of research and analysis	Plans: Regularly places dummy orders	Plans: Determines, in conjunction with the Catalog Manager/ Coordinator, the appropriate prices for all products
Plans: If results are not met, determines strategy for meeting them	Plans: Visits warehouse per catalog drop (prior to catalog drop) to confirm readiness for catalog mailing and order taking	Plans: Keeps abreast of all sales analysis and product quality problems in the warehouse and makes recommendations for any policy or procedure changes
Plans: Is aware of and responsible for postal considerations, such as the weight of the catalog and the proper preparation for optimal delivery	Reports: Responsible for fulfillment report set maintenance and upgrading	Plans: Makes recommendations for pagination
Plans: Prepares financial plan and keeps updated based on changes in mailing plan and actual results		Plans: Working with product sales results, the financial plan and the mailing plan, creates a yearly product strategy

CATALOG MANAGER/ COORDINATOR	ANALYSIS/OPERATIONS MANAGER/COORDINATOR	MERCHANDISER
Plans: Prepares mailing and circulation plans for all list segments, including testing grids and catalog themes, per list segment		Plans: Works with existing resources to determine which products are appropriate for the catalog
Plans: Regularly places dummy orders and makes recommendations for any necessary corrective action or marketing advantage		
Plans: Reviews overall sales results and creates marketing strategies for leveraging buyers and converting non-buyers		
Plans: Sets goals, objectives and oversees the implementation of strategies to attain these goals		
Plans: Via Analysis/Operations Manager/Coordinator, solicits input from customer service and recommends policies and procedures		
Schedules: All aspects of each catalog, internally and externally, and makes certain that all phases of the schedule are adhered to		

While there are a variety of management configurations that a small catalog business might choose, our experience has shown that this one is most often used. The Catalog Manager/Coordinator is usually the owner or, if the catalog is owned by a parent, the liaison between the catalog operation and the parent.

Since the merchandise is the lifeblood of any catalog, having an on-staff merchant is generally deemed a top priority. It is hard to be a good merchant, or run a business effectively, without reliable analysis. Hence, the third person in this trio oversees or actually does the analysis as well as supervising the warehouse.

As this is a very simple organization, no organization chart has been provided for Exhibit 8.2.

Expanding the Organization

As the catalog grows, so does the need for more personnel. Most companies realize that even though they may need more people, they do not necessarily need them full-time. Therefore, they will look for outside resources or part-timers to handle some positions.

Exhibit 8.3 Job Descriptions as Catalog Grows

CATALOG MANAGEMENT	
Internal Liaison	**Catalog Manager/Coordinator**
Most Important: Keeps lines of communication open and constant between the parent and the independent catalog company	*Most Important:* Planning, Coordination with All Team Members and Outside Resources, Budget and Schedule Control
Coordinates: Keeps catalog team apprised of corporate feedback, relevant direction or policy revisions and merchandising issues	Budgets: Keeps creative and production on budget and up to quality standards
Coordinates: Keeps parent company apprised of catalog marketing and creative direction	Coordinates: All elements, is the hub of the project
Plans: Stays well informed about company-initiated new product development and merchandise trends	Coordinates: Is key contact with marketing consultants
	Coordinates: Keeps all team members informed of key elements, such as mailing plan, sales results, research
	Directs: Oversees catalog creative and production, both print and Internet
	Directs: Digital content system for archiving creative
	Organizes: Creates product pagination, both print and Internet
	Organizes: Prepares, with materials provided by Merchandiser, complete folders for Agency hand-off meeting
	Plans: Coordinates and directs all research
	Plans: Determines and writes long-term plans for the catalog
	Plans: Determines types and frequency of research and analysis
	Plans: If results are not met, determines strategy for meeting them
	Plans: Is aware of and responsible for postal considerations, such as the weight of the catalog and the proper preparation for optimal delivery
	Plans: Prepares financial plan and keeps updated based on changes in mailing plan, web site sales and actual results
	Plans: Regularly places dummy orders and makes recommendations for any necessary corrective action or marketing advantages
	Plans: Schedules all aspects of each catalog, print and Internet, internally and externally, and makes certain that all phases of the schedule are adhered to
	Plans: Sets goals, objectives and oversees the implementation of strategies to attain these goals
	Plans: Via Analysis/Operations Manager/Coordinator, solicits input from customer service and recommends policies and procedures; makes certain that postal checks are received by the right people at the right time
	Schedules: All aspects of each catalog, print and Internet, internally and externally, and makes certain that all phases of the schedule are adhered to

MERCHANDISING		
Merchandiser	Merchandise Rebuyer	Merchandise Development Manager
Most Important: Product Development and Timely Updates on Any Product Problems that Might Affect Sales	***Most Important:*** Handles all product paper work and coordinates with the warehouse for optimum inventory control	***Most Important:*** Provides a steady stream of new product based on sales analysis
Coordinates: Reviews purchase orders	Coordinates: Makes team aware of any quality or delivery problems which may affect the re-running of a product or any other relevant happenings	Plans: Keeps abreast of all sales analysis and product quality problems in the warehouse and makes recommendations for any policy or procedure changes
Organizes: Creates all Merchandise Information Forms (Chapter 10) in order to provide sufficient information for product selection and for copy writing purposes	Coordinates: Traffics all paper work	Controls: All aspects of each product's quality and price controls, from prototype to warehouse samples
Other: Handles corporate needs for merchandise (PR, employee discounts, etc.)	Coordinates: Writes all purchase orders and follows up on outstanding information needed for creative and/or fulfillment center	Develops: Finds applicable resources for the production of the products
Plans: Arranges for back-up merchandise and initial delivery terms	Negotiates: Terms for all aspects of merchandise, including returns, allowances, COG, delivery terms, etc.	Organizes: Has acceptable, timely samples for pagination and merchandise photography
Plans: Creates bundles and cross references	Negotiates: Works with all merchandise vendors for initial and subsequent price negotiations and quality control	Plans: Works with existing resources to determine which products are appropriate for the catalog
Plans: Determines, in conjunction with the Catalog Manager/Coordinator, the appropriate prices for all products in all mediums		
Plans: Makes recommendations for pagination, print and Interent		
Plans: Working with product sales results, the financial plan and the mailing plan, creates a yearly product strategy (Chapter 10)		

CIRCULATION/DATABASE	OPERATIONS
Manager Circulation/Database	**Analysis/Operations Manager/Coordinator**
Most Important: Understands, directs and makes best use of whom to contact, when and with what offers	*Most Important:* Providing Understandable Statistical Information to Team and Staying in Control of Operations
Plans: Creates an acquisition plan for the gathering of more potential buyers, includes print and e-mail	Budgets: Reviews and negotiates invoices and contract with fulfillment and analytical service bureaus
Plans: Prepares mailing and circulation plans for all list segments, including testing grids and catalog themes, per list segment	Coordinates: With service bureaus to direct and obtain analytical reports
Plans: Reviews overall sales results and creates marketing strategies for leveraging buyers and converting non-buyers	Coordinates: Is liaison between internal resources and appropriate service bureaus
Reports: Designs relevant reporting structures for outside resources	Coordinates: Is the catalog's representative to any database operation
Reports: Prepare reports on the effectiveness of the various media used and makes recommendations based on the analysis of such reports	Coordinates: Makes certain that all printed materials which will be used by the fulfillment house (such as order forms) are reviewed by the fulfillment house prior to mailing
Plans: Keeps abreast of all current and upcoming Internet developments	Coordinates: Minimum of weekly contact with warehouse for review of any outstanding issues
	Coordinates: Provides inventory status information to Catalog Manager/Coordinator and Merchandise Manager/Coordinator
	Plans and Coordinates: Working in conjunction with the Merchandiser, develops inventory projections and monitors warehouse inventory levels
	Plans and Coordinates: Works with warehouse and Merchandiser in determining and maintaining product quality levels
	Plans: Directs and oversees warehouse operations and recommendations for policies
	Plans: Implements and oversees all analysis
	Plans: Proactive involvement with service bureau on the development and maintenance of the database
	Plans: Regularly places dummy orders
	Plans: Visits warehouse per catalog drop (prior to catalog drop) to confirm readiness for catalog mailing and order taking
	Reports: Responsible for fulfillment report, set maintenance and upgrading

Note that many jobs are still outsourced. At this stage for this particular catalog, only the Internal Liaison, Catalog Manager/Coordinator, Merchandiser, Merchandise Rebuyer, Merchandise Development Manager, Manager of Circulation/Database and Analysis/ Operations Manager/Coordinator are internal. Naturally, the Internal Liaison would not be needed if this catalog were independent. More than likely, this position is part-time.

Exhibit 8.4 Organization Chart for Exhibit 8.3

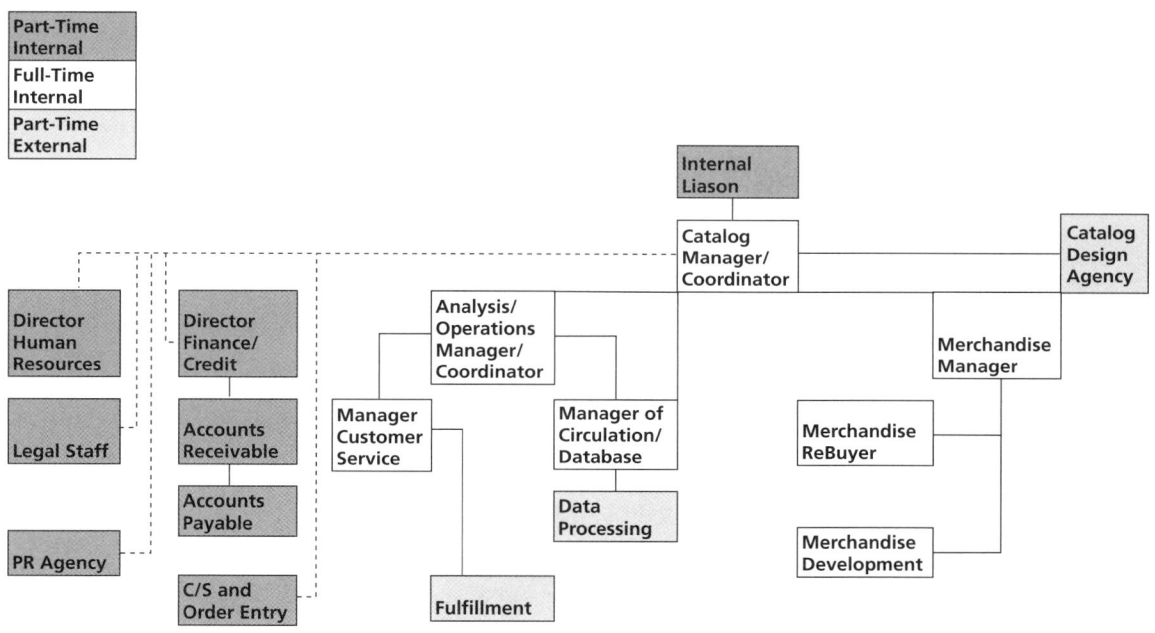

Exhibit 8.5 Expanded, Internal Organization Chart

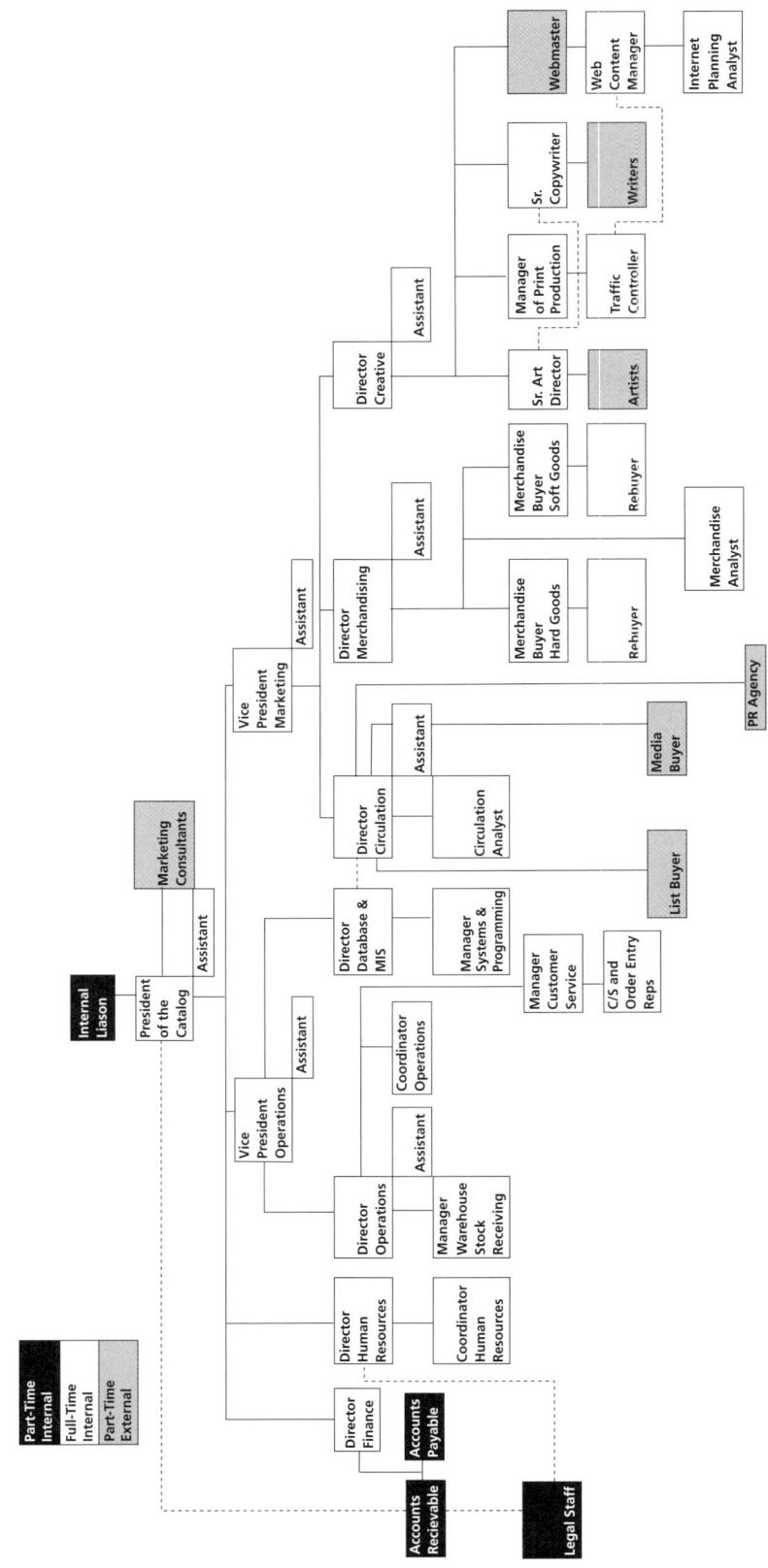

Though every company structures their organization in a distinctive manner, this chart, in Exhibit 8.4, will give you a basic understanding of the major areas that will need to be addressed. There is a trend toward not using assistants as extensively as shown, but, if desired, they would appear in the locations noted. This chart illustrates a catalog company that has a parent and access to some of the parent's personnel resource. Exhibit 8.5 depicts an organization chart for an extensive start-up.

In order to keep costs under control, the PR Agency, Artists, Writers, Webmaster, and Buyer List Media functions are outsourced. See below for corresponding job descriptions.

Job Descriptions for Exhibit 8.5

Internal Liaison

Responsible for keeping the lines of communication open and constant between the associated companies and the independent catalog company. Should keep catalog team apprised of corporate feedback, relevant direction or policy revisions, and merchandising issues. Should keep parent company apprised of catalog marketing and creative direction. Should stay well informed about company-initiated new product development and merchandise trends. Reports to the parent company.

President of the Catalog

In addition to running The Catalog Company, the President must spend time and effort on long-term planning. Will act as the direct link to the associated companies and investors. Will represent The Catalog Company at board meetings. Responsible for setting company goals/objective and overseeing the implementation of strategies to attain these goals. Coordinates with, but is independent of, Liaison. Reports to the parent company.

Executive Assistant

Responsible for executing the President's correspondence and maintaining his/her schedule. Must be committed to maintaining confidential information. Reports to the President of the Catalog.

Vice President of Marketing

Has overall responsibility for creating, producing, and marketing the catalog. Keeps abreast of postal implications. Overseeing the Director of Circulation, the Director of Merchandising, and the Director of Creative, this position establishes company strategies and delegates tactical implementation methods to meet company objectives. Reports to the President of the Catalog and works closely, as needed, with outside consultants.

Administrative Assistant to Marketing Vice President

Distributes intra-company correspondence and assists in marketing department's organization and internal information flow. Acts as gatekeeper for the Vice President of Marketing and manages his/her agenda, travel, appointments, and schedules. Reports to Vice President of Marketing.

Vice President of Operations

Supervises the personnel responsible for the different areas that pertain to the customer order process. The areas that fall under the supervision of this function include:

- Telephone and order taking.
- Mail handling and order processing.
- Physical distribution.
- Customer service.
- Systems and programming.

This position would work closely with other company executives involved in finance, marketing, and merchandising. Responsibility includes assurance that the catalog's operations have the flexibility, capacity, systems, and equipment to meet planned growth and marketing programs. Initial responsibility will include warehouse development and equipment selection and purchasing. Reports to the President of the Catalog.

Director of Operations

Oversees processing of orders and general operations. Manages mail opening, data entry, cash handling, and customer service functions. This includes:

- Providing schedules, goals, work procedures, and administering deadlines.
- Establishing personnel levels and types and quantity of supplies.
- Expediting resolution of system emergencies.
- Assisting in resolving various problems relative to specific orders.
- Creating and updating forms and equipment to meet needs of assorted operations areas.
- Developing new work procedures for newly created jobs and refining existing job procedures.

This position also provides long-range organization planning and acts as an advisor and liaison to merchandising and marketing. Reports to Vice President of Operations.

Director of Database and Management Information Systems

As start-up, will work with consultants to purchase and develop the systems to contain and maintain the catalog operations database, sales reports, and customer order/inquiry information. Will be responsible for internal training on the equipment.

Ongoing, will function as troubleshooter for any system problems that might or will happen. Will also update the equipment and software, keeping up with the evolving catalog operations. Responsible for ongoing training as new systems are implemented. Reports directly to the Vice President of Operations and works closely with the Director of Circulation.

Manager of Systems and Programming

Responsible for cost and time estimates, feasibility studies, as well as design and implementation of new or customized systems and programs. Assists in determining user specifications and requirements. Can encode, test, debug, and document programs. Though not indicated in the organization chart, may have system analyst and or programmer reporting to him/her. Reports to the Vice President of Operations.

Coordinator of Operations

Makes sure that all aspects of the day-to-day operations (including customer service, order taking, entry, and processing, and physical distribution) are running smoothly and according to company policy. Should devise and implement efficiency measures as needed. Reports to the Director of Operations.

Manager of Customer Service

Supervises the customer service staff. Is influential in establishing customer service policies. Is responsible for establishing departmental personnel needs and schedules, hiring and training customer service personnel. Will handle difficult or problematic customer issues. Assures that company policies and professionalism are being adhered to. Makes sure telephone representatives are technically trained so that they are able to talk intelligently with their customers about the product line. Reports to Director of Operations.

Manager of Warehouse, Stock and Receiving

Manages the catalog merchandise stock retrieval process, including planning for shipments and delivery driver dealings. Specifically includes:

- Reviewing and filing purchase orders for future reference.
- Keeping the merchandise buyers apprised of any merchandise quality-related issues.
- Keeping merchandise buyers apprised of count and/or pattern discrepancies.
- Organizing the incoming merchandise and putting on designated shelves.

Reports to the Director of Operations.

Customer Service and Order Entry Representatives

Handles basic customer inquiries received by mail, telephone, fax, or Internet in accordance with established company policies and procedures. Performs support duties necessary for the effectiveness and successful operation of the department. Specific duties include:

- Solving basic problems regarding a customer's account.
- Investigating customer inquiries and complaints.
- Making necessary adjustments or taking the action required to solve the customer's problem.
- Notifying the customer of actions taken.
- Acting as a product information specialist.

This function reports to the Manager of Customer Service.

Director of Merchandising

In charge of all merchandise decisions, including these functions:

- Merchandise strategy.
- Supervising and advising buyers.
- Negotiating terms with vendors.
- Making final selections of merchandise to be offered per channel.

- Determining merchandise pricing per channel.
- Suggesting merchandise products to be sourced.
- Overseeing quantities and quality of purchases.

Reports to the Vice President of Marketing.

Merchandise Buyer, Hard Goods

Sources the hard goods category of products offered in the catalog. Conducts negotiations with vendors, including arranging back-up merchandise and delivery terms. Needs to keep the Coordinator of Operations apprised of merchandise delivery dates. Must review purchase orders. Reports to the Director of Merchandising.

Merchandise Buyer, Soft Goods

Sources the soft goods category of products offered in the catalog. Conducts negotiations with vendors, including arranging back-up merchandise and delivery terms. Needs to keep the Coordinator of Operations apprised of merchandise delivery dates. Must review purchase orders. Reports to the Director of Merchandising.

Merchandise Rebuyer

Works with buyers to coordinate and traffic the paperwork associated with product reordering. Will fill out purchase orders, distribute them, and then follow up with the vendors and operations on delivery. Needs to be aware of any vendor policy changes, such as price terns. Will report to the relevant Merchandise Buyers on any discontinued product or change in design or delivery problems.

Merchandise Analyst

Working in conjunction with the Director of Merchandising and the Buyers, develops inventory projections and monitors warehouse inventory levels. Works with warehouse and buyers in determining and maintaining product quality levels. Implements and oversees all merchandise analysis. Reports to the Director of Merchandising.

Director of Circulation

Working with marketing, determines the catalog and promotional print mail and e-mail schedules and quantities with regard to corporate objectives. This function works with outside media buyers to select the best sources for name acquisition. Will coordinate with marketing, merchandise buyers, Webmaster, and printers to anticipated quantity of customer contacts expected. Is aware of and abides by all relevant rules and regulations concerning consumer contact. If the catalog rents its list, this position is responsible for assuring that the list rental income is sufficient and that the list is handled to protect consumers' privacy. Reports and makes contract strategy recommendations to Vice President of Marketing.

Circulation Analyst

Prepares reports on the effectiveness of the various media utilized and makes recommendations based on the analysis of such reports. Will also be responsible for designing relevant, requested reporting structures. Uses historical and current data to project, by medium, sales, customer attrition rates, and inventory needs. Develops customer segmentation models. Reports to the Director of Circulation and will have contact with the marketing department.

List Buyer

Often takes the form of an outside business, a List Brokerage Company. Makes rental recommendations on the basis of past results and available names. Works with The Catalog Company to select lists for testing and rolls out. Is responsible for placing the orders received from the Director of Circulation and following up on services rendered. Reports to the Director of Circulation.

Media Buyer

Often takes the form of an outside business, a Media Buying Company. Makes print and electronic advertising recommendations to marketing department on the basis of past results. Is responsible for placing the orders received from the Director of Circulation and following up on services rendered, including the collection of tear sheets from space ads. Must also provide art and web team with creative specs and schedules and traffic finished materials to the appropriate media. Reports to the Director of Circulation.

Internet Planning Analyst

Plans, implements, and oversees Internet systems. Determines and recommends necessary upgrades or improvements. Supports development of technical standards and application uses. Attempts to determine and resolve Internet problems before they arise. Works with Circulation Analyst to assist in providing analysis of site results and effectiveness. Reports to Web Content Manager.

Director of Creative

Acts as main contact between creative and production/suppliers/merchants. Sets creative direction and oversees the overall catalog creative progress. Relays the creative directions and specifications to the art, copy, and web teams. Presents the works to the marketing department. Reports to the Vice President of Marketing.

Manager of Print Production

Requests estimates from photographers, printers, separators, and service bureaus. Selects suppliers for each creative project. Secures specifications and provides art team with this information. Sets production schedules. Reviews digital art prior to releasing it to the separator or printer. Reviews separations and goes to press to oversee the printing of the catalog. Is main contact for productions suppliers. Manages digital assets. Reports to the Director of Creative.

Traffic Controller

Prepares and electronically distributes internal creative and production schedules for the catalog, printed and Internet, and related collateral. Makes sure that the schedules are being adhered to and that all parties that need to approve the creative have seen it. Reports to all creative departments and provides regular updates on scheduling. Works closely with the Web Content Manager. Reports to the Manager of Production.

Senior Copywriter

Works with Director of Creative and Senior Art Director to develop concepts for the catalog and web creative. Sets copy tone for the projects. Prepares a copy element style guide for writers to follow for consistency. Delegates and manages the copywriting work. Reports to the Director of Creative.

Writers

Following the direction provided by the Senior Copywriter and adhering to the Style Guide, writes copy for all sales and customer communications. Reports to the Senior Copywriter.

Senior Art Director

Works with the Senior Copywriter. Prepares comprehensive layout designs as a template for the rest of the catalog. Delegates the artwork and then manages the artists in the creation of the catalog creative. Makes sure the artists adhere to the specifications provided by the Director of Creative, Marketing Department, and Printer. Supervises photography shoots and reviews color separations. Works with the Manager of Print Production and appropriate resources to manage digital assets. Reports to the Director of Creative.

Artists

Following the direction provided by the Senior Art Director, creates layouts, gives direction and reviews computer-generated layouts. Makes all necessary color breaks, type, and photography-specific indications for digital production. Reports to Director of Creative.

Webmaster

Determines user's needs, strategies, and goals and creates web pages that meet those needs and monitors to assure effectiveness of efforts. Directs and implements internal and external web pages and applications. Must have expertise in operating systems and a digital production environment. Ensures that all aspects are stable, well designed, effective and up-to-date. Working with Traffic Controller, adheres to all schedules. Reports to the Director of Creative.

Web Content Manager

In conjunction with the Marketing Department, develops and provides content for the catalog's web site. Responsible for gathering information, internally and externally, in order to act as editor of the site's content. Making improvements as needed, designs graphics for the site. Establishes and maintains links. Should be comfortable with the technical aspects of the web site. Reports to the Webmaster.

Director of Finance

Responsible for cash flow, profit-and-loss projections, financial analysis, and banking relationships. If applicable, will open and establish credit/charge card accounts for customer orders. Will also plan and maintain customer payment options. Reports to the President.

Accounts Receivable

Maintains sales reports and sales projections. Works closely with the order processors to keep apprised of outstanding receivables. Reports to the Director of Finance.

Accounts Payable

Pays outstanding debts and keeps track of cash flow. Works closely with the product purchasing department to anticipate large invoices for merchandise purchases. Reports to the Director of Finance.

Legal Staff (Attorneys)

Reviews contracts; advises on legalities of promotions and Federal Trade Commission (FTC) regulations. May also review catalog copy to ascertain that unsubstantiated promises are not being made. Writes and reviews vendor contracts. Will keep the company informed of tax regulations as they pertain to The Catalog. Will report and work directly with the President of the Catalog.

PR (Public Relations) Agency

In charge of generating positive promotion for The Catalog Company. Works in conjunction with the marketing and circulation departments for possible tie-ins. Promotion should span the media choices—electronic, print, and other. Should make public relations strategy recommendations and be proactive in initiating opportunity. Reports to Direct of Circulation.

Director of Human Resources

Responsible for determining internal personnel budget allocations and overseeing all aspects related to personnel such as:

- Meeting with department heads to determine staffing needs.
- Recruiting and interviewing prospective employees.
- Yearly reviews.
- Benefits package and supplier negotiations.
- Hiring, firing, promotions.
- Employee manual preparation and ongoing adjustments as needed.
- Employee issue resolutions.
- Holiday scheduling.
- Distributing paychecks.
- Keeping track of employee sick days, personal days.

In charge of personnel policies designed for small independent company; not influenced by existing parent company policies. Reports to President and works with Legal Staff.

Coordinator of Human Resources

Works for the Director of Human Resources by coordinating all aspects of day-to-day personnel functions. This includes filling out and trafficking such items as insurance forms. Will distribute paychecks and arrange appointments with employees for reviews, issue discussion, etc. Will be a contact for outside benefit suppliers. Reports to Director of Human Resources.

9 Developing Your Strategy: Brainstorming and Positioning

Strategies for building a successful catalog business need to be defined in detail. And updated regularly. The overall game plan must look at now and the near future by understanding exactly what the creative will look like and represent, how much and what merchandise will be offered, to whom the catalog will be mailed and at what time of year, and what special promotions or other approaches, if any, will be needed. Plus how all of these elements will interact with whatever selling modes the catalog has chosen.

Think linearly and start at the beginning. How do external and internal factors affect what a catalog will actually become? How do incubated ideas come to fruition, be corralled and turned into functional, useful data that is responsible for the birth of a catalog? One effective method for developing a strategy is to turn to the talent that lies within your organization and your external supplier team and start your strategy with a Brainstorming Session.

Brainstorming/Planning Sessions

Webster's defines brainstorming as "a method of problem-solving in which all members of a group spontaneously contribute ideas." The problem with this definition is that, when followed accurately, a brainstorming session will produce only that—a bunch of spontaneous ideas.

To get real value out of a brainstorming session, you need to organize it in a way that:

1. Every person contributes somewhat equally.

2. You know precisely what to do with all the resulting, brilliant ideas.

First, stand back and understand the real reason behind the brainstorming session. Our experience has shown us that the most common reason is to determine an overall strategic plan.

Exhibit 9.1 Strategic Planning Diagram

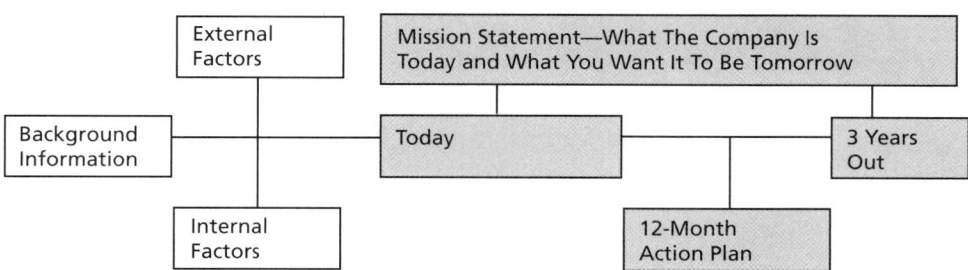

To properly prepare, first collect information noted in the white boxes in Exhibit 9.1:

1. Background information, such as top-line status of particular programs, sales as they relate to competition, current problem and potential opportunities.

2. External factors, such as environmental concerns, potential outside cost increases, and buying patterns.

3. Internal factors, such as staff capabilities, equipment needs, budget constraints, or opportunities.

All items with white boxes should be put together in an organized package and distributed approximately one week in advance to those who will be attending the brainstorming meeting. The items with gray backgrounds will be what you will be creating in the brainstorming session.

In order for attendees to fully understand what they will be expected to do in the session, you will need an outline, also distributed a week in advance. Exhibit 9.2 illustrates the typical subjects covered in a one-to-two day session. In Exhibit 9.3, the explanation of 9.2, you see an adaptation that includes the actual time to be allocated per section. This is not uncommon, and if this is done, a member of the brainstorming team should be assigned the role of timekeeper. This person should stringently attempt to keep the group moving from topic to topic based on the timetable. One of our clients, Betty Crocker Enterprises, a division of General Mills, used to bring a Betty Crocker timer and big wooden spoon to pound on the table when the time was up. It worked!

When using the *Outline for Strategic Planning/Brainstorming Session*, the leader of the group typically spends 15 minutes making certain that all attendees are familiar with each others' roles, not just their titles. This form should include the names of those attending, the location, and the times of the meeting.

The leader also summarizes the main purpose of the meeting, including its ultimate goal(s) and how the meeting will be run (see Exhibit 9.4). Presenters augment the comments of the session leader by adding pertinent information as it applies to their particular area of expertise. The italic type under *Topic* in Exhibit 9.3 gives examples of what each presenter would address. The *Time Allocation* column shows an example of the total time frame for both the presenter and interactive discussion.

The session leader should touch base with the individual presenters after information about the meeting has been received and several days before the meeting. The reason for the pre-session talks is to assure that each presenter is clear on what they will be covering during the presentation and the time they are allocated for their presentation.

To recap, what you will need to distribute one week prior to the meeting is:

1. Background information.

2. A summation of external factors.

3. A summation of internal factors.

4. A completed outline for the Strategic Planning/Brainstorming Session (Exhibit 9.3).

5. Rules for Strategic Planning/Brainstorming Sessions (Exhibit 9.4).

Exhibit 9.2 Strategic Planning/Brainstorming Outline (Form Only)

Outline for Strategic Planning/Brainstorming Session

I. Introduction

II. Major Company Objective

   A. Sales

   B. Image

   C. Profitability

   D. Sales mix (off page, retail, Internet)

   E. Other

III. How to Achieve the Objectives
   A. Understanding the market
   B. Status of database
   C. Being/staying competitive
   D. Increase average order
   E. Increase response
   F. Increase frequency
   G. Other

IV. Methodology for Attracting First Order
   A. Acquisition methods
   B. Policies
   C. Product/offers
   D. Timing
   E. Pricing
   F. Tie-ins
   G. Other

V. Methodology for Converting to Repeat Purchase
   A. Acknowledgment of customer's place in purchase cycle
   B. Product/offers
   C. Timing
   D. Pricing
   E. Services
   F. Other

VI. Creating a Distinctive Brand Personality
   A. Synergy in all selling avenues
   B. Graphics
   C. Organization
   D. Services
   E. Product offerings

       F. "Voice"
       G. Interactive
       H. Social considerations, ethics
       I. Consistency
       J. Authority
       K. Other

VII. Watching/Cutting/Controlling Costs
       A. Catalog
       B. Product
       C. Operations
       D. Overhead
       E. Other

VIII. Making Best Use of Employees
       A. Resources
       B. Empowerment
       C. Training
       D. Motivation
       E. Communication
       F. Company culture
       G. Other

IX. Leveraging Product/Merchandise
       A. Margins
       B. Frequency
       C. Current mix
       D. Future mix
       E. Effect on creative
       F. Determination of offerings in each selling avenue
       G. Other

X. Using Operations as a Marketing Tool
   A. Customer service
   B. VIP Clubs
   C. Guarantee
   D. Stock positions
   E. Credit
   F. Humanize
   G. Departmental interfaces
   H. Integration with all selling avenues
   I. Environmentally sensitive
   J. Other

XI. Analytical Needs
   A. Real needs versus desires
   B. Costs
   C. Impact/real value
   D. Actionable
   E. Other

XII. Round-Up
   A. Determination of top goals
   B. Assigning responsibilities
   C. Assigning time frames

Exhibit 9.3 Strategic Planning/Brainstorming Outline (Example of an Adapted and Completed Form)

Strategic Planning/Brainstorming Session

Company Name: ABC Company

Date/Time: Monday, 00/00/00, 8:30AM–4:45PM and Tuesday 00/00/00, 8:30AM–2:30PM

Place: Conference Room B, Third Floor, Main Building

Major Outcome Desired: After interactive discussion will prioritize recommendations, assign responsibility, and time frames.

Attendees:

Jerry Hones, Controller

May Smelt, Merchandise Manager

Maria Learning, Creative Director

Susan Keith, Art Director

Ben Lesto, Copywriter

Janet Yu, Marketing Manager (overall session leader)

Jeff Sanchez, Operations Manager

Yolanda Elder, Customer Service Director

Jonathon Martenson, Database Director

Katerina Nelson, Analytical Director

Marsha Fielding, Human Resources Director

Presenter makes minimal opening statement; rest of time per subject is interactive participation by all attendees.

Topic	Time Allocation	Presenter
DAY ONE		
Breakfast (rolls, coffee, tea)	8:30–9:00	
Introduction *State reasons team is at the session.* *Recap materials that were previously distributed.* *Introduce all attendees; include what they do and why they were chosen to be here.*	9:00–9:30	J. Yu
Major Company Objective: • Sales. • Image. • Profitability. • Sales mix (off page, retail, Internet). • Other. *Simplified statements of the above; a recap only, answer questions, but keep elaboration minimal.*	9:30–10:00	J. Hones M. Learning
How to Achieve the Objectives: • Understanding the market. • Status of database. • Being/staying competitive. • Increase average order. • Increase response. • Increase frequency. • Other. *Report on status of database and competitive date only; rest interactive.*	10:00–11:00	J. Yu J. Martenson
Break	11:00–11:15	
Methodology for Attracting First Order: • Acquisition methods. • Policies. • Product/offers. • Timing. • Pricing. • Tie-ins. • Other. *Simplified current strategies, products and offers; a recap only, answer questions, but keep elaboration minimal.*	11:15–12:15	J. Martenson M. Smelt
Lunch	12:15–1:00	
Methodology for Converting to Repeat Purchase: • Acknowledgment of customer's place in purchase cycle. • Product/offers. • Timing. • Pricing. • Services. • Other. *Simplified recap of current policies, merchandising pricing, and buying cycles.*	1:00–2:00	J. Martenson M. Smelt

Topic	Time Allocation	Presenter
DAY ONE		
Creating a Distinctive Brand Personality: • Synergy in all selling avenues. • Graphics. • Organization. • Services. • Pproduct offerings. • "Voice." • Interactive. • Social considerations, ethics. • Consistency. • Authority. • Other. *Simplified current strategies, products and offers; a recap only, answer questions but keep elaboration minimal.*	2:00–3:00	J. Yu J. Martenson
Break	3:00–3:15	
Watching/Cutting/Controlling Costs: • Catalog. • Product. • Operations. • Overhead. • Other. *Simplified statements of the above; a recap only, answer questions but keep elaboration minimal.*	3:15–4:00	J. Hones
Making Best Use of Employees: • Resources. • Empowerment. • Training. • Motivation. • Communication. • Company culture. • Other. *Simplified statements of the above; a recap only, answer questions, but keep elaboration minimal.*	4:00–4:45	M. Fielding
DAY TWO		
Breakfast (rolls, coffee, tea)	8:30–9:00	
Leveraging Product/Merchandise: • Margins. • Frequency of new product introduction. • Current mix. • Future mix. • Effect on creative. • Determination of offerings in each selling avenue. • Other. *Simplified statements of the above; a recap only, answer questions, but keep elaboration minimal.*	9:00–10:00	M. Smelt

Topic	Time Allocation	Presenter
DAY TWO		
Using Operations as a Marketing Tool: • Customer service. • VIP Clubs. • Guarantee. • Stock positions. • Credit. • Humanize. • Departmental interfaces. • Integration with all selling avenues. • Environmentally sensitive. • Other. *Simplified statements of the above; a recap only, answer questions, but keep elaboration minimal.*	10:00–10:45	J. Sanchez
Break	10:45–11:00	
Analytical Needs: • Real needs versus desires. • Costs. • Actionable. • Impact/real value. *Simplified statements of the above; a recap only, answer questions, but keep elaboration minimal.*	11:00–12:00	K. Nelson
Lunch	12:00–12:45	
Round-Up: • Determination of top goals. • Assigning responsibilities. • Assigning time frames. (See text below)	12:45–2:30	J. Yu

The *Round-Up* is the most critical element of the entire process: Doing it right will garner strategies and tactics that will be pertinent for years. Doing it wrong can mean that you have just wasted valuable staff time and effort.

Before we clarify exactly what the outcome of any brainstorming session should contain, let's look at how the session itself should be run.

You will need white boards or paper on which ideas can be transcribed. You will need pens and, if using paper, masking tape to hang the paper on which the ideas will be displayed. Today, some companies use a computer and display the ideas on a screen for all to see. Whatever form you use, you will need to be able to see all the ideas from Days One and Two's efforts at once. Most likely, this will be in the form of large sheets of white paper taped to walls with masking tape.

The leader writes all the ideas on the paper. Each page must be clearly numbered to keep pages in order. Some use different colored pens for the different categories, which aids in sorting though a mass of brainstorming thoughts.

At the *Round-Up* time, all sheets should be put on the walls and attendees told to review them. Attendees are usually asked to grade those that they feel will provide the most benefit for the money. Most often they are asked to pick their top five. The session leader sorts these out and a new list is drawn up.

The new list is the final outcome, but it doesn't stop there. It *must* have key personnel assigned to follow up the strategies and tactics displayed on the list. In addition, each task must have a real date assigned to it and someone in the group assigned follow-up (FOL) in order to make certain that the task has been completed. This person will also issue a report summarizing what everyone has agreed to do.

All information from the session should be transcribed and circulated to attendees. Even if an idea did not make it this time, it can be reconsidered in the future.

Exhibit 9.4 Rules Checklist

Rules for Strategic Brainstorming Sessions:

1. There are **no** negative ideas. Every idea, no matter how far-fetched or impractical, is a good one.

2. Freewheeling is the right approach. In fact, we want wild and crazy ideas. It's easier to tone down than pump up. A wild idea often triggers other ideas from other folks.

3. Build on other people's ideas and make them better. Don't step on someone else's idea, but make the idea grow! Try thinking like this: Restate the idea in your own words—make sure you understand what the other person really said. Then, see what you can do to improve the idea.

4. Listen first, then speak. Don't interrupt.

5. No side conversations allowed. Respect the person speaking.

6. Participate! One person cannot do it alone and every idea or thought is important.

7. Quantity is important! The more idea alternatives generated, the greater the number of good ideas. It's better to whittle down 300 ideas than select from just a few.

Positioning Statement

Positioning is the term used to describe how a catalog represents itself to the market. A Positioning Statement is a written document that details the why and what behind the chosen positioning, e g., what factors went into deciding why this way of presenting the catalog is correct and why is it superior to that of the competition. A positioning statement indicates what the catalog wants the image to be; a strategic plan, in part, determines the particulars of how that positioning is going to come about.

If a catalog is part of an overall company, the catalog company positioning will almost always be an extension of any position statement that is already in existence for the parent company. If the catalog company is an independent or privately held business, the catalog company positioning statement will reflect that entity's individual personality.

Without a positioning statement it is impossible to concretely and consistently know what your company stands for in the eyes of both your employees and your customers. Take the time to solidify what it is about your catalog that makes it stand apart from all the others.

Exhibit 9.5 Positioning Statement Outline

POSITIONING STATEMENT
for

_____
(name of catalog)

_____
(date)

_____
(written by)

1. What is the product?
2. At whom is the product now aimed?
3. What is the consumer perception of the product area as it relates to this product?
4. Who are the competitors?
5. What are the unique benefits of the product (i.e., how does the product differ from the competition)?
6. What is the unique selling proposition?
7. What are the credibility factors?
8. What factors in the sociological environment affect the product?
9. What factors in the economic environment affect the product?
10. Do any legal considerations affect the product?

Based on the above information, create one all-encompassing tag line.

The positioning statement should be delivered to all team members in its blank form (Exhibit 9.5). Accompanying it should be Exhibit 9.6, which provides a useful explanation of what each of the questions mean. Completed forms should be collected by the person who will take the input and create one master document.

People who should be part of the input include creative, merchandising, customer service, operations, and anyone else who has dealings with, or input to, the customer. You will most likely be surprised to see that even though everyone believes that they are "on the same page," they are not. This exercise takes the best from all team members and creates one document that clearly states the image that the catalog company wants its customers to see and understand.

When writing a Positioning Statement for a catalog company, do not think of the catalog as simply a printed or electronic shopping aid. Think of it more like you would a product that you could find on any shelf in any store. This method of viewing a catalog as a product helps you to see it as a consumer sees it . . . as just one more option in a field of many choices. Therefore, your catalog "product" must have unique attributes—from the items it offers in the catalog to the service it provides after the sale—that make it a distinctive, desired choice.

Exhibit 9.6 Positioning Statement Explanation

POSITIONING STATEMENT
for

_____
(name of catalog)

_____
(date)

_____
(written by)

1. What is the product?
   State the type of catalog, characteristics, equities, products, services, and feelings that the catalog inspires. The catalog itself is the product that is being marketed. Do not think of this question as dealing with only the products that are offered in the catalog.

2. At whom is the product (catalog) now aimed?
   Profile the target audience including attitudes, behaviors, and characteristics.

3. What is the consumer perception of the product area as it relates to this product (catalog)?
   Product and services of this method of distribution (catalog, Internet, retail—all that apply) as they relate to the particular product line, including attitudes and feelings. Example: how does the target audience feel about buying shoes via this catalog and its web site)

4. Who are the competitors?
   Key competitors including retail, sales force, Internet, wholesale. Strengths and weaknesses, both real and perceived.

5. What are the unique benefits of the product (i.e., how does the product differ from the competition)?
   Identify the unique, differentiating, important discovery about the target and their relationship to the product (catalog).

6. What is the unique selling proposition?
   The single most motivating and unique reason or aspiration for the target audience to buy from this catalog. "Why should I buy something from this catalog?" "What's in it for me?"

7. What are the credibility factors?
   What is the primary fact that gives the prospect a reason to believe the selling proposition?

8. What factors in the sociological environment affect the product?
   Elements/emotions in the life of the target that influence attitudes toward purchase.

9. What factors in the economic environment affect the product?
   Financial considerations as they relate to the product.

10. Do any legal considerations affect the product?
    Legal constraints/concerns.

Based on the above information, create one, all-encompassing tag line.

Exhibit 9.7 Positioning Statement Example, Consumer

POSITIONING STATEMENT

for

The Company of Women

00/00/00

Written by Karen O'Donnelly

1. What is the product?
   A socially aware catalog of personal and gift products that will inspire and help today's women take control of their lives and respond effectively to their changing roles in society.

2. At whom is the product now aimed?
   Financially and socially secure females interested in combining their purchasing power with the aim of ending violence against women and supporting women-owned businesses.

3. What is the consumer perception of the product area as it relates to this product?
   - The catalog is a communication device, providing potentially desirous products plus a link with a worthwhile endeavor—helping other women.
   - The product area has enough breadth and depth to be inviting to both customers and non-customers and price points are rational.
   - The products are designed to appeal emotionally as much, if not more, than practically.

4. Who are the competitors?
   - Other worthwhile non-profit causes, such as public broadcasting, that use the sale of goods to raise funds.
   - Women's bookstores.
   - Non-traditional catalogs, such as EFG Company and HIJK Company.
   - More traditional catalogs targeted primarily at women and offering the same core products.

5. What are the unique benefits of the product (i.e., how does the product differ from the competition)?
   The purchase of these products benefits a worthwhile cause and allows the purchaser to buy for herself or as a gift while helping others. The catalog also celebrates womanhood.

6. What is the unique selling proposition?
   Highly targeted, emotionally appealing, largely exclusive product line that provides customers with products that "advertise" their feelings while allowing them to support a worthwhile cause.

7. What are the credibility factors?
   - The fact that the Company of Women is five years old.
   - Association with a respected women's shelter.
   - All products are made by women.
   - A growing customer base.
   - The credentials of its staff, directors, and consultant.
   - Audited financial statement available to the public.

8. What factors in the sociological environment affect the product?
   The prevalence of violence and discrimination against women.

9. What factors in the economic environment affect the product?
   - The increase in the number of women working today and the related decrease in leisure time to spend shopping at retail locations.
   - The increasing emphasis on value, thus making the emotional appeal of the product more important.
   - The proliferation of catalogs; positioning, therefore, must fully use the emotional appeal of the product's social agenda to sway purchasers from selecting similar products from competitors.
   - The difficulty of raising working capital.

10. Do any legal considerations affect the product?
    - Product liability issues may affect merchandising decisions.
    - Invasion-of-privacy issues, postal requirements, and industry self-regulation may influence the company's marketing program.

Potential Tag Line: Just for women, about women, by women

Exhibit 9.8 Positioning Statement Example, Business-to-Business

1. What is the product?
   A user-friendly, small business-oriented catalog offering a selection of paper and paper-related products designed to enhance the users' business with a minimal amount of effort. They will be offered in low-hurdle quantities and prices. All products and service policies will be backed with the highest level of service.

2. At whom is the product now aimed?
   In order of anticipated sales volume:
   - Small to mid-size printers, including quick printers and in-plant printers.
   - Designers who cater to small companies.
   - Influencers in paper choices.
   - Owners/managers of photo labs.
   - MIS professionals/departments.

3. What is the user perception of the product area as it relates to this product?
   - This catalog offers a comprehensive selection of papers and paper-related products not traditionally or readily available to smaller printers and design firms.
   - The non-paper products are hard to find because they are unique in their solutions to the market's needs.
   - Paper products are a combination of the familiar and the exotic and can be easily purchased in desired quantities, which is not the case with the traditional avenue of purchase.
   - Paper products offered will supplement the catalog user's paper reps, not replace them.

4. Who are the competitors?
   - Paper merchants.
   - Paper manufacturers.
   - Large retail discounters, such as Staples.
   - Small, independent stationery shops.
   - Niche catalogs catering to one particular, non-paper line, e.g. display.

5. What are the unique benefits of the product (i.e., how does the product differ from the competition)?
   - One-source purchase.
   - Availability of smaller quantities.
   - More education within the catalog.
   - Relevant, higher level of sales/technical support.
   - Subsequent promotions for loyalty building.
   - Consumer involvement in product selection (sizes, brand, and packaging).
   - Same day delivery for much of the country.

6. What is the unique selling proposition?
   Knowledgeable, readily available, targeted selection of highly useful paper and paper-related products designed to save the small business owner time and hassle. Backed by superior service and customer-attuned policies.

7. What are the credibility factors?
   - Network of knowledgeable resources.
   - Customer service/information staff.
   - Product depth and presentation.
   - Service policies.

8. What factors in the sociological environment affect the product?
   - Increased acceptance and choice of shopping via catalog and the web.
   - Need for one reliable, centralized, knowledgeable source for paper and paper-related products.

9. What factors in the economic environment affect the product?
   - Tendency to understaff resulting in less time to merchandise.
   - The proliferation of catalogs; positioning, therefore, must fully use the huge, but easy-to-understand selection quickly available and in smaller quantities than the norm to sway purchasers from selecting similar products from competitors.
   - The difficulty of raising working capital.

10. Do any legal considerations affect the product?
    - Federal Trade Commission rules and regulation.
    - Licensing of designs.

Potential Tag Line: THE Complete, FAST Source for Paper

10 Merchandising

Merchandising can be divided into two main areas: 1) *procurement* and 2) *selection*. Procurement can be further divided into two additional categories: 1) *sourcing*, where the merchant finds items that are already manufactured by other companies; and 2) *development*, where the merchant actually creates items that are specifically made for the cataloger. Developed items can be produced by the catalog company itself or another manufacturer. Selection is when determination is made of exactly what will run in the particular issue of the catalog. In order to make the selection, merchants need to have decided what will be rerun (pick-up) and have all the new samples available for pagination.

Pagination, a major part of the final selection, includes the determination of products that will be featured in the catalogs, the prices of the products, the pages on which the products will appear, and the combinations of products on those pages.

Product Strategy

Before you even step a foot into a buying office, merchandise show floor room, or a manufacturing facility, you've got to have a plan. Not just a verbal plan, but a written one that outlines exactly what you plan to offer for the year. That plan must be based on existing sales, marketing ambitions, and fulfillment capabilities. This needs to be done on a year-to-past-year basis per issue with an overall look at the needs of the all of the catalogs.

One of the major reasons for such a plan is that merchants need to fully understand, per issue, who the catalog is going to and what the expectations for sales are. For instance, if the catalog is going mostly to the house list, the merchandising and/or marketing team may well decide to offer more new products than they would for a catalog that went largely to prospects.

Suggested space allocations (how much space a particular product should be given) are based on analysis that shows what product performed best in the space it occupied.

Exhibit 10.1 Product Strategy Form for One Issue

PRODUCT STRATEGY

Current Issue Specifications

Issue Name/Title: _____

In-Mail Date: _____

In-Home Date: _____

Total Circulation: _____

Percentages of Total Circulation:

- rental prospects _____
- requests (0–12 months) _____
- house total _____
    - 1x buyer _____
    - 2x multi-buyer _____
    - 3x multi-buyer _____
    - 4x+ multi-buyer _____
    - inactive (including requests older than 12 months) _____

Current Issue Year-to-Year Comparison

Anticipated Demand:

    current year _____   past year _____

Anticipated ROS:

    current year _____   past year _____

Number of Pages

    current year _____   past year _____

Number of Products (pictures)

    current year _____   past year _____

Number of New Products

    current year _____   past year _____

Average Margin

    current year _____   past year _____

Current Issue Overall Goals

Price Range _____

Product Categories _____

Margin _____

New versus Repeat _____

Specific Strategy Per Category By Page and Item Number Allocation

(Category) *Strategy* (in paragraph format)

Category Goals

Price Range_____

Space Allocation _____

Margin _____

Allocations

Number of Pages

    current year _____ past year _____

Number of Products (pictures)

    current year _____ past year _____

Exhibit 10.2 Product Strategy Form One Issue Example

(Shows plan for the one issue only; also would need to be done per catalog and for the entire year. Two categories that would not be correct for a fall catalog—Outdoor Decor and Outdoor Furniture—are shown here as these categories would appear in the strategy for the year.)

PRODUCT STRATEGY for ABC Catalog, October, 2005 Issue
Current Issue Specifications

Issue Name/Title: _____ October, 2005 _____
In-Mail Date: _____ 10/20/05 _____
In-Home Date: _____ 10/26/05 _____
Circulation: _____ 1,000,000 _____

Percentages of Circulation:
- rental prospects ___ 200,000 ___
- requests (0–12 months) ___ 50,000 ___
- house total ___ 750,000 ___
    - 1x buyer ___ 250,000 ___
    - 2x multi-buyer ___ 200,000 ___
    - 3x multi-buyer ___ 150,000 ___
    - 4x+ multi-buyer ___ 75,000 ___
    - inactive (including requests older than 12 months) ___ 75,000 ___

Year-to-Year Comparison past year is for October 2004)

Anticipated Demand:
    current year (05) $2,100,000   past year (04) $1,700,000

Anticipated ROS:
    current year 5 percent   past year 4 percent

Number of Pages
    current year 102   past year 80

Number of Products (pictures w/o inserts)
    current year 683   past year 661

Number of New Products
    current year 86   past year 134

Average Margin
    current year 62.7 percent   past year 60.9 percent

Overall Goals for Year (based on space allocation sales)

Price Range: In general, add more items in the higher price ranges, such as $225–$269 and decrease items under $40; see specific categories.

Product Categories: Eliminate Linens, Bed & Bath except for top products that will be placed in Bath Decor; significantly increase Seasonal; reduce Table Accessories, Decorative; marginally increase Indoor & Outdoor Furniture (in season), slightly increase Floor Coverings and Entertaining. Other categories maintained in percentage space allocated.

Of the top 50 best sellers in gross dollars, 32 percent came from Indoor and Outdoor Furniture. 22 percent came from Floor Coverings, 16 percent from Entertaining and 15 percent from Seasonal. Even taking into consideration the number of items offered in those categories, it is clear that ABC Catalog should concentrate its merchandising on Furnishings.

The categories are:

- Bath decor
- Entertaining
- Floor coverings
- Furniture
- Lamps
- Linens, bed & bath
- Outdoor decor
- Outdoor furniture
- Seasonal
- Table accessories, decorative
- Table accessories, useful
- Toiletries
- Wall decor

Margin: increase by 1.8 percent overall
New versus Repeat: Move to 13 percent new versus last year's 22.6 percent.

Specific Strategy Per Category By Page and Item Number Allocation

Category Goals for Bath Decor

Price Range: Add $15–$39.99 with the highest concentration in $15–$19.99 and $30.00–$39.99; reduce all other categories.

Space Allocation: Decrease minimally

Number of Pages
 current year 4.00   past year 4.25
Number of Products (pictures)
 current year 30   past year 30
Margin: 65.2 percent

Category Goals for Entertaining

Price Range: Add $35–$49.99 with the highest concentration in $45–$49.99; reduce all other categories, especially those in under $19.99 and $90+.

Space Allocation: Increase

Number of Pages
 current year 7.25   past year 5.00
Number of Products (pictures)
 current year 51   past year 35
Margin: 61.5 percent

Category Goals for Floor Coverings

Price Range: Add $225–$249.99 with the highest concentration in $240–$249.00; hold allocation in all other categories.

Space Allocation: Increase

Number of Pages
 current year 8.00   past year 6.00
Number of Products (pictures)
 current year 48   past year 42
Margin: 66.1 percent

Category Goals for Furniture
Price Range: Add $225–$269.99 with the highest concentration in $225–$229.99; hold allocation in all other categories.
Space Allocation: Increase significantly
Number of Pages
 current year _30.75_ past year _20.5_
Number of Products (pictures)
 current year _231_ past year _237_
Margin: _62.9 percent_

Category Goals for Lamps
Price Range: Add $50–$74.99 and $100; reduce $30.00–$59.99.
Space Allocation: Maintain
Number of Pages
 current year _5.25_ past year _5.25_
Number of Products (pictures)
 current year _36_ past year _36_
Margin: _63.4 percent_

Category Goals for Outdoor Decor (HOLD FOR SPRING—DOES NOT RUN IN FALL)
Price Range: Add $40.00–$59.99 with emphasis on $40–$49.99; add minimally to $400–$499; decrease all others.
Space Allocation: Increase minimally
Number of Pages
 current year _5.25_ past year _5.00_
Number of Products (pictures)
 current year _38_ past year _35_
Margin: _63.8 percent_

Category Goals for Outdoor Furniture (HOLD FOR SPRING—DOES NOT RUN IN FALL)
Price Range: Add $140.00–$199.99 with emphasis on $140–$149.99; add minimally to the 400–$499 range; decrease all others.
Space Allocation: Increase minimally
Number of Pages
 current year _6.50_ past year _5.00_
Number of Products (pictures)
 current year _33_ past year _31_
Margin: _58.5 percent_

Category Goals for Seasonal
Price Range: Add $20–$49.99 and $60.00–$74.99; decrease all others.
Space Allocation: Increase significantly; concentrate on product that is representative of the best selling categories
Number of Pages
 current year _12.00_ past year _5.00_
Number of Products (pictures)
 current year _84_ past year _35_
Margin: _65.7 percent_

Category Goals for Table Accessories, Decorative
Price Range: Hold $25–$49.99 with the highest concentration in $40–$49.00; decrease allocation in all other categories.
Space Allocation: Decrease
Number of Pages
    current year 4.00   past year 6.00
Number of Products (pictures)
    current year 28   past year 42
Margin: 58.5 percent

Category Goals for Table Accessories, Useful
Price Range: Add $25–$89.99 with the highest concentration in $40–$49.00; hold allocation in all other categories.
Space Allocation: Increase
Number of Pages
    current year 7.75   past year 6.00
Number of Products (pictures)
    current year 54   past year 42
Margin: 62.1 percent

Category Goals for Toiletries
Price Range: Hold $15–$49.99 with the highest concentration in $25–$39.99; decrease allocation in all other categories.
Space Allocation: Increase
Number of Pages
    current year 7.00   past year 6.00
Number of Products (pictures)
    current year 50   past year 48
Margin: 59.7 percent

Category Goals for Wall Decor
Price Range: Add $125–$149.99 with the highest concentration in $140–$149.00; hold allocation in all other categories.
Space Allocation: Increase
Number of Pages
    current year 6.25   past year 6.00
Number of Products (pictures)
    current year 50   past year 48
Margin: 59.5 percent

Merchandise Criteria

Now that the game plan is written, it is time to start sourcing and/or developing product. Every merchant should have a written list of criteria by which they judge each and every new item prior to recommending it for catalog insertion. Though many merchants will insist that such a list exists in their head, we believe that writing it down creates tighter criteria and helps to avoid oversights. The list should be regularly updated as customer product needs are continually refined.

Exhibit 10.3 Merchandise Initial Selection Criteria Checklist

---

☐ Quality.
  ___ a. Does the product fit the image of the company?
  ___ b. Will the customer be so enthused about the quality that she eagerly looks forward to buying more goods from this company?
  ___ c. Does the item appear to be worth as much, or even more, than the retail price?

☐ Price.
  ___ a. Does this price seem fair to the customers and prospects?
  ___ b. Is this price in line with the competition in all areas, be they printed catalog, retail, or Internet?
  ___ c. Does this price fit your catalog's image?
  ___ d. Price comes before profitability. How your customer views your prices is more important to your future bottom line than a few extra points of margin, even though extra points are extremely valuable.

☐ Profitability.
  ___ a. Will this item meet the margin criteria you have established and your Product Strategy?
  ___ b. Will it generate enough revenue to pay for the space it is given in the catalog?

- ☐ Availability.
    - ___ a. Will you be able to get more of the item should it become a best seller? In what time frame and at what cost?
    - ___ b. Is the item in this country or must you consider overseas costs and logistics?
    - ___ c. Can your fulfillment department handle the demand you are planning in the time period in which the item will be running?
    - ___ d. If the item is out of stock, you will not only antagonize, and even lose a customer, but also may significantly increase customer service, operating, and fulfillment costs.
- ☐ Exclusivity.
    - ___ a. Is it yours and yours alone? This is a key selling factor.
    - ___ b. Can you, through some minor modifications, adapt an existing product to make it exclusive?
- ☐ Uniqueness.
    - ___ a. Uniqueness is different from Exclusivity. In this situation, it really means hard-to-find. Is this item not regularly or easily available in other catalogs, stores, or easily found on the Internet?
    - ___ b. Unless you design and make it yourself, it is almost impossible these days to have a totally unique item. The key here is to make sure that the item is exotic enough not to be found at the local chain store or in every competitor's catalog.
- ☐ Vendor cooperation/reliability.
    - ___ a. Top consideration: Will the vendor work with you on price? Give up all or most of the items listed below in "c" if you can get a rock bottom cost of goods.
    - ___ b. Also critical is his or her reliability when it comes to delivering the quality you need in the agreed-upon time frame.
    - ___ c. Will the vendor work with you in other areas of negotiation?
        - Advertising allowance/discount—A percentage off the base price. Catalogers have historically reasoned that their catalogs are like magazines since they provide "ads" for the products.

- Back-ups—Allowing catalogers to place a small initial order with a guarantee that two to three times that number will be available to the catalog if it is needed.
- Photographic allowances—Dollar credits that can be used against the cost of actually shooting the photograph.
- Rebates/co-op payments—Partial refunds of purchases and co-op payments that are usually associated with particular promotions.
- Forward dating invoices—Where you don't pay for the goods until well after they actually arrive.
- Lenient policies and/or bending minimum order policies for less inventory risk.

☐ Photographic potential.
  ___ a. Will it look great in the catalog and on a computer screen?
  ___ b. How will it fare in retail if you have stores?
  ___ c. Does it shoot true to quality or look better than it actually is? You do not want the customer disappointed because the wallet looked like leather but was actually plastic.

☐ Cross-selling ability.
  ___ a. Does it appeal to all channels of your distribution: Catalog, Internet, or retail?
  ___ b. Does this item work well with others in the catalog, creating the opportunity for the customer to buy more than one product? Two examples: A printer with a computer, and a scarf with mittens.

☐ Mix factor.
  ___ a. Are you making yourself too reliant on a few vendors? While you do not want to complicate accounting by dealing with hundreds of vendors, relying too strongly on too few vendors can spell disaster if one of the vendors has problems.
  ___ b. Are you following your Product Strategy Plan and not overemphasizing certain categories just because they are easier to find?
  ___ c. Are you always looking for new, but complementary, category opportunities?

The Difference Between a Buyer and a Merchandiser

You can have the prettiest catalog in the world, being mailed to the smartest selection of lists ever known, and it still won't work if the merchandiser doesn't get it. What makes a great merchant? And what is the difference between a merchandiser and a buyer?

Generally speaking, a buyer is the person who follows the direction of the merchandiser. (See Chapter 11) This can take the form of sourcing and/or handling the negotiation and reordering. The merchandiser is the one who develops the strategy and pricing for products to be offered. The merchant alone can create the merchandise strategy, but it is most often done in conjunction with the marketing department.

To be a truly superior merchandiser you've got to first have predictive instincts that know, just at the right time, what the customer wants that year, that season, and at that price.

 Exhibit 10.4 Smart Merchandiser's Four Part To Do List

TO DO LIST

Part One

- ☐ Have a game plan (Exhibits 10.1 and 10.2). This means a written strategy based on known sales for the year before. Written in combination with circulation plans, it helps explain the reasoning behind your movement to increase/decrease/test categories and price ranges.

- ☐ Get the right analysis. It's scary how many people still do minimal analysis. You must have price point and category direction to avoid spinning your wheels in the market. And, you must have a clear idea of returns and customer complaints per product.

- ☐ Have written criteria (Exhibit 10.3 and Exhibit 10.5). First, document what is critical to the initial selection. Then, determine the attributes your best sellers have by assigning values to each criterion and creating a final selection critical checklist.

- ☐ Think add-on. Using your best sellers as a guide, think about what products would work with the item (not more of the same, but in addition). For instance, if a high-style dish drainer is selling, try a complementary high-style draining board. But watch your mix. Due to sales direction, a common trap is to add too many similar products, which results in splitting rather than adding to sales.

- ☐ Review again and again for cross-sell opportunities. Putting complementary items together helps overcome consumer indecision because it takes the guesswork out of the equation.

- ☐ Remember that one point in margin can make a major difference in the bottom line; negotiate like crazy.

- ☐ Make something out of a product that it wasn't before. Just one example is gardening rocks. They are only rocks, but with the addition of a clever maxim, they become decorative assets.

- ☐ Extend the use of a product from its accepted use. Products for those with arthritis, such as large-grip pens, have had excellent success in mainstream usage. Some catalogers have taken utilitarian, cafeteria-style stoneware and presented it as the "new" alternative to more traditional tableware.

- ☐ Know what is "hot" by subscribing to every relevant trade publication in your business, as well as to consumer publications that feature new products, e.g., some travel magazines highlight new products.

- ☐ Think beyond your regular resources. Lighting "found" in a restaurant turned into a top 20 seller; just make sure that small vendors can meet the demand.

Part Two

If you are hiring outside help (non-staff personnel), give them the tools they need to make the right choices:

- ☐ Positioning statement and/or charter and mission; include any company philosophy, e.g., the company makes it a point to be environmentally-friendly and would not run any products that jeopardizes this environmentally-friendly stance.

- ☐ Demographics and psychographics.

- ☐ Percentages of price points and categories to be filled *and* to be avoided.

- ☐ Objectives of this particular issue (can be the same as the game plan).

- ☐ The number of products that will be run and how many samples will be needed from which to select. (You will usually need three to five samples for every one that is selected.)

☐ Quantities expected to be ordered. (Initially, this is a rough estimate. The quantities should become more specific as it becomes clearer that the item is a strong contender for inclusion in the catalog.)

☐ Information about any existing relationships the company has with vendors.

☐ When samples are needed for initial review, final review, photography, and inventory.

Part Three

Make sure marketing is involved. Provide:

☐ Weekly reports of what has been sourced, why, from whom, and at what cost.

☐ Opportunity to review samples as they arrive. While this is a merchant responsibility, marketing needs to look at them, too, as merchants need marketing input on what is on target and what is not. The last thing you want is hundreds of samples that do not fit the overall company criteria and to learn of it only on the day of product selection!

☐ Filled out merchandise information forms, which indicate all the details about the item, including its benefits. Don't forget any laws and regulations relating to the specific product.

☐ Specifics about the sampling, e.g., is it on memo (credit) or must it be paid for. (If on memo, be sure to understand the terms under which the merchandise must be returned in order not to have to pay for it.)

☐ The name of the person/company to which merchandise must be returned and the preferred method of return.

Part Four

In addition, freelance merchants, just like those on staff, need to:

☐ Negotiate terms and conditions.

☐ Provide information so that the company can write purchase orders.

☐ Follow up on delivery of samples and completion of merchandise information form.

You probably do not want to use this valuable, and not inexpensive, talent to unpack the samples. Have someone on staff, or a temporary person, unpack, log, and tag the items with relevant information (cost, suggested retail, any advertising allowances, etc.).

Vendor Contracts

First and foremost, get a contract lawyer to write your contracts with your vendor. A lawyer is worth the money to make sure that every potential pitfall is addressed. Exhibit 10.5 provides a starting point to identify the contractual areas you will need to consider. If at all possible, do not cut a purchase order until you have all the rules and regulations in a contract.

Exhibit 10.5 Contract Considerations Checklist

- ☐ Price—Be sure you and your vendor understand exactly what is covered in the cost of goods (e.g., excise tax, sales commissions) for what time period, and for what quantity commitments.

- ☐ Quantity—Not just its effect on price, but what will happen should you be over- or under-delivered.

- ☐ Delivery—What happens if the item is not delivered within the time your contract states it is needed?

- ☐ Warranty—In addition to all warranties that are expressed or implied by law, also get a promise that each product:

    ___ Will be suitable for the use intended.

    ___ Will be free from defects that could create a life, health, or property-threatening hazard.

    ___ Will be labeled and packed for shipment in accordance with all laws and your specified needs.

    ___ Doesn't infringe on anyone else's right, trademarks, and proprietary rights in general.

    ___ Possesses all performance qualities and characteristics claimed by the vendor or product advertisements. The contract must assure you that the vendor has filed continuing guarantees with the appropriate referral agencies under all applicable federal statues. The contract should also guarantee that the product does not violate any federal, state, or local statue, rule or regulations, and that you will be supplied with all current warranties for the merchandise you purchase.

- ☐ Defective or nonconforming merchandise—You need the right to return it at full price value. It can either be repaired to your liking, replaced, or have the full value refunded. Vendor must pay all costs that you incur, such as shipping and packing.

- ☐ Indemnification and damages—The vendor, not the cataloger, should be held responsible for any claims, lawsuits, damages, judgments, and expenses (including those of attorneys) that might arise in connection with a product sold through the catalog.

- ☐ Insurance—Get a current certificate of insurance from the vendor. This needs to insure you for any losses or damages for a five-year period following delivery.

- ☐ Termination for default—You can, in writing, terminate the whole or any part of an order if the vendor fails to make delivery in the time specified, fails to perform in accordance with the contract, becomes insolvent, or is the subject of certain kinds of proceedings under law.

- ☐ Underwriters Laboratory listings and other approvals—When it is required by law, vendors must provide approvals and ratings of their merchandise from testing or rating institutions; these must be provided to you at the vendor's expense.

- ☐ Inspection and acceptance or rejection—You have the right to reject any merchandise that does not fit the specifications you have previously set. Shipping of unspecified merchandise is considered a breach of contract. You can either return the goods or make the vendor correctly replace them at no cost you. You can also sue for damages on the rejected goods and cancel any unfulfilled part of an order.

Final Selection and Pagination

Every cataloger approaches this important function somewhat differently. Some use actual samples of every item, whether it is new or pick-up. Some use only pictures of items and tack them to a wall grid that represents the different pages in the catalog. The pagination process can take several hours to several days.

There can be one pagination per book, or, as is shown in Exhibit 10.6, there can be two. A new cataloger who had the need and the time for a more extensive review would most likely use multiple paginations. If at all possible, give yourself time to re-evaluate your selections. This can mean selecting in the morning and reviewing in the afternoon or taking two days, one for initial selection, one for refinement.

Exhibit 10.6 Product Review and Pagination Plan Outline

Purpose:

    a. To determine exactly which products will be offered per catalog, on what pages, and at what price points.

    b. To allow a review by all team members, including fulfillment and creative (if possible or feasible) and a consensus to be achieved *prior* to beginning work on the catalog.

Process:

Day One—Initial Pagination

    a. All new products under consideration should be physically displayed by category on large tables. If actual products are not used, photos should be readily accessible in category folders.

    b. All pick-ups (previously run products) should be noted and shown either through actual samples or photo reproduction.

    c. New products should be ticketed with essential information, such as retail price, advertising allowances, co-op dollars, etc.

    d. Buyers should have had their sources prepared prior to this meeting, (using the Merchandise Information Form (MIF) in Exhibit 10.9) or, as much information about the product as is available.

    e. Spread Record Sheets (Exhibit 10.14) should be filled out as completely as possible (all products must be listed). When complete, copies will be given to all creative team members. This should be complete by the end of Day One.

    f. Determination is made of exactly what products go on what spreads, keeping in mind price points and categories needed to meet the numbers in the business plan, as well as offering balanced category testing and cross-sell opportunities. If necessary, a mini P&L is performed on debatable entries.

    g. Products are taken from the tables where they are in categories and put on tables that indicate spreads. Alternately, if only photos are used, the photos are put on the wall grid that represents all the pages in the catalog. If photos are not available, simply use sticky notes with the name of the product written on it.

Day Two—Initial Pagination

a. Continuation of process as outlined on Day One.

b. Coordinator determines what information is missing and creates a deadline for when it must be received for the product to be run.

c. Spreadsheets are updated with all information available.

d. Histograms (Exhibit 10.16) of product categories and price points are tabulated and corrective action is taken as needed.

e. Products are re-evaluated for their ability to fall in the correct category and price point, based on the business plan and/or product strategy (Exhibit 10.17).

f. If necessary, products are replaced by others to meet the criteria.

g. Determination is made of what is missing and what is needed for final pagination.

Day Three—For Final Pagination

a. New products are reviewed and incorporated into the spreads.

b. Creative review occurs after the spreads have been tweaked and finalized as this allows all to visually and verbally sign-off on agreed-to products.

c. Art team views the product, while product manager explains to the team why this product is special (use either MIF in Exhibit 10.9 or Exhibit 10.11 as a guide).

d. Features and space allocations are recommended by the product team to the creative team and noted on the spreadsheets.

e. Propping and any other relevant creative handling is recommended by the creative team to the product team and recorded on the spreads.

Materials Needed:

a. All information specific to the product to be offered (either version of the MIF).

b. List and examples (actual samples or photos) of what items are to be picked-up.

c. Spreadsheets.

d. Histograms of merchandise categories and price points.

e. Cost of the book in the mail and circulation quantity.

f. Any written merchandising strategy.

Attended by the following staff for length of time noted:

Function	Day
Buyers	All days
Artists	Final pagination
Photographer	Final pagination
Writers	Final pagination
Fulfillment Manager (to check for any potential fulfillment problems)	Final pagination
Coordinator of the Project	All days
Marketing Manager	All days
Merchandiser	All days
Catalog Consultant	All days

Time Allocated: Three working days, plus follow-up time.

Follow-Up: Materials Needed

Function	Person Responsible
All MIF sheets and corresponding creative material, such as previously written copy and images of new products, should be put into individual folders by spread and made available to the artists and writers.	Coordinator
Histograms should be reviewed to determine if product mix should be altered.	Merchandiser

Allocated Follow-Up Time: Three to Five Working Days

Exhibit 10.7 evolves from Exhibit 10.3. You will note how some of the criteria are the same as Exhibit 10.3, but others have been added or changed somewhat. This illustrates how a cataloger would make similar adaptations for their particular catalog.

Most catalogers would not have the time or manpower to use this form for every product, but you can use it when you feel uneasy about a particular entry or if there is disagreement as to the value of adding the product to the catalog. It can be especially useful if there are concerns about a particular product during pagination.

To make this form work, take the weight that you have assigned to *Criteria* multipled by the *Value* you believe this item has. This will give you the *Value to the Catalog*.

Exhibit 10.7 Final Selection Merchandise Criteria Form

Product description: _____

Projected order quantity: _____   Est. Retail Price: $ _____

Targeted customers: _____

At a minimum, must meet the following guidelines:

Shipping cost not to exceed _____ percent of sales price (fill in percent that is right for your catalog).

Appropriateness to targeted customers and prospects.

Criteria	Weight Percent	Value	Value	Value	Value	Value	Times Weight	Value to Catalog
Profitability		1	2	3	4	5		
Cross-sell potential		1	2	3	4	5		
Uniqueness		1	2	3	4	5		
Quality (value/image)		1	2	3	4	5		
Inventory requirements		1	2	3	4	5		
Merchandise fit		1	2	3	4	5		
Availability		1	2	3	4	5		
Reorder potential		1	2	3	4	5		
Photographic clarity		1	2	3	4	5		
Minimal space needed to show properly		1	2	3	4	5		
TOTAL								

0 = lowest, 5 = highest

Scores: 0–20 Unacceptable product
  21–30 Re-evaluate; other considerations
  31–40 Add to catalog
  41–50 Sure to be a winner!

Exhibit 10.8 Final Selection Merchandise Criteria Form Example

Product description: <u>Silver lawn chair</u>

Projected order quantity: <u> 500 </u>   Est. Retail Price <u> $100 </u>

Targeted customers: <u>Urban and suburban male/female, upscale, design-oriented,</u>
<u>our main customer profile</u>

At a minimum, must meet the following guidelines:

Shipping cost not to exceed <u> 1 percent </u> of sales price.

Appropriateness to targeted customers and prospects.

Criteria	Weight Percent	Value	Value	Value	Value	Value	Times Weight	Value to Catalog
Profitability	25%	1	**2**	3	4	5	2.50	5
Cross-sell potential	15%	1	2	3	**4**	5	1.50	6
Uniqueness	12.5%	1	2	**3**	4	5	1.25	3.75
Quality (value/image)	12.5%	1	2	3	4	**5**	1.25	6.25
Inventory requirements	10%	1	2	**3**	4	5	1.00	3
Merchandise fit	10%	1	2	3	4	**5**	1.00	5
Availability	5%	1	**2**	3	4	5	.50	1
Reorder potential	5%	1	**2**	3	4	5	.50	1
Photographic clarity	2.5%	1	2	3	4	**5**	.25	1.25
Minimal space needed to show properly	2.5%	**1**	2	3	4	5	.25	.25
TOTAL	100%							32.50

0 = lowest, 5 = highest

Scores: 0–20 Unacceptable product
21–30 Re-evaluate; other considerations
31–40 Add to catalog
41–50 Sure to be a winner!

Merchandise Information Forms

As noted in Exhibit 10.6, one of the elements needed for pagination is a Merchandise Information Form (MIF). The vendors fill out these forms. The best scenario is to have them completed prior to pagination; then all the relevant information is available at your fingertips (assuming you bring these files to the pagination!).

MIFs do not replace a contract, but they are a binding document. As with all documents, you would adapt the MIF to fit your particular product line. You will need one filled out form per product.

Exhibit 10.9 Merchandise Information Form, Long Version

ABC Catalog Company
123 Main Street
Anywhere, USA 00000
#000-000-0000

Our Catalog No.: _____
Promotional Time Period: From: _____
To: _____

A. Your product, listed below, is being considered to be featured in _____ during the period from _____ to _____. In order to make our final decision and develop strong selling copy for your product, we must have COMPLETE AND ACCURATE information. Please complete this form and return it IMMEDIATELY to the address shown above.

Incomplete information will affect the likelihood of your product being run in the ABC Catalog.

Product/Mfg. No.: _____ Item Name: _____

B. MANUFACTURER
Name: _____
Address: _____
City: _____ State: _____ Zip: _____
Voice Mail No.: _____ E-Mail: _____
Principal: _____

Sales Agent (if applicable)
Name: _____
Address: _____
City: _____ State: _____ Zip: _____
Voice Mail No.: _____ E-Mail: _____
Principal: _____

Our orders should be sent to: ☐ Manufacturer _____
                                 ☐ Sales _____
                                 ☐ Other (Specify) _____

To trace shipments, contact: _____
Will you furnish us with free samples? _____
If not, specify charge per unit $: _____
How do you handle returns? _____
    Prior approval required? ☐ YES   ☐ NO
    Return to whom or department, specifically: _____

C. PRICING INFORMATION
    Suggested retail price $ _____   Usual printed catalog retail $ _____
    Usual web site catalog retail $ _____
    Range of actual national retail prices: From: $ _____   To: $ _____

        Wholesale cost (before discounts): $_____
        Catalog/advertising allowance: _____%   minus $_____
        Quantity discount: _____%   based on _____ # pcs.   minus $_____
        Net wholesale cost: $_____
        Payment Terms (include any discount): _____

    Our catalogs are active for six months from issue date.
        a. Will your item be available for this period? ☐ YES   ☐ NO
        b. Will you maintain your price for this period? ☐ YES   ☐ NO

D. SHIPPING INFORMATION
    F.O.B point: _____
    What freight allowance is made? _____
    Master Pack: Quantity: _____   Carton: _____   Carton Weight _____
    Dimensions: Length: _____   Width: _____   Height: _____
    Individual product carton size: (Specify each dimension) _____
    Can this carton be shipped/mailed? ☐ YES   ☐ NO
    If not, can you provide shippers? ☐ YES   ☐ NO   At what cost? _____

E. PRODUCT DESCRIPTION
    Product country of origin: _____   Fabricator country of origin: _____
    Is this product imported? ☐ YES   ☐ NO
    Colors available: _____
    How long has this item been on the market? _____
    Dimensions of product: L _____   W _____   H _____   D/Dia _____
    If electric, is it UL approved? ☐ YES   ☐ NO Fiber content: _____
    Vat dyed? ☐ YES   ☐ NO   Machine wash? ☐ YES   ☐ NO
    Machine dry? ☐ YES   ☐ NO   Wrinkle resistant? ☐ YES   ☐ NO
    Other characteristics: _____

Fabric care recommended: _____

Size equivalents P ☐   S ☐   M ☐   L ☐   XL ☐   XXL ☐

If European sizing, state US equivalents: _____

Description of item (also include descriptive advertising material and be as specific as possible):
_____
_____

If item or part of item is gold-plated, specify:
_____ Karat   _____ Gold   _____ Gold-plated   _____ Electroplated

F. DELIVERY AND AVAILABILITY

Shipping time required from receipt of our original order: _____

Lead-time required on reorders: _____

Can you drop ship to customers? ☐ YES   ☐ NO   Charges $_____

What is your normal on-hand supply? _____

Is this an item you will be continuing? ☐ YES   ☐ NO

    This item will be available from: _____ to: _____

State dates that you can grant us exclusivity: _____

    ☐ We cannot grant exclusivity on this product.

Does the manufacturer carry liability insurance? ☐ YES   ☐ NO

Limit of insurance carrier: $_____   Carrier name _____

G. PHOTOGRAPHIC ALLOWANCE

Will you allow an allowance of $200 per photo for photography? ☐ YES   ☐ NO

H. SELLER'S WARRANTY

This merchandise conforms to all laws, federal and states, as to labeling, brands, and so on. We agree to indemnify against any claims arising from violation of trademark, patents, or similar law, or from damage or injury to person or property caused by a defect.

    It is understood that the commitment made above and the terms and conditions on the back of this form constitute an agreement for the promotion period indicated.

Signature _____   Date _____

Title _____

SEND THE ABOVE DATA AND COMPLETED FORM TO:

ABC Catalog Company

123 Main Street

Anywhere, USA 00000

ATTN: Name of Merchandiser

Advertising Aids: Please return with completed forms any catalog sheets, descriptive material, and so forth, that will enable our layout and copywriting staff to do a better job in presenting your product. You are most knowledgeable about your own merchandise, its special features, uses, and so on, and we solicit your suggestions and comments.

Exhibit 10.10 Merchandise Information Form Explanation

A. Fill in Section A with name, season, and year of the catalog in which you are considering offering the merchandise. Next, indicate the time frame for which you want the rest of the merchandise. Now provide this partially completed form to all vendors.

B. Note that in Section B the manufacturer of the item may not be the sales representative. Make sure you know specifically to whom you should address questions, purchase orders, and so forth.
Section B also asks for free (also called Memo) samples. Know the return policy for samples up front to stop confusion and wasted sampling dollars.

C. Section C gives you insight into the current retail and direct marketing price structure so you can determine if this product's "normal" pricing works within your catalog's image and product strategy.

D. Section D helps you know what the cost of freighting the item will be to your warehouse. This is a cost that is too frequently overlooked when items are being selected, as it can significantly and negatively affect the bottom line. If the vendor provides well-priced reusable cartons, be certain that they reflect your catalog's image.

E. Section E will help provide the information you need for well-written copy and it helps confirm the features and benefits you believed that the product had when you first showed an interest in it. You will not necessarily need such specifics as "Vat-dyed"; again, adjust to your catalog's needs. For example, a children's catalog would need to know what age ranges were appropriate per product.

F. Section F makes certain that the timing of orders works with your needs and reinforces the need for vendor liability insurance.

G. Section G asks for photographic assistance. While this can add extra dollars in your pocket, spend the greatest effort on getting the lowest cost of goods.

Because the Long Version is, indeed, quite long, some catalogers cut it to a smaller version. This version works harder at getting copy information. Some adapt the longer version by using the *Selling Points* section from Exhibit 10.11. Customize as you see fit.

Exhibit 10.11 Merchandise Information Form, Short Version

ABC Catalog Company Date sent to vendor: _____
123 Main Street Date completed by vendor: _____
Anywhere, USA 00000
#000-000-0000

A. CATALOG
   a. Issue date and name: _____
   b. Promotional time period: _____

B. PRODUCT DESCRIPTIONS
   a. Item name:
   b. Product/ Mfg. no.:
   c. Article no.:
   d. Retail price (be specific as to what is included, e.g., set of four, in the price)_____
      "Going price" _____ Where? _____
   e. New? ☐ YES ☐ NO How new? _____
   f. Exclusive to ABC Catalog? ☐ YES ☐ NO
   g. Availability? _____

C. SELLING POINTS
   a. Write a brief statement indicating what you believe is *the single most important selling benefit* of the product or service: _____
   _____
   _____

   b. List additional benefits in order of importance: _____
   _____

   c. List product features; be as specific as possible in describing the product: _____
   _____

   d. Specify size/dimension of product:
      Height: _____ Width: _____ Length: _____ Depth: _____ Diameter: _____
   e. List colors and other options being offered: _____
   _____

   ADDITIONAL COMMENTS/INFORMATION: _____
   _____

D. VENDOR INFORMATION
   Name: _____ Title: _____
   Address: _____
   City: _____ State: _____ Zip: _____ Country: _____
   Phone: _____ E-mail: _____ Fax: _____

Pick-Up and Pagination Considerations

Besides the physical process of moving items from table to table—or pictures of items on a grid representing catalog pages—what goes into deciding which items will appear on which pages?

The first consideration is what is to be picked up. Which items have earned their way into another version of the catalog? Here's a checklist of what to consider before making a decision to pick up or not.

Exhibit 10.12 Pick-Up Checklist

- ☐ Contribution—Did it pay for its space? Has this item generated a profit or, at a minimum, contributed enough to be in the top percentile of offerings?

- ☐ Quality—Has the vendor maintained or even improved the quality?

- ☐ Reliability—Has the vendor proven itself to be reliable in every way?

- ☐ Price—Has the vendor maintained the price? If not, do you believe that your customers and prospects will believe that the product is worth the price increase? Or is it worth it to absorb the cost and live with a lower margin?

- ☐ Audience Profile—Has your customer changed? Are their needs moving in another direction?

- ☐ Wearout—Is this item losing its appeal? Products have faster wear than ever before; don't keep a waning item as you will almost always get more sales out of new one.

Exhibit 10.13 Pagination Pointers Checklist

- ☐ Know the sales goal—Understand and work the numbers to know how much each product needs to generate in the space allocated; this can be a general number, not absolutely specific to the inch.

    Using some very simplified math, here's the general concept: A 64-page catalog costs $1.00 a book in-the-mail, and there are plans to mail 1,000,000 copies; therefore, that catalog costs $1 million dollars. Each of its 64-pages costs $15,625. If there are, on average, seven items a page, each item has to do $2,232 net dollars. If the margin were 50 percent that would mean each item would have to earn about $45,000. As you consider an item, know your numbers—has this item, or one like it, ever done $45,000 or better? If not, don't run it.

- ☐ Cost of goods/margins—Does the item provide enough margin? Are you being certain to take inbound freight in costs into consideration (out-bound freight costs should be covered or offset by the shipping and handling charge to the customer)? Put higher margin items in traditionally higher pulling spaces:

    ___ front cover

    ___ back cover

    ___ upper right-hand corner of spreads

    ___ around the order form (if bound-in)

- ☐ Return rate—What has the return rate been on this item? Even if it has paid for its space, the ill will created with customers may mean it needs to be rested until the reason(s) for the returns are resolved.

- ☐ Space allocation—Does this item require an unusually high amount of space? Will it be able to pull in enough dollars to pay for that additional space? If it is a marginal item in other ways, but takes a minute amount of space, maybe it should be reconsidered as its tiny space means it will have to pull in less money.

- ☐ Units sold—While paying for its space is important, it is not the only consideration. Items that have the power to pull in many units help increase the overall response and can be responsible for bringing new customers into the fold. Selecting merchandise to run is a balance between sales, sales per square inch, units sold, and margins.

- ☐ Photographic quality—How well is this item going to photograph? Will the photo be able to capture the major benefits behind the reasons it was initially chosen? To show this product well, will the photography need cost more than the norm?

Tools for Staying Organized and On Track

Most merchants maintain all information regarding the sample items on a database and then simply bring that information on a laptop to the pagination. The spreads that the merchants use are generally a table with these headings: *Manufacturer, Manufacturer's Product Number, Cost, Retail, Allowances*, and *Terms*.

By adapting the merchant's product databases, a *Spread Record* can be constructed for use by all team members. The purpose of a spread record is to act as a control that alerts everyone to exactly what is going to be on a spread. This helps avoid layouts that are missing products, alternate colors, correct prices, and so on.

All parts of the spread, other than the *Importance on Page* and *Comments/Props* sections, are completed by the merchant as each item is selected. Since records that the merchant already had are being used, you should not have to do much more than rearrange (cut and paste) items on to new electronic spreadsheets.

Since direction will be needed on how the items should be shown, it is always advantageous to have the artist and the photographer on hand for their valuable input. Some artists can actually rough out the spreads during pagination. This is highly useful, as it allows merchants to make appropriate changes before the real layouts are begun.

It usually helps to actually name the spread something other than just its page numbers, as pages can be rearranged, causing future confusion if, say a spread numbered 4–5 was later moved to the 10–11 position.

SKU indicates the *Stock-Keeping Unit* number that is assigned by the warehouse for product fulfillment and tracking.

Mfg. is the company producing the product. As you may be running many similar products, try to make the descriptions as individual as possible.

If the spread also needs to have editorial, be sure to allow for it on the *Spread Record Sheets*.

Spread Record Sheets would be given in a folder (marked with the spread name/number) and containing all the copy found on the MIFs and any other advertising materials sent by the vendor. If digital photos are taken during the pagination, these pictures can, for further clarification, be inserted into the spreadsheets.

Exhibit 10.14 Spread Record Sheet

SKU	Mfg.	Description	Color(s)	Sizes	Cost	Retail	Importance on Page	Comments/ Props

Exhibit 10.15 Spread Record Sheet Example

SKU	Mfg.	Description	Color(s)	Sizes	Cost	Retail	Importance on Page	Comments/ Props
999978	Shoes Unlimited	Clog Loafers w/ Ribbed Soles	Brown Black Red	6–11	$20	$49	5	Need to show ridges on the bottom of the sole, color swatches; doesn't need props or model.
456780	Best of the Best	5-pocket Jean	Denim Khaki White Black	6–16	$36	$79	3	Need to show front and back pockets, color swatches; show on model.
456889	Able Garments	Tiny-ribbed Turtleneck	Burgundy White Black Navy blue	XS, S, M, L, XL, XXL	$12	$32	3	Show alone and as the prop under the jacket; used burgundy as the prop, show all colors (including burgundy) in lay down shot.
222346	Able Garments	Lycra LS T-Shirts	White Black Yellow Lime Light blue	XS, S, M, L, XL, XXL	$6	$15	2	Show all colors in lay down shot.
232096	Ready to Wear	Barn Jacket	Tan Black	S, M, L, XL	$40	$85	1	Feature; show on model.
667842	Western+	Lizard-Look Belt	Brown	S, M, L, XL, XXL (state size equivalents)	$17	$39	6	Feature on model; show clearly enough that we do not have to show again.

Simple Price Point Histograms can give you a quick read on whether or not you have stayed on plan. Exhibit 10.17 represents sales per price point, but it could just as easily be based on the product strategy. Note that prices points can be in any range; this is determined by the number of products you offer. Just be sure that you have a rational number of items per price point.

Exhibit 10.16 shows what price points were produced in an initial pagination. As you can see, it has not met the sales goals. Therefore, it would need to be edited to provide a catalog product offering based on past performance and/or product strategy. Most probable changes would be to reduce the offerings in the $20.01–$40.00 range and attempt to increase the products in the higher price points. If this catalog went ahead with the pagination as is, it is highly likely that it would cause a lower average order than the catalog has previously seen.

The same histogram exercise should be done for categories to check if categories are on plan.

Exhibit 10.16 Initial Pagination Histogram

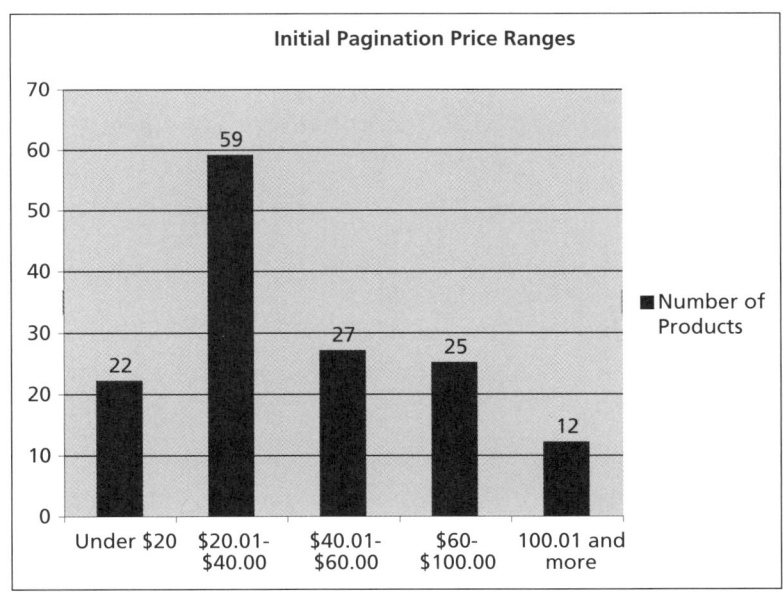

Exhibit 10.17 Optimal Price Range Histogram

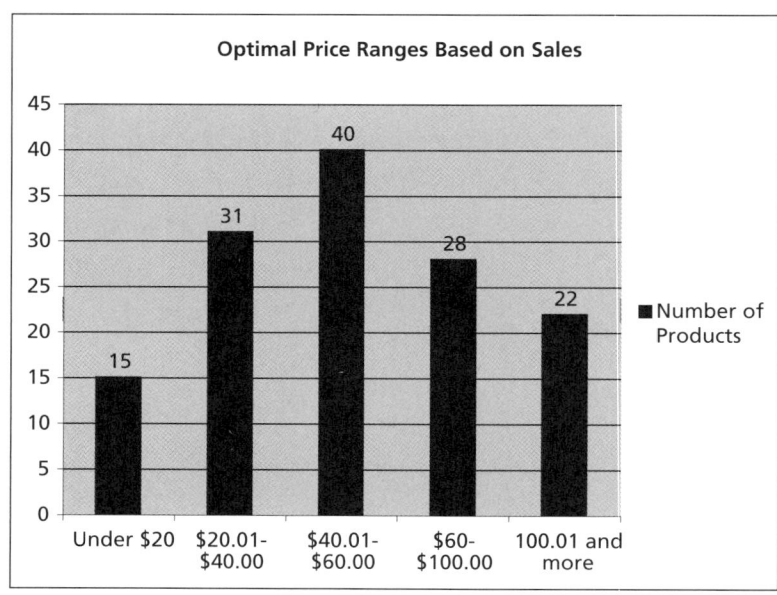

Managing Merchandise Across Channels

Sourcing and selecting merchandise has taken on an added element—the merchandise needed will, hopefully, have the potential for sales in every avenue in which you sell. Unfortunately, experience has shown that what sells at the retail level sometimes does not do as well by direct and vice versa. Prices on the Internet can sometimes be lower for the same item sold via other methods. Therefore, it is critical to keep analysis records per channel so you can source and order accordingly.

Coordinating data from every channel is a challenge. It will undoubtedly require EAI or enterprise application integration that allows data from different areas, even if collected on different systems, to be integrated. There are many management systems available, and the list of companies offering such systems continues to grow. You can find an expert specializing in coordination of software and systems by attending industry trade shows and through recommendations and advertisements. This is a highly specialized area; make sure that your expert has full knowledge of current systems and the needs of a multi-channel cataloger.

11 Creative and Production

Creative is often considered "the fun part" of developing the catalog, where your imagination can run wild and excitement rules. Not entirely true. Basic rules and regulations apply to this area just as they do for less glamorous ones. For starters, creative should not begin without a solid understanding of production requirements.

Overview of the Process

To get an overview of the process, see Exhinit 11.1 for the flow from product selection (pagination) to in-the-mail. For a detailed schedule, see Exhibit 6.1. Though the work flow is shown in a linear manner, in reality many items can be happening concurrently. See Chapter 6 for more on scheduling.

Every company has its own way of creating and producing a catalog. Some use digital photography; others still work with film. Over 50 percent, according to *Catalog Age's 2004 Benchmark Study*, do a combination of both. Some have the photos available prior to the first layouts; others insert the photos after the first round of layouts. Some have copy first round; others have partial copy, and so on. Exhibit 11.1 shows you the basic steps.

What should come first—the copy or the layout? There is no set answer to this question, but usually a very dense catalog (one with a lot of products) will write the copy first as the artist must plan space for a great deal of copy. A less dense, more fashion-forward catalog often leads with the layout, and the copy is written to fit.

In some cases, the photography comes first, with the digital images being sent directly to the artist's computer. The artist then makes adjustments that he or she feels should be done, such as adding shadows, highlights, special effects, and color corrections.

Due to the fact that new developments seem to be happening every day in digital production, there is no set way to produce a catalog. Some catalogers use agencies or freelancers that handle every detail. Some use an agency or a freelancer for just part of the process and do the rest in house. Some do everything in house, including separations.

Generally speaking, catalogs that have higher circulations have in-house creative departments and those with lower circulations use outside agencies. The number of pages per catalog also affects this. Many large catalog companies also use outside agencies so they can manage it as a variable cost (this is especially beneficial if production is seasonal). Bottom line: In-house creative departments are the best bet only when you have enough work to keep them busy full-time.

Exhibit 11.1 Basic Creative/Production Work Flow

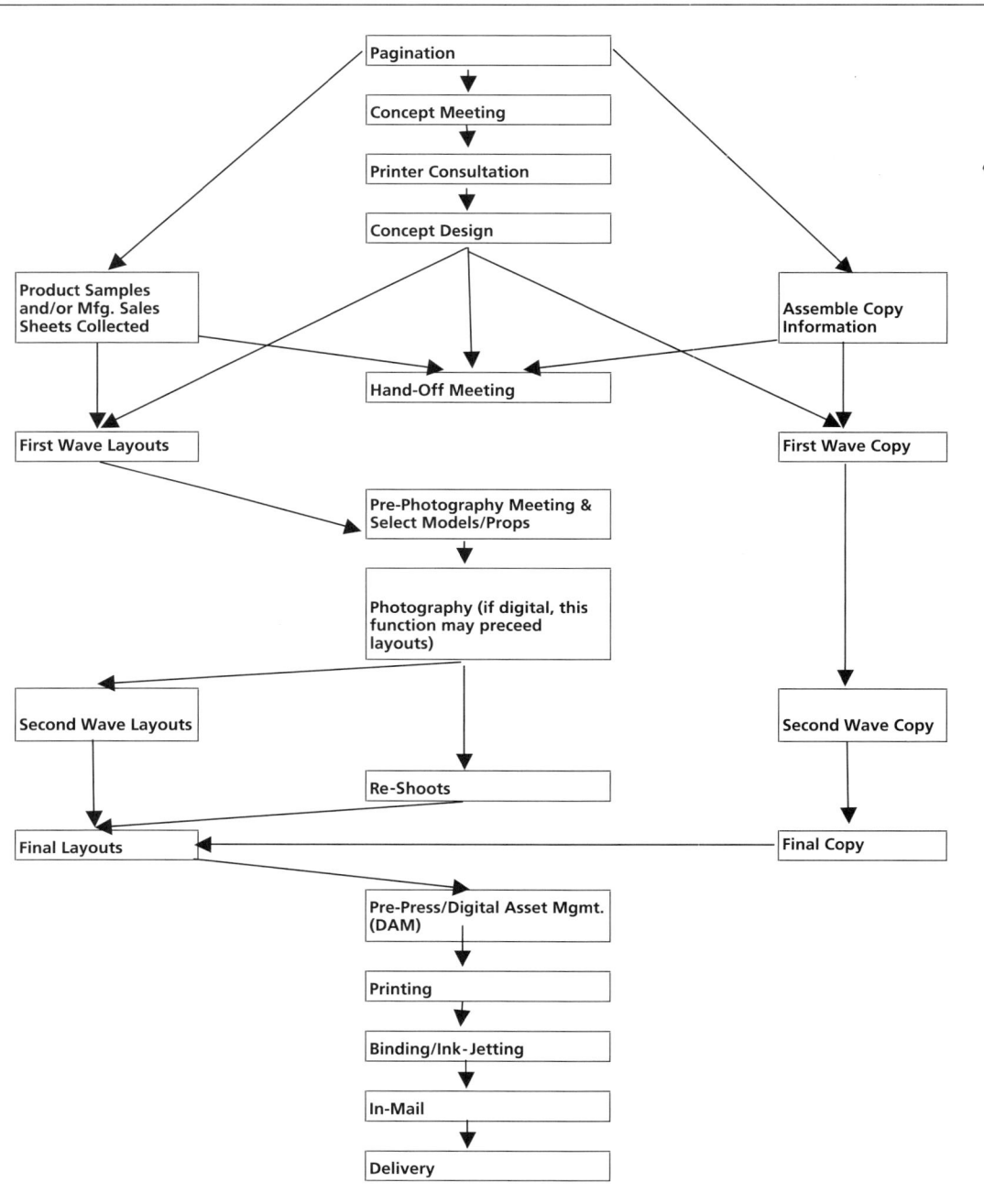

Exhibit 11.2 Basic Creative/Production Explanation

⇨ Pagination.

- The collection and selection of merchandise as described in Chapter 10, *Merchandising*.

⇨ Concept Meeting.

- This meeting only occurs when a new catalog or new creative direction is needed. The marketing team gives the creative team a Positioning Statement and Creative Strategy Outline to produce several design options. Verbal discussion should make certain that creative has a clear idea of goals, images and so on.

⇨ Printer Consultation.

- The creative/production team meets with a printer to be certain that the design cost efficiently fits the needs of the press on which the catalog will be printed and allows for any limitations, such as the space needed for ink-jetting.

⇨ Concept Design.

- This meeting is to review creative concepts, based on direction given in the Concept Meeting, that show how the actual layouts might look. Discussion determines the pluses and minuses of the concepts in order for them to go to the next stage, actual layouts. Concepts may or may not include photos of real products. Some concepts strive to show an image direction that will not work with existing photos and so images from magazines or other sources are used for illustrative purposes.
- Concepts should work in conjunction with web design for a consistent company image.

⇨ Product Samples and/or Manufacturers' Sales Sheets Collected.

- This is the time to get everything you can lay your hands on, including filled out MIFs (Chapter 10, *Merchandising*), so that you can have an efficient, useful hand-off meeting.

⇨ Assemble Copy Information.

- Make certain that copy information is more than just a listing of features. Provide the writer with benefits and all the little details, like accurate product measurements.

⇨ Creative Hand-off.
- This is when all items should come together and be "handed-off" to the creative team.

⇨ First Wave Layouts.
- Most of the time, first wave layouts will include PU (pick-up) photography and PU copy; for new items, photo space will most likely be either blank or, if the photography is digital, may show an actual photo of the product (this photo will not necessarily be the final choice, but one that is used for position only).

⇨ First Wave Copy.
- Some companies prefer to read the first round of copy in manuscript form, but more and more catalogers want to see copy in the initial layouts. It is also becoming more common to proof copy within a database "portal" or spreadsheet, as copy databases become more prevalent, especially with the advent of the web (and the need to repurpose, centralize, and synchronize copy/price revisions).

⇨ Pre-Photography Meeting & Select Models/Props.
- Bringing the photographer into the equation early on is a smart move. The artist and the photographer can work as a team to determine backgrounds, props, mood, location, models, and so on. With this kind of pre-planning, the layouts tend to look more like the original concepts, plus there are less re-shoots. This is the time to decide which shots will be shot digital and which will be shot with film.

⇨ Photography.
- The artist/designer and a catalog representative should be at the location or set as the photography takes place. Without a catalog representative present, last minutes decisions can be made erroneously, translating into costly and time consuming re-shoots. More and more companies are turning to digital photography for its cost and time efficiencies, as well as the fact that digital is needed for web images. (According to *Catalog Age*, in 2004, 43 percent of catalogers used digital photography exclusively, as opposed to 29 percent in 2002, and only 15 percent in 2000.)

⇨ Second Wave Layouts.
  - The revisions desired by the merchandise/marketing teams are incorporated into new layouts that reflect these changes. Even if all photography and copy were not in the first round, they should be in this second wave.

⇨ Second Wave Copy.
  - Copy suggestions made by the team are incorporated into the layouts.

⇨ Re-shoots.
  - Photos that are deemed unacceptable because they do not show the product well enough or do not meet the image of the catalog are re-shot in film or digital.

⇨ Final Copy.
  - Last chance for revisions, double checking prices and SKU numbers, and making sure that there are no typos.

⇨ Final Layouts.
  - Re-shoots and any other changes are incorporated for what should be the last look before the catalog is released to the separator or an in-house desktop color separator (CS) (if separations are being used).

⇨ Pre-Press/Digital Asset Management (DAM).
  - May or may not involve separating the layouts into film. Most companies are now going computer-to-plate via PDF (Portable Document Format files that embed all fonts and images in one file that can be opened on any computer using the free, downloadable Adobe Acrobat® Reader®.) or application files (all images, documents, and fonts are collected by QuarkXpress or Adobe InDesign®) that are copied to CD-ROM or delivered via FTP over the Internet. By eliminating film, production time is saved and last-minute revisions are quicker to make. Digital Asset Management, also called DCM (Digital Content Management) is a fancy way of saying put all your digital content in an electronic file cabinet that allows you to easily repurpose content.

⇨ Printing.
  - The actual printing of the catalog and, if separate, its order form.

⇨ Binding/Ink-jetting.
- Putting the catalog together with saddle stitching or perfect binding, addressing it and inserting any order forms or other inserts.

⇨ In-Mail.
- The time period from the catalog leaving the bindery to being received by the consumer in their home or office.

⇨ Delivery/In-Home.
- The actual expected delivery date of the catalog by the recipient.

Creative Strategy

The more relevant information provided to your creative staff, the more efficient and on target the copy and the layout will be. As much as possible of Exhibit 11.3 should be provided in writing to the creative staff at the concept meeting. Naturally, all these elements will have been discussed and prepared in advance by the marketing and merchandising teams.

Many of the areas in Exhibit 11.3 have been discussed in other chapters of this book. The areas that have not been discussed will be detailed in specific exhibits.

Exhibit 11.3 Creative Strategy Outline

I. Target Customer.
    A. Demographics of House File.
        1. Attitudes.
            a. Key characteristics.
            b. Key motivations.
    B. Demographics of Prospects (core and peripheral).
        1. Attitudes.
            a. Key characteristics.
            b. Key motivations.

II. Positioning (see Chapter 9).

   A. Differentiation.

      1. Positioning statement.

   B. Advantages/Disadvantages.

III. Competition (see Chapter 4)

   A. Major Strengths/Weaknesses per Segment (retail, wholesale, mail, Internet).

      1. Creative.

      2. Merchandise.

      3. Service.

      4. Overall positioning.

IV. Merchandising/Product Offering (see Chapter 10).

   A. Key Product Attributes.

   B. Strategy for the Year.

   C. Value Proposition.

      1. Offers/promotions.

      2. Bundles.

   D. Pagination (including editorial).

V. Creative Model.

   A. Brand Statement.

      1. Overall tone.

      2. Usage & frequency.

   B. Body.

      1. Density.

      2. Number of pages.

      3. Format.

      4. Graphic design approach.

      5. Copy "voice."

      6. Promotional influence.

VI. Contact Strategy (see Chapter 12).

　　A. Relationship to Other Mailings.

　　B. Theme per Issue/Drop/Contact.

Customer Profiles

Exhibit 11.4 Customer Profile Example

A. Demographics of House File.
50+, primarily female, high concentration in Midwest, married, no children at home, $65M HHI (household income).

1. Attitudes.

   a. Key characteristics.
      (1) Conservative.
      (2) Frugal.
      (3) Religious.
      (4) Have traditional values.
      (5) Do not shop much by Internet.
      (6) Can be retired so have more free time.

   b. Key motivations.
      (1) Value.
      (2) Caring attitude.
      (3) Traditional values.

B. Demographics of Prospects, Core.
35–50, mostly female, married and single, can have older children/teenagers at home, $85M HHI for married, $75M HHI for single.

1. Attitudes, Core.

   a. Key characteristics.
      (1) Willing to try new things.
      (2) Wants value, but will spend more if there is something special about it.
      (3) Expects top-rate service.
      (4) Expect easy to use, fun web site.
      (5) Time crunched.

b. Key motivations.
   (1) New items that are different and/or better in some way.
   (2) Rewards, such as savings for ordering the second time.
   (3) A friendly phone personality.
   (4) Entertaining, quick/efficient Internet site.

C. Demographics of Prospects, Peripheral.
Small to mid-size businesses who order lots of customer gifts, mostly service businesses.

1. Attitudes, Peripheral.

   a. Key characteristics.
      (1) Cost-conscious.
      (2) Busy, don't have time to spend selecting a lot of different gifts for customers and employees.

   b. Key motivations.
      (1) Want gift that is cost-efficient, but impressive/memorable.
      (2) Reliable service.
      (3) Timely delivery.
      (4) Easy to find correct gift choice and order it quickly.

Brand Statement

Exhibit 11.5 Creative Model Example

A. Brand Statement.

1. Overall tone.

   a. Traditional value illustrations that show the people behind the products.

   b. Charming visuals that illustrate quality product.

   c. Show recipients enjoying their gifts.

   d. Use some old time photos from the original store.

   e. Down-to-earth, attractive, but not flashy.

2. Usage & frequency.

   a. Company name, phone number, and Internet site alternate on every page.

   b. Show company name brand up close.

   c. Show attractive, branded packaging throughout.

A. Body.

   1. Density.

      a. Average four items per page, some more and some less dense.

   2. Number of pages.

      a. 68 pages, separate cover for holiday.

      b. Other issues 48 pages, self cover.

   3. Format.

      a. 8″ × 10.5″.

      b. May add smaller size for special holidays.

   4. Graphic design approach.

      a. Allow room for editorial throughout.
         i. Have quarter page lead-in editorial on page two.

      b. Have "hero" spreads, which are much less dense and show the product up close and beautiful.

      c. Sans serif typeface for editorial, modern serif for body copy and headlines.

      d. Short headline, not on every page.

      e. Use excellent lighting in photography to bring out texture.

      f. Keep backgrounds simple (no patterns or locations).
         (1) Product needs to be the star.
         (2) Editorial photos can set the mood.

   5. Copy "voice."

      a. Warm and friendly, but also knowledgeable and seductive.
         (1) Be specific about exactly what comes with each gift.

b. Use benefit lead-in copy subheads.

c. Use testimonials throughout.

6. Promotional influence.

a. As gifts are often bought on price, make prices bold and end prices with 95 cents.

b. Use seasonal savings in Contact Strategy.

c. Use testimonials that support product value.

Pre-Consulting with the Printer

Before you start the design, know the parameters under which it will be printed, bound, and ink-jetted. One of the common mistakes is designing a back cover that does not allow for ink-jetting both an address and a marketing message that is targeted to the specific segment to which that catalog is being mailed.

Every printer has its own list of what they think is important but Exhibit 11.6 provides a useful guide and explanation. This exhibit can also double as a checklist for getting a price quote.

Exhibit 11.6 Printer Checklist and Explanation

☐ Trim size—What will the exact size of the catalog be after it is printed and trimmed, e.g., 8″ × 10.5″?

☐ Quantity—How many catalogs are you printing per version, per drop, and in-home date?

☐ Versions—How many versions of the catalog are there, e.g., do some customers get different covers than others or more pages than non-customers?

☐ Paper—What kind and weight of paper is the catalog going to be printed on? Who is providing the paper, you or the printer? Are there extra printer charges if you supply the paper? If you supply it, what happens to the leftover paper?

- ☐ Preparation—What are you supplying to the printer for them to print from (see Exhibit 11.32, *Digital File Information Checklist*, from Banta).

- ☐ Proofs—Are you going to get proofs from the printer before going on-press? What form will they take?

- ☐ Colors—How many colors is this job, the usual four colors? Though not used that often, some catalogers have opted for more than four colors and, if this were your choice, you would need to use a press that could print more than four colors at once.

- ☐ Ink coverage—How much ink coverage is the printer putting into their price; this will affect the cost of the job and/or the design.

- ☐ Binding—What kind of binding (most often saddle-stitching) is being used? Are you binding in other items like an order form or a special coupon? Make sure that your design complies with the printer's capabilities and do not have a design element that could cause a slow-down in the bindery function.

- ☐ Will you be using a "dot whack" on the cover?

- ☐ What are the restrictions for ink-jetting the address and special marketing message, if applicable? (e.g., how far from spine and trim? Does it need to be perpendicular or parallel to the spine?). Most printers can provide a template.

- ☐ Are all the catalogs mailing or are some being sent elsewhere? This is also important to know as there is a FOB (Freight on Board) charge that you should be aware of early on for shipping to destinations. Entry point optimization may save postage dollars even after freight is considered to move to the BMC (Bulk Mail Center) or SCF (Sectional Center Facility) destination post offices.

- ☐ Schedule—When do you have to have what at the printer? Missing a press date by a day does not mean that you go on press the next day. If you are late, it could be a week or more before you are fit into the overall schedule.

- ☐ Terms of sale—What is the method of payment and when is it due? Most typical is Net 30 though some printers offer early pay discounts.

The Hand-Off Meeting

This is where it all comes together. Attended by artists, writers, marketing and merchandising representatives, as well as account executives if an outside agency is creating the catalog, a well-conducted hand-off meeting is key to the efficient, accurate construction of catalog creative. Here's just one example of a practical checklist, compliments of Ambrosi, a Chicago-based agency.

Exhibit 11.7 Client Turn-In Checklist (Ambrosi)

The following information is necessary for the agency to begin creating layouts.

- ☐ Complete market information.
- ☐ Pagination and folio information.
- ☐ Page/item allocation.
- ☐ Merchandise item numbers.
- ☐ Pricing information.
- ☐ Headline/subhead information.
- ☐ Prioritization of messages.
- ☐ Specific product styling or propping information.
- ☐ Vendor hi-res images.
- ☐ Pick-up image numbers.
- ☐ Actual samples.

Source: Reprinted with permission of Ambrosi, a Seven Worldwide Company.

Exhibit 11.8 Client Turn-In Checklist Explanation

- ☐ Complete market information—See Exhibit 11.3: *Creative Strategy Outline.*

- ☐ Pagination and folio information—See Chapter 10: *Merchandising.*

- ☐ Page/item allocation—See Exhibit 10.14: *Spread Record Sheets.*

- ☐ Merchandise item numbers—See Exhibit 10.14: *Spread Record Sheet.*

- ☐ Pricing information—See Exhibit 10.14: *Spread Record Sheet.*

- ☐ Headline/subhead information—See Exhibit 11.3: *Creative Strategy Outline.*

- ☐ Prioritization of messages—See Exhibit 11.3: *Creative Strategy Outline.*

- ☐ Specific product styling or propping information—See Exhibit 10.14: *Spread Record Sheets.*

- ☐ Vendor hi-res images—Is the vendor supplying images of sufficient quality? For which items?

- ☐ Pick-up image numbers—This will usually be found either on the agency's database or at an in-house or other supplier digital asset management (DAM) system.

- ☐ Actual samples—Real product samples, preferably not prototypes, as they can be inaccurate when the item is actually produced.

Source: Checklist is reprinted with permission of Ambrosi, a Seven Worldwide Company; explanations are the author's.

Writing Great Copy

If you remember these three things, you will have 90 percent of what you need to write copy that really sells.

1. The absolutely number one most important asset to writing great copy is taking the time to unearth what really makes this item special. Prioritize the benefits you discover, and then turn them into copy that starts with the best benefit first and continues on with each benefit in descending order. The most important benefit can be the headline or the lead-in sentence; either way it needs to be out front as much as possible.

2. As most catalogs give minimal space to copy, one of the hardest parts can be composing scintillating prose in only a few lines of copy. Don't let that get in your way. Write exactly what you feel about the item, then go back and cut and refine. But write down all the brilliant ideas down before chopping away!

3. Skip words like "beautiful," "quality," "value." They are so overused they hardly have meaning anymore. Dig down and say *why* it is a value, not just that it is (Example: "Rated #1 in its price range by an independent consumer advocate society").

Here are some more pointers:

Exhibit 11.9 Best Selling Copy Checklist

☐ Put yourself in the customer's mindset. Really understand who the customer is and attempt to unearth their motivations (best discovered through customer research). Then meet them. (Example: "Moms tell us our exclusive diaper bag is the most efficient ever.")

☐ Get to the point. Even if the style for your catalog is writing long copy, make sure that every word specifically adds an incentive to purchase.

☐ Don't exaggerate. Yes, you want to enhance the product by succinctly describing its benefits, but overselling only encourages returns. Remember, inaccurate statements can also have negative legal connotations.

- ☐ Use eye-catching tools such as:
    - ___ Captions that go in or under the picture and point out a benefit that is not evident in a photo. (Example: "Comes in designer colors, too.")
    - ___ Call-outs that generally have a line drawn from the words to a particular attribute of the product. (Example: "Self-cleans.")
    - ___ "Exclusive," not just the word, but really playing up that the customer can only find it here.
    - ___ Cross-sell other items that make sense with the product. (Example: "Check out the headset on page 9; it's perfect for this phone.")
- ☐ Be positive and directive. Positively state why someone should buy this product. (Example: "Buy one for a friend and one for yourself.")
- ☐ If you have legitimate comparisons, use them. (Example: "Scans faster than any other scanner of comparable price.")
- ☐ Keep your copy style consistent. Too often a catalog is written by more than one person, each with her own style. Having more than one copy style does not create a distinctive personality for the catalog. Decide what your style should be (follow the *Creative Strategy Outline* in Exhibit 11.3.) and make sure all writers stick with it.
- ☐ Be aware of your competitors' positioning. While you don't want to let your competition drive your approach, you should understand the pluses and minuses of their individual style.
- ☐ Think poetry. Copy has a rhythm that, when spoken, falls off the tongue in a lovely, natural manner.
- ☐ AND THE LAST TEST—read the copy without the photo. Does it still sell? You've done it!

Sizzling and Smart Layouts

To have layouts that generate top sales, you and your artists need to work as a team. Easily said, but how to actually go about it?

Exhibit 11.10 Checklist of What an Artist Needs from You

- ☐ Completed and verbally explained Creative Strategy.
- ☐ Positioning Statement that includes customer profile.
- ☐ Clear and complete information on what items belong on what pages. (See Exhibit 10.14: *Spread Record Sheet*)
- ☐ Clear direction of what items are most and least important on a spread and how they should be handled photographically.
- ☐ Complete and approved copy.
- ☐ An accurate, realistic schedule of exactly when you would like to see what. (This can be generated by the art team, but needs to have a solid OK from the cataloger before proceeding.)
- ☐ Agreement of and written production specifications, such as whether or not there are two covers, a separate order form, and so on.
- ☐ How many cover ideas you expect to see per cover (as the cover is the door to the store, this often gets several possible creative designs before the one to be used is decided upon).

Exhibit 11.11 Checklist of What You Need from an Artist

- ☐ Someone who listens and understands your Creative Strategy and Positioning and actually appreciates that you have gone to the effort to produce these guidelines.
- ☐ Experience in the design of catalogs or a sincere willingness to understand the basics of good catalog design.
- ☐ An ability to prepare digital material to the standards necessary for the printer or separator.
- ☐ An ability to stay on schedule.
- ☐ A desire for a top quality product in design, photography and production.
- ☐ A willingness and ability to stay up-to-date with electronic changes.
- ☐ Sensitively to the importance of showing products scaled in a way that helps the customer understand their actual size.
- ☐ Expertise in eye-flow, the process by which the layout directs the eye across the entire layout, often in a "U" formation.
- ☐ An understanding of the key selling spots in the catalog and how to use them. These are best supplied by the cataloger based on the tracking of actual sales, but they are often:
  - ___ Front cover.
  - ___ Back cover.
  - ___ Inside front cover.
  - ___ Around a bound-in order form.
  - ___ Upper right-hand corner of right-hand pages.
  - ___ Upper left-hand corner of left-hand pages.
- ☐ An understanding that when everything is the same size, nothing is shown, therefore some items (best sellers, new potential best sellers) must be featured based on input from the Spreadsheets.
- ☐ Attention to detail, e.g. getting the prices right.

☐ Consistency, e.g. keeping key elements, such as product key codes, in the same, easy-for-the customer-to-find spot.

☐ Knowing when and when not to use hot spot techniques. (They must fit the overall Creative Strategy and Positioning); hot spots can include:
   ___ Tinted backgrounds.
   ___ Bullets in the front of copy.
   ___ Colored type.
   ___ Correctly shown insets of products shown in a different manner, e.g., an inset photo of a model with a dress only plus a feature photo of the same model wearing the dress and the jacket that is included with it. Insets must be attached to the picture, not free floating.
   ___ When to use illustrations, usually for added explanation of a product in use, its size or impact (such as an illustrated front cover).

☐ An understanding of readable typefaces that also support the overall positioning. These should be as consistent as possible with typefaces used on the web site (don't let web site typeface limitations grossly influence your printed catalog type choices).

☐ An affinity for pacing. Pages should not all contain the same amount of products, but should have an ebb and flow that keeps the reader interested.

☐ A willingness to, in conjunction with the cataloger and copywriter, create a Style Guide (see Exhibit 11.16),

Making Sure Everything Is Accurate

It helps to have checklists against which you can check your work. Here are a few valuable ones, requiring only minor explanations, used by Ambrosi.

Exhibit 11.12 Layout Review Checklist (Ambrosi)

- ☐ All product information on a page is accurate.
- ☐ Correct item numbers.
- ☐ Logos correct.
- ☐ Prioritization of messages is accurate.
- ☐ Product space allocation in correct.
- ☐ Line art (illustrations) reflects merchandise.
- ☐ Photo art direction notes are accurate.
- ☐ Folio and pagination information is correct (right page numbers and right product on right pages).
- ☐ Headlines/subheads message appropriate.
- ☐ Creative and marketing strategy have been met.

Source: Reprinted with permission of Ambrosi, a Seven Worldwide Company.

The following checklist is for the stages before the final proof (usually one original and one to two revisions)

Exhibit 11. 13 Art & Copy Review Checklist (Ambrosi)

- ☐ Correct merchandise on the page, i.e., photography, pick-up, vendor, etc.
- ☐ Merchandise is shot accurately, all pieces accounted for, color accurate, etc.
- ☐ Correct copy.
- ☐ Correct logos.
- ☐ Correct pricing.
- ☐ Item numbers correct (key codes that match the photo to the copy).
- ☐ SKU numbers accurate (the Stock Keeping Unit number).
- ☐ Market alt information accurate (refers to different versions or pages within a catalog, e.g., one version may have different prices than another).

Source: Reprinted with permission of Ambrosi, a Seven Worldwide Company.

Exhibit 11.14 Change Form

AMBROSI CHANGE FORM 9/2002

Today's Date: _____
Requested By: _____
Job Number: _____
Page Number: _____

Ambrosi Client: _____
Traffic Coordinator: _____
Account Executive: _____

Change Information

Type of Change:
- ☐ Merchandise
- ☐ Photography
- ☐ Price
- ☐ Copy
- ☐ Pagination
- ☐ Layout/Structure

Description of Change:

_____
_____
_____
_____
_____

Additional Instructions:

_____
_____
_____

Current Phase:
- ☐ Pre Production
- ☐ Layout Proof
- ☐ Art/Copy Proof
- ☐ Final Proof
- ☐ Pre-Press

Reflect Change On:
- ☐ Layout Proof
- ☐ Art/Copy Proof
- ☐ Final Proof
- ☐ Pre-Press

Distribution: (Initial and date when changes are implemented. Return original to TC.)

CD:	INITIAL/DATE:	CC:	
ACD:	INITIAL/DATE:	QA:	
SAD:	INITIAL/DATE:	Prod:	
AD:	INITIAL/DATE:	SC:	
CW:	INITIAL/DATE:	Folio:	
DES:	INITIAL/DATE:		

Form 00100 07/2004

Source: Reprinted with permission of Ambrosi, a Seven Worldwide Company.

The *Change Form* indicates changes to be made at the various stages, such as turnover, the time period in which the cataloger turns over their changes. Distribution initials refer to the following:

D	=	Creative Director, the head of all creative, including copy.
ACD	=	Associate Creative Director, works with Creative Director on overall creative direction; ensures team executes against strategy.
SAD	=	Sr. Art Director, develops the visual look and feel of the covers and pages, photography; develops layouts.
AD	=	Art Director, works with Sr. Art Director on covers, pages, layouts, photography.
CW	=	Copywriter, the writer.
DES	=	Designer, builds electronic layouts, pulling in all art and copy, implements changes and prepares files for pre-press.
QA	=	Quality Assurance, the triple checker for accuracy and quality.
Prod	=	Production, pre-press, printing, and bindery.
SC	=	Sample Coordinator, the person who assembles and sees that samples are in the right place at the right time.
Folio	=	The page in the catalog to which the change applies.
TC	=	Traffic Coordinator, the person who makes all the pieces come together.

The final proof is the last proof before the catalog is released to the printer.

Exhibit 11.15 Final Proof Review Checklist (Ambrosi)

☐ Check that changes from Art & Copy Review have been executed exactly.

☐ Correct copy.

☐ Correct logos.

☐ Correct pricing.

☐ All legal copy issues have been addressed.

Source: Reprinted with permission of Ambrosi, a Seven Worldwide Company.

Style Guides = Professional Consistency

Once, when we worked with a large, well-known computer company, someone from the company took us into a room to show us something most interesting. There on the wall were hundreds of faxes from all over the world. Though they were all from this same computer company, every fax looked different. There was no brand consistency and reinforcement. This, as illustrated by all the faxes in one room, was a big no-no.

In this day of ever-increasing competition, you want every single piece of correspondence to have the same look and feel. That same company put together a style guide that, with some adaptations necessary for each country, added all-important consistency to the lowly fax form and every other document issued by that company.

Exhibit 11.16 provides a checklist of the areas you will mostly likely need to address for your printed catalog. This list can also be easily adapted for a web site, as consistency is just as critical in this medium.

Exhibit 11.16 Style Guide Checklist

OVERALL

- □ *Organization*
    - ___ How will the catalog be organized? By product category? By price point? By themes?
    - ___ Will the catalog require category headers or headlines? How will they be formatted? Rules (lines)? Text?
    - ___ How will text be handled? Caps? Caps and lower case? Type size, font, weight? Color differentiation?
    - ___ How are the table of contents and index handled? Are they used at all?
    - ___ Where are page numbers located? What is their type size, font, weight? Must they be on every page?

- □ *Ordering Information*
    - ___ What will it consist of? Alternating message or same on every page?
    - ___ How frequently will these messages appear?
    - ___ Where do the messages go exactly? Front cover? Order form? What location per page?
    - ___ What type size, font?
    - ___ Any design with the information?

COVER
- ☐ *Elements*
  - ___ What elements will always be required on the cover?
  - ___ How do these items need to be represented?

- ☐ *Logo/Company Name*
  - ___ Where does it go?
  - ___ How big is it?
  - ___ Can it move around or must it always be in the same place? Where?
  - ___ Can anything be shown with it? What? Can it be attached to the logo or just next to it?
  - ___ What colors can be used in what parts?

- ☐ *Tag Line*
  - ___ Where does it go?
  - ___ What type font, size and weight?
  - ___ Can the color change?

- ☐ *Issue Date*
  - ___ Is one used?
  - ___ Where?
  - ___ What type font, size and weight?

- ☐ *Special Offer(s)*
  - ___ Will this ever occur?
  - ___ If so, should there be a consistent placement?
  - ___ What type font, size, weight? Use pictorial?

- ☐ *Product Reference*
  - ___ If product is shown, will page references be used?
  - ___ If yes, where? On the cover with the product or a separate listing on the back cover or inside front cover? In more than one location?
  - ___ What type font, size and weight? Will a photo of the product on the cover be re-shown in this reference?

- ☐ *Strategic Theme*
  - ___ How will the cover reflect the theme of the particular issue?

GENERAL COPY

☐ *Capitalization/Punctuation*

___ Will the standard rules of grammar, capitalization and punctuation for narrative copy be followed?

☐ *Abbreviations*

___ What will the rule be for abbreviations?

☐ *Hyphens*

___ Will hyphens be used to finish a word that won't fit at the end of a sentence?

☐ *Numbers*

___ Should these be spelled out? Where? In body copy? In charts? In captions? In call-outs?

___ Which numbers does this apply to? Measurements? Years? Styles? Quantities?

☐ *Trademarks/Logos*

___ How and when should registration marks® and/or trademarks™ be used?

___ Should vendor trademarks/logos appear on products?

___ How shall trademarks be used in conjunction with the catalog company's logo?

☐ *Type*

___ Type size, style, and face should be noted in parentheses near specific copy elements throughout the style guide.

___ Where not specifically indicated, type elements may change for graphic effect (this should be kept to a minimum).

BODY COPY

☐ *Type*

___ Use specific font? Point size? Leading?

___ What format (right justified, left justified, centered)?

☐ *Capitalization*

___ Should standard capitalization rules be followed?

___ How should first letters of each word, including hyphenated words in item lead-ins, item lines, and charts, be treated? How should the first word in incomplete sentences in body copy be treated?

___ If key letters are used, should they be capitalized?

☐ *Punctuation*

___ Should standard punctuation rules be used?

___ Should incomplete sentences have periods?

___ Should a semicolon be used to separate a series of similar elements in a list?

___ Should exclamation points ever be used?

___ Should hyphens and/or a series of periods be used between thoughts/
incomplete sentences?

___ Should the number of commas in one sentence be limited?

___ Should series commas be used before "and"?

☐ *Elements of SKU Line*

___ What should the basic elements be?

___ In what order should they be listed? Item lead-ins? Copy? Item line? Price line? Price only? Keying?

___ How are any abbreviations handled?

___ What type font, size, weight?

___ How should capitalization/lower case be handled?

___ For each SKU line, determine the type font, weight, color, for the SKU and price. What about the items? Cap head? Weight? How should items be ordered and placed in relationship to rest of the body copy? How should hyphens be used and placed? Use dollar sign with price? Use consistent .99 prices ending with decimal points? How should sets/groups be indicated in the line? Can abbreviations be use? If so, when? How does all of this coordinate with the operations department's needs?

☐ *Sale Prices*

___ What should the basic elements be?

___ What font and size?

___ What color?

- *Guarantee*
    - ___ Frequency of placement? Consistent location? Where?
    - ___ How is the heading treated? Color? Boxed or set off in some other manner? What?
    - ___ Should icons be incorporated? What position do they have in relationship to the copy? Do they replace the copy?
    - ___ Is the same wording used throughout or is the guarantee spelled out in greater detail in the ordering area or in some other area?

- *Regular Body Copy*
    - ___ Is the first sentence bold, cap and lower case, or simply handled the same as the rest of the paragraph?
    - ___ Indented? If indented, first paragraph only, or subsequent paragraphs as well or only?
    - ___ Does ampersand ever replace "and"?
    - ___ Are numbers used as words or numerals? Does this differ per use?
    - ___ If photography contains more than one product, how should they be identified?

- *Category Headers*
    - ___ Bold? Italic?
    - ___ Logo-like treatment?
    - ___ Boxed?
    - ___ Caps and lower case?
    - ___ Colors?
    - ___ Subhead/Category Lead-in Paragraphs?
    - ___ Bold? Italic? Caps and lower case?
    - ___ Indented?

MISCELLANEOUS COPY

- *Bursts/Banners/Special Items (such as "New" and "Exclusive")*
    - ___ Are words all cap or cap and lower case?
    - ___ Should punctuation be used? What punctuation?
    - ___ Should type be italic? Bold? Is type consistent with body copy and/or header, or a separate design element?

- *Phone Numbers, Web Addresses and Hours for Ordering*
    - ___ Frequency?
    - ___ Consistently placed? Where?
    - ___ Type font, size, weight, color?

- *Call-outs*
    - ___ Type size, leading and font?
    - ___ If sentence, use end punctuation and initial cap? If not a sentence, should any end punctuation be used?
    - ___ Italic? Does type match body copy and/or headers?

- *Captions*
    - ___ Type size, leading and font?
    - ___ Write as labels or short sentences?
    - ___ Capitalize first word? Use end punctuation?
    - ___ Place directly under photos or inside photos?

- *Editorial Elements*
    - ___ Type size, leading, and font for head? For body?
    - ___ Use quotes and relevant punctuation?
    - ___ If endorsements are used, are city, state and/or title abbreviated?
    - ___ Tinted backgrounds? Rules around area?

- *Cross-References*
    - ___ Part of body copy? Separate line?
    - ___ Same type size and font as body copy?

- *Letter*
    - ___ Where will this appear in the catalog?
    - ___ Who signs?
    - ___ Will a photo be part of it?
    - ___ Format? Type font, size, and weight?

- *Icons*
    - ___ Specifically, how are they used?
    - ___ Size? Color(s)? Type font, size, weight?

Photography Types and Techniques, Preparation Forms, and Legalities

There are two basic types of photography: film and digital. Because digital can speed up the production process, costs less than film, and has image resolutions that meet or exceed traditional separations, it is quickly becoming the standard. Fashion photography is the latest to come on board, as new digital cameras can provide the feeling of movement, along with fabric detail, that digital had previously been missing. In addition, the proliferation of laptops and smaller/lighter digital cameras has made it easier to capture digital images on location.

However, some catalogers, such as food catalogers, still believe that they cannot, at this time, get the richness they need in their photography by using digital. If you use film, it will eventually have to be digitized for pre-press and for Internet use. This extra step and cost is one of the main reasons for the popularity of digital.

Don't assume anything in photography. Preparation here is as all-important as knowing exactly what your rights, now and in the future, are to the photography you are about to purchase.

Techniques

When we use the word "techniques" here, what we are talking about is the style of photography and terminology for the various shot choices. The layout artist will most likely have already decided the latter category, but a good photographer will also give input as to whether or not he feels that this treatment will show the product to its best advantage.

Though there are variations, there are two main styles, both based on how the photos are lighted:

1. Flat.
2. In-depth.

Flat photography has a more traditional look and, literally, because the light is evenly distributed on the product and its surroundings, makes the products look flat on the page. This style is most often used for lower-end catalogs.

In-depth photography will strive to give each item real dimension or depth. This means that you will see shadows on the product itself, behind, or around the product and everything in the shot is not in focus (also known as "shallow depth of field") to produce an overall feeling of depth in the photo as well as directing the eye to key features (in sharp focus).

Terminology includes the following:

- *Silhouette*, called silo for short. This is a photo of the product outlined on the page; it has no background. This is a fairly inexpensive method of shooting and, because there is no background, the product can usually be shown a little larger than it could be if it had a background.

- *Lay-down* is just what it sounds like. The product is laid on a seamless or another simple background, and shot. The stylist makes certain that the item, usually a garment, has the appropriate folds and tucks to give it depth and an "alive" feeling.

- *On-figure* means that the garment is being shown on a model.

- *In-use* means that the item is being shown as it might be used in a home, office, or whatever appropriate location.

- *Location* means the atmosphere surrounding the product. This can be an important consideration as it helps sets the mood/theme for the catalog.

- *Single item* means one product to a shot.

- *Group shot* mean several items to a shot. It is generally inadvisable to have more than three items to a shot.

- *Insets* are the smaller size photos that show a particular attribute, section or alternate view; they are used in conjunction with a larger photo showing the entire product.

Preparation

The more time you spend up front dotting every "I" and crossing every "T", the less time you will spend in expensive and sometimes frustrating re-shoots. Further, your photography will be more than just pictures on paper; it will bring the product to life for the customer and exemplify your catalog's positioning.

Exhibit 11.17 Photography Preparation Checklist

First

- ☐ Check out catalogs or other sources and determine the style you want.
- ☐ Talk with other catalogers who can give you firsthand recommendations.
- ☐ Visit booths of photography resources at major industry events.

Second

- ☐ Review portfolios and recent references for:
  - ___ Dependability—The photographer does what she says she will when she says she will.
  - ___ Accuracy—Shows the right photo on the right background in the right size with the right props and so on.
  - ___ Ability to stay on schedule—Includes make-up time if needed.
  - ___ Budget Consciousness—Keeps on budget and keeps a sharp eye on quality control.
  - ___ Creative interpretation—Takes direction from artists, but makes that direction even better by constructively making recommendations.
  - ___ Knowledgeability—Knowledge of, and ability to access and use, the newest, but most appropriate equipment for your needs.
  - ___ Usefulness—Helps with other resources, such as stylists and locations.

Third

- ☐ Check out the studio—Neatness and organization count.
- ☐ Get a quote that includes:
  - ___ Photo fee.
  - ___ Film and processing (if relevant).
  - ___ Expenses.
  - ___ Usage rights.

___ Location and/or studio fees (if relevant).

___ Prop and/or background costs.

___ Re-shoot policy.

___ Weather delays policy.

___ Overtime policy.

___ Policy regarding postponement and cancellation should either of these become necessary.

___ Terms of usage—Are images for catalog use only? Can they be used for advertisements or other promotions?

___ Ownership of images—Beyond usage, who owns the photographs?

___ Loss and damage in case of loss or damage to the original images.

___ Indemnification for lost merchandise if it disappears during the photography shoot.

___ Payment and collection terms.

___ Sales, use, and transit tax.

Other areas that simple forms can help plan are the actual shooting and propping schedules. Sometimes more than one photographer and/or stylist is working on your catalog. These checklists clarify who will do what and the necessary time frames. Just create a simple grid with the items shown in Exhibits 11.18 and 11.19 as headers.

Exhibit 11.18 Shooting Schedule Checklist

☐ Catalog page number.

☐ Day/date of shot.

☐ Time allocated per shot.

☐ Product to be shot.

☐ How will clothing products be transported?

☐ Stylist responsible.

☐ Prop to be used.

☐ Model to be used.

☐ Schedule a test-fitting prior to the shoot.

☐ Where will models change (will you need to rent a van or trailer)?

☐ Will you require separate hair and make-up artists/stylists?

☐ Photographer responsible.

☐ Product manager or art director to supervise.

Exhibit 11.19 Prop Background Checklist

☐ Day/date needed on set or location.

☐ Catalog page number.

☐ Product for each prop/background.

☐ Prop to be used.

☐ Background to be used.

☐ Stylist responsible.

☐ Product manager or catalog representative responsible.

Exhibit 11.20 Pre-Production Meeting Checklist

AMBROSI

Pre-Production Meeting Checklist

CLIENT:_____   JOB#:_____

Art Director and/or Account Manager:_____

Pre-Pro Date:_____   First Scheduled Shoot Day:_____

Last Scheduled Shoot Day:_____   No. of days scheduled for photo:_____

Post Mortem Date:_____   Reshoot window:_____

Merchandise

Total shot count @ pre-pro:_____   # of shots not merch complete:_____

Info Available @ Pre-Pro:
(Y) Yes / (N) No/ (NA) Not Applicable

_____Final Layouts*
_____Set/Background Requirements
_____Work Orders
_____Prop Shopping List
_____Styling Guidelines
_____Tentative Shoot Schedule
_____Photo Deadlines
_____Merch Info
_____Digital issues
_____($) Cost Estimate

Pre-Pro Attendees:
(Y) Yes / (N) No / (NA) Not Applicable

Producer: _____
Art Director: _____
Photo Art Dir.:   _____
Stylist: _____
Photographer: _____
Photographer: _____
Merch Coord.:   _____
Digital Coord.:   _____
Account Rep: _____
Bus Manager: _____
Other: _____

*Final layouts <u>must</u> include all mech #'s, all image names and accurate PAD notes.

Topics Covered:
(Y) Yes / (N) No/ (NA) Not Applicable

_____What specific merch is in each shot
_____What background will be used for each shot
_____What props/styling will be needed for each shot
_____Set Construction-are Work Orders drawn up and in hands of Producer
_____Photo Issues – lighting direction etc.

Additional Comments:
_____
_____
_____
_____

Source: Reprinted with permission of Ambrosi, a Seven Worldwide Company.

To assure accuracy and avoid revisions, it is hard to have too many checklists. Exhibit 11.20, Pre-Production Meeting Checklist, is used in the meeting with the photographer and it combines many of the elements listed in the Shooting Schedule Checklist and Prop Background Checklist. This checklist makes it clear exactly what tools, such as final layouts, will be used in the meeting, who will
attend and what topics will be covered.

Re-shoots

While nobody likes them, you would be foolish not to allow time for redoing some photos. Re-shoots are caused by a variety of factors, the two most important being:

1. Lack of preparation.

2. Lack of a qualified catalog representative available during the first shoot.

Be certain that you agree in writing, prior to the shoot, about what constitutes a re-shoot and who pays for it.

Though most of our clients have been terrific, we once had a soon-to-be-resigned client whose only explanation for wanting to have fashion photography redone was that, "it just wasn't right." When asked for guidance on what would be right, nothing was forthcoming. This kind of communication will doom you to excessive re-shoots, a waste of time and money. Before moving forward, get firm agreements from all involved on what is to be shot.

Exhibit 11.21 Re-Shoot/New Photo Request Form

AMBROSI — RESHOOT/NEW PHOTO REQUEST FORM

Today's Date: _____ Client Name: _____
Requested By: _____ Job Number: _____
Page Number: _____ Mrkt/Version: _____
Acct. Executive: _____ AE Approval: _____

Stage Requested At:	☐ Finalized Layout Proof	☐ Art/Copy Proof	☐ Final Proof	☐ Other

AESTHETIC RESHOOT	☐ NEW PHOTO REQUEST
Image Name:	Merchandise Number:
☐ Purge Original Image	☐ Archive Original Image
Non-Billable: ☐ AAI Driven ☐ Client Driven	Billable: ☐ Client Driven

REASON FOR RESHOOT/RESHOOT INSTRUCTIONS:

PAD INSTRUCTIONS: | **MERCHANDISE DESCRIPTION:**

DISTRIBUTION:

PAD:	CD:
IC:	AE:
Producer:	Merch. Coord:
TC:	Digital Coord:

REVISED 12/04/03

Form 00007 07/2004

Source: Reprinted with permission of Ambrosi, a Seven Worldwide Company.

Dan Morrissey, co-president of Ambrosi, heads an agency with over 190,000 square feet of studio facilities including a digital imaging group that works twenty-four hours, seven days a week. Who better to talk to about what should be covered in a digital photography checklist?

Exhibit 11.22 Digital Photography Checklist

☐ Match your shots and the level of aesthetic quality you require to the appropriate photographic medium.

    ___ As previously discussed, not all products, due to the need for detail, are good candidates for digital. Dan also points out that location photography can have hazards, such as blowing sand at a beach, which can damage the digital equipment.

☐ Consider all the costs in your photography estimate.

    ___ Yep, you save the cost of film separations and scanning, but Dan alerts to the costs of a learning curve and, should you decide to do your own photography, the cost of equipment, its upkeep and updates

    ___ Don't forget about retouching/digital imaging costs and the need to convert digital images from RGB (Red, Green, Blue) to CMYK (Cyan, Magenta, Yellow, Black) for optimal color quality.

☐ Spend time with your photography studio to understand exactly what they can and can not do.

    ___ Know what technology is available now and what is coming.

    ___ Make the creative staff speak in plain English so you get a true grasp of capabilities.

☐ Understand quality assurance and your studio's process orientation.

    ___ Know your studio's record for re-shoots and its capacity for same. (Of course, what you want here is the impossible dream: Little re-shoot experience, but fast turn-around when you do need re-shoots.)

___ Review the systems in place to handle and track your merchandise.

☐ This is not unlike the overall checklist (Exhibit 11.17). You want to know when everything is due and when it will be back; Dan suggests that bar coding can be useful for tracking this information.

___ Check the studio's record for hitting its release dates.

☐ And check references that back up the claims.

___ Ask what kind of color management system is in place for capture as well as retouch/digital imaging. Make sure images are saved with color profile information so accurate color can be maintained when you need to convert from one color space to another (e.g., converting from CMYK to RGB for your web site or from web to sheet fed presses.)

☐ Take charge when using a commercial studio.

___ Bottom line—understand the studio's capacity and real abilities as they apply to your catalog.

Source: Dan Morrissey, Ambrosi, a Seven Worldwide Company.

Locations

For some catalogs, location provides a key component to their overall positioning. Work with your photographer to help determine places with which he has had positive experience. Additionally, should you choose, he can recommend a Location Scout, someone who, for a fee, will find and setup arrangements at locations for you.

Exhibit 11.23 lists some pointers to help your location shoot go smoothly.

Exhibit 11.23 Location Photography Checklist

☐ Match your location to your market. For the most part, the main reason for a location shoot is to provide something with which your customers can identify or aspire to.

☐ Before starting to look, prep yourself with details that will be asked; knowing what the parameters are can help you get better prices.

___ How many rooms will you need, and for how long per room? Don't forget that you're going to need a secure room for equipment and samples.

___ What are your approximate flight schedules?

☐ July in the Caribbean, winter in Alaska will get better rates than vice versa.

☐ Talk to the right people.

___ You want the PR or marketing department of the hotel's corporate office, not someone at the individual hotel you have tentatively selected.

___ Know what permits are needed; a location scout is invaluable here and your photographer may know; double check that information is accurate and up-to-date.

☐ Be flexible.

___ A chain may have options in similar, but not exact locations, which may be cheaper than your initial location choice.

___ Be open to promoting the hotel and/or airline if you can get a better deal.

___ Go for group rates with airlines and hotels.

___ Understand any weight requirements and be ready to make adaptations or other arrangements. Some things may need to be shipped ahead of the shoot dates.

☐ Going abroad has even more details to manage.

___ Proper documentation is a MUST.

☐ Passports, any necessary visas. Check the web site of the U.S. State Department (http://www.state.gov)

☐ Talk with customs to know exactly what documents you need for merchandise and equipment for *each* country in which you will be shooting.

___ Regularly check what vaccinations or other health measures might be necessary. (Check the web site of the Centers for Disease Control and Prevention at http://www.cdc.gov.

___ Stay up to date on any alerts regarding the safety of a country (U.S. State Department web site.)

☐ Allow enough time for all of this preparation; it always takes longer than you think it will.

Forms and Legalities

Keep abreast of the latest laws regarding usage, most often of photos, models, and locations, but ask about every element involved in the photography. It is not unheard of for stylists (those that arrange props and garments and/or apply make-up) to ask for a usage fee. Fees are generally based on use (catalog, magazine ads, web page) and/or circulation (catalog quantity, magazine circulation).

Exhibits 11.24 through 11.26 give examples of the types of forms you need. While any signed form is better than none, the smartest approach is to get a lawyer to approve or to create one. Forms can be provided by the cataloger or the photographer and would most likely have the name and contact information of the company providing the services listed at the top of the form. You may not be able to get agreement on all of the elements listed; negotiate as best you can.

Exhibit 11.24 Photography Release Form

This document confirms the agreement between (Cataloger), as well as anyone authorized by (Cataloger), and (Photographer) for photographs or videotapes (the Property). For valuable consideration received, (Photographer) hereby irrevocably grants to (Cataloger) perpetually, exclusively, and for all media throughout the world (including print, non-theatrical, catalog, CD-ROM, Internet and any other electronic medium presently in existence or invented in the future), the right to use and incorporate (alone or together with other materials), in whole or in part, photographs and/or video footage taken by (Photographer) as a result of your agreement with (Cataloger).

You agree that (Photographer) will not bring or consent to others bringing claim or action against (Cataloger) on the grounds that anything contained in the Property, or in the advertising and publicity used in connection herewith, is defamatory, reflects adversely on (Cataloger), violates any other right whatsoever, including without limitation, rights of privacy and publicity. You release (Cataloger), its directors, officers, successors, and assigns from and against any and all claims, demands, actions, causes of actions, suits, costs, expenses, liabilities, and damages whatsoever that (Photographer) may hereafter have against (Cataloger) in connection with the Property.

This agreement shall not obligate (Cataloger) to use the Property or to use any of the rights granted hereunder, or to prepare, produce, exhibit, distribute or exploit the Property.

(Cataloger) shall have the right to assign its rights hereunder, without (Photographer) consent in whole or in part, to any person, firm or corporation.

AGREED TO AND ACCEPTED this _____ day of _____, 20_____

_____ _____
Authorized Catalog Representative Signature   Witness

_____ _____
Photographer or Authorized Photographer   Witness
Representative Signature

_____ _____
Printed name of Authorized Catalog Representative   Printed Name of Photographer or
                                                     Authorized Photographer Representative

Contact information for Photographer
(if the form is provided by the Cataloger)

_____
_____
_____

Exhibit 11.25 Model Release Form

(If the person signing this form is under 18 years of age, delete the line that states the signatory is 18 and add a line for a parent/guardian to sign.)

For valuable consideration received, I grant permission to (Cataloger), or anyone authorized by (Cataloger), to use my picture in all forms of print, web sites, or any other form of electronic media currently in existence or invented in the future.

I waive any right to inspect or approve the photographs or electronic matter that may be used in conjunction with (Cataloger) now or in the future, whether that use is known to me or unknown, and I waive any rights to future royalties or further compensation arising from or related to the use of the photographs. All negatives or positives, together with the prints and any electronic or digital media, shall constitute (Cataloger's) sole property.

I release and hold harmless (Cataloger) from and against any claims, damages or liability arising from or related to the use of the photographs, including, but not limited to any re-use, distortion, blurring, alteration, optical illusion, or use in composite form, either intentionally or otherwise, that may occur or happen in the finished product.

I am 18 years of age or older and am competent to contract in my own name. I have read this release before signing it and fully understand the contents, meaning and impact of the release.

Model _____

Street Address _____

City _____ State _____ Zip _____

Phone _____ E-mail _____

Exhibit 11.26 Location Release Form

I (Owner/Qualified Agent) grant to (Cataloger, herein referred to as Lessee) the use of the premises described as follows:

_____

_____

Together with access to and from said premises, for the purpose of photographing said premises and/or recording sound for such motion picture scenes as lessee may desire, or for such other purposes directly related to motion picture production as lessee may desire. The undersigned warrants that he/she is the owner/agent of said promises, and he/she is fully authorized to enter into this agreement and has the right to grant lessee the use of said premises and each and all of the rights herein granted.

Lessee may take possession of premises on or about _____ (date) at _____ (time) and may continue in possession until _____ (date) at _____ (time).

Lessee shall leave said premises in substantially as good condition, allowing for reasonable wear and tear and use of said premises for the purposes herein permitted, as when received by the Lessee.

Lessee shall own all rights of every kind in and to all photographs and recordings made by Lessee on or about said premises and shall have the right to use such photographs or recordings in any manner it may desire without limitation or restrictions of any kind.

_____	_____
Owner/Qualified Agent Signature	Date
_____	
Owner/Qualified Agent Printed Name	
_____	_____
Address	Contact person representing owner/agent on premises
_____	_____
City/State/Zip	Phone
_____	_____
Phone	E-mail
_____	
E-mail	

Using an Outside Agency

If you choose to use an outside resource for your creative and production, you should first require contenders to complete a RFP (Request for Proposal), sometimes also called a RFP (Request for Quote). The larger your business, the more willing an agency will be to go through the process of completing an RFP and providing potential layouts for your catalog.

But, even small companies can create a less detailed version of the RFP, as it is a valuable tool in assessing the capabilities and character of the companies you are considering hiring. Additionally, it allows you to detail exactly what you are expecting from the agency and what they can expect from you.

As with all forms, this RFP should be adapted to your particular needs.

Exhibit 11.27 RFP for Creative Agency Outline

Catalog Name
Request for Proposal (RFP)
(date)

> Round One: Deadline and date
>
> Round Two: Steps and related dates

Confidentiality Statement

   Overview

      I. Selected Agency Will Be Awarded the Following:

         A. Initial Catalog Project and Date.

         B. Initial Scope of Work for Selected Agency (for which an estimate is needed).

            1. Concepts.

            2. Photography.

            3. Selection/supervision/purchase.

            4. Proofreading.

5. Separations, if needed.

6. Printing/bindery.

7. Mail plan input.

II. Selection Process Will Be in Two Rounds:
Preliminary Screening for All Agencies.

A. Screening Quote Should Include:

1. Outline of methodology and process.

2. Biographies of all involved in process.

3. Relevant references.

4. Relevant samples.

5. Philosophy of doing business; discuss.

6. State critical points for success or failure of a superior working relationship during the preparation of a catalog.

7. Standard contract including costs.

8. Timing.

9. Internet capabilities.

10. Other direct marketing capabilities.

B. Your Requirements of (Cataloger).
Please indicate as completely as possible.

III. Concepts for Top Two Agencies Only.

A. Scope of Work for the Second Phase of This Project Will Include:

1. Concepts.

2. Creative Brief and Rationale.

IV. Role of (Cataloger) (for concepts and thereafter).

A. List of elements and personnel the cataloger will provide.

B. Role of Agency.

V. Future Scope of Work for Selected Agency.

VI. Confirmation of Process and Contact Information.

Exhibit 11.28 RFP for Creative Agency Example

Catalog Name
Request for Proposal (RFP)
(date)

> Round One: **Deadline for RFP answer (date)**
>
> Round Two:
> 1. Agency notified that they have made it to concept level (date).
> 2. Deadline for concepts required in Round Two (date).
>   (Round Two will apply to two agencies only)
> 3. Agency awarded contract: (date).

ALL MATERIAL IN THIS RFP IS CONFIDENTIAL
(Please sign the enclosed confidentiality agreement and fax back to the (Cataloger) name on the last page of this RFP before beginning the RFP).

Overview

Up to five direct marketing, catalog agencies are being requested to participate in a *preliminary review* (Round One) to determine which agencies will be asked to present concepts (Round Two) for the (Cataloger) catalog redesign. Your response to this RFP (Round One) will become a legally binding part of any Sales Agreement entered into as a result of this bid process. We reserve the right to reject any and all responses. The information in this RFP and responses to it are confidential.

After reviewing the RFP's (Round One), two agencies will be asked to move to Round Two, concept presentation. The agency selected from these concepts (Round Two) will become (Cataloger) Catalog Agency of Record.

I. Selected Agency Will Be Awarded the Following:

   A. Initial Catalog Project for (Date) first drop mailing (there will be three drops).

      1. Prepare through digital files and in conjunction with (Cataloger) and their catalog consultant, (Name), a 48 + 4 page, 4-color catalog, 8" × 11" (or equivalent) plus 4 page, full size order form.

2. Select and supervise all suppliers needed through in-mail production of the catalog; (Cataloger) will supply paper or provide paper specs and resource.

B. Initial Scope of Work for Selected Agency (for which an estimate is needed).
   1. Concepts, layout, and copy for (Name of Catalog).
      a. Product categories to be:
         (1) Female apparel.
         (2) Jewelry.
         (3) Accessories, such as scarves and handbags.
         (4) Shoes.
   2. Photography.
      a. Assume 150 photos.
      b. Assume 9 location shots.
      c. Assume 26 with models.
   3. Select, supervise/monitor, and/or buy all aspects including:
      a. Layouts.
      b. Copy.
      c. Photography.
         (1) Strongly request digital.
         (2) Must know costs for unlimited and limited usage, including Internet, advertising, and public relations.
         (3) Must be able to digitally store all art.
   4. Professional proofreading service.
   5. Separations including current forms of proofing systems.
      a. Indicate your equipment and retrieval process.
      b. If you wish to use a direct-to-plate process, explain why and your experience with this process.
   6. Printing, 48+4 page.
      a. 250M, 350M, and 500M quantities (assume all three drops will be printed at once and held on the floor).
      b. Three cover changes (quantities per cover TBD).
      c. #3 grade, 60# interior, 70# outer 4.
      d. 4-page, 4/4 60# offset bound-in order form.
      e. Bindery/mailing (inkjet).

       f. On-press supervision by the agency is required:
- (1) Please this cost separately.
- (2) This should be a flat fee.
- (3) No commissions are allowed.

       g. Agency will be responsible for selecting a printer with extensive, reliable catalog printing experience and a good track record of advice on postal requirements and delivery.

7. Mail plan.
    a. Agency will be provided an initial mail plan by (Cataloger), but input is expected and desired.
    b. Should agency become Agency of Record, they will be responsible for implementation of the agreed-to mail plan.

Size of catalog, number of pages, number of photographs, etc., are all speculative at this stage. They may be adapted based on research and analysis. The specifications shown are to provide consistency in quoting and as representative of the current catalog and its potential page count.

Please break out day rate costs for on-press and bindery supervision (no commissions).

Please indicate if there are any costs should (Cataloger) ever wish to take possession of all art files.

  II. Selection Process Will Be in Two Rounds: Preliminary Screening for All Agencies.

    A. Screening Quote Should Include:

1. Outline of methodology and process.
    a. Think proactive; e.g., we expect the agency to anticipate any potential problems and not only alert (Cataloger), but provide viable solution options.
2. Biographies of all involved in process, including how replacements might be handled if client determines that those selected are not acceptable.
    a. Agency will be required to have:
        (1) Project manager.
        (2) Account supervisor.

(3) Account executive.
(4) Production staff.
(5) Internet strategist.

3. Relevant references.

4. Relevant samples.

5. Philosophy of doing business; discuss.
    a. Your communication abilities (the way the agency prefers to communicate and how effective the agency feels that it is at communication).
    b. Proactive stance.
    c. How you look out for your clients' interests.
    d. How you work with consultants, etc.
    e. If possible, provide real examples for all of #5.

6. State critical points for success or failure of a superior working relationship during the preparation of a catalog.

7. Standard contract.
    a. Any brochures or other information about your company.
        (1) What are your standard hours of operation?
        (2) How many personnel do you have overall? (If possible, provide an organization chart)
    b. Are any of the agency contacts with which we would be dealing part-time and/or freelance?
    c. Price all costs of all services.
        (1) Explain billing process (project, hourly, retainer, daily, etc.)
        (2) Allow for multiple reviews by client (initial reviews can take up to 7 days; this will be condensed as the process with the chosen agency becomes more familiar).
    d. Estimated travel costs.
    e. Estimated outside production costs.
    f. Payment process and terms, including early payment discounts.
        (1) Include to whom each area is paid, e.g., is printer paid directly?

8. Timing.
    a. Interim and final dates (see suggested schedule, attached).
        (1) Both copy and layouts must be seen in waves, not as one whole until the final.
    b. How you plan to assure on-time delivery and adherence to budget.
9. Internet capabilities including e-commerce tactics.
10. Solo mailing capabilities.
    a. (Cataloger) may wish to do alternate mailings in the future.

B. Your Requirements of (Cataloger)
Please indicate as completely as possible.

III. Concepts for Top Two Agencies Only (This is for the two agencies that move forward after the initial screening and is shown here simply to allow the agencies a full understanding of (Cataloger's) needs).
Scope of Work for the Second Phase of This Project Will Include:

A. Concepts
   1. Create concepts executable in
      a. Two spreads.
         (1) One interior spread.
         (2) Inside front cover.
      b. Cover.
         (1) Up to three versions, agency's choice of how many they wish to present.
      c. Copy examples (several each, must fit into spread layout examples).
         (1) Sell copy.
         (2) Editorial copy.

B. Creative Brief and Rationale.
   1. Agency will be required to provide creative brief and rationale of work for concept presentations.
   A fee of ($) will be paid to selected agencies for concept work as outlined. These concepts will be used in a focus group presentation on (Date).

IV. Role of (Cataloger) (for concepts and thereafter)
  A. Provide:
    1. Preliminary schedule (see attached).
    2. Drop date(s) currently planned for.
    3. Materials in timely manner.
       a. Product information (based on agency-supplied informational outline).
       b. Marketing strategy.
       c. Positioning statement.
       d. Creative critique.
       e. Demographics.
    4. Dedicated (Cataloger) catalog liaison, (Name of Liaison), for:
       a. Clear direction.
       b. Coordination within (Cataloger) catalog team.
       c. Timely review.
          (1) Assume one review with (name people who will be reviewing the catalog).
          (2) Revisions based on that review.
          (3) One review with team.
          (4) Revisions based on that review.
          (5) (Catalog liaison name) will be contact for all reviews, revisions.
              NOTE: (Cataloger) retains the rights to all submitted materials.
  B. Role of Agency.
    1. Review client-supplied materials.
    2. Create catalogs as outlined in timely manner.
       a) Provide and adhere to schedule.
    3. Be proactive in approach to all, such as providing informational outline for copy.
    4. Provide and maintain acceptable budget.
    5. Timely alerts as to budget status.

V. Future Scope of Work for Selected Agency:

   A. Additional catalogs per year (quantity and frequency not yet determined).

   B. Potential customer acquisition activities such as ad design for space, inserts, etc.

   C. Creative production of interim mailings.

   D. Potential assistance in electronic media.

   E. Potential assistance in research.

   F. Potential assistance in telemarketing.

VI. To Confirm, the Process Is:

   A. *Round One Deadline for RFP answer* (Date)

      1. Send back the signed Confidentiality Agreement.
      2. Provide the completed RFP as outlined.
      3. Send relevant samples.

      Please provide an original and one copy of your response and samples to: (Catalog liaison name and contact information).
      Also provide one copy to: (Catalog consultant name and contact information).

   B. **Round Two (only for agencies selected out of Round One).** *Agency* notified that they have made it to Round Two:

      1. Deadline for concepts (Date).
      2. Agency awarded contract (Date).
      3. Concept development (Date).
      4. Re-bid with more complete information provided by client.

Exhibit 11.29 Pointers on the RFP

⇨ As this is a relatively complex form, many areas have been filled in as examples; you would, of course, adapt the data that is currently shown.

⇨ State exactly what areas you expect the agency to handle.

⇨ Give as accurate a summation of the elements of your planned catalog as possible, e.g., the number and type of photos.

⇨ When it comes to separations and printing, find out if the agency is planning either:

- Film separations. (The process in which a digital art is separated into separate films representing the colors being used; the films are then used to create plates that allow the press to print the catalog content.)
- Direct to plate digital. (The process in which a data file is sent electronically to the printer and turned into plates without the film separation stage.)

⇨ Digital retrieval has become an important asset (see more discussion on this later in this chapter); check to be certain that this element is available.

⇨ Be certain that someone either from the agency or from your establishment goes on press with your job.

⇨ You can negotiate the rate for the concepts; do not expect them to come for nothing.

⇨ Agencies will often do more concept work than you request, but be sure to request the minimum as is outlined in Exhibit 11.28.

⇨ By preparing your own creative/production schedule, you alert the potential agencies as to how much time you will need for turn-around, a critical element that they would not have knowledge of if you did not provide it

⇨ Be sure to mention what capabilities, aside from catalog creative and production, that you want now and may want in the future.

⇨ Make your communication channels are clear, e.g., who at your company will be working on what in the catalog process that relates to the agency.

⇨ Let the agency know how their role might expand with you should the relationship on the initial project go well.

⇨ Summarize and confirm everything in the RFP; it is a complicated document and a summary helps everyone to be on the same page.

Actually choosing the agencies to move to Round Two and then, in the next step, deciding which one will win the account can be an emotional and frustrating process. Though such a judgment cannot be reduced to numbers, we have found that using an evaluation form helps to crystallize the pros and cons of the contenders. Sometimes this form is filled out by individual catalog team members; sometimes it is completed as part of an interactive meeting at which all suggest scores and discuss the reasoning behind their choices. The criteria and the value assigned the criteria would be adjusted per company.

Exhibit 11.30 Catalog Agency Evaluation Form

Agency (in alpha order)	Completed Materials (followed layout directions)	Ease of Working Relationship	Most Appropriate for (cataloger) Image	Shows Understanding of (cataloger) Products & Positioning	Appears to Have Greatest DM Skills	Appears to Have Greatest Design Sense (innovation, creativity)	Costs
Contender #1							
Contender #2							

AREA	VALUE
Completed Materials	10
Ease of Working Relationship	15
Most Appropriate Design/Copy for (cataloger) Image	20
Shows Understanding of (cataloger) Products & Positioning	15
Appears to Have Greatest DM Skills	15
Appears to Have Greatest Design Sense	15
Cost	10

Exhibit 11.31 Catalog Agency Evaluation Form Completed

Agency (in alpha order)	Completed Materials (followed layout directions)	Ease of Working Relationship	Most Appropriate for (cataloger) Image	Shows Understanding of (cataloger) Products & Positioning	Appears to Have Greatest DM Skills	Appears to Have Greatest Design Sense (innovation, creativity)	Costs (value)
Contender #1	5	8	5	6	7	7	7
Contender #2	2	5	7	8	4	9	2

Contender #1

AREA	Value	Score	Final
Completed Materials	10	5	50
Ease of Working Relationship	15	8	120
Most Appropriate Design/Copy for (cataloger) Image	20	5	100
Shows Understanding of (cataloger) Products & Positioning	15	6	90
Appears to Have Greatest DM Skills	15	7	105
Appears to Have Greatest Design Sense	15	7	105
Cost (value)	10	7	70
TOTAL			640

Contender #2

AREA	Value	Score	Final
Completed Materials	10	2	20
Ease of Working Relationship	15	5	75
Most Appropriate Design/Copy for (cataloger) Image	20	7	140
Shows Understanding of (cataloger) Products & Positioning	15	8	120
Appears to Have Greatest DM Skills	15	4	60
Appears to Have Greatest Design Sense	15	9	135
Cost (value)	10	2	20
TOTAL			550

Pre-Press and DAM (Digital Asset Management)

It is most often the artist who creates the digital files that are handed-off to the printer for reproduction. As previously noted, prior to beginning the creative, art preparation includes a discussion with the printer. Exhibit 11.6 indicates that one of the most important items is for the artist and the printer to agree on the format in which the digital materials will be received. Exhibit 11.32 shows a Digital File Information Checklist (DFIC) that details the areas that need to be addressed.

Exhibit 11.32—Digital File Information Checklist (DFIC)

BANTA

Digital File Information Checklist (DFIC)

Company _____ Phone _____ E-mail _____
Contact _____ Banta CSR _____ Fax _____
Title _____ Checklist Completed By _____ Date _____

Note: Please take the time to fill out this brief checklist. Although we realize this information might not be readily available, it's required to process each digital job submitted for high-resolution output. Failure to complete this form will most certainly result in additional preflight charges.

System Software

☐ Mac /v 8/9/X _____ ☐ Windows /v 95/98/NT/ME/2000/XP _____ ☐ Other, please list _____ /v _____

File Medium

☐ Zip 100mb ☐ DLT
☐ Zip 250mb ☐ Portable Hard Drive
☐ Jaz 1gb ☐ Compact Disk (CD)
☐ Jaz 2gb ☐ Other _____
☐ DVD/DVD-RAM   Number of disks? _____

◆ **Digital File Transfer**
☐ E-mail (midprep@athenet.net)
☐ FTP (midprep.banta.com or ftp.corp225.banta.com)
☐ Other _____

Note: Please submit with a completed Digital File Transfer Form.

File/Page Specifications

◆ **File Format Submitted**
☐ PDF (See Banta PDF specs)
☐ CT/LW
☐ TIFF-IT
☐ DCS/2
☐ PostScript (See Banta specs)
☐ Application
☐ Other _____

Page Dimensions _____
Total Page Count _____
No. of Prelim. Pages _____
No. of Blank Pages _____

Note: If applicable, please indicate position of blank pages under "Special Instructions."

☐ Cover
☐ Insert
☐ Text

◆ **Page Layout Software** (if application files)
☐ Quark /v _____
☐ PageMaker /v _____
☐ FrameMaker /v _____
☐ InDesign /v _____
☐ Other _____ /v _____

◆ **Images/Illustrations**
☐ N/A Text Only
☐ Illustrator /v _____
☐ FreeHand /v _____
☐ PhotoShop /v _____
☐ Corel Draw /v _____
☐ Other _____ /v _____

◆ ☐ Trial or test previously submitted?   Date: _____

◆ **Page Margins**
Top _____
Bottom _____
Outside _____
Inside _____
Other _____

◆ **Color Breakdown**
☐ PMS Colors - Describe: _____
☐ 4/C Process
☐ Cyan
☐ Magenta
☐ Yellow
☐ Black
☐ Other _____

Scanning

◆ Are there images to be scanned?
☐ Yes ☐ N/A
Total Count? _____
☐ Halftone ☐ Four-Color
☐ Line Art ☐ Placed Electronically
☐ Stripped In ☐ To Disk

◆ Specific scanning instructions?
☐ Yes
☐ N/A
☐ Scan for best results

◆ Are transparencies or reflective art:
☐ Tagged and properly identified?
☐ Scaled?
☐ Horizon line identified?
☐ N/A

Source: Banta Corporation. Reproduced with permission.

Data Management

Note: You must choose at least one of the options noted below. Please be advised there will be additional cost associated with file copy, management, or retrieval. Please contact your Banta sales or service representative to customize a data-management program specific to your needs.

- ☐ Destroy digital files after job is complete.
- ☐ Manage digital files for reprint.
- ☐ Copy files and return to customer.
  Disks burned as: ☐ Mac ☐ Windows ☐ Other
  You must also select either "Destroy Files" or "Manage Files" to be done after the files are copied:
  ☐ Destroy Files or ☐ Manage Files

Customer Checklist

*Note: The correct answer is **bold** and underscored; the incorrect answer will undoubtedly be associated with additional cost. If you have any concerns regarding these questions or require further information, please do not hesitate to contact your Banta sales or service representative immediately. You may also refer to our Digital File Requirements & Guidelines information sheet for detailed explanations as to the significance of these questions.*

Question	Yes	No	Other
Are files clearly identified for output? Folios contained in file used in file name: i.e., 001-016.pdf	☐ **Yes**	☐ No	
Are files organized into press sections?	☐ **Yes**	☐ No	
Are files compressed? If yes, with what program/format? _____	☐ Yes	☐ **No**	
Complete set of same-size, updated laser proofs? Generated from file submitted: i.e., if submitting PDF, lasers from PDF not application file.	☐ **Yes**	☐ No	
Final trim size correct?	☐ **Yes**	☐ No	Dimensions: _____
If applicable, are blank pages included in your files?	☐ **Yes**	☐ No	☐ N/A
Is image or text which does not bleed closer than 1/4" to final trim?	☐ Yes	☐ **No**	☐ N/A
Are hairline (.25 pt.) rules used? For belt, rules less than .5 pt?	☐ Yes	☐ **No**	☐ N/A
Does margin allow for drill or perf, if applicable?	☐ **Yes**	☐ No	☐ N/A
Has bleed (3/16" min.) been added?	☐ **Yes**	☐ No	☐ N/A
Are all screen and printer fonts provided?	☐ **Yes**	☐ No	☐ N/A Embedded / PDF/ Locked
Are any TrueType fonts used in the job?	☐ Yes	☐ **No**	
Are customized fonts used in the job?	☐ Yes	☐ **No**	
Are fonts stylized using menu commands (i.e., italic, bold, etc.)?	☐ Yes	☐ **No**	
Are digital files trapped?	☐ **Yes**	☐ Add Trap	☐ Leave "as is"
Are all images included?	☐ **Yes**	☐ No	☐ N/A Text Only/PDF/Locked
Do files conform to color breakdown?	☐ **Yes**	☐ No	
Are grayscale TIFFs colorized in page layout program?	☐ Yes	☐ **No**	
Are RGB images included or embedded in the job?	☐ Yes	☐ **No**	☐ N/A Text Only
Are screen shots used?	☐ Yes	☐ **No**	☐ N/A Text Only
If so, was GCR applied?	☐ **Yes**	☐ No	☐ N/A Text Only
Are there unique images named alike?	☐ Yes	☐ **No**	☐ N/A Text Only/PDF/Locked
Are TIFF images used in transparent (fill of none) picture boxes?	☐ Yes	☐ **No**	
If Xtensions or Plug-ins are used, are they included?	☐ Yes	☐ **Included**	☐ N/A
Film picked up or stripped in?	☐ Yes	☐ **No**	☐ N/A

Special Instructions
Please note (or attach) anything specific to the job here:

Internal Use Only:

Code: _____ Salesperson: _____ Service Director: _____

Job No.: _____ Phone: _____ Phone: _____

Fax: _____ Fax: _____

Note: Please route all correspondence and materials through your Banta customer service representative.

Source: Banta Corporation. Reproduced with permission.

Exhibit 11.33 DFIC Explanation

Marketers do not need to know exactly what all the electronic terminology, such as Zip, 100mb or DCS/2, means, but they do need to know that their creative team explicitly, completely, and accurately has made this information available to the production team.

- ⇨ System Software—Indicate what type of computer the files were created on.

- ⇨ File Medium—What type of file will be delivered to the printer?

- ⇨ File Page Specifications—What format has been used, how many pages are there, and in what sizes? Are there intro pages or blank pages? What software was used to create the pages? Are there images and/or illustrations on the file? What are the page margins and in what colors will this job be printed?

- ⇨ Scanning—Are all items in the electronic materials provided or must some items, such as photos, still be scanned to create the necessary digital formats? If so, exactly what must be scanned?

- ⇨ Data Management—What should be done with the files after the production team has used them?

- ⇨ Customer Checklist—An excellent list of all the items that must be addressed BEFORE releasing the digital material to the production team. It helps if you are familiar with the terms used, but most marketers do not need to have detailed knowledge. Just be certain that your creative team is using such a checklist as it will greatly aid in avoiding last minute misunderstandings, errors, and delays.

- ⇨ Special Instructions—Anything that is unusual or different about this job.

The DFIC Explanation touches on the complexity of keeping track of thousands of pages of images, plus thousands of individual photographs. Contemporary catalogers mail more frequently than in the past, creating even more pages, photos, copy, and images that must, somehow, be readily, accurately, and easily accessible. With all the materials moving from one issue to another and one place to another, DAM can help keep your catalog production consistent, exact and more time efficient.

One of DAM's main benefits is that it can help communications, as all the information needed can be stored in one place that is accessible by marketing, merchandising, creative, and production. For instance, merchants can update prices in the database rather than going to the copywriter or artist directly. Then, when the artist goes to create the latest catalog or update the web site, she will have the most current prices at hand.

As with most other creative and production functions, DAM can be outsourced or handled internally. Some choose to use an outside service to handle all graphic files; others may choose an internal system that manages graphics as well as scheduling and trafficking. Attend direct marketing trade shows as they almost always have a variety of exhibiters and speakers on the subject.

This is a fast-moving area with new and better methods seemingly available every day, but here is a checklist of potential attributes to help you get a start on determining what features might be right for your needs.

Exhibit 11.34 DAM Potential Features Checklist

☐ Exactly how do you want to use the system, e.g., for digital asset management only or also as an aid in trafficking and scheduling?

☐ Do you need to repurpose content or just manage files?

☐ Who will need to have access?

☐ How will updates be handled? Are they in real time?

☐ Can approvals be made on screen? For instance, R. R. Donnelley offers on screen soft proofing that can be calibrated to your specifications for web offset printing.

☐ How efficient and applicable is the search function? For instance, can you use both single word and word combinations to search?

☐ In what formats can files be archived?

☐ Can you view files in full size?

☐ How well does the system integrate with existing systems used in all channels?

☐ Are some repetitive layouts functions automated, e.g., price tables?

- ☐ Will the supplier of the DAM system help you fully understand your ROI (how this is going to pay for itself and when)?
- ☐ Can the system be used off-the-shelf or will it have to be customized?
- ☐ Do you need a web interface in order to link with outside departments and/or resources?
- ☐ What are the security controls?
- ☐ Do you want to be able to group images from multiple categories together so that you can choose from many options in one "glance"?
- ☐ How does the required disk space fit with your equipment?
- ☐ Do you need remote storage for security or other factors such as equipment redundancy and back-up?
- ☐ If the system is going to be used internally, what is the learning curve, e. g, how simple is the system to master and who is doing the teaching?

Printing Types and Selection Guidelines

In essence, there are two kinds of printing for catalogers:

1. Offset—A rubber plate transfers ink to paper; the printing plate can be made from film or direct laser imaging of plates.

2. Gravure—Wells on a copper cylinder hold the ink that is transferred directly to the paper; used for runs in the millions.

Within offset, there is also sheet fed and web type printing (except in Europe, all gravure is web printed). Sheet fed feeds one sheet at a time and is only for very small runs (under 50,000). Web offset is the most commonly used method for catalogers. Webs use a roll of paper rather than individual sheets so it is faster than sheet fed. In addition, webs sometimes have equipment attached to them that allow the catalog to be bound in one automated process just moments after it is printed.

We have previously looked at a checklist (Exhibit 11.6) for what should go into a printing quote. But what should you look for in a printer?

Exhibit 11.35 Selecting a Printer Checklist

☐ Use a catalog printer. Catalog printers' expertise covers much more than just ink on paper. Catalog printers are well versed in techniques that help you achieve the highest possible postal discount as well as making certain that the catalogs are prepared for the post office in a way that expedites delivery.

☐ Don't buy on price alone. A printer who is proactive in helping you understand their equipment, paper, and mail preparation for your catalog is more important than the cheapest price, as they can save you many thousands through the right press efficiencies and lower costs for paper and postage, as well as help you get a better response to the catalog because correct addresses have been applied to the catalog, allowing higher deliverability.

☐ Go to press with your job or send someone who knows your product line and can do an excellent press approval. After spending thousands of dollars to produce the catalog up to this point, now is not the time to step back from the process.

☐ Consider a contract. Well-negotiated contracts can help you keep your prices reasonable and guarantee press time.

☐ Look for a close relationship with one knowledgeable representative. Don't allow yourself to be tossed from one person to another. Insist on a rep who can be there with advice and assistance, who will alert you of new developments, and will follow every detail of your job from the second it arrives until it is delivered in-home.

☐ If you are buying anything (separations, paper, inserts) from another source, be certain that this printer is willing to work with the outside resources to make sure that they are correct and compatible with the printer's equipment. Understand if there are any extra charges from the printer to you if you provide catalog "parts" from other resources.

Paper Primer

The two major categories of paper are:

1. Coated—Smoother paper that doesn't absorb ink as much as uncoated paper. Can be shiny or matte.

2. Uncoated—Rough paper usually used for order forms or stationery. Absorbs ink.

Catalogers almost always use coated paper in a variety of types, grades, and pound weights. To fully understand paper, the absolutely best thing you can do is to get to know a paper rep or a knowledgeable printer. Their extensive expertise is free and they can be found at trade shows or in the Yellow Pages. To choose paper for your catalog you need to know the grade, the weight, and the type. Before printing your catalog, always get paper samples both printed and unprinted. The unprinted example allows you to check one paper's characteristics against another; the printed samples allow you to see how well the paper prints.

All paper is made from pulp. The better papers are made from virgin bulb; the lesser papers are made from ground wood pulp. To help understand the degree of pulp in a paper, it is graded one to five. Simply put, the lower the number, the higher the quality of (less pulp or no groundwood) paper. The higher the number, the less refined the paper, leaving more ground wood pulp (that, in some cases, you can actually see with the naked eye.) To save on costs, most catalogers opt for a four or five grade ground wood paper.

Next, we come to the weight of the paper. Cover weights are measured differently than text weights. According to Bob Hovan of R.R. Donnelly, this is where one of the greatest confusions in papers comes into play. He notes that too often customers order a cover weight using the terminology for text weight papers and are surprised when the paper they selected is not what they thought it should be. Bob says, "Don't use the terms cover weight and text weight interchangeably. They are distinctly different. 65# cover weighs 119#, which is more than 100# text when translated to the same basis size, e. g., 20" × 26" for cover or 25" × 38" for 'book' or 'text,' which are some of the most commons sheet sizes for weight comparison."

In this case of text and cover weights, the lower the weight, the lighter the paper. Paper weights run from the low 20's # weight to 100#. The higher the weight, the higher the cost, and the higher quality the image. According to *Catalog Age's 2004 Benchmark Study*, the most widely used weight by catalogers for the body of the book is in the 30# to 40# range.

Cover texts run from 65# to 120# and can go even heavier into point ranges, such as 12 point. Be careful. Some of the heavier weights can be very difficult to run on a web press and may need to be relegated to a higher cost sheet fed press. Again, talk with your printer prior to committing to a paper.

It is not unusual for a cataloger to use a separate cover in a slightly higher weight and grade than what is used in the body of the book. A separate cover requires its own signature. Signatures are the forms that automatically come off a web press; they are most often in forms of 16 pages, but a cover, of course, would be a quarter of a 16-page form, or four pages. Not all catalogs use separate covers. Many just use the same weight as, or slightly higher than, the body of the book. As postage costs are based on weight, understand the postal implications before making a final determination on your paper choices. Currently 3.3 ounces is the cut-off for piece or pound rate on non-letter standard mail.

Different paper manufacturers have a great breadth and depth of weights, grades, and types. For instance, some papers, while relatively lightweight, are designed to bulk up, giving the feeling that the paper is heavier than it actually is. A paper merchant or printer can walk you though the extensive types and their benefits. Exhibit 11.36 will give you a quick idea of important paper basics.

In addition, there are a variety of recycled papers available. For a paper to be considered recycled by the government, it must be 50 percent total recycled post-consumer. Recycled paper, while no longer as expensive as it once was, can still be hard to get, especially if you are aiming for paper based on the government guidelines. Because of the shortage, you will often see environmentally-conscious catalogers being somewhat creative. One example, as reported by *Direct*, states that the National Wildlife Federation uses 15 percent post-consumer for the body of the catalog while the order form is 20 percent to 30 percent.

Exhibit 11.36 Paper Checklist

There are some basic characteristics that will give you a quick idea of what to look for when selecting the right paper for your catalog.

☐ Strength—You don't want a paper that tears on press.

☐ Color—We all use white papers, but there are many degrees of whiteness. Lower grades, due to higher ground wood pulp content, can appear more yellow than higher grades. The whiter the paper, the truer the color, but you must balance cost with color accuracy.

- ☐ Brightness—A combination of the color of the paper and its whiteness. The brighter the paper, the more the colors will pop.

- ☐ Opacity—Can you see the graphics on one side of the paper through the other? This, called show-through, is the result of poor opacity.

- ☐ Smoothness and printability—How even is the paper's surface? The smoother the paper, the better the quality of the printing "laydown."

- ☐ Gloss—This is a measurement of how much light is reflected; the more light reflected, the stronger the color.

- ☐ Affordability—Of course you want the best of all of the above, but you also want a handsome bottom line, so balance what qualities you really need to make the sales. Even upscale catalogs can find that higher end papers will not generate enough sales to pay for their additional costs.

Bindery Overview

This is where it all comes together: The catalog, any inserts, versions, addressing, and personalizing. Usually catalogs are bound and personalized in the same printing facility as your catalog was printed. If they are not, allow for the additional cost and time of shipping. If two parties are involved, as with any other such teamwork, make sure all parties understand the schedule, how items are to be shipped, what is to be shipped, and what is to be done with the items after they have been received.

Exhibit 11.37 Basic Bindery Checklist

For your bindery, be prepared to answer every question in writing.

- ☐ Mailing name/title?

- ☐ Mailing date or dates?

- ☐ Quantity to be mailed per list segment and per version within that list segment?

- ☐ Codes for each list segment and version?

- ☐ Cover changes? Order forms? Inserts other than just an order form? Envelopes? Outer wraps? What goes with what list/version?

- ☐ Total number of catalogs to be mailed? How many to be sent to another distribution area? Where? In what time frame?

- ☐ What is to be done with leftover catalogs? Where should they be sent, in what quantities, and in what time frame?

- ☐ What method should be used to ship catalogs by destination type, e.g., warehouse versus mailed buyer list?

- ☐ What postage format should be used? If indicia, who supplies the permit number, you or the bindery?

- ☐ Description, source-code format and expected arrival date of mailing lists?

- ☐ For shipped packages, tell the bindery to identify the contents on the outside of the package as well as indicate the quantity within.

- ☐ Are there any advertising messages? Has the amount of words and space been previously cleared with the bindery so that it fits their capabilities?

- ☐ When is the postage check due and to what postmaster should the check be written? Specifically, to whom should the check be sent?

Web Design

There is no doubt that this is the hottest and fastest-changing area in catalog marketing. Every day new exhibits predict the power of the web and usability studies unearth new methods for improving your web site. But even with all this turmoil there are some basics that need to be in your web site. Use the following *Critique Form* in Exhibit 11.38 to assess and correct your web site.

Exhibit 11.38 Internet Catalog Critique Form

HOME PAGE On a scale of 1 to 5, with 5 being the highest, rank the following:						
1. The home page has a selling proposition that is compelling enough to remain on the site.	1	2	3	4	5	NA
2. The objective of the home page (what steps the site wishes the user to take next) is quickly conveyed above the fold (90 percent of visitors to the home page will not scroll below the fold).	1	2	3	4	5	NA
3. The home page clearly explains the purpose of this site.	1	2	3	4	5	NA
4. The home page can be quickly scanned and acted upon, e.g., it has easy-to-follow eye flow.	1	2	3	4	5	NA
5. Company logo is displayed in the traditional upper left-hand or top area and the logo links back to the home page.	1	2	3	4	5	NA
6. Search is easy to find and above the fold.	1	2	3	4	5	NA
7. The home page uses a simple search button with a box for entering the search item that is to be found.	1	2	3	4	5	NA
8. Navigation buttons are simple, easy to spot, and inviting.	1	2	3	4	5	NA
9. An 800-number is easily located in the traditional upper left-hand area.	1	2	3	4	5	NA
10. To ensure download time is sufficiently fast, page size is sufficiently small, under 100k, ideally at 40k.	1	2	3	4	5	NA
11. Privacy and security notices are at the bottom, below the fold.	1	2	3	4	5	NA
12. Color is used well to direct the eye and call attention to key points; it is balanced with white space that "frames" important elements.	1	2	3	4	5	NA
13. There is a clear call to action, one major objective per page.	1	2	3	4	5	NA
14. The page is free of unnecessary and distracting elements such as animated gifs, blinks, pop-ups, and pop-unders.	1	2	3	4	5	NA
15. Global information is easy to find and use.	1	2	3	4	5	NA
TOTAL FOR HOME PAGE	1	2	3	4	5	

DESIGN: SELLING PAGES (Those pages on which merchandise is offered for sale)	
1. The pages have good eye flow; the user knows what to look at first, second, etc.	1 2 3 4 5 NA
2. The relevant copy is above the fold, easy to find, and read.	1 2 3 4 5 NA
3. Prices are easy to find and read.	1 2 3 4 5 NA
4. The photos or illustrations used are above the fold and of sufficient size and clarity to facilitate a purchase decision.	1 2 3 4 5 NA
5. Space is well used; products are shown to their best advantage and can be upsized if appropriate and needed.	1 2 3 4 5 NA
6. Creative techniques (unusual type treatments, illustrations, small copy statements, etc.) do not get in the way of selling the products.	1 2 3 4 5 NA
7. Typefaces are readable for all site users.	1 2 3 4 5 NA
8. Download time is sufficiently fast.	1 2 3 4 5 NA
9. It is easy to navigate from one page to the next. The site clearly shows the reader how to navigate from one page/product to a related or complementary one.	1 2 3 4 5 NA
10. There are useful merchandise links.	1 2 3 4 5 NA
11. There is an easy-to-use search function on every page.	1 2 3 4 5 NA
12. It is obvious how to return to the home page.	1 2 3 4 5 NA
13. A format, such as tabs (like those used in a printed address book), is used to highlight particular categories or selling points.	1 2 3 4 5 NA
TOTAL FOR DESIGN PAGES	1 2 3 4 5

COPY: SELLING PAGES	
1. The copy makes you want to buy the product and can be easily scanned for key details (bullets, short paragraphs, drill down links are used for quickly digestible tidbits).	1 2 3 4 5 NA
2. There is sufficient information (sizes, colors, configurations) to buy online; if not, information is immediately provided on whom to contact and how.	1 2 3 4 5 NA
3. The copy is believable.	1 2 3 4 5 NA
4. The copy appears correct for the target audience and speaks with an understanding of the customer, not in arcane company lingo.	1 2 3 4 5 NA
5. The copy is grammatically correct and has no typos.	1 2 3 4 5 NA
6. Product pages are mini-home pages that allow customers to easily move forward no matter what page they land on.	1 2 3 4 5 NA
7. Provides shipping information and rationale as early as possible.	1 2 3 4 5 NA
TOTAL FOR COPY PAGES	1 2 3 4 5

MARKETING						
1. It feels easy, safe, and smart to order on this site.	1	2	3	4	5	NA
2. The entire site makes and reinforces the company's positioning; its creative is in concert with the printed catalog.	1	2	3	4	5	NA
3. The company's brand identity and personality are clear.	1	2	3	4	5	NA
4. There is a consistent customer focus throughout the site.	1	2	3	4	5	NA
5. The merchandise reflects the company's positioning.	1	2	3	4	5	NA
6. The site is fun/entertaining, holds repeat usage value.	1	2	3	4	5	NA
7. The links (to other sites) promoted are useful and non-competitive.	1	2	3	4	5	NA
8. There is an easy-to-spot e-mail collection device.	1	2	3	4	5	NA
9. The overall design allows for the eccentricities of different browsers.	1	2	3	4	5	NA
10. The site is fast, smooth, professional, consistent, and gives the user a positive first impression of your brand.	1	2	3	4	5	NA
11. All links are simple to use and formatted in a traditional manner, i.e., links underlined and blue and visited links change color.	1	2	3	4	5	NA
12. The good stuff is at the top of the page; think of the design as a folded newspaper.	1	2	3	4	5	NA
13. It is easy to quickly scan each page.	1	2	3	4	5	NA
14. There is a place for customer feedback.	1	2	3	4	5	NA
15. Individual pages deep link to search engines so customers can enter the site on any page.	1	2	3	4	5	NA
16. Usability studies are undertaken to understand what is and is not working on the site.	1	2	3	4	5	NA
TOTAL FOR MARKETING PAGES	1	2	3	4	5	

EDITORIAL PAGES (Any commentary, special services, chat rooms, etc., that this particular site provides)						
1. The editorial adds another dimension to the site and gives the user a reason to enjoy this site now and in the future.	1	2	3	4	5	NA
2. The pages have good eye flow; the user knows what to look at first, second, etc.	1	2	3	4	5	NA
3. The editorial makes a natural tie-in with the sponsoring company.	1	2	3	4	5	NA
4. The editorial has real value for the user.	1	2	3	4	5	NA
5. The editorial enhances the company.	1	2	3	4	5	NA
6. Creative techniques (unusual type treatments, illustrations, small copy statements, etc.) do not get in the way.	1	2	3	4	5	NA
7. Typefaces are readable for all.	1	2	3	4	5	NA
8. Download time is sufficiently fast.	1	2	3	4	5	NA
9. It is easy to navigate from one page to the next.	1	2	3	4	5	NA
10. There are useful merchandise links.	1	2	3	4	5	NA
11. It is obvious how to return to the home page.	1	2	3	4	5	NA
12. Content pages are designed for Search Engine Optimization (SEO), e.g., title pages have descriptive titles of 50–70 characters.	1	2	3	4	5	NA
13. Older content is clearly dated and not retired in order for spiders to have more content to access, resulting in higher ratings.	1	2	3	4	5	NA
TOTAL FOR EDITORIAL PAGES	1	2	3	4	5	

MERCHANDISING	
1. The products offered are appropriate for the catalog's market.	1 2 3 4 5 NA
2. The merchandise is consistent with the marketing goal.	1 2 3 4 5 NA
3. The direction from page to page is rational and easy to follow.	1 2 3 4 5 NA
4. The depth of merchandise is sufficient, but not so overwhelming as to be confusing.	1 2 3 4 5 NA
5. The breadth of merchandise is sufficient and easy to navigate.	1 2 3 4 5 NA
6. You can easily and efficiently order the merchandise online.	1 2 3 4 5 NA
TOTAL FOR MERCHANDISING PAGES	1 2 3 4 5

NAVIGATION AIDS	
1. The search engine allows quick and correct information gathering.	1 2 3 4 5 NA
2. Each page has useful navigation buttons.	1 2 3 4 5 NA
3. Each page reinforces the identity of the company behind the site	1 2 3 4 5 NA
4. There is a useful text-based site map, useful both to the customer and to the search spiders and bots, e.g., the map contains meaningful titles and headlines.	1 2 3 4 5 NA
5. There are easy-to-use help buttons.	1 2 3 4 5 NA
6. The site logo links to the site home page.	1 2 3 4 5 NA
7. Text links clearly indicate where they will take the person who selects them.	1 2 3 4 5 NA
8. The site is consistent throughout, keeping elements in the same places.	1 2 3 4 5 NA
TOTAL FOR NAVIGATION AIDS	1 2 3 4 5

SHOPPING CART	
1. Appears friendly and easy to complete.	1 2 3 4 5 NA
2. Includes clearly and highly visible security notice.	1 2 3 4 5 NA
3. Shows a thorough guarantee.	1 2 3 4 5 NA
4. Takes user through process in simple steps, allowing them the option of canceling the order before confirming it.	1 2 3 4 5 NA
5. Provides standard shipping time information and speedier options in an easy-to-see manner.	1 2 3 4 5 NA
6. Doesn't lose the customer if they hit the back button.	1 2 3 4 5 NA
7. Totals order including appropriate sales tax (if applicable) and allowances for coupons or other deductions.	1 2 3 4 5 NA
8. Allows broken orders (can have part of order go to gift recipient and part to user).	1 2 3 4 5 NA
9. Has full gift service (order, wrap, certificates).	1 2 3 4 5 NA
10. Gives alternative service phone numbers if customer should choose to telephone.	1 2 3 4 5 NA
11. Has easy-to-use place for written service questions/comments via e-mail.	1 2 3 4 5 NA
12. Makes all charges (shipping, tax, etc.) extremely clear in easy-to-read type.	1 2 3 4 5 NA
13. If a password is required, password holders can request help in remembering their password.	1 2 3 4 5 NA
14. Has online credit, leasing, bill me later, etc. options applicable to the particular audience.	1 2 3 4 5 NA
15. Offers real-time credit authorization.	1 2 3 4 5 NA
16. Gives customer prompt notification and details of order by return mail.	1 2 3 4 5 NA
TOTAL FOR SHOPPING CART	1 2 3 4 5

OVERALL SCORE	1 2 3 4 5

12 Customer Acquisition and Leveraging

Catalog marketers, for whom this book is written, are not usually the people responsible for the circulation strategy. That responsibility is most often handled by the Circulation Manager and her staff (Exhibit 12.4). However, without understanding to whom the catalog is being mailed, no department—merchandising, creative, or operations—can effectively do their job.

See the simplified flow chart, Exhibit 12.1, *Influence of Circulation on Other Functions,* for an idea of how Circulation affects other functions.

Exhibit 12.1 Influence of Circulation on Other Functions

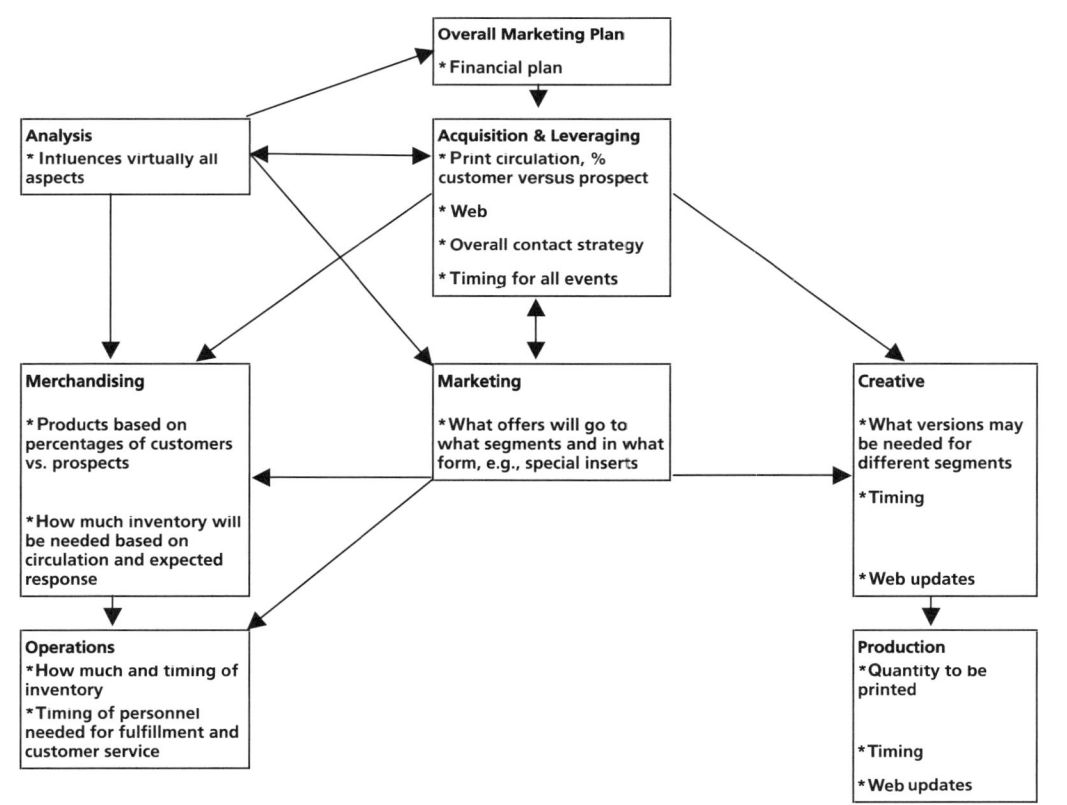

For a catalog marketer to optimize customer acquisition and leveraging, you need three major tools:

1. Input into and a firm understanding of a real circulation and contact strategy that addresses both new customer acquisition and leveraging of the existing customer.

2. Truly informative analytical reports that allow you to understand the effectiveness of past strategies for both new customer acquisition and leveraging of the existing customer.

3. An ongoing, yearly customer acquisition strategy that includes methods other than list rental.

Customer Acquisition

List Rental

For the greatest part of cataloging history, the major method of acquiring new customers has been through the rental of other catalogers' lists of customer names. This process has been handled quite simply: The cataloger, via a list manager, makes their catalog customer names available for an agreed-upon rental fee, plus an agreement about the number of times the list can be used, and time frame in which the list can be used. Every list available for rental has a list card that details specifics about the list. List brokers specializing in catalog marketing work with a cataloger to select the right mix of lists per catalog mail date.

For a catalog marketer, list cards contain extremely useful information beyond info needed for renting the list.

Exhibit 12.2 List Rental Card Checklist of Terms and Their Explanation

☐ Updated: How new is the information on the card? Should include "data verified" date that indicates the recency of the information.

☐ Selections with Counts: The quantity of names by segment, and last purchase, e. g., how many 0–6 month buyers, how many 7–12 month buyers, how many 0–6 month, who spend $50+ or $75+, and so on. Many lists also break out by type of product purchased, e.g., jewelry, home decor, etc. Be aware of how recent selections are. This area also states rental cost per thousand and minimum rental quantity.

Beyond telling you how many names you can rent by segment, *Selections with Counts* can help you understand the growth of the business, as businesses that do not have increasing counts can indicate a company that has reached a plateau or is failing to invest in the segmentation and upkeep of the file.

- ☐ Average Order: The average purchase amount. To get a very basic idea of what a company's yearly sales are, take the average order multiplied by the number of buyers over one year. This formula assumes that buyers only buy once a year, which is not often the case. But the formula does allow you to understand the minimum sales of companies that are not public and whose sales figures are unavailable.

- ☐ Other Selections: Indicates costs/per 1,000 for areas such as key coding, gender, geographic, average order, etc.

- ☐ Summary Description: Top line demographic of the audience and the catalog, such as gender and the average unit of sale offered in the catalog.

- ☐ Data Card Description: More detailed description and demographics of the customers of this particular catalog. Important information for marketers about the makeup of both competing and non-competing catalogs.

- ☐ List source: How the list came to be direct mail, print advertising, Internet and the percentage contribution of each medium as a source for the list.

- ☐ Method of addressing: The form in which the names will be provided to the service bureau. Some examples are mag tape, diskettes, and electronic transfer.

- ☐ Maintenance: How often the list is updated.

Other than individually renting catalog lists, there are also co-op databases. Co-op databases typically merge all members' names into a large database. Members' names are modeled to determine which names from other catalog members should be pulled for your rental. These models can be based on your catalog's house file demographics, purchase behavior, product affinity, and channel of purchase. The model output will give names similar to your catalog's buyers and, based on the model, appear to be most likely to buy from your catalog.

In addition, there are lifestyle databases. These databases typically divide into groups that are named to describe them in a definitive way. Again, these are specific to the database, but examples are:

- Affluents.
- City Centers.
- Elite Suburbs.
- Inner Suburbs.
- Landed Gentry.
- Middle America.
- Rustic Living.

Lifestyle databases are most often used to aggregate consumer preferences and psychographic similarities that go beyond basic demographic information. For instance, while it is useful to know "How many homeowners are in a City or SCF (Sectional Center Facility) or zip code," it can be even more useful to know *how* they live.

Circulation Plan

Using rented lists, most often from other catalogers and the co-op databases, a catalog puts together a *Circulation Plan*, usually in conjunction with their list broker, which details, by year, every mailing by lists used, quantities, and expected returns.

Exhibit 12.3 Circulation Plan Form

Drop 1 - In-Home Date
Drop 1 - In-Mail Date

HOUSE FILE	SEGMENTS	Gross Circulation	Net Circulation	Expected Response Rate	Expected Average Order	Expected Demand, Net Circulation	Expected $/Book	Demand	Orders Prior to Degradation	Expected Degradation in Response Rate if Remailed	Demand Less Expected Degradation if Remailed
Internet and Catalog	Total buyers (entire list)										
Catalog	Total buyers										
	0-6 month										
	7-12 month										
	13-24 month										
	24+ months										
Internet	Total buyers										
	0-6 month										
	7-12 month										
	13-24 month										
	24+ months										
Gift Recipients	Total										
	0-6 month										
	7-12 month										
	13-24 month										
	24+ months										
Requestors	Total										
	0-6 month										
	7-12 month										
	13-24 month										
	24+ months										
SUB-TOTAL HOUSE											

Exhibit 12.3 Circulation Plan Form (continued)

RENTALS											
Co-op Databases (include test of segment per database) SEGMENTS	Gross Circulation	Net Circulation	Expected Response Rate	Expected Average Order	Expected Demand, Net Circulation	Expected $/Book	Demand	Orders Prior to Degradation	Expected Degradation in Response Rate if Remailed	Demand Less Expected Degradation if Remailed
ABC Database										
Best Ever Database										
One and Only Database										
Smarter Than Ever Database										
You Can't Beat This Database										

SUB-TOTAL DATABASE MODELS

Rental List Breakout	SELECTS										
Ms. Smith	0-6 month										
Who knows	0-6 months, $75+										
Neverland	0-6 months, $75+										
Neverland	7-12 months, $75+										
Peter Pan II	0-6 months, $75+										
JuneBug	0-6 months, $75+										

TOTALS FOR RENTAL TESTS

Rental List Continuations	SELECTS										
Marilyn's Closet	12 month $100+										
Little BoBeep	12 month Children's Mdse $100+ (est.qty.)										
Make Believe	7-12 month $50+										
Nanny's Favorite	12 month Holiday Mdse										
Cartoons Galore	6 month Female $100+										
Back to Wonderland	0-6 month $100+										

TOTAL RENTAL CONTINUATIONS

TOTALS FOR DROP 1

Exhibit 12.4 Circulation Plan Explanation

- ⇨ Create a plan for every drop/date that the catalog is mailed; Exhibit 12.3 shows one drop only.
- ⇨ Indicate both the in-home date (when the catalog arrives at the consumer or business) and the date that the catalog goes in the mail; work with your printer to help determine how to create a schedule that allows for your desired in-home dates (Exhibits 12.5 and 12.6).
- ⇨ Break out all segments of all list types to be mailed.
    - Some segments will be mailed more than one time.
        - —These segments would be those that have proven profitability in the past or appear likely to be high achievers.
    - Some tests will be repeated at different drop times.
        - —This helps assure that a poor- or well-performing list is not overlooked because it does better or worse in a particular time period.
- ⇨ Indicate the circulation per segment pre- and post-merge/purge as dollars generated per segment will change substantially when multi-buyers and duplicates are eliminated.
    - Merge/purge net numbers will be estimates at this stage; as real numbers are known, the circulation plan will be adapted.
    - The circulation manager will work with the service bureau handling the lists to determine merge/purge specifics such as what segments should have priority over others in the identification and coded retention of multi-buyers.
- ⇨ Determine the expected:
    - Response rate.
    - Average order.
    - Demand. (This is the dollar amount generated whether orders are actually fulfilled or not; it is important to know how many orders were received prior to back orders and other problems in order to know the effectiveness of each list segment.)

- $/Book factors out the variations in response rate and average order size, producing a common factor—*Sales per Catalog Mailed*. Response rate data alone is not sufficient, and average order size alone is not the complete sales picture. Further, this allows marketers to see how well the list did without the potential distortion of a higher circulation.

⇨ Degradation is shown as some lists may be mailed more than once in a time period; each time the list is mailed again, there is almost always some degradation in response.

Exhibit 12.5 Circulation Plan Example

Drop 1 - In-Home Date Drop 1 - In-Mail Date	SEGMENTS	Gross Circulation	Net Circulation	Expected Response Rate	Expected Average Order	Expected Demand, Net Circulation	Expected $/Book	Orders Prior to Degradation	Expected Degradation in Response Rate if Remailed	Demand Less Expected Degradation if Remailed
HOUSE FILE										
Internet and Catalog	Total buyers (entire list)									
Catalog	Total buyers	19,500	19,500							
	0-6 month	3,500	3,500	4.0%	$150	$21,000	$6.00	140	2.8%	$14,700
	7-12 month	8,000	8,000	4.0%	$150	$48,000	$6.00	320	2.8%	$33,600
	13-24 month	3,000	3,000	3.0%	$140	$12,600	$4.20	90	2.1%	$8,820
	24+ months	5,000	5,000	2.0%	$130	$13,000	$2.60	100	1.4%	$9,100
Internet	Total buyers	7,300	7,050							
	0-6 month	2,500	2,250	3.0%	$130	$9,750	$4.33	68	2.1%	$6,825
	7-12 month	3,500	3,500	2.5%	$130	$11,375	$3.25	88	1.8%	$7,963
	13-24 month	1,300	1,300	1.0%	$120	$1,560	$1.20	13	0.7%	$1,092
	24+ months	0	0							
Gift Recipients	Total	3,900	3,700							
	0-6 month	700	500	2.0%	$100	$1,400	$2.80	10	1.4%	$980
	7-12 month	1,600	1,600	2.0%	$100	$3,200	$2.00	32	1.4%	$2,240
	13-24 month	600	600	1.5%	$90	$810	$1.35	9	1.1%	$567
	24+ months	1,000	1,000	1.0%	$90	$900	$0.90	10	0.7%	$630
Requestors	Total	7,000	7,000							
	0-6 month	2,000	2,000	2.0%	$130	$5,200	$2.60	40	1.4%	$3,640
	7-12 month	5,000	5,000	1.5%	$130	$9,750	$1.95	75	1.1%	$6,825
	13-24 month	0	0							
	24+ months	0	0							
SUB-TOTAL HOUSE		37,700	37,250							

(M/P Priority 1)

Exhibit 12.5 Circulation Plan Example (continued)

RENTALS Co-op Databases (include test of segment per database)	SEGMENTS	Gross Circulation	Net Circulation	Expected Response Rate	Expected Average Order	Expected Demand, Net Circulation	Expected $/Book	Orders Prior to Degradation	Expected Degradation in Response Rate if Remailed	Demand Less Expected Degradation if Remailed
ABC Database		25,000	22,500	3.00%	$120	$90,000	$4.00	675	2.1%	$63,000
Best Ever Database		25,000	22,500	3.00%	$120	$90,000	$4.00	675	2.1%	$63,000
One and Only Database		25,000	22,500	3.00%	$120	$90,000	$4.00	675	2.1%	$63,000
Smarter Than Ever Database		25,000	22,500	3.00%	$120	$90,000	$4.00	675	2.1%	$63,000
You Can't Beat This Database		#####	22,500	3.00%	$120	$90,000	$4.00	675	2.1%	$63,000
SUB-TOTAL DATABASE MODELS		125,000	112,500							
(M/P Priority 3)										
Rental List Breakout	**SELECTS**									
Ms. Smith	0-6 month	10,000	9,500	1.5%	$110	$16,500	$1.74	143	1.1%	$11,550
Who knows	0-6 months, $75+	10,000	9,500	1.5%	$110	$16,500	$1.74	143	1.1%	$11,550
Neverland	0-6 months, $75+	10,000	9,500	1.5%	$110	$16,500	$1.74	143	1.1%	$11,550
Neverland	7-12 months, $75+	10,000	9,500	1.5%	$110	$16,500	$1.74	143	1.1%	$11,550
Peter Pan II	0-6 months, $75+	10,000	9,500	1.5%	$110	$16,500	$1.74	143	1.1%	$11,550
JuneBug	0-6 months, $75+	10,000	9,500	1.5%	$110	$16,500	$1.74	143	1.1%	$11,550
TOTALS FOR RENTAL TESTS		60,000	57,000							
Rental List Continuations	**SELECTS**									
Marilyn's Closet	12 month $100+	15,000	14,250	1.75%	$125.00	$32,813		249	1.2%	$22,969
Little BoBeep	12 month Children's Mdse $100+ (est.qty.)	15,000	14,250	1.75%	$125.00	$32,813	$2.30	249	1.2%	$22,969
Make Believe	7-12 month $50+	15,000	14,250	1.75%	$125.00	$32,813	$2.30	249	1.2%	$22,969
Nanny's Favorite	12 month Holiday Mdse	15,000	14,250	1.75%	$125.00	$32,813	$2.30	249	1.2%	$22,969
Cartoons Galore	6 month Female $100+	15,000	14,250	1.75%	$125.00	$32,813	$2.30	249	1.2%	$22,969
Back to Wonderland	0-6 month $100+	15,000	14,250	1.75%	$125.00	$32,813	$2.30	249	1.2%	$22,969
TOTAL RENTAL CONTINUATIONS		90,000	85,500							
(M/P priority 2)										
TOTALS FOR DROP 1		312,700	292,250			$884,420	$3.03			$619,094

Exhibit 12.6 Circulation Plan Summary Form

Drop Number	In-Mail Date	In-Home Date	Gross Circulation	Net Circulation	Demand	$/Catalog	Demand after Degradation Due to Remails	$/Catalog after Degradation Due to Remails

Exhibit 12.7 Circulation Plan Summary Example

Drop Number	In-Mail Date	In-Home Date	Gross Circulation	Net Circulation	Demand	$/Catalog	Demand after Degradation Due to Remails	$/Catalog after Degradation Due to Remails
1	12/26 to 12/29	1/2 to 1/4	312,700	292,750	$884,420	$3.03		
2	2/26 to 2/27	3/1 to 3/3	312,700	292,750			$619,094.0	$2.12
3	5/4 to 5/6	5/13 to 5/16	750,000	637,500	$1,593,750	$2.50		
4	8/26 to 8/28	9/5 to 9/8	750,000	600,000			$1,200,000	$2.00
5	10/1 to 10/4	10/6 to 10/9	750,000	600,000	$1,200,000	$2.00		
6	11/15 to 11/18	11/22 to 11/25	1,000,000	750,000	$2,550,000	$3.40		

Drops 2 and 4 are re-mails so show degradation

The Circulation Plan Summary basically summarizes all the data from the main circulation plan. Note that drops two and four are re-mails, meaning that the catalog is sent at two different times. Re-mails, while very cost efficient because the creative, production and lists costs are amortized over both the initial mailings and the re-mails, will almost always have decreased demand due to the fact that the recipient has seen the catalog before. Still, even with a lower response rate, the fact that the remail basically has only postage cost, means that a re-mail often nets more than the mailing that preceded it.

Exhibit 12.8 Reverse Timeline Form (Estee Marketing Group, Inc.)

This is the form that Estee Marketing Group, Inc. provides to its clients in order for the clients to have one concise document that outlines the critical quantities and dates per list and activity.

(date) (catalog company name)	Drop 1 "A"	Drop 2 "B"	Drop 3 "C"	Drop 4 "D"	Drop 5 "E"	Drop 6 "F"
Mailing Date(s):	(first date)	(second date)	(third date)	(foruth date)	(fifth date)	(sixth date)
NET TO BE MAILED						
BUYERS						
NON-BUYERS						
SPECIAL INTERNALS:						
M/B Quantities Pending Results Merge #1:						
EXTERNAL DATABASE ALLIANCE MODELS:						
RENTALS/EXCHANGES						

MAILING DATE	(first date)	(second date)	(third date)	(foruth date)	(fifth date)	(sixth date)
MERGE AT PRINTER						
ALL TAPES DUE AT MERGE						
ORDER LISTS						
FINAL LIST-OF-LISTS						
UPDATED FILE TO MODEL COS.						
CUT FILE						
CIRC PLAN FINAL						
CIRC PLAN OUTLINE	(date)	(date)	(date)	(date)	(date)	(date)

contact info at lifestyle database	contact info at other list supplier
contact info at service bureau	contact info at other list supplier or service bureau

Exhibit 12.9 Reverse Timeline Example (Estee Marketing Group, Inc.)

3-Aug-05 ABC Catalog Company	Drop 1 "A"	Drop 2 "B"	Drop 3 "C"	Drop 4 "D"	Drop 5 "E"	Drop 6 "F"
Mailing Date(s):	**27-Dec-05**	**27-Mar-06**	**30-May-06**	**20-Aug-06**	**1-Oct-06**	**5-Nov-06**
NET TO BE MAILED	**489,923**	**419,866**	**298,041**	**597,506**	**336,250**	**580,890**
BUYERS	194,915	55,421	175,324	168,123	113,621	206,444
NON-BUYERS	32,447	15,272	11,772	9,609	11,884	34,108
SPECIAL INTERNALS	69,839	-	-	87,416	-	67,890
MULTI-BUYERS	26,075	-	23,123	-	24,839	-
CO-OP DATABASE NAMES	91,824	184,897	87,822	239,818	150,920	272,448
RENTALS/EXCHANGES	74,823	164,276	-	92,540	34,986	-

MAILING DATE	27-Dec-05	27-Mar-06	30-May-06	20-Aug-06	01-Oct-06	05-Nov-06
MERGE AT PRINTER	17-Dec-05	20-Feb-06	13-May-06	31-Jul-06	16-Sep-06	21-Oct-06
ALL TAPES DUE AT MERGE	**06-Dec-05**	**10-Feb-06**	n/a	**21-Jul-06**	**08-Sep-06**	**13-Oct-06**
ORDER LISTS	26-Nov-05	01-Feb-06	n/a	14-Jul-06	01-Sep-06	02-Oct-06
FINAL LIST-OF-LISTS	26-Nov-05	01-Feb-06	n/a	14-Jul-06	01-Sep-06	02-Oct-06
UPDATED FILE TO ABACUS		22-Jan-06	n/a	03-Jul-06		03-Oct-06
CUT FILE	**23-Oct-05**	**22-Jan-06**	n/a	**20-Jun-06**	**03-Sep-06**	**30-Sep-06**
CIRC PLAN FINAL	26-Nov-05	28-Jan-06	n/a		08-Sep-06	01-Oct-06
CIRC PLAN OUTLINE	01-Nov-05	10-Jan-06	n/a		27-Jun-06	27-Jun-06

Pull Marketing

Some feel that catalogers have entered a time in which *Pull Marketing* will become more important than *Push Marketing*. Pull marketing is defined as techniques that make the customer come to you. Push marketing, simply explained, is pushing the customer to take action, such as sending catalogs to prospects. Due to the fact that list prospecting generally has not been responding as well as in the past, marketers have been more aggressively investigating methods of pull marketing.

As pull marketing requires that you make the customer come to you, it is essential that you understand what motivates a customer to choose a particular catalog over another one. See *Researching your Competition* (Chapter 4) for one smart way to get first-hand information. In addition, many database companies provide modeling techniques that create useful customer profiles that can help you better understand your customers' needs.

Exhibit 12.10 Pull Marketing, Checklist of Potential Avenues

- ☐ Web site, a growing opportunity.
    1. Search helps new customers find your site.
        a. Be totally up-to-date on how search engines determine rankings on unpaid searches then make your entire site as friendly as possible to search engine spiders.
        b. Be prepared to pay for searches in order to get top listings.
            (1) Generally works best with focused merchandising.
        c. Track your results and know which methods of search provide the highest repeat income.
        d. Make your product and information search on your web site totally complete, including words that may be misspelled and helpful references (Example "Did you mean (word)?").
    2. See Chapter 11, Exhibit 11.38, Internet Catalog Critique Form.

- ☐ Extranet Sites, basically an extension of a company's private Intranet. network. These can be shared, when authorized, with outside resources; some business-to-business catalogers have very successfully

created company-specific extranets for the sale of the catalogs' customized product line to the companies with such Intranet networks. Some pointers for success:
1. Be clear on the purpose of the site.
2. Understand your audience's needs in this environment.
3. Be willing to make the time and personnel commitment, including, if needed, any in-depth training necessary to make the site effective.
4. Make a commitment to heavy content and frequent updates.
5. Test and measure the ROI.
6. As this is a partnership, see Alliances in this checklist for other valuable considerations.

☐ Viral Marketing, a kind of an electronic endorsement, can also be called "word of mouth." This acquisition method relies on the old saying "I told two friends, they told two friends, etc." Viral marketing has become a greater tool due to users sending messages from person to person via the Internet.) Some pointers:
1. Give something away (meaningful incentives, games, sweepstakes opportunity, coupons, sneak previews, etc.).
   a. Do it legally.
   b. Plan ahead so you don't overextend and become unable to deliver the catalog and/or the freebie.
2. Be outrageous or terribly clever, cool, or fun enough so that readers want to pass the info on.
   a. Humor and controversy are hard to pull off, but if you do, they work like wildfire.
3. Make it easy for the reader to pass the message on and encourage them to forward to friends.
4. Use some of your other partnerships, such as tie-ins, affiliates, and alliances, to also promote your viral marketing.
5. Track and evaluate results.
6. Have a back-up plan in case it gets out of hand or goes wrong in some way.

☐ Tie-ins use specific PR stories or other such highly noticeable approaches to help define the business and attract consumers who previously may not have considered this catalog; examples are:
1. Cause-related, such as the environment.
2. Health-related, such as Breast Cancer tie-in.

3. Ethnic-related, such as Black History Month.
4. Trade organizations related to your target market.

See Alliances for some considerations prior to tying-in with another company.

☐ Affiliates are most often part of another company's Internet site; they can provide an implied endorsement and, often, access to a new market. Questions to ask before moving into a potential relationship:
1. Is the site relevant and image correct?
2. Is there an easy-to-use interface?
3. How reliable is the support?
4. Are there easy-to-use links?
5. How complete is the reporting?
6. Is the potential affiliate trustworthy with good references?
7. Can you effectively police the relationship?

☐ Alliances are a close association of two or more companies to advance common interests or causes. Questions to ask in this case are:
1. Does the partner in the alliance have a complementary but not competitive product?
2. Does the target audience fit with your growth strategy?
3. Does this opportunity provide high potential for expansion into a new market?
4. Is the new market large enough to contribute a sufficient audience?
5. Is the partner small enough to give sufficient attention to the project and large enough to be economically stable?
6. Does the potential partner have a similar business philosophy and ethics?
7. Is this the appropriate image for our catalog?
8. Is the partner willing to share responsibilities and costs?
9. Is there a complementary report structure?
10. Is there a clear-cut understanding of who owns names generated from this venture?
11. What is our data-sharing comfort level?
12. Do both parties have a clear understanding, preferably in writing, of what is considered "success"?

☐ Endorsements are very powerful, as they can help attract those who would not have discovered your catalog without an endorsement and they can enhance brand recall. There are three basic kinds:
1. Customer—Those customers who write to tell you how wonderful your catalog is.
2. Authority—Most often membership organizations.
3. Celebrity—Match carefully and be certain they have credibility with your market.

All endorsements have legal considerations. Check with the FTC (Federal Trade Commission) and the BBB (Better Business Bureau) for laws and guidelines. Both can be found on the Internet.

☐ PR—See separate section, which follows.

Public Relations

All of the acquisition methods outlined in Exhibit 12.10 work best if teamed with public relations (PR). Historian and author Daniel J. Boorstin says, "Some are born great, some achieve greatness, and some hire PR officers." With the Internet, getting PR for your catalog is harder and easier than ever before: harder because there is more competition, easier because there are more avenues and methods of approaching those opportunities.

For starters, have a game plan. PR has to be a fully realized, coordinated effort to have a meaningful effect.

And don't forget to have a section of your web site devoted to PR. Here, those looking for news and current info about your catalog can get quick access. This info needn't be in a key sales position; one alternate possibility is to include it in the same area as, or as part of, "About Us."

Exhibit 12.11 PR Game Plan

TO DO LIST

- ☐ Make sure the goals and objectives of your press releases are the same as those of your parent company and are consistent with your image overall.

- ☐ As one shots are unproductive, create a plan for the entire year that optimizes tie-ins with events, introductions, occasions, and so on.

- ☐ Create a list of the publications that you believe are right for your market:
  a. Keep it up-to-date.
  b. Read the publications so that you know what kinds of stories and writing style they are looking for.
  c. If you offer an exclusive story to one publication, honor that commitment.

- ☐ Keep your release to one page, usually no more than 400 words.

- ☐ Don't overreach; understand how well the respondents convert to buyers and to long-term customers before creating a program that has extremely high exposure.

- ☐ Keep abreast of what your competition is doing:
  a. Do your own searching or look into hiring a clipping service.

- ☐ Create your own releases (Exhibit 12.12) or use the online forms available at publications' web sites (Exhibit 12.13).

- ☐ Follow up any communication with a phone call within a week if by mail, within a day or two if by Internet.

Exhibit 12.12 Printed Press Release Outline

- ⇨ Can be mailed or sent by e-mail.
- ⇨ Complete contact info at the top of the release; it should include:
  - Contact Name.
  - Name of Organization or Company.
  - Phone Number.
  - Fax Number.
  - E-mail Address.
  - Web page URL.
- ⇨ Headline that summarizes and sells.
- ⇨ Dateline—who, what, why, time, and place.
- ⇨ A few "sell paragraphs" (see Exhibit 12.14).
- ⇨ Background information.
- ⇨ Boilerplate about the company.

Exhibit 12.13 Online Press Release Outline

An online press release will often be the type where it provides directions on how to complete the required spaces. Below are examples of the data entry fields; be prepared before you start filling out the form.

- ⇨ Contact Name.
- ⇨ Name of Organization or Company.
- ⇨ Phone Number.
- ⇨ Fax Number.
- ⇨ E-mail Address.
- ⇨ Web page URL.
- ⇨ Department (select the desired one from the list that may be provided).

⇨ Preferred publication date.

⇨ Subject of Press Release.

⇨ Event (if applicable, include who, what, why, time, and place).

⇨ Press Release.

⇨ Additional Comments.

Exhibit 12.14 Press Release Copy Checklist

☐ As with catalog copy, start with the most exciting information first:

___ Sell benefits, not features.

☐ Don't oversell, but don't be dry either.

☐ Keep to the point.

☐ Make sure all your facts are accurate.

☐ Rewrite and cut until it succinctly sizzles . . . and sounds perfect for the publication it is going to.

___ Is it really newsworthy?

___ Does it have the potential of leading to more coverage?

Media Planning

Like PR, control your media plan both in terms of exposure and budget. Build a plan so that you test categories rather than individual publications. In other words, it would be wiser to test ads in several different media categories so you can get a reading of the print media universe for your product.

For example, if you are trying to reach adult women, you may want to test one ad in a shelter magazine, one in mass media such as FSIs (Free Standing Inserts, most often seen as part of the Sunday newspaper), and one in a woman's general interest publication, and so on. In order to establish the right creative approach to successfully sell your product through print advertising, some publications offer A/B tests.

A/B tests allow you to test two different versions of an ad in the same issue of the same magazine in order to determine which version generates the highest initial response and the most profitable long-term buyer. While there is often a hefty production charge attached to this test, it is usually worth paying in order to establish a control ad.

The wisest choice, if your budget allows it, is to work with a media consultant. These specialists can often save you money both in budget and in avoiding errors. If you wish to create your own plan, you first need an overview that answers reasons behind the plan and its overall direction. Exhibit 12.15 is beneficial whether you hire an expert or do the plan yourself. Exhibits 12.16 and 12.17 help you to organize and evaluate your plan.

Both for printed and Internet media, there are companies that offer online planning tools as well as software programs. These tools can assist in determining the online mix, managing multiple campaigns, and capturing as well as measuring results. You or your Circulation Manager can find them at industry conferences, recommendations, or through web site searches.

There are, of course, many other forms of pull media such as billboards and TV advertisements. However, print and the Internet are the two most common forms of pull media for acquisition. The *Media Plan Overview Checklist* would apply to virtually all forms of media.

Exhibit 12.15 Media Plan Overview Checklist

- ☐ Major objective of campaign—Are you looking for direct sales, image building, hits to the web site, conversions, etc.? If there is more than one objective, rank in order of importance.

- ☐ Target audience—Key demographics and psychographics.

- ☐ Success criteria—Is there an overall financial goal? Immediate sales? Internet activity? Purchasing behavior change? What? If more than one, rank in order of importance.

- ☐ Research—Will any kind of research be utilized pre- and post-campaign to determine purchasing behavior changes due to the campaign?

- ☐ Campaign—What is the main message of the advertising? Budget by time frame and medium. How much are you willing to spend, where, when?

- ☐ Schedule—What is the schedule that will be needed to accomplish this aspect of our plan?

Exhibit 12.16 Printed Media Plan Form

Target Market(s) _____

Description of Market(s) _____
_____
_____
_____

Rationale for Market Selection _____
_____
_____
_____

Time Frame and Overall Budget for this Market: Time Frame _____ Budget _____

Summary Description of Campaign _____
_____
_____

DATE ON COVER _____

Publication Name	Rationale for Publication	Date on Stands	Circulation	Net Cost (mail order rates when available)	Net CPM (cost per thousand)	Ad size and color
TOTALS						

DATE ON COVER _____

Publication Name	Rationale for Publication	Date on Stands	Circulation	Net Cost (mail order rates when available)	Net CPM (cost per thousand)	Ad size and color
TOTALS						

DATE ON COVER _____

Publication Name	Rationale for Publication	Date on Stands	Circulation	Net Cost (mail order rates when available)	Net CPM (cost per thousand)	Ad size and color
TOTALS						
GRAND TOTALS						

This form is used for planning and budgeting; it could easily be adapted to a production form by adding a column for date art is due. In addition, for some media plans, the issue editorial, such as Cosmetic Make-Over Issue, might be a consideration in what months the ads ran.

Exhibit 12.17 Printed Media Plan Example

Target Market(s): Fashion-attuned female, 18–35

Description of Market(s): Two major type fashion magazine, the traditional that editorializes fashion and the new form that shows fashion and a listing of exactly where it can be found; the latter version also often does product comparisons. One health-oriented magazine

Rationale for Market Selection: Test two different types of publications both in the fashion-conscious area; test health category, especially based on tie-in with Support the Cure and skin care products promoted in the ad. In addition, all publications are with one publisher and will attempt to negotiate lower rates

Time Frame and Overall Budget for this Market: Time Frame: Aug, Sept, Oct   Budget: $250,000

Summary Description of Campaign: Tie-in our association with Support the Cure, especially in October (Breast Cancer Month), web traffic generator, purchase of 5 skin care products (shown in the ad) on web or by toll-free number gives portion to Support the Cure

DATE ON COVER   August

Publication Name	Rationale for Publication	Date on Stands	Circulation	Net Cost (mail order rates when available)	Net CPM (cost per thousand)	Ad size and color
Lucky, Inc.	Target market, hot shopping magazine	7/12	970,652	$22,353/per insertion for 3 insertions	$23.03	1/3 vertical 2 color
Self	Dedicated to total well-being, incorporating health and beauty, fitness and nutrition	7/26	1,300,000	$38,245 per insertion	$29.42	1/3 vertical 2 color
Allure	Called The Beauty Expert, guides consumer in beauty selections	7/26	1,031,407	$21,654 per insertion for 3 insertions	$20.99	1/3 vertical 2 color
TOTALS			3,302,059	$82,252	$24.92	

Publication Name	Rationale for Publication	Date on Stands	Circulation	Net Cost (mail order rates when available)	Net CPM (cost per thousand)	Ad size and color
Lucky, Inc.	Target market, hot shopping magazine	8/9	970,652	$22,353/per insertion for 3 insertions	$23.03	1/3 vertical 2 color
Allure	Called The Beauty Expert, guides consumer in beauty selections	8/23	1,031,407	$21,654 per insertion for 3 insertions	$20.99	1/3 vertical 2 color
Vogue	Long-term fashion icon, high circ, decent cost per M	8/24	1,275,359	$34,455 for one insertion	$27.02	1/3 vertical, 2 color
TOTALS			3,277,418	$78,452	$23.94	

DATE ON COVER September

Publication Name	Rationale for Publication	Date on Stands	Circulation	Net Cost (mail order rates when available)	Net CPM (cost per thousand)	Ad size and color
Lucky, Inc.	Target market, hot shopping magazine	9/13	970,652	$22,353/per insertion, for 3 insertions	$23.03	1/3 vertical 2 color
Self	Dedicated to total well-being, incorporating health and beauty, fitness and nutrition	9/27	1,300,000	$38,245 per insertion	$29.42	1/3 vertical 2 color
Allure	Called The Beauty Expert, guides consumer in beauty selections	9/27	1,031,407	$21,654 per insertion for 3 insertions	$20.99	1/3 vertical 2 color
TOTALS			3,302,059	$82,252	$24.92	
GRAND TOTALS			9,881,536	$242,966	$24.59	

DATE ON COVER October

There are more variables to consider when creating a marketing plan for the web. Rimm-Kaufman, a web marketing firm, has provided an evaluation checklist (Exhibit 12.18), an evaluation explanation (Exhibit 12.19) and an example (Exhibit 12.20) of how their company puts a plan together.

Exhibit 12.18 Internet Marketing Deal Evaluation Checklist

- ☐ Deal Lead.
- ☐ Venue Name.
- ☐ Recommendation & Next Steps.
- ☐ Description of Test.
- ☐ Previous/Related Tests with Ad Provider or Similar Provider.
- ☐ Deal & Payment Structure.
- ☐ Deal Economics: Revenue and Cost Expectations.
- ☐ Success Metrics & Time Period.
- ☐ Merchandising Angle, Needs & Lead.
- ☐ Creative Angle, Needs & Lead.
- ☐ Strategic Considerations.
- ☐ Customer Service Issues.
- ☐ Vendor Relations Issues.
- ☐ Competitive Considerations.
- ☐ Tracking: How, When.
- ☐ Whose Cart, Who Is Merchant-of-Record, Who Bills CC (credit card)?
- ☐ Delayed Sales, Frauds, Cancels, No Cookies, Call-ins.
- ☐ Downside Marketing Risk: Worst Case & Response.
- ☐ Upside Marketing Potential: Scalability & Rollout.
- ☐ Contract & Legal: Downside Legal Risk, Worse Case & Response.
- ☐ Marketing Needs and Marketing Lead.
- ☐ IT Needs and IT Lead.
- ☐ Culture: Corporate Appropriateness.
- ☐ Culture: Venue Credibility & Venue Relations.

Source: Alan Rimm-Kaufmann, principal of the web consulting firm The Rimm-Kaufman Group

Exhibit 12.19 Internet Marketing Deal Evaluation Explanation

Deal Lead
The "owner" of the deal, typically a marketing person, who serves as internal deal "production cop" and primary external liaison.

Venue Name
Self-explanatory.

Recommendation & Next Steps
It is helpful to start with the conclusion: should the retailer sign this deal, and if so, under what circumstances?

Description of Test
A brief summary of how the proposed advertising works.

Previous/Related Tests with Ad Provider or Similar Provider
Self-explanatory.

Deal & Payment Structure
Web advertising deals involve a variety of payment forms: fixed-cost, CPM (cost per thousand impressions), CPC (cost per click), CPA (cost per action), CPO (cost per order), rev-share (revenue sharing), or a hybrid of these.

It's essential the retailer understand the tracking on which these fees are based. Whose click counts are taken as authoritative to determine CPC costs? How are discrepancies handled? For CPO and rev-share deals, how are orders counted? Are immediate web frauds included? Subsequent credit card declines? Later returns? What about orders into the call center?

Deal Economics: Revenue and Cost Expectations
The details of what we can expect to make and spend.

Success Metrics & Time Period
Smart retailers define what constitutes "success" in advance. This helps evaluating deals as they progress, and ensures clear internal communication as to what the deal is expected to produce.

It is often helpful to define at least two success metrics: one related to volume (typically, a minimum sales threshold), and one related to efficiency (typically, a cost-per-order measure, or an advertising-to-sales-ratio measure).

Merchandising Angle, Needs, & Lead

Your Merchandising Team should be involved in every web deal from its beginning, keeping an eye on pricing, margin, presentation, and selection issues.

Each deal should have a dedicated Merchandising Lead, an individual who "owns" the deal from the merchandising perspective.

Creative Angle, Needs, & Lead

Each deal should have a dedicated Creative Lead, an individual who "owns" the deal from the creative perspective.

Web creative can include advertising banners in various shapes and sizes, ad text copy, etc., and dedicated landing pages (where the customer arrives within the site).

Strategic Considerations

Retailers sometimes need to do a deal for strategic reasons, even if the economics are uncertain or poor. In such cases, it is helpful to document in advance why the deal should nonetheless go forward, and what the retailer hopes to achieve.

Customer Service Issues

Smart web retailers evaluate every deal from the customer perspective.

Will the advertising or ordering process confuse new customers, or alienate existing customers? Does the deal involve awkward site mechanics or awkward cart mechanics? Does the deal place undue work on the customer, or place the customer in a confusing situation?

Vendor Relations Issues

Some retailers have contractual relationships with their vendors that might prohibit certain kinds of advertising.

Typical concerns could include auctions (which could generate sales below suggested retail price) and use of vendor's trademarks, images, and intellectual property in online advertising.

Competitive Considerations

Does this web deal put the retailer at an advantage or disadvantage relative to their competitors?

Tracking: How, When

Web tracking is a complex and subtle issue.

Retailer should consider the following questions: Does the tracking involve changes to the retailer site? To the retailer's session logic? Does the tracking involve cookies? (A cookie is a small file placed by a web server on a visitor's computer. It can contain just about anything; commonly, a cookie contains a long random tracking string, used so the server can recognize the same visitor across a session and across visits.)

If so, are they site cookies or "third-party" cookies? (A third-party cookie is when a site "A" shows an image or makes a call to site "B," and site "B" uses that opportunity to place a cookie on the user's machine, even though the user is still on site "A"). Many browsers permit users to refuse third-party cookies, making third-party cookies less effective for tracking. Are the cookies persistent, and for what duration? How will the tracking handle visitors who do not accept cookies, or who purge cookies, or who use cookie-removing software? If the tracking involves source codes in the URLs, can every page on the retailer's site handle these inbound parameters? Does the tracking involve JavaScript, and how will the tracking respond to users who have turned off this technology? What if a visitor e-mails a tracking link to a friend—will this confuse the tracking; will this release a private offer onto the full Internet, thus allowing anyone who acquires the e-mail to use the offer, even if the retailer intended the offer or coupon or discount or merchandise credit to be private and used only by the intended original recipient? Can the tracking be hacked or cracked by customers or competitors?

Whose Cart, Who is Merchant-Of-Record, Who Bills CC (Credit Card)
Some web deals involve the retailer taking the sale elsewhere, through a partner's shopping cart. If not handled well, this can lead to customer service issues. If the partner bills the customer's credit card, the retailer will not be able to handle and issue returns directly. Regardless of whose cart takes the order, and regardless of which entity bills the credit card, it essential to establish which entity is the merchant-of-record for legal purposes, such as sales tax collection.

Delayed Sales, Frauds, Cancels, No Cookies, Call-Ins
Regardless of the deal structure, the retailer needs a clear understanding of revenues attributed to the deal. While "sales" seems at first a straightforward concept, there are numerous subtleties: What about sales that come some time after the initial click? What about frauds and cancels? What about sales to visitors who do not accept cookies? And what about spillover sales into the call center?

Downside Marketing Risk: Worst Case & Response
It is helpful to assess the worst-case marketing scenario: what's the worst thing that could occur from a performance perspective? Often, this is the "zero sales" scenario. If this were to occur, what would be the implications for the deal, and how would the retailer respond?

Upside Marketing Potential: Scalability & Rollout
On the other hand, if the test is successful, to what extent can the retailer grow the deal? What is the potential for scaling?

Contract & Legal: Downside Legal Risk, Worst Case & Response
Good lawyers are often pessimists. As with any contract, look for potential pitfalls and traps. Web contracts often hinge on technical tracking issues; ensure terms such as "order," "click," and "visit" are clearly defined.

Marketing Needs and Marketing Lead
Each deal should have a dedicated Marketing Lead, an individual who "owns" the deal from the marketing perspective. Often, this is the same individual as the Deal Lead.

IT Needs and IT Lead
Most web deals involve some IT (Information technology) effort. And most web retailers report that web IT effort is their scarcest resource. Pay careful attention to the implementation time required from your IT team, as well as ongoing maintenance programming.

Culture: Corporate Appropriateness
Is the deal appropriate with the corporate culture? Concerns might include ad syndication to adult web sites, association with unsavory advertising technologies (adware, scumware, spyware); excessive promotion or discounting inconsistent with the retailer's brand, etc.

Culture: Venue Credibility & Venue Relations
Some advertising partners are a pleasure to work with: easy IT implementation, fair contract, reasonable negotiation and accommodation. Other advertising partners are more difficult. While not a deal-breaking criterion, the friendliness and ease of working with an online partner is a significant consideration.

Source: Alan Rimm-Kaufmann, principal of the web consulting firm The Rimm-Kaufman Group

Exhibit 12.20 Internet Marketing Deal Evaluation Example

Today's Date: Nov 26

Deal Lead: Tim G, Marketing Dept

Venue Name: WidgetBid.com

Recommendation & Next Steps:
Go forward with deal, if they'll provide a 30-day out (deal breaker). Negotiate for lower (zero) fixed monthly cost & lower rev-share to account for frauds and cancels.

Description of Test
WidgetBid.com is an eBay competitor that only sells widgets and widget accessories. They're advertising aggressively to generate traffic to their site among widget enthusiasts, both in the B2B (business-to-business) trades and in the B2C (business-to-consumer) popular press. While they only have a fraction of the traffic of larger auction sites, their focus makes them interesting to us.

They're actively looking for major widget retailers for their site, and so they approached us.

If we sign a 12-month deal, they'll offer us "gold" level placement (whatever that means—supposedly extra banners, highlighted listings in auction results, etc.) at "bronze" level pricing, and they'll waive the customary $15K integration fee as in this case it is hard for us to see that they have any real up-front integration costs to cover.

Previous/Related Tests with Ad Provider or Similar Provider
None—we've never worked with them before.

Deal & Payment Structure
Hybrid: $15k integration fee (waived), $2,500 per month base (ongoing), plus 15 percent rev-share.

Deal Economics: Revenue and Cost Expectations
They claim 100k widget visits per month, with 10 percent leading to an auction sale. At a $200 AOV (average order value), they're currently at $2 mil/month gross sales ($24 mil/year) & projecting growth. They're suggesting we'd sell something like $200k/month ($2.4 mil/year). Ad cost = $2,500/month + 15percent = $30k + $360k = $390k

Their expectations:
$2.4 mil / year sales.
390 k / year ad cost.
(16.25% cost/sales ratio).

Success Metrics & Time Period

Efficiency: as this is a customer acquisition play, we'll go to marginal breakeven.

So, "success" is:

(tracked net sales—COGs (cost of goods)—10 percent variable—ad expense)

The above formula must = above zero.

Scale: if the deal isn't at least $200k in Year One sales, not worth the bother.

It's a 12-month deal with no out. Negotiate a 30-day out (deal breaker if not). Deal must be successful in 90 days or exercise out and end deal at 120 days.

Merchandising Angle, Needs, & Lead

They want to run all our widget SKUs (no accessories), so no selection issues.

We'll need to establish and pass them "reserve prices" on every SKU—the price below which we won't sell.

Wendy B. from Merchandising will handle setting & monitoring reserve pricing.

Creative Angle, Needs, & Lead

They want thumbnail images, full images, and a 100-character copy block. We have these already going out to other advertising partners, so nothing special here. Tim G. of Marketing will handle.

Strategic Considerations

They're claiming all our competitors will be there and if we're not there we'll lose out; if we don't start with them early, we might not be able to get in later.

All claims highly dubious—they'd be happy for our ad spend at any point, we think.

Customer Service Issues

As the order completes on our site with our cart just like all of our other web orders, there are no issues here.

Vendor Relations Issues

As an authorized reseller, all of our vendors have approved us to auction their goods. No issues.

Competitive Considerations

See "Strategic Issues" above.
  No issues.

Tracking: How, When

As usual, inbound traffic to our site would carry our customer tracking tag.[1] As usual, this would tag resulting orders to the appropriate deal. Will report weekly sales from this deal from the standard weekly source-code report.

  Tim G to handle marketing economics calculations, and reporting out monthly.

Whose Cart, Who is Merchant-Of-Record, Who Bills CC

Our cart, we take the sale, we bill the credit card. No issues.

Delayed Sales, Frauds, Cancels, No Cookies, Call-Ins

As the deal is written, we pay them rev-share on all immediate sales, including frauds and cancels.

  Negotiate a rev-share reduction (say, from 15 percent to 12 percent) to address frauds, cancels, and returns.

  We don't pay rev-share on folks who come back and order later, or folks who order by phone. (Push the call center in any banner art!)

Downside Marketing Risk: Worst Case & Response

If we didn't get a 30 day out, was stuck in the deal for the full 12 months, and NOTHING sold: we'd be out $30k in ad expense, we'd have wasted a person-week in marketing and a person-week in IT; we'd have wasted legal review of contract.

Upside Marketing Potential: Scalability & Rollout

If test successful, could increase scale by adding widget accessory SKUs and possibly reducing reserve price to increase volume, if margins support it.

---

[1] A customer tracking tag links to a given product page, such as www.oursite/product/prodview?item=12345. In order to do this, a tag representing the test, in this case WBID (which would stand for WIDGETBID), would be attached to an "src=venue" tag which would then look like www.oursite/product/prodview?item=12345&src=WBID.

Contract & Legal: Downside Legal Risk, Worst Case & Response
Contract is reasonable, except for the following two concerns from Legal:
1. Negotiate 30-day out, without cause.
2. Make indemnification and non-disclosure clauses reciprocal.

Marketing Needs and Marketing Lead
Tim G

IT Needs and IT Lead
Ralph P

XML[2] data feed (their spec) of item names, URLs, thumbnails, full images, short copy, price, reserve price, ship cost.

Reporting handled by Marketing (Tim G) via weekly sales source report.

Culture: Corporate Appropriateness
No issues.

Culture: Venue Credibility & Venue Relations
They've been fair in the sales pitch, and reasonable in discussing Legal.
Ralph says their IT docs seem reasonable and well-thought out.
No red flags, no issues.

---

[2] XML stands for Extensible Markup Language—it is a verbose and precise data exchange readable by computers and humans.

Source: Alan Rimm-Kaufmann, principal of the web consulting firm The Rimm-Kaufmann Group.

Leveraging

Increasing the purchase behavior of your customer should be your number-one goal. It is almost always more cost efficient to motivate customers to more frequent and greater purchases than it is to acquire new customers. Think in a triad (catalog, Internet, and retail) form, allowing customers to purchase from you by any means available.

House List Hygiene

Before you can put together a strategy for leveraging your customers, you have to be certain that your house list is in tip-top shape. Your service bureau, working under the direction of the Circulation Manager, will be responsible for maintaining your list properly. Major areas that the service bureau will address are:

- Merge/Purge—The de-duplication of names on the lists in order to avoid duplicate catalogs going to one person.

- Address Updating and Standardizing—In order to get the highest delivery rate and best postal discounts. Inaccurately recorded street addresses that cannot be corrected will be deleted as "undeliverable." It is very important that your order entry staff fully appreciate the importance of accurate address keying.

Real Contact Strategy

A *Contact Strategy* is different from a *Circulation Plan* in that it is a written document that details every contact with customers and prospects planned for a particular time period, often one year. Circulation Plans are list and quantity specific. Contract Strategies are offer-specific.

A circulation plan is the first step in creating a contact strategy as it lists all the segments to which your catalog will be mailed. The purpose of a contact strategy is to show exactly how many times, and what offers, are going to a customer in a given time period, thus the document can be quite extensive. The examples shown in Exhibits 12.21 and 12.22 illustrate a two-month period; ideally the strategy would actually cover an entire year. Headings shown, such as *Catalog Offer* and *Internet Offer*, should, naturally be adapted to your particular needs.

Exhibit 12.21 Customer Contact Strategy Overview Form

HOUSE FILE	SEGMENTS	(time period)						(time period)				
		CATALOG & OFFER DATE	CATALOG OFFER	INTERNET DATE	INTERNET OFFER	OTHER DATE	OFFER OTHER THAN INTERNET & CATALOG	CATALOG & OFFER DATE	CATALOG OFFER	INTERNET DATE	INTERNET OFFER	OTHER DATE	OFFER OTHER THAN INTERNET & CATALOG
Catalog		VERSION, IN-HOME DATE						VERSION, IN-HOME DATE					
MULTI BUYERS	0-6 month												
	7-12 month												
	13-24 month												
	24+ months												
SINGLE BUYERS	0-6 month												
	7-12 month												
	13-24 month												
	24+ months												
Internet	0-6 month												
	7-12 month												
	13-24 month												
	24+ months												
Gift Recipients	0-6 month												
	7-12 month												
	13-24 month												
	24+ months												
Requestors	0-6 month												
	7-12 month												
	13-24 month												
	24+ months												

Exhibit 12.22 Customer Contact Strategy Overview Example

All offers have "order by" date

JANUARY, FEBRUARY / JANUARY / MARCH

HOUSE FILE	SEGMENTS	CATALOG & OFFER DATE (VERSION, IN-HOME DATE)	CATALOG OFFER	INTERNET DATE	INTERNET OFFER	OTHER DATE	OFFER OTHER THAN INTERNET & CATALOG	CATALOG & OFFER DATE (VERSION, IN-HOME DATE)	CATALOG OFFER	INTERNET DATE	INTERNET OFFER	OTHER DATE	OFFER OTHER THAN INTERNET & CATALOG
Catalog				**INTERNET**				**INTERNET**					
MULTI BUYERS	0-6 month	Spring Catalog, cover test, 1/2-1/4	announcement of birthday, special day registration	1/6 and 1/7	promote fall/holiday clearance savings for customers only on Internet	none	none	New Spring cover, repaginate one signature, 3/1-3/3	none	3/4-3/6	fashion alert	none	none
	7-12 month	Spring Catalog, sale insert, 1/2-1/4	reactivation sticker, 20% off, all	1/6 and 1/7	e-mail reactivation message, 20% off, to all names with e-mail addresses	none	none	New Spring cover, repaginate one signature, 3/1-3/3	reactivation sticker, 20% off, $50+ buyers only	3/4-3/6	reminder re 20% off	in-home 2/25	postcard premailing with 20% savings
	13-24 month	Spring Catalog, 1/2-1/4	reactivation sticker, 20% off, $75+ buyers only	1/6 and 1/7	e-mail reactivation message, 20% off, to all names with e-mail addresses	none	none	do not mail	none	3/4-3/6	offer free S&H if order online	none	none
	24+ months	Spring Catalog, 1/2-1/4	reactivation sticker, 20% off, $75+ buyers only	1/6 and 1/7	e-mail reactivation message, 20% off, to all names with e-mail addresses	none	postcard mailing promoting store sale	do not mail	none	3/4-3/6	none	none	none
SINGLE BUYERS	0-6 month	Spring Catalog, cover test	no offer	1/6 and 1/7	promote fall/holiday savings on Internet, reminder of limited time to buy	1/10-1/13	postcard mailing promoting store sale	New Spring cover, repaginate one signature, 3/1-3/3	free S&H on orders over $75	3/4-3/6	reminder free S&H on orders over $75	none	none
	7-12 month	Spring Catalog, sale insert, 1/2-1/4	reactivation sticker, 20% off, $50+ buyers only	1/6 and 1/7	e-mail reactivation message, 20% off, to all names with e-mail addresses	1/10-1/13	postcard mailing promoting store sale	New Spring cover, repaginate one signature, 3/1-3/3	free S&H on orders over $75	3/4-3/6	reminder free S&H on orders over $75	none	none
	13-24 month	Spring Catalog, 1/2-1/4	reactivation sticker, 20% off, $75+ buyers only	1/6 and 1/7	e-mail reactivation message, 20% off, to all names with e-mail addresses	none	none	do not mail	none	3/4-3/6	none	none	none
	24+ months	Spring Catalog, 1/2-1/4	reactivation sticker, 20% off, $75+ buyers only	1/6 and 1/7	e-mail reactivation message, 20% off, to all names with e-mail addresses	none	none	do not mail	none	3/4-3/6	none	none	none
Internet													
	0-6 month	Spring Catalog, 1/4	new customer, thank you discount 10% off	1/6 and 1/7	Thank You for your order, no offer	none	postcard mailing promoting store sale	New Spring cover, repaginate one signature, 3/1-3/3	Thank You for your order, no offer	3/4-3/6	base new emphasis on past history, recommend complementary item to past purchase	none	none
	7-12 month	Spring Catalog, 1/4	no offer	1/6 and 1/7	Thank You order confirmation with offer additional 10% off next order	none	none	New Spring cover, repaginate one signature, 3/1-3/3	Thank You order confirmation with offer additional 10% off next order	3/4-3/6	reminder re 10% off	none	none

Exhibit 12.22 Customer Contact Strategy Overview Example (continued)

Segment		Catalog	Offer/Sticker	Date	E-mail/Reminder	Date	Other Mailing	New Catalog	Extended Offer	Date	Reminder		
	13-24 month	Spring Catalog, 1/2-1/4	reactivation sticker, 20% off, $75+ buyers only	1/6 and 1/7	reminder of 20% off	none		New Spring cover, repaginate one signature, 3/1-3/3	Extended time for 20% off, printed sticker	3/4-3/6	reminder re 20% off	none	none
	24+ months	Spring Catalog, 1/2-1/4	reactivation sticker, 20% off, $75+ buyers only	1/6 and 1/7	reminder of 20% off	none	none	New Spring cover, repaginate one signature, 3/1-3/3	Extended time for 20% off, printed sticker	3/4-3/6	reminder re 20% off	none	none
Gift Recipients													
	0-6 month	Spring Catalog, sale insert, 1/2-1/4	Play up sales insert	1/6 and 1/7	promote fall/holiday savings on Internet, reminder of limited time to buy	1/10-1/13	postcard mailing promoting store sale	New Spring cover, repaginate one signature, 3/1-3/3	Extended time for 20% off, printed sticker	3/4-3/6	reminder re 20% off	none	none
	7-12 month	Spring Catalog, 1/2-1/4		1/6 and 1/7	e-mail activation message, 20% off first order, to all names with e-mail addresses	1/10-1/13	postcard mailing promoting store sale	New Spring cover, repaginate one signature, 3/1-3/3	Extended time for 20% off, printed sticker	3/4-3/6	reminder re 20% off	none	none
	13-24 month	Spring Catalog, 1/2-1/4	no offer	1/2-1/4	e-mail activation message, 20% off first order, to all names with e-mail addresses	none	none	**do not mail**	no offer	3/4-3/6	none	none	none
	24+ months	do not mail	no offer	1/2-1/4	e-mail activation message, 20% off first order, to all names with e-mail addresses	none	none	**do not mail**	no offer	3/4-3/6	none	none	none
Requestors													
	0-6 month	Spring Catalog, 1/2-1/4	conversion sticker, 20% off, no dollar qualifier	1/6 and 1/7	e-mail activation message, 20% off first order, to all names with e-mail addresses	1/10-1/13	postcard mailing promoting store sale	New Spring cover, repaginate one signature, 3/1-3/3	Extended time for 20% off, printed sticker	3/4-3/6	reminder re 20% off	none	none
	7-12 month	Spring Catalog, 1/2-1/4	conversion sticker, 20% off, no dollar qualifier	1/6 and 1/7	e-mail activation message, 20% off first order, to all names with e-mail addresses	1/10-1/13	postcard mailing promoting store sale	New Spring cover, repaginate one signature, 3/1-3/3	Extended time for 20% off, printed sticker	3/4-3/6	reminder re 20% off	none	none
	13-24 month	Spring Catalog, 1/2-1/4	Last Chance, 20% off, order by or discontinue mailing catalog	1/6 and 1/7	Last Chance, activation message, 20% reminder off to all names with e-mail addresses	none	none	**do not mail**	none	3/4-3/6	Sorry that you have chosen no more catalogs, one last chance, free S&H	none	none
	24+ months	Spring Catalog, 1/2-1/4	Last Chance, 20% off, order by or discontinue mailing catalog	1/6 and 1/7	Last Chance, activation message, 20% off reminder to all names with e-mail addresses	none	none	**do not mail**	none	3/4-3/6	Sorry that you have chosen no more catalogs, one last chance, free S&H	none	none

All tests noted should be tested against controls and/or other offers. All offers should have "order by" dates. Any promotional offers sent to rental lists should be submitted to the list owner in order to receive advance permission to make the offer.

E-mail offers most likely would be more extensive than shown and, unlike other contact forms, are sometimes wisely added to the contact plan at the "last moment." A prime example would be using an e-mail to help lift a mailing that is not performing up to expectations.

Timing is estimated and would depend on the quantity mailed and on the web site's database. Less performing segments are mailed less and given more incentives than high performing segments.

Offers

A cataloger should constantly be testing offers. Exhibits 12.21 and 12.22 show a contact strategy for customer leveraging, but a similar approach can be taken with prospects. As you generally do not contact the same prospects repeatedly, there is no need to create a complicated chart. Areas to address:

- Continually look for new offers that will better the ones previously used.
- Have an ongoing testing program.
- Re-test offers that did not work in the past as incentives can work differently in different time periods and to different list segments.
- Be certain that all tests are statistically valid.
- Be certain that the cost of the offer is weighed against the lift in response and average order.

Reactivation

There is no one that does not agree that keeping customers actively buying should be one of your first priorities. Yet too many catalogers overlook the opportunity, through incentives and other techniques, to keep customers buying. Exhibit 12.22 Contact Strategy Overview Example shows some methods and possible timing.

Your List as a Profit Center

The majority of catalogers rent their list to parties that are pre-approved by the cataloger. For the most part, catalogers do not rent to competitors, though a number of catalogers do as they feel that their catalog is strong enough to handle the competition. The income from list rentals can, for some, become a significant part of the catalogers' revenue. However, because of the concerns about more catalogs in the mailbox competing for the consumers' dollar, some catalogers do not make their list available.

One advantage of having a list to rent to other mailers is that your list broker can arrange list trades that are less expensive than rentals, thus lowering the in-the-mail cost of your catalog. But also keep in mind that exchanges will lower your income from list rentals to the other parties. You are substituting a barter arrangement for a sale, and neither is without some cost.

Exhibit 12.23 House List Rental Checklist

☐ Make certain that you know exactly who is renting the list.

☐ Be clear on exactly what you are renting (quantities, segments).

☐ Understand how many times the renter is allowed by you to use the list.

☐ Clarify what dates the renter is allowed to mail.

☐ Know and agree to the method of payment and its timing.

☐ Approve mailing content before allowing the renter to rent your list.

☐ Decoy the list rentals to audit exactly what your customers are receiving—and when. If the decoy sample differs from the "clearance sample," immediately contact your List Manager. Your List Manager will advise you on an equitable solution, usually involving an extra payment to you.

E-Mail Marketing

Corresponding with customers via e-mail is an effective method of gaining additional sales and, if done right, can increase brand loyalty. Permission-based e-mail, in which you have received permission from the customer to e-mail them, has, as you might expect, a higher conversion rate than non-permission based e-mail. E-marketing laws are constantly being reviewed, changed, and changed again. Stay up-to-date on them.

It is not just that e-mail is relatively inexpensive, it is also that, done correctly, it can appear to be a personal benefit to the customer. Understand that e-mail marketing will not have the same sales curve you are used to in your print catalog, as orders tend to be active for only a few days. Here is a checklist of areas to which you should be attuned.

Exhibit 12.24 E-Mail Marketing Checklist

☐ Look into every form of communication as a potential sales avenue; possibilities:

    ___ Order confirmations.

    ___ Shipping notifications.

    ___ Returns received notifications.

    ___ Bill (for those who pay by e-mail).

    ___ Statements (for those who pay by e-mail).

☐ Keep the offer "above the fold" (the part of the screen that you see without scrolling).

☐ Put other important factors, such as the guarantee and shipping costs, at the bottom.

☐ Keep the offer relevant by offering products in which you know, based on history, that the customer has an interest.

☐ Customize your offer depending on the type of connection, e.g., keep dial-up connections simpler and faster to load than broadband connections.

☐ Constantly test offers and incentives.

- ☐ Include the Search function so that those who do not immediately see what they want can find it easily.

- ☐ Make certain that the customer knows who you are in the subject line; lack of clarity can be construed as spam mail.

- ☐ Carefully monitor the timing so that it does not seem overwhelming to the customer, but timely, e.g., an exciting pre-announcement of a catalog that is about to arrive.

- ☐ An increase in opt-outs is one sign that you are over e-mailing.

- ☐ Remember to use e-mail to drive all channels.

- ☐ Use e-mail to reinforce offers in the catalog and/or stores.

- ☐ Keep e-mail consistent with your overall brand image.

- ☐ While e-mail is an excellent way to move excess inventory, make sure that this contact is part of your contact plan, not an isolated message and not a message that, due to timing, may negatively affect a full price catalog.

- ☐ Keep your e-mail list as up-to-date and clean as you do your mailing list, eliminating inactives and correcting addresses.

Loyalty Programs

One way to help assure repeat purchases is to lock in customers via a program that is tailored to meet their desires. Such programs can definitely add to a customer's retention and frequency of purchase, but the key here is to create something that has true value to the customer.

There are really two types of loyalty programs: 1) hard, and 2) soft. The hard type of loyalty program is of the formal sort, such as reward and membership clubs. Reward clubs are most often based on points; membership clubs often require a yearly fee.

The soft type of loyalty program allows customers to access or be provided with services they value, such as a wedding registry, a relevant newsletter, or pre-notification of a customers-only sale. Handled correctly, cataloger after cataloger has found that loyalty programs work. But first, you need a well-thought out plan.

Exhibit 12.25 Loyalty Club Plan Checklist

☐ How will success be determined? Are the goals financial? Added multi-buyers? Increased frequency of purchase?

☐ What are the basic elements of the program?

    ___ What will the program consist of in order to meet the goals?

    ___ What will be tested and to whom?

    ___ What will the program be called?

☐ What will the offer be?

    ___ What will the major offer be?

    ___ Will there be other discounts or offers than the major one?

☐ What systems will be needed?

    ___ What information needs to be collected at launch?

    ___ What information needs to be collected during the program?

☐ What will the creative consist of?

    ___ Printed

    ___ Telemarketing

☐ How will renewals be encouraged?

☐ Through what media will the offer be proposed to the consumer?

☐ What will be the exit strategy if the program doesn't work and some customers have signed up?

☐ What is the timing?

☐ What are the administrative needs?

Exhibit 12.26 Loyalty Club Plan Example

    I. Objective.
        A. An ongoing loyalty program that will increase multi buyers by 50 percent.
        B. By year two, 80 percent of customers should be members.
   II. Elements.
        A. Keep the program simple for the customer to understand and use.
        B. No cumbersome hard-to-keep-track-of points, just savings based on easy-to-understand criteria.
        C. Will test on:
            1. 50 percent of buyers, 0–12 month, 7–12 month, $75+, 13–24 month, $75+.
            2. 50 percent of all requestors, 0–12 month.
        D. Be especially alert to any seasonality as it affects initial sign-up and conversion.
        E. Name will be ABC Catalog's VIP Club.
  III. Offer.
        A. No fee, membership is free.
        B. Points must be used in one year (year from first purchase)
        C. 5 percent discount after spending $400 year, 10 percent discount for anything over $400; can be used in conjunction with other ongoing catalog discounts.
        D. Free shipping and handling after reaching the $400 a year mark.
        E. Free e-mail alerts pre-mailing for sales and other events.
        F. No proprietary credit card at this time; can add in Year Two or Three if program successful.
        G. Will not include discount coupons or offers from other companies.
  IV. Systems.
        A. Daily, weekly, and monthly reports that track conversions.
        B. Software to alert when the customer's points are about to expire.
        C. Software to tag customer when they become a member:
            1. Must work in conjunction with telemarketing and e-mail program.

D. Software to note birthdays and anniversary of the length of time they have been a customer.
E. Will need dedicated Customer Service Reps for initial sales and all FOL including renewals.

V. Creative.
   A. Printed:
      1. Sticker on front cover plus insert between pages two and three.
         a. Plan retail store coupon insertions for year.
      2. E-mail message campaign.
         a. Need to test number of e-mails needed for "subscription" to program.
         b. Have ongoing electronic coupons to drive to stores.
      3. Renewals (points about to expire) will get combination effort.
         a. Inkjet on back cover.
            (1) Different message for those that meet $ goal and those that did not.
         b. Test cover change announcing renewal time.
         c. Thank you letter to those that automatically renew.
   B. Respondent package.
      1. Simple letter of appreciation that restates advantages that come with membership.
   C. Telemarketing, in-bound only.
      1. Script for initial sell to non-members.
      2. Script for renewal.

VI. Media.
   A. Catalog.
   B. Web site.

VII. Exit strategy.
   A. Letter or e-mail to those that signed up explaining that the program is discontinued.
      1. Offer apology and discount coupon.

VIII. Timing.
   A. Need to initiate within 3 months.

IX. Administrative needs.
   A. John Murphy will head team with Tamika Jannis coordinating.

Package Inserts

Package inserts are advertising flyers or extra copies of catalogs that are inserted into outgoing catalog packages. They can be inserted in your catalog or, for a fee, small inserts can be inserted into other catalogers' catalogs.

Exhibit 12.27 Package Insert Pointers

- ⇨ Check the size carefully—due to weight considerations (extra weight can increase the cost of sending the package to the customer).

- ⇨ Know how many other, and what types of, offers will be in the package with your offer.

- ⇨ Work with a broker experienced in package inserts; this is not the same expertise as list rental.

- ⇨ Keep the cost low; the response on inserts is usually much less than a catalog—usually 2/10 to 4/10 of 1 percent.

- ⇨ Test offers.

- ⇨ If selling product, keep the price very low so that there are no price hurdles to purchase.

- ⇨ Understand how fast or slow the insertion of the package inserts will be (speed of delivery is, of course, based on number of orders fulfilled).

- ⇨ Test putting your own catalog in your outgoing packages.

- ⇨ Code everything carefully to fully understand the short and long term value of this method.

Code Tracking

All methods of acquisition need to be tracked as tightly as possible. Print ads, for instance, can have a separate phone or extension number and a slightly modified, separate web address. Offers may have a unique code; be certain that customer service reps are aware of any campaigns and what their role in collecting the code should be.

13 Operations as a Marketing Tool

Marketing does not stop when the catalog goes into the mail. The overall experience is what customers remember. More than one customer has been lost due to poor product fulfillment and/or customer service. Further, it's not just what is in the package that makes an impression; it's how the package looks when it arrives. Keeping an open dialogue between marketing and operations is critical to a seamless and top quality experience for the customer.

To begin with, it helps if the marketer has an idea of the overall process, what goes into such key functions as forecasting and how operational reports can affect the rest of the catalog team. The areas that your operations staff will most likely be monitoring are:

- Shipping and handling costs.
- Direct labor fulfillment costs.
- Labor required to meet fulfillment objectives.
- Customer service issues.
- Speed and efficiency of output.

When viewed from a marketing position, the cost of operations is less of an immediate concern than is the effect of operations on customers' experiences with both their initial and repeat purchases. Nevertheless, it is advisable to work with the operations department to understand what marketing strategies mean in terms of personnel and dollar commitments. Further, some key areas, such as forecasting, when to raise delivery charges, and whether or not to offer gift-wrap will most likely fall under marketing's domain.

Operations and Fulfillment Magazine, (http://www.opsandfulfillment.com) is an excellent resource that can help you learn more about operations, which is also called the "back end" of the business.

Exhibit 13.1 Operations Flow Chart

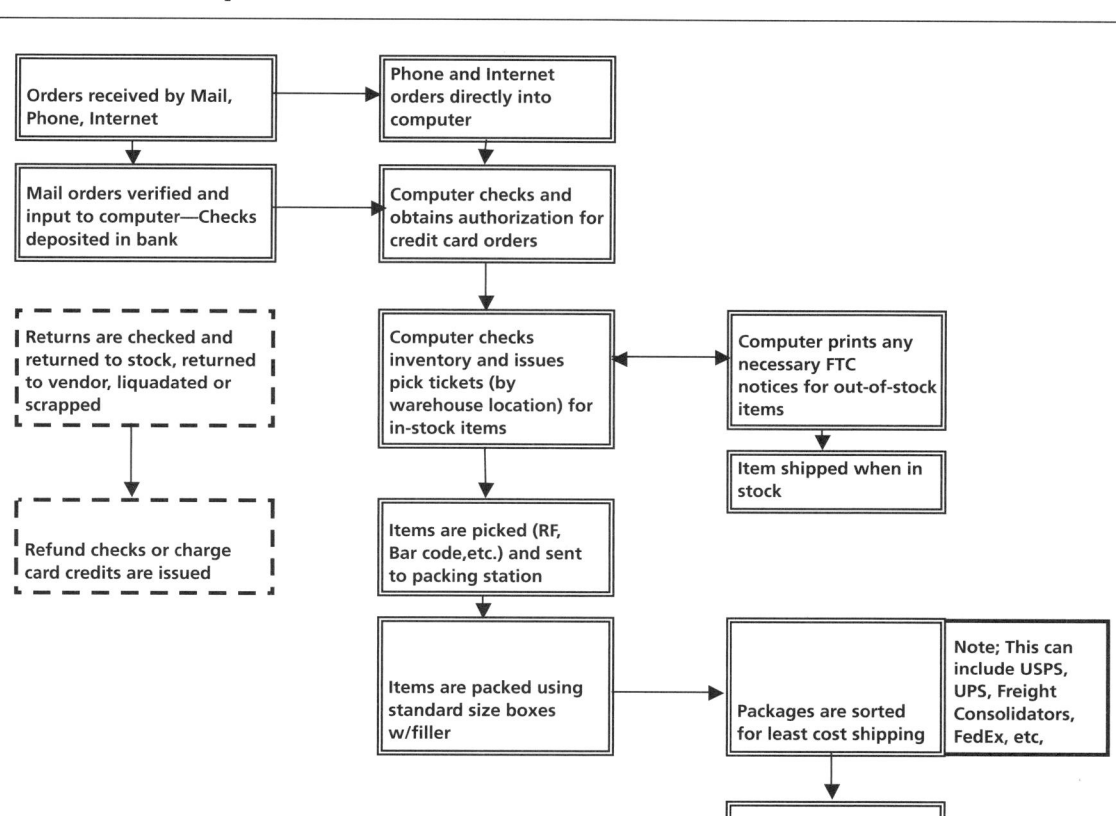

Key elements that have serious impact on current and future sales are:

1. Forecasting.

2. Timely reports.

3. Customer service policies.

4. Delivery costs.

5. Shipping options.

6. Packaging.

Forecasting

Marketers and merchants, as well as customers, need product forecasting that is as accurate as possible. Determining exactly how many of an item, in what sizes, and in what colors must be inventoried for the catalog is not an easy assignment, but it is one that gets more accurate as experience and past data grow. But even with experience, there are factors that can heavily influence what will and will not sell. Exhibits 13.2 and 13.3 provide checklists of the key areas that should be considered when developing your forecast.

A variety of software programs are available to assist in forecasting, but many catalogers find that the current programs are more attuned to the needs of retailers than to those of catalogers. As a result, catalogers often will develop their own forecasting tools using Excel spreadsheets that link to the various elements, such as daily sales, that go into forecasting.

 Exhibit 13.2 Forecasting Influencers

TO DO LIST

☐ Pre-mail Plans

___ Circulation plan—To whom is the catalog going, what is the mix of prospects (who respond less) and house file (who respond more)? What segments of the house file is the catalog going to: The high-spending, multi-buyers or the less receptive, single buyers? Is the mailing arriving in-home on the planned for dates or will a wrong in-home date negatively affect sales?

___ Contact strategy—How frequently are the customers receiving catalog mailings and how many versions of the catalog are they getting? What can be expected in wear-out due to multiple exposures of the same items and/or creative?

☐ Creative/Marketing

___ Offers—What kinds of incentives are being used to increase orders?

___ Product placement in the catalog—Where is the product on the page: A key location or in a spot that traditionally draws fewer sales?

___ Price—Has the price changed, increased, or decreased, and has it stayed competitive with the competition for the same or similar item?

☐ Analysis

___ History of the same or similar item—What has this product, or something like it, done in sales in the past?

___ Seasonality—Is this the right time of year for the product?

___ Source of the order—What percentages of orders by source are expected and, as different sources have different responses, what will the effect be?

___ Life cycle—In what phase of the life cycle is this product?

☐ Outside Forces

___ Trends—Are the consumer trends that have affected product sales no longer in play?

___ Weather—Is the weather (actual or forecast) likely to increase or decrease the demand for particular products?

___ Unforeseen events—Has an election, tragedy, or some other event caused a change in orders in the past? Keep a record so that you can use this change in response data in the future.

☐ Operations

___ Back orders—Has the catalog been less than ideal in getting products to customers in a timely manner? Back orders often mean lower customer response in subsequent mailings.

___ Warehouse space/staffing—For the items to be ordered are there any limitations on the warehouse space or the necessary staff, including the call center?

___ Reorder time frame/availability—Due to long lead times, must an item be ordered in larger volume than it would be otherwise?

___ Up-sell—How proficient are your customer service reps at selling additional items to the caller when they place an order?

Exhibit 13.3 Forecasting Criteria Checklist

☐ Time definition—Do you and your warehouse agree on exactly when a week starts (Monday, Sunday, other)?

☐ Measuring accuracy—What percentage of accuracy in projections are you shooting for? How can you constantly improve your percentage?

☐ The Big Picture—Do the projections match and/or support the marketing plan?

☐ Cash flow—Will the cash flow support the projections?

☐ Insurance—Will the insurance coverage support the projections?

☐ Employee time—What is the cost of employee time in cutting multiple orders?

☐ Patterns—Are there any patterns in the sales that you can apply to the forecast?

☐ Assumptions—What are the assumptions you are using for the projections? For instance, what are you assuming will be the weekly back order and returns rate over the time period of the catalog? How much can be recycled into inventory?

☐ Formulas—Have you triple-checked them to be certain that they are correct?

☐ Reality check—Has anyone other than the forecaster reviewed the numbers?

☐ History—Has the analytical history been taken into account? (See Chapter 14, *Basic Analysis*)

Reports that forecasters use to determine what quantities to order and when can also be useful in understanding negative influences (e.g., back orders due to a particular vendor) as well as opportunities (e.g., seasonality trends).

Exhibit 13.4 Forecasting Spreadsheet Form

Product Name and Item Number

Minimum reorder quantity per color

Circulation Quantity/% Breakout:

Buyers
Requests
Models
Rentals
Totals

Offer & Percentage (if applicable):   Remail % (if applicable):

Color	Size	Size Splits	Expected Gross Sales	Original Expected Return %	Actual Return % to Date	Actual Returns to Date	Return Recyle %	On Hand	Expected Net Demand	Ordered (P.O.'s Cut)	Sold Out and Cancels	Possible Future Buys	Open to Buy
Hunter Green													
Red													
Sky Blue													
Marine Blue													

Exhibit 13.5 Forecasting Spreadsheet Example

Product Name and Item Number

Fleece Bathrobe   p12354

Minimum reorder quantity per color   10

Circulation Quantity/% Breakout:

Buyers   340000   40%
Requests   85000   10%
Models   212500   25%
Rentals   212500   25%
Totals   850000

Offer & Percentage (if applicabl no offer   Remail % (if applicable   20%

Color	Size	Size Splits	Expected Gross Sales	Original Expected Return %	Actual Return % to Date	Actual Returns to Date	Return Recyle %	On Hand	Expected Net Demand	Ordered (P.O.'s Cut)	Sold Out and Cancels	Possible Future Buys	Open to Buy
Hunter Green	S, M, L, XL	S 15%	75	8%	9%	7	5%	43	69	25	0	0	0
Red	S, M, L, XL	M 50%	250	10%	11%	28	5%	114	224	50	0	0	60
Sky Blue	S, M, L, XL	L 20%	100	8%	8%	8	5%	54	92	25	0	0	0
Marine Blue	S, M, L, XL	XL 15%	75	6%	5%	4	5%	42	71	25	0	0	0

Exhibit 13.6 Forecasting Spreadsheet Explanation

- *Product Name and Item Number*—Product description and its identifying item number.
- *Minimum Reorder Quantity per Color*—How many of each?
- *Circulation Quantity/% Breakout*—How many catalogs, and what percentages, will be mailed to customers and prospects?
- *Offer & Percentage*—What offers, if any, are being made (e.g., 10 percent off) and what percentage of the mailing is getting the offer?
- *Re-mail Percentage*—What percentage of the recipients will see this catalog more than once, thus reducing the demand?
- *Color*—What quantities are anticipated for each color (by code number)?
- *Size*—What sizes and quantities are anticipated for each size?
- *Size Splits*—What is the percentage breakout of sizes?
- *Expected Gross Sales*—What is the anticipated sale for each product?
- *Original Expected Return %*—What quantities are the expected returns by size and color?
- *Actual Return Percentage to Date*—What percentage was actually returned?
- *Actual Returns to Date*—What are the returns at the date of this report?
- *Return Recycle %*—What percentage of the returns can go back into stock?
- *On Hand*—What quantity is on hand at the time of this report?
- *Expected Net Demand*—What is the overall anticipated sell quantity minus returns, cancels, plus restocks? (If restocking can be done in the necessary time period, this may be applicable to future catalog issues only.)
- *Ordered*—What are the quantities for which purchase orders have been cut?

⇨ *Sold Out and Cancels*—What is the number of items not sold due to lack of inventory and inability to be restocked?

⇨ *Possible Future Buys*—What is the likelihood of additional sales?

⇨ *Open to Buy*—What needs to be purchased?

Response Curves

Response curves show the trajectory of orders from when they are first received until the end of the time frame that the catalog covers. Response curves are the basis for projecting how many orders will be received over time and are determined using past sales history. Initially, historical data is shown on the charts. Then, the expected weekly results are plotted, both as weekly and cumulatively, using the percentage or orders per week from the historical data. The circulation data is used to normalize the curves to each other so that there is a measurement of apples to apples. As results come in, they are re-plotted as actual and the curve is adjusted to predict the number of orders or demand dollars based on the variance in the curves.

Percent done is the common phrase used when referring to what percent of catalog sales have already been received. If you know how much you have already sold, you can then understand what is yet to be sold, and how close you are to meeting your projections. Response curves should be done for a catalog as a whole, as well as for each category and each price range. Some catalogers also do response curves for each item.

Response curves are affected by frequency of mailing, number of catalog pages, price points, and circulation as well as all the other factors outlined in forecasting.

Exhibit 13.7 shows that this particular printed catalog outperformed previous catalogs at Week Four, but it also had a sharper tail-off than previous catalogs.

Web marketing can cause some positive adjustments to be made to the curve. Because web marketing is fast, decisions that affect the bottom line and forecasting can be made on a dime (usually one to two times per week). Alan Rimm-Kaufman, principal of the web consulting firm The Rimm-Kaufman Group, points out that "slow, late or poor performing catalogs can be assisted plus or minus 20 percent by cranking up the web marketing. If a catalog is performing great, cut back on the web marketing to avoid crashing the call center and fulfillment." In addition, products that aren't selling can quickly find themselves moving at a discount on the web.

Exhibit 13.7 Weekly Response Curve Example (Individual Weeks)

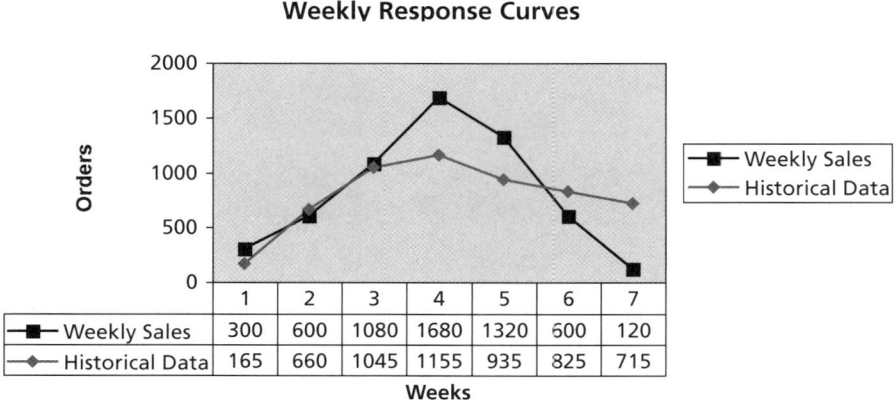

Exhibit 13.8 Cumulative Response Curve Example (Cumulative Weeks)

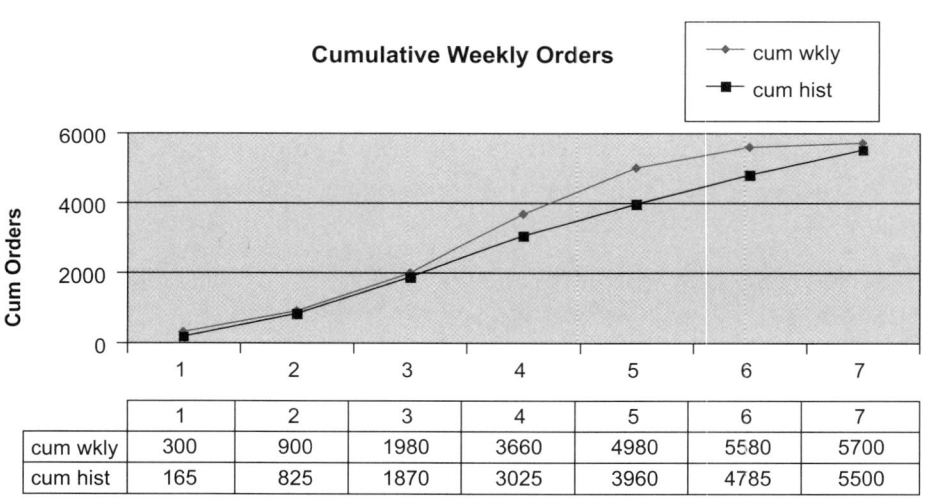

Timely Reports

Marketing and merchandising will use daily, weekly, and monthly reports to compare to past selling seasons in order to ascertain successes and failures . . . and create the response curve.

Exhibit 13.9 Daily Sales Report Form

Day of the Week	Daily Demand	Daily Orders	Daily Demand % per Week	Daily Order % per Week	Historical Order % per Day for same week	Variance= +/- percent
Monday						
Tuesday						
Wednesday						
Thursday						
Friday						
Saturday						
Sunday						

Exhibit 13.10 Daily Sales Report Example

Day of the Week	Daily Demand	Daily Orders	Daily Demand % per Week	Daily Order % per Week	Historical Order % per Day for same week	Variance= +/- percent
Monday	$20,000	143	20.0%	18.0%	17.0%	-1.0%
Tuesday	$7,000	50	7.0%	7.0%	7.0%	0.0%
Wednesday	$11,000	79	11.0%	11.0%	10.0%	-1.0%
Thursday	$12,000	86	12.0%	10.0%	9.0%	-1.0%
Friday	$20,000	143	20.0%	20.0%	18.0%	-2.0%
Saturday	$15,000	107	15.0%	20.0%	23.0%	3.0%
Sunday	$15,000	107	15.0%	14.0%	16.0%	2.0%

Example is shown for end of week

Exhibit 13.11 Weekly Sales Report Form

Day of the Week	Daily Demand	Daily Orders	Daily Demand % per Week	Daily Order % per Week	Historical Order % per Day (week) for same week (catalog)	Order Variance= +/- percent	Cum Weekly Orders	Expected Cat Orders
Monday								
Tuesday								
Wednesday								
Thursday								
Friday								
Saturday								
Sunday								
Week 1 Totals								
Monday								
Tuesday								
Wednesday								
Thursday								
Friday								
Saturday								
Sunday								
Week 2 Totals								

Exhibit 13.12 Weekly Sales Report Example

Day of the Week	Daily Demand	Daily Orders	Daily Demand % per Week	Daily Order % per Week	Historical Order % per Day (week) for same week (catalog)	Order Variance= +/- percent	Cum Weekly Orders	Expected Cat Orders
Monday	$20,000	143	20.0%	18.0%	17.0%	-1.0%		
Tuesday	$7,000	50	7.0%	7.0%	7.0%	0.0%		
Wednesday	$11,000	79	11.0%	11.0%	10.0%	-1.0%		
Thursday	$12,000	86	12.0%	10.0%	9.0%	-1.0%		
Friday	$20,000	143	20.0%	20.0%	18.0%	-2.0%		
Saturday	$15,000	107	15.0%	20.0%	23.0%	3.0%		
Sunday	$15,000	107	15.0%	14.0%	16.0%	2.0%		
Week 1 Totals	**$100,000**	**714**			**11.0%**		**714**	**6,494**
Monday	$45,874	270	24.3%	21.2%	17.0%	-4.2%		
Tuesday	$12,091	86	6.4%	6.8%	7.0%	0.2%		
Wednesday	$19,000	136	10.1%	10.6%	10.0%	-0.6%		
Thursday	$20,727	148	11.0%	11.6%	9.0%	-2.6%		
Friday	$34,545	247	18.3%	19.4%	18.0%	-1.4%		
Saturday	$30,878	203	16.3%	15.9%	23.0%	7.1%		
Sunday	$25,909	185	13.7%	14.5%	16.0%	1.5%		
Week 2 Totals	**$189,025**	**1,275**			**19.0%**		**1,989**	**6,631**

In addition, you would construct a monthly sales report following the two above examples.

Customer Service Policies

It goes without saying that a bad experience with a company can turn a customer into a lifelong activist against your catalog. From personal experience, I know that there are two catalog companies I will never, ever order from again . . . and I have made sure that all my friends don't order from either of these catalogs. Poor customer service can easily result in negative viral marketing.

To help ensure a positive experience for the customer, first fully understand what the policies for handling customers are. Policies can be different for a web site and for a catalog, as web sites allow for fast, inexpensive communication. Before establishing or adapting policies there are three key bits of information that you will need:

1. Federal Trade Commission (FTC) rules and regulations affect some policies, so stay abreast of all that relate.

2. Input from your customer service team, as they are the ones that hear firsthand what customers want and what they don't like.

3. Industry "Best Practices" so that you have a gauge against which to create or judge policies as they apply to your company.

Customer service inquiries tend to fall into six categories, three associated with pre-orders and three associated with post-orders:

Pre:

1. Desire to apply refund or credit to purchase.

2. Privacy—How do you use my name?

3. More information about a particular product.

Post:

1. Status of an order.

2. Cancellation or change in order.

3. Need to return.

Exhibit 13.13 Customer Policies Checklist

- ☐ Order Processing.
  - ___ If a customer underpays by check, will the shipment still be sent? By how much can they underpay? If paying by credit card, will the amount just be added to the charge? What if they overpay?
  - ___ What if there is a credit card problem?
  - ___ How long will shipments be held waiting so that all items can be shipped at once?
  - ___ Is an order confirmation sent? By e-mail? By mail?
  - ___ How will you handle an incomplete order?
  - ___ Credit charges will be submitted only after the package has shipped.*
  - ___ No merchandise substitutions will be made unless this is clearly explained in the catalog or on the web site.*
- ☐ Product Delivery Considerations.
  - ___ Will the original have to be returned before the customer is sent a replacement?
  - ___ How do you handle a customer who claims to have returned an item that has not been received?
  - ___ If a customer claims to have not received the item, will another item be sent?
  - ___ How are customers notified of back orders?
  - ___ Will packages be marked in a way to alert customers if the shipment is one of many because not everything is being shipped at the same time?
  - ___ What happens if the product arrives after the time that the customer expected and needed it? Will we accept a cancel? Who pays the return delivery costs?
  - ___ What happens if the product is damaged in transit?

* These are not questions, but legal mandates and must be honored by your catalog.

Operations as a Marketing Tool 333

          ___ What happens if pieces or parts are missing in the package containing the product?

   ☐ Satisfaction Considerations.

          ___ Under what conditions will the customer pay the return postage?

          ___ How quickly are refunds made?

          ___ If a customer has been waiting for a back-ordered item, will it be delivered via the fastest delivery possible at no extra cost to the customer?

          ___ How will we assure the customer that their privacy is protected?

Now create a written document that records your answers to the questions in Exhibit 13.13 and determine if this is a company you will want to buy from regularly. Make sure the answer is "yes" by creating a written document that explicitly outlines the answers in a method that understands that even customers in error are customers you want to retain.

Exhibit 13.14 Customer Phone and E-mail Representative Checklist

   ☐ Customer perception of speed in assistance.

          ___ How quickly and customer-attuned are complaints or questions answered? Operations has call reports that indicate time on the phone, time waiting to speak with a CSR (customer service rep), number of rings before pick up, abandoned shopping carts, and so on.

              Operations is, understandably, sometimes more interested in making certain that costs are under control than making certain that customers are being well-served. Read the reports, regularly communicate with your Operations Manager, and understand the service level your customers are actually getting.

          ___ Is there an expected turnaround time for customer service and complaints? Create timeline for each and break out your complaints by source.

          ___ How many contacts does a customer have to make to address an inquiry or resolve a complaint?

- [ ] Operation efficiencies versus customer needs.
    - ___ What is your contact-to-order ratio and what makes it change over time? This can be positively affected by something like an ad for catalog requests (which takes seconds to process) or negatively by less than explanatory descriptive copy (which can take a long time to explain).
    - ___ Is an automated response, in which customers have to pick a number to select a department, the right image for us? If you use an automated response, is it easy to navigate, and does it include the option to speak directly to a person?
    - ___ Are you listening in on calls and sampling correspondence? You need to know exactly how customers are being handled. Alert customers that you are monitoring the call in order to create better service (customer notification is the law).
- [ ] Education and training.
    - ___ Have your customer service reps (CSRs) had sufficient training time? Invest in creating educated representatives so that all reps can speak knowledgeably about all areas of your company, including product usage, specs and compatibility, offers and service policies.
    - ___ Have your CSRs had sufficient time to be familiar with the current catalog and web site? This means being certain that the reps have access to all sales avenues.
    - ___ How aware are your CSRs of current offers? Not knowing about an offer that is running makes the rep and the catalog seem careless.
    - ___ Are you specific about how the CSR should handle individual situations? Be clear as to what the course of action should be.
    - ___ Do you make certain that your CSRs have and properly use authority? CSRs need to know that they have the power to make decisions. This means adequate training must happen first, so the CSRs know exactly when they should use their own judgment and when they need to speak with a supervisor. Create a decision table or branching diagram that gives clear guidance on what the CSRs should do about each problem.

___ Are CSRs trained to respectfully and fully capture the codes that represent the source of the order? Without code capture, marketers will not understand what customer acquisition methods perform best.

☐ The work environment.

___ Are you asking your CSRs to multi-task? Some people are better at some things than others; if you can, use different people for different customer needs, such as handling complaints versus taking orders, writing versus talking. Leave the multi-tasking to other departments.

___ Are you a role model? Your attitude influences the attitudes of others. If you are concerned about the customer, it will be clear that customer care is ingrained in the company as a whole.

___ Do you have the latest, or at least current, technological support? Are your different avenues of purchase (web site, catalog, store) integrated? You cannot be competitive if your CSRs are unable to do their job well due to lack of proper systems and equipment.

___ How comfortable/functional is the environment in which your CSRs work? It is easier to be friendly and productive if the everyday tools (chair, headphone, computer screen, for example) are designed to be easy on the user.

___ Are you supportive of your staff? Make it clear to your CSRs how important they are to the company as a whole.

___ Do you offer incentives? Determine the greatest motivation for your staff, (recognition, money, time off), and offer it.

Back Orders

Some level of back orders is necessary in order to properly maintain the appropriate inventory levels. No back orders would mean that your inventory investment is too high, resulting in more items than you will actually sell. The probable balance, usually measured by the initial fill rate (what percentage of orders have the appropriate merchandise to ship them complete), is what you are seeking.

So, there will be some back orders. How they are handled will make or break the customer relationship.

Exhibit 13.15 Back Orders

TO DO LIST

☐ Collect Shadow Demand—Make certain that your reporting system is capturing demand, not just the actual number of orders filled, which can be a smaller number once the CSR has told the customer that the product is not available immediately. In order to plan merchandising, the cataloger needs to know what the customer wanted, not just what they were shipped.

☐ Provide a Real Time Delivery—Let CSRs know exactly when you expect the item to be in stock so that they can tell the customer a real delivery date and attempt to save the order. This can also help cut down on extra customer service time in the future, as customers will call and e-mail less if they receive accurate information when they place the order.

☐ Substitution Sell—When an item goes out of stock, have an alternate ready to suggest as a replacement. Remember, legally you cannot *automatically* substitute items without including this policy in writing in the catalog. Also, be very careful that your offer of a replacement item does not appear to be a "bait and switch."

☐ Bonuses—Offer customers who have items on back order an apology and back it up with a discount on future purchases.

FTC Mail Order Rule

The United States Postal Service is an excellent source for information on the legalities that concern the mail. Here is their take on a critical Federal Trade Commission (FTC) rule regarding out-of-stock products:

The Mail-Order Merchandise Rule

The mail-order rule adopted by the Federal Trade Commission in October 1975 provides that when you order by mail:

- You must receive the merchandise when the seller says you will.

- If you are not promised delivery within a certain time period, the seller must ship the merchandise to you no later than 30 days after your order comes in.

- If you don't receive it shortly after that 30-day period, you can cancel your order and get your money back.

How the Rule Works

The seller must notify you if the promised delivery date (or the 30-day limit) cannot be met. The seller must also tell you what the new shipping date will be and give you the option to cancel the order and receive a full refund or agree to the new shipping date. The seller must also give you a free way to send back your answer, such as a stamped envelope or a postage-paid postcard. *If you don't answer, it means that you agree to the shipping delay.*

The seller must tell you if the shipping delay is going to be more than 30 days. You then can agree to the delay or, if you do not agree, the seller must return your money by the end of the first 30 days of the delay.

If you cancel a prepaid order, the seller must mail you the refund within seven business days. Where there is a credit sale, the seller must adjust your account within one billing cycle.

To view the ruling in its entirety, go to FTC web site (http://www.ftc.gov) and see *A Business Guide to the Federal Trade Commission's Mail or Telephone Order Merchandise Rule,* produced in cooperation with the Direct Marketing Association. When it comes to any issues of a legal nature, work with a lawyer familiar with the catalog business.

Returns

Like it or not, returns will happen. For high-fashion catalogs, overall returns should not exceed 30 percent but can be even higher. For gift catalogs, returns are most often under 10 percent. Even though it seems like making returns easy for the customer is counterproductive, this is not the case. Catalogs typically include a form that indicates the item that was purchased and provides an area for return information. Generally, the return form will also have a ready-made label addressed to the cataloger, so the customer can complete it, apply the label to the package, and add postage or take it to a carrier such as USPS.

Some catalogers provide the ultimate customer convenience by using a form that allows customers to charge the return cost to the charge card on which they made the purchase. The label provided is, in essence, "prepaid" so, after the return label has been affixed, the package can just be dropped in a mailbox or left at the post office.

Exhibit 13.16 Return Form Checklist

☐ Is there an easy-to-detach label that the customer can apply to the package to be returned?

☐ Is the form inserted into the package on top of the product so that the customer can easily see it?

☐ Are the "Reasons for the Return" explicit enough to provide useful information to the cataloger as to why this item is being returned?

☐ Are the how-to-return instructions direct and simple so that the customer feels like this is a relatively simple process?

☐ Is an acknowledgement mailed or e-mailed to the customer when the item is received back in stock?

☐ Does the acknowledgement give the customer a bonus for ordering again?

It is critical that marketers and merchandisers be fully aware of why products are being returned. This allows catalogers to be able to take corrective action to minimize returns and increase customer satisfaction. The next two forms detail not only what will happen to the returns, but, more importantly, why the items were returned. For instance, napkin holders may need better packaging to protect them from delivery damage and the ABC Ltd. Company needs to do a better job of quality control on the measuring spoons.

Exhibit 13.17 Returns by Vendor Form

Item No.	Description	Vendor Name	YTD Sales	MTD Sales	Qty On Hand	Total Returns	Return Rate %	Return to Stock	Return to Vendor	Scrap or Liquidate

Item No.	Description	Vendor Name	Damaged by Carrier	Not as Expected	Did Not Work as Advertised	Wrong Size	Wrong Color	Wrong Style	Manufacturer Defect

Exhibit 13.18 Returns by Vendor Examples

Item No.	Description	Vendor Name	YTD Sales	MTD Sales	Qty On Hand	Total Returns	Return Rate %	Return to Stock	Return to Vendor	Scrap or Liquidate
123456	English Tea Kettle	ABC Ltd.	31	18	51	10	32.26	2	8	0
344567	Thermal Carafe	ABC Ltd.	13	9	60	1	7.69	1	0	0
567865	Measuring Spoons Set	ABC Ltd.	848	641	1751	101	11.91	10	91	0
203457	Paper Towel Holder	ABC Ltd.	284	23	97	10	3.52	5	4	1
777948	Napkin Holders	Wilson Ltd.	5052	0	40	139	2.75	110	24	5
173699	Gravy Dish	Wilson Ltd.	1530	75	455	40	2.61	30	5	4

Item No.	Description	Vendor Name	Damaged by Carrier	Not as Expected	Did Not Work as Advertised	Wrong Size	Wrong Color	Wrong Style	Manufacturer Defect
123456	English Tea Kettle	ABC Ltd.	0	0	2	0	0	1	7
344567	Thermal Carafe	ABC Ltd.	0	0	0	0	1	0	0
567865	Measuring Spoons Set	ABC Ltd.	0	0	10	0	0	0	129
203457	Paper Towel Holder	ABC Ltd.	1	1	3	1	0	0	4
777948	Napkin Holders	Wilson Ltd.	5	5	50	18	20	22	24
173699	Gravy Dish	Wilson Ltd.	4	4	25	0	2	0	4	5

Delivery Costs

One of the reasons customers used to avoid shopping by mail was the lack of "instant gratification" caused by slow shipping times. Due in part to the fast response mindset fostered by the online shopping experience, now catalogers are getting packages in the mail within hours of receipt of the orders. Customers expect it "now" and are often willing to pay a premium for overnight or two-day delivery.

Operations continually balances the most efficient method of shipping to meet the customers' needs with the costs to the cataloger and the customer. Shipping costs need to have their own individual P&Ls so that operations is aware of what is being spent on fulfillment as well as what is being recovered through charges to the customer.

Don't overpromise on delivery times. Some catalogers who have done so have run aground of FTC rules and regulations, resulting in fines of hundreds of thousands of dollars. Make certain that you are abiding by the most current FTC rules and regulations. Currently, the FTC requires that products be fulfilled within 30 days unless the cataloger notifies customers promptly of back orders.

Also be aware that the FTC is especially concerned that shipping charges represent justifiable expenses. Make certain that you can authenticate the costs you assign to the shipping and handling (S&H) process. Have a written policy on how shipping and handling rates are set. Any extra charges should be stated to the customer clearly and at the time the order is placed. If shipping is included in the price of the item, say so. Again, keep current with FTC rules, regulations, and guidance.

Exhibit 13.19 Shipping Costs versus Revenue Form

ACTUAL SHIPPING COSTS				CHARGED SHIPPING AMOUNT			DIFFERENCE
Carrier Code	Carrier	Sum Of Shipping Costs	Sum of Packages Count	Carrier Code	Carrier	Sum Of Amount	

Total Actual Shipping
Total Charged Shipping
Net Loss

==========

Exhibit 13.20 Shipping Costs versus Revenue Example

ACTUAL SHIPPING COSTS				CHARGED SHIPPING AMOUNT			DIFFERENCE
Carrier Code	Carrier	Sum Of shipping_costs	Sum of package_count	Carrier Code	Carrier	Sum Of amount	
5F06	5 FedEx Standard Overnight	$39,727	5,886	5F06	5 FedEx Standard Overnight	$39,496	($231)
P03	USPS First Class Priority	$282	52	P03	USPS First Class Priority	$83	($199)
5F65	5 FedEx Int'l Priority	$3,663	52	5F65	5 FedEx Int'l Priority	$147	($3,516)
5U12	5 UPS Residential	$115,508	21,374	5U12	5 UPS Residential	$100,376	($15,132)
5U01	5 UPS Next Day Air	$5,567	170	5U01	5 UPS Next Day Air	$1,670	($3,897)
5U21	5 UPS 3 Day Service	$325	171	5U21	5 UPS 3 Day Service	$325	$0
5F11	5 FedEx Economy 2 Day	$17,743	2,896	5F11	5 FedEx Economy 2 Day	$36,496	$18,753
5U07	5 UPS 2nd Day Air	$43,078	3,760	5U07	5 UPS 2nd Day Air	$11,259	($31,820)
5F01	5 FedEx Priority Overnight	$2,052	219	5F01	5 FedEx Priority Overnight	$927	($1,125)

Total Actual Shipping $227,945
Total Charged Shipping $190,780
Net Loss   ($37,165)   ==========   ($37,165)

Exhibit 13.20 shows a catalog that needs to either raise delivery costs to the customer or lower their costs of shipping.

Packaging

Think about how you react when you receive a package delivery in your home or office. If the package is clean and tidy, it conveys the feeling that the company behind the packaging cares. If it is torn or damaged in some way, the recipient can easily have concerns about both the contents and any company that would pack the product in a way that harm could occur. Regularly order and ship different size products from your catalog so that you see firsthand if the packaging supports or distorts the overall image.

Exhibit 13.21 Packaging Checklist

- ☐ Outside attractive? Coordinate labels and any other package art with the overall image in color, typeface, and graphics.

- ☐ Not messy when opened? You, too, probably hate opening a package when the contents spill all over your floor. While packing peanuts are efficient packaging materials, and can be relatively environmentally friendly, make certain that they are used in such a way as to be an acceptable nuisance to the customer.

- ☐ Environmentally-friendly? Be realistic about how truly friendly to the environment your packaging can be. Strides have been made in creating packaging that is less tough on the environment, but nothing is perfect yet.

- ☐ Exterior of package? When there is an option for the item, what form of shipping package will be used, e.g., soft pack envelopes, boxes? Does it sufficiently protect the item and enhance the catalog's image? Does your particular product line (e.g., personal, electronics) suggest using unidentifiable packaging?

- ☐ Extra goodies? Are you putting a catalog into every package for potential add-on orders, and then monitoring the sales results? Are you providing a surprise freebie that may help the customer remember this catalog over others? Are you reminding the customer of their wise choice?

☐ Reusable? Can the customer reuse the packaging if they have to send it back?

Inserts

Some catalogs insert sales flyers into outgoing packages. These inserts can be the catalog company's advertisements or inserts from another direct marketer. From the customer's viewpoint, the important thing is that the inserts do not overwhelm the item in the package, making the packaging look cluttered. Ideally, any advertising in the package should be put into an envelope, so that all inserts are neatly held in one place.

(For using inserts as part of your customer acquisition policy, see Chapter 12, *Customer Acquisition and Leveraging*.)

Gift-Wrap, Cards, and Certificates

There is no doubt that customers like the convenience of having gifts wrapped and sent to friends. Even more important, is the increased use of gift certificates. Too often services such as gift-wrap and certificates are poorly thought out. Perhaps this is the reason too many catalogs choose not to picture these services.

If you offer gift products, make certain that the wrap, cards, and certificates are of a gift-giving quality that reflects memorably on the catalog and the company. Then highlight this advantage in your catalog.

Exhibit 13.22 Gift-Wrap, Cards, and Certificates Checklist

☐ Is it necessary to provide gift-wrap year-round?

☐ Does the gift-wrap add to the image of the company?

☐ Is the cost of the gift-wrap reasonable in customers' minds?

☐ Is the cost of the gift-wrap and the labor involved in wrapping the items covered by the cost to the customer?

☐ How much additional time must be allowed for the gift-wrap?

☐ Is the card hardwritten or computer generated? If computer generated, is the message located in a part of the packaging that is easy for customers to see? Some computerized packing slips bury the giver information, resulting in unnecessary customer service calls because the giftee does not understand who sent them the package.

☐ Have you made sure that no catalogs are added to the gift packages (because the catalog can show the recipient the cost of their gift)?

☐ Are the gift certificates attractive? Do they come in an envelope with a catalog for ordering?

☐ Are the gift certificate denomination amounts customer-friendly?

14 Basic Analysis

Without proper analysis, a catalog cannot plot a path for strong growth. Analysis affects virtually every aspect of a catalog, determining what merchandise to run, what lists to rent, what offers to make, how much to spend on the creative, what seasons to mail, and so on.

Yet too much analysis is almost as bad as too little. We have all seen "doorstop" reports that contain so much data nobody actually reads them. The well-run catalog carefully picks and chooses the reports to be read by the marketing department, making certain that those reports are relatively easy to read, and whose conclusions are actionable; i.e., future actions can be taken based on the information they provide.

Analysis is an invaluable guide, but it is not an absolute. This is especially true with *Square Inch Analysis*, a form of analysis that tells the cataloger how effectively space in the catalog was utilized. We have seen catalogs that took the results of square inch analysis literally; they are very ugly catalogs that do not support the brand statement.

In all analyses, allow for channels other than the printed catalog. Always include, where the data is present, the Internet (may need to be based on matching the names of who ordered to the lists that were rented, retail and advertising space names and/or sales).

Data Capture

No analysis can be done correctly if the data is not available.

Exhibit 14.1 Data Capture Checklist

- ☐ Date order received.
- ☐ Method of ordering.
    - ___ Mail.
    - ___ Phone.
    - ___ Electronic.
    - ___ Fax.
- ☐ Payment method.
    - ___ Check or Money Order.
    - ___ Credit card.
    - ___ Other.
- ☐ Source code.
- ☐ Mailing code.
- ☐ Order number assigned.
- ☐ Name of sold-to.
- ☐ Address of sold-to.
- ☐ Name and address of ship-to.
- ☐ Phone number, day and evening.
- ☐ E-mail address for confirmations.
- ☐ Date keyed.
- ☐ Items ordered.
    - ___ Quantity.
    - ___ Date shipped.
    - ___ Item description matches SKU number?
- ☐ Total payment amount.
    - ___ Sales tax.
    - ___ Delivery charges.
    - ___ Merchandise amount.
    - ___ Correct price and delivery charge?

☐ Date and quantity of items returned.

☐ Date and amount of refunds.

☐ Privacy requests.

☐ What about offers?

☐ What about list data?

Exhibit 14.2 Data Capture Explanation

⇨ Date order received.

⇨ Method of ordering.
- Mail.
- Phone.
- Electronic.
- Fax.

⇨ Payment method.
- Check or Money Order.
- Credit card—Are the numbers correct and current?
- Other—Such as credit from previous purchase, reward for bonus points, etc.

⇨ Source code—Where did the customer originate?

⇨ Mailing code—Which segment, including offers, did the order come from?

⇨ Order number assigned—Most systems will assign and display a unique number for each order as the orders are entered.

⇨ Name of sold-to—Is the title of the person (Ms. Mrs., Mr., Dr.) correct?

⇨ Address of sold-to.

⇨ Name and address of ship-to—If different from sold to.

⇨ Phone number, day and evening.

⇨ E-mail address for confirmations.

⇨ Date keyed—When order was entered into system.

⇨ Items ordered—Break out by demand?
- Quantity.
- Date shipped.
- Item description matches SKU number?

⇨ Total payment amount.
- Sales tax.
- Delivery charges.
- Merchandise amount.
- Correct price and delivery charge?
- Discounts or refunds?

⇨ Date and quantity of items returned.

⇨ Date and amount of refunds.

⇨ Privacy requests—If the customer wants their name removed from the mailing list.

⇨ What about offers? Break out effect of offer on segments that. received the offer versus those that did not.

⇨ What about list data? Break out by list used.

To increase the accuracy of order entry, be certain that order forms, shopping cart, SKU lines, and any ordering data in the catalog or on the web site is presented in the way that the service reps actually capture the data. In addition, the work area needs outlined in Chapter 13, Exhibit 13.14, *Customer Phone and E-Mail Representative Checklist*, apply here.

Merchandise

Without analysis, a merchant is flying blind. Catalogers have traditionally relied heavily on square inch analysis, which literally measures the number of square inches (manually or with electronic design programs that measure for you) the catalog contains and then allocates the amount of space used to sell a product (its photo and its copy) and "charges" that product for the cost of that space.

Any space that does not sell a product, such as editorial or an order form, is allocated against all the spaces that do sell product. The cost of the catalog is based on its "in-the-mail" cost that covers creative and production, including bindery, lists, and postage costs. It does not cover overhead. Square inch analysis breaks down into three major types:

1. Individual products.

2. Category.

3. Price points.

The basic philosophy behind square inch analysis is that merchants will want to increase the space or offering of those items, categories, and price points that pay for their space and decrease those that don't. Take care in evaluating results that these factors are also taken into consideration:

- Seasonality—Some products and/or categories will only work in certain seasons.
- Position in the catalog—A product may not pay for its space because it is in the wrong place, but when moved to the right location it becomes a money-maker.

A critical point to remember with square inch analysis: It is a guide only and should not be taken literally. Catalogs that are designed to exact square inch allocation can be unattractive, as they seldom have the eye flow that a catalog should have. Let the analysis strongly direct the space, but not absolutely rule it.

Exhibit 14.4 is based on demand. If you wished to base it on net sales, add two columns, one for returns and one for net sales. At the item level, sizes, colors, etc. are rolled-up. Instead of doing the analysis at the item level, the color/size/SKU level allows for color and size parameters.

Exhibit 14.3 Item Level Square Inch Analysis Form

Item Number	Description	Category	Subcategory	Items Sold	Retail	Gross Demand	Demand Margin	Inches of Space	Cost of Space	Marketing Contribution	% Demand	% Margin	% Space	Demand Index	Margin Index

Exhibit 14.4 Item Level Square Inch Analysis Example

Item Number	Description	Category	Sub-category	Items Sold	Retail	Gross Demand	Demand Margin	Inches of Space	Cost of Space	Marketing Contribution	% Demand	% Margin	% Space	Demand Index	Margin Index
1	Cardigan	Apparel	Women's	350	39.95	$13,983	$6,292	12.5	$3,125	$3,167	13.4%	11.7%	9.9%	135	119
2	Ski Jacket	Apparel	Men's	25	185.00	$4,625	$2,544	10	$2,500	$44	4.4%	4.7%	7.9%	56	60
3	Blender	Kitchen		173	59.95	$10,371	$4,667	17	$4,250	$417	9.9%	8.7%	13.4%	74	65
4	Lawn Santa	Seasonal		501	29.95	$15,005	$8,253	22	$5,500	$2,753	14.4%	15.4%	17.4%	83	88
5	Elec. Cooler (cars)	Automotive	Gadgets	110	59.95	$6,595	$2,968	7	$1,750	$1,218	6.3%	5.5%	5.5%	114	100
6	Xmas Wreath	Seasonal		232	79.95	$18,532	$10,193	15	$3,750	$6,443	17.7%	19.0%	11.9%	150	160
7	Silver Frame	Gifts		272	39.95	$10,858	$4,886	8	$2,000	$2,886	10.4%	9.1%	6.3%	164	144
8	Tee	Apparel	Women's	356	17.95	$6,390	$3,834	10	$2,500	$1,334	6.1%	7.2%	7.9%	77	90
9	Polo	Apparel	Men's	299	29.95	$8,953	$4,029	9	$2,250	$1,779	8.6%	7.5%	7.1%	120	106
10	Charm Bracelet	Jewelry		131	69.95	$9,163	$5,956	16	$4,000	$1,956	8.8%	11.1%	12.6%	69	88
etc.				=======		=======	=======	=======	=======	=======	=======	=======	=======		
				2,449		$104,476	$53,622	126.5	$31,625	$21,997	100.0%	100.0%	100.0%		

Exhibit 14.5 Item Level Square Inch Analysis Explanation

- Item Number—The product identification number.
- Description—A concise narrative of the item.
- Category—The category into which this item belongs.
- Subcategory—The item may also belong to a subcategory.
- Items Sold—How many were sold.
- Retail—The selling price.
- Gross Demand—Is the total dollar value of orders even if not fulfilled.
- Demand Margin—The gross demand less the COG (cost of goods).
- Inches of Space—How many inches the particular item and its copy occupied in the catalog.
- Cost of Space—How much did that space cost "in-the-mail."
- Marketing Contribution—The gross margin less the cost of space (measure both text and photo) for the item.
- Percent Demand—The demand for the item divided by the demand for the entire catalog times 100.
- Percent Margin—The margin for the item divided by the margin for the entire catalog times 100.
- Percent Space—The space for the item divided by the space for the entire catalog.
- Demand Index—Determined by dividing the percent demand by the percent space times 100.
- Margin Index—Determined by dividing the percent margin by the percent space times 100.

The score of 100 in this index is the average. Products that do better than 100 should be considered for repeat and/or extension. Products that do less should be considered for deletion, a different placement, or improved presentation. Index does not indicate profitability; it merely helps the merchant's understanding of how products rank in effectiveness for the space they occupy.

Exhibit 14.6 Category Level Square Inch Analysis Form

Category Name	Description (if needed)	Gross Demand	Demand Margin	Space	Cost of Space	Marketing Contribution	% Demand	% Margin	% Space	Demand Index	Margin Index

Exhibit 14.7 Category Level Square Inch Analysis Example

Category Name	Description (if needed)	Gross Demand	Demand Margin	Space	Cost of Space	Marketing Contribution	% Demand	% Margin	% Space	Demand Index	Margin Index
A	Kitchen	$816,456	$367,405	479	$167,776	$199,629	42.3%	39.0%	28.1%	150	138
B	Bed and Bath	$58,979	$35,387	71	$24,924	$10,464	3.1%	3.8%	4.2%	73	90
C	Women's Apparel	$470,602	$258,831	490.21	$171,574	$87,258	24.4%	27.5%	28.8%	85	95
D	Garden	$68,695	$30,913	92.76	$32,466	($1,553)	3.6%	3.3%	5.4%	65	60
E	Kids	$87,164	$39,224	117.67	$41,185	($1,961)	4.5%	4.2%	6.9%	65	60
F	Misc	$2,913	$1,311	4.12	$1,442	($131)	0.2%	0.1%	0.2%	62	57
G	Toys	$37,701	$22,621	14.82	$5,187	$17,434	2.0%	2.4%	0.9%	225	276
H	Tabletop	$33,243	$19,946	42.46	$14,861	$5,085	1.7%	2.1%	2.5%	69	85
I	Seasonal	$159,393	$71,727	187.35	$65,573	$6,154	8.3%	7.6%	11.0%	75	69
J	Men's Apparel	$111,783	$50,302	155.06	$54,271	($3,969)	5.8%	5.3%	9.1%	64	59
K	Home Décor	$81,903	$45,047	48.02	$16,807	$28,240	4.2%	4.8%	2.8%	151	169
		=======	=======	=======	=======	=======					
		$1,928,832	$942,713	1,703	$596,064	$346,649					

All items in the catalog are assigned categories. Having too many categories can sometimes mean that there are not enough items in each category to give you meaningful analytical results. Therefore, keep main categories to an informative minimum, and use sub-categories to help better understand all the levels of products. The explanation for Exhibit 14.4: Item Level Square Inch Analysis form is the same, without individual product items, as it is for *Exhibit 14.5: Item Level Square Inch Analysis Explanation.*

At the category level, the retail selling price is not shown. Because the categories are listed for the individual items in the item-level report, category reports can be obtained by sorting on these categories. Then category totals are obtained by summing the demand, margin and space columns.

Strangely, price points are really price ranges, but the two terms—price points and price ranges—are used interchangeably in cataloging. Price point ranges analyzed would vary, dependent on the price points offered in the catalog.

The examples shown in Exhibits 14.7 and 14.9 are based on demand and assume that the space is $350 per inch.

Exhibit 14.8 Square Inch Price Point Analysis Form

Price Point	Items Sold	Gross Demand	Demand Margin	Space	Cost of Space	Marketing Contribution	% Demand	% Margin	% Space	Demand Index	Margin Index
0-19.99											
20.00-39.99											
40.00-59.99											
60.00-79.99											
80.00-99.99											
100.00-149.99											
150.00-199.99											
200.00-299.99											
300.00+											

Exhibit 14.9 Square Inch Price Point Analysis Example

Price Point	Items Sold	Gross Demand	Demand Margin	Space	Cost of Space	Marketing Contribution	% Demand	% Margin	% Space	Demand Index	Margin Index
0-19.99	53,128	$602,500	$271,125	350	$122,500	$148,625	28.3%	24.1%	21.9%	129	110
20.00-39.99	21,955	$468,249	$257,537	325	$113,750	$143,787	22.0%	22.9%	20.3%	108	113
40.00-59.99	7,814	$281,106	$168,664	200	$70,000	$98,664	13.2%	15.0%	12.5%	106	120
60.00-79.99	414	$36,807	$20,244	80	$28,000	($7,756)	1.7%	1.8%	5.0%	35	36
80.00-99.99	2,870	$206,545	$92,945	100	$35,000	$57,945	9.7%	8.3%	6.3%	155	132
100.00-149.99	20	$1,984	$893	50	$17,500	($16,607)	0.1%	0.1%	3.1%	3	3
150.00-199.99	1,260	$114,314	$62,873	150	$52,500	$10,373	5.4%	5.6%	9.4%	57	60
200.00-299.99	1,542	$275,524	$165,314	245	$85,750	$79,564	12.9%	14.7%	15.3%	85	96
300.00+	209	$141,777	$85,066	100	$35,000	$50,066	6.7%	7.6%	6.3%	107	121
	========	========	========	========	========	========					
	89,212	$2,128,806	$1,124,661	1600	$560,000	$564,661					

Exhibit 14.10 Categories versus Price Form

CATEGORIES	PRICE RANGES									
	0-20	21-40	41-60	61-80	81-100	101-150	151-200	201-300	301+	TOTAL	% returns
Gross Sales											
Net Sales											
Sales Index											
Margin Index											
# of Items sold											
Items per cat.											
ALL	0-20	21-40	41-60	61-80	81-100	101-150	151-200	201-300	301+	TOTAL	% returns
Gross Sales											
Net Sales											
Sales Index											
Margin Index											
# of Items sold											
Items per cat.											

This form is a simple method of comparing the combination of categories and price points. It provides insight into price resistance for a given category and/or shows where merchants can expand offerings.

In Exhibit 14.11, some examples of how to read this analysis are: the Category "A" offering could be expanded in the $101–$150 range. Because the $81–$100 range did so well in Category "K" the higher range of $101–$150 should be tested, as the next higher range of $61–80 should be for Category "G" as it did exceptionally well in the next lower range. Category "C" did poorly in all price points and should most likely be reduced in units offered overall.

Exhibit 14.11 Categories versus Price Example

CATEGORIES	PRICE RANGES										
A	0-20	21-40	41-60	61-80	81-100	101-150	151-200	201-300	301+	TOTAL	% returns
Gross Sales	$318,431	$195,759	$63,305		$77,526		$97,082	$190,768	$73,585	$1,016,456	
Net Sales	$302,053	$189,018	$61,519		$72,649		$94,202	$178,053	$29,970	$927,464	9.6%
Sales Index	239	172	84		126		226	165	143		
Margin Index	228	180	62		127		286	172	58		
# of Items sold	28,630	9,305	2,011		1,297		854	1,119	103	43,319	
Items per cat.	24	18	7		5		4	9	3		
B	0-20	21-40	41-60	61-80	81-100	101-150	151-200	201-300	301+	TOTAL	% returns
Gross Sales	$24,700	$6,567		$14,703	$13,009					$58,979	
Net Sales	$21,158	$6,229		$4,869	$12,808					$45,064	30.9%
Sales Index	181	41		92	31						
Margin Index	185	51		41	35						
# of Items sold	1,937	227		97	181					2,442	
Items per cat.	2	1		1	1						
C	0-20	21-40	41-60	61-80	81-100	101-150	151-200	201-300	301+	TOTAL	% returns
Gross Sales	201690	118488	$93,598		56826					470,602	
Net Sales	$188,445	$113,535	$89,224		$53,398					444,602	5.8%
Sales Index	114	59	60		75						
Margin Index	94	62	53		84						
# of Items sold	17968	5566	2773		742					27,049	
Items per cat.	41	29	16		6						
D	0-20	21-40	41-60	61-80	81-100	101-150	151-200	201-300	301+	TOTAL	% returns
Gross Sales	$2,847	$14,871	$26,813	$4,407	$19,757					$68,695	
Net Sales	$2,672	$14,540	$25,765	$4,173	$18,755					$65,905	4.2%
Sales Index	$39	112	86	207	32						
Margin Index	$60	163	84	466	41						
# of Items sold	$209	572	640	55	235					1,711	
Items per cat.	$2	3	11	2	3						
E	0-20	21-40	41-60	61-80	81-100	101-150	151-200	201-300	301+	TOTAL	% returns
Gross Sales	$3,331	$23,684	$48,530	$1,017		$1,984		$8,618		$87,164	
Net Sales	$3,057	$22,646	$44,875	$972		$1,634		$8,298		$81,482	7.0%
Sales Index	21	49	128	6		46		38			
Margin Index	-1	41	136	7		39		43			
# of Items sold	301	981	1,229	20		20		50		2,601	
Items per cat.	6	11	7	1		1		2			
F	0-20	21-40	41-60	61-80	81-100	101-150	151-200	201-300	301+	TOTAL	% returns
Gross Sales			2913							2,913	
Net Sales			$1,880							1,880	54.9%
Sales Index			57								
Margin Index			44								
# of Items sold			43							43	
Items per cat.			2								
G	0-20	21-40	41-60	61-80	81-100	101-150	151-200	201-300	301+	TOTAL	% returns
Gross Sales	11316	13151	$13,234							$37,701	
Net Sales	$10,377	$12,509	$11,256							34,142	10.4%

Exhibit 14.11 Categories versus Price Example (continued)

	0-20	21-40	41-60	61-80	81-100	101-150	151-200	201-300	301+	TOTAL	% returns
Sales Index	333	176	177								
Margin Index	529	252	204								
# of Items sold	800	495	268							1,563	
Items per cat.	2	4	4								
H	0-20	21-40	41-60	61-80	81-100	101-150	151-200	201-300	301+	TOTAL	% returns
Gross Sales	$322	$15,798	$8,643	$2,200			$1,905	$4,375		$33,243	
Net Sales	$322	$13,904	$8,367	$2,153			$1,773	$4,055		$30,574	8.7%
Sales Index	9	377	73	39			14	32			
Margin Index	4	407	102	38			11	30			
# of Items sold	71	612	256	43			13	23		1,018	
Items per cat.	1	1	1	1			1	1			
I	0-20	21-40	41-60	61-80	81-100	101-150	151-200	201-300	301+	TOTAL	% returns
Gross Sales	$1,184	$71,839	$5,250		$6,012			$71,763	$3,345	$159,393	
Net Sales	$1,184	$61,832	$5,090		$3,013			$69,553	$2,970	$143,642	11.0%
Sales Index	7	125	43		62			82	7		
Margin Index	3	157	44		98			106	8		
# of Items sold	204	3909	159		79			350	10	4,711	
Items per cat.	3	4	1		1			5	1		
J	0-20	21-40	41-60	61-80	81-100	101-150	151-200	201-300	301+	TOTAL	% returns
Gross Sales	$12,508	$3,656	$15,445				$15,327		$64,847	$111,783	
Net Sales	$12,345	$3,430	$11,923				$14,557		$60,527	$102,782	8.8%
Sales Index	100	40	208				52		49		
Margin Index	119	-14	144				24		38		
# of Items sold	1235	105	393				393		96	2,222	
Items per cat.	2	2	2				3		4		
K	0-20	21-40	41-60	61-80	81-100	101-150	151-200	201-300	301+	TOTAL	% returns
Gross Sales	$26,197	$4,436	$3,375	$14,480	$33,415					$81,903	
Net Sales	$20,731	$4,279	$2,454	$13,735	$30,003					$71,202	15.0%
Sales Index	72	79	158	136	677						
Margin Index	63	125	242	275	920						
# of Items sold	1773	183	42	199	336					2,533	
Items per cat.	8	3	2	10	1						
ALL	0-20	21-40	41-60	61-80	81-100	101-150	151-200	201-300	301+	TOTAL	% returns
Gross Sales	$602,526	$468,249	$281,106	$36,807	$206,545	$1,984	$114,314	$275,524	$141,777	$2,128,832	
Net Sales	$562,344	$441,922	$262,353	$25,902	$190,626	$1,634	$110,532	$259,959	$93,467	$1,948,739	9.2%
Sales Index	101	112	98	44	91	4	27	29	18		
Margin Index	117	129	101	83	131	4	29	32	9		
# of Items sold	53,128	21,955	7,814	414	2,870	20	1,260	1,542	209	89,212	
Items per cat.	91	76	53	15	17	1	8	17	8		

Circulation

Based on Chapter 12 (*Customer Acquisition and Leveraging*) you have planned and implemented a circulation plan to a variety of lists and their segments. Now is the time to determine which lists provide the highest return.

Exhibit 14.12 Basic List Segment Analysis Form

(showing unknown allocation)

Drop Code	List Segment Description	Selects	Raw Data						Adjusted for Unknowns				
			Pre-Merge Quantity	Mailed Quantity	Orders	Demand	Response Rate	Average Order	Orders	Demand	Response Rate	Average Order	$/Catalog
	Unknowns												
Totals													

Known	
Factors	

For individual list segments, this form shows the raw data and adjusted (for unknowns) data that enables the calculation of *Response Rates*, *Average Orders* and *Dollars/Catalog*.

Exhibit 14.13 Basic List Segment Analysis Example

(showing unknown allocation)

Drop A				Raw Data						Adjusted for Unknowns			
Code	List Segment Description	Selects	Pre-Merge Quantity	Mailed Quantity	Orders	Demand	Response Rate	Average Order		Orders	Demand	Response Rate	Average Order	$/Catalog
100	Catalog Multi-Buyers	0 to 36 months	7000	7000	350	$70,000	5.00%	$200		387	$77,906	5.52%	$202	$11.13
101	Catalog Single Buyers	0 to 18 months	20000	19700	788	$137,900	4.00%	$175		870	$153,475	4.42%	$176	$7.79
102	Internet Buyers	0 to 12 months	5000	4800	192	$26,880	4.00%	$140		212	$29,916	4.42%	$141	$6.23
103	Requesters	0 to 12 months	3000	2700	68	$10,125	2.50%	$150		75	$11,269	2.76%	$151	$4.17
104	Gift Recipients	0 to 12 months	3000	2500	38	$4,688	1.50%	$125		41	$5,217	1.66%	$126	$2.09
200	Rental A	0 to 6 Mo., $100+	20000	18000	225	$28,125	1.25%	$125		249	$31,301	1.38%	$126	$1.74
201	Rental B	0 to 6 Mo., $100+	20000	18000	225	$28,125	1.25%	$125		249	$31,301	1.38%	$126	$1.74
202	Rental C	0 to 6 Mo., $100+	20000	18000	144	$12,960	0.80%	$90		159	$14,424	0.88%	$91	$0.80
203	Rental D	0 to 6 Mo., $100+	20000	18000	360	$46,800	2.00%	$130		398	$52,086	2.21%	$131	$2.89
204	Rental D2	7 to 12 Mo., $100+	10000	9000	153	$15,300	1.70%	$100		169	$17,028	1.88%	$101	$1.89
300	Model A	Insert Type of Models	25000	21250	638	$86,063	3.00%	$135		704	$95,783	3.31%	$136	$4.51
301	Model B	Insert Type of Models	25000	21250	425	$53,125	2.00%	$125		469	$59,125	2.21%	$126	$2.78
302	Model C	Insert Type of Models	25000	21250	319	$39,844	1.50%	$125		352	$44,344	1.66%	$126	$2.09
303	Model D	Insert Type of Models	25000	21250	213	$21,250	1.00%	$100		235	$23,650	1.10%	$101	$1.11
304	Model E	Insert Type of Models	25000	21250	213	$29,750	1.00%	$140		235	$33,110	1.10%	$141	$1.56
999	Unknowns				455	$69,000								
Totals			253000	223950	4,803	$679,934		$142		4,803	$679,934	2.14%	$142	$3.04

	Known	4,348	610,934
	Factors	1.105	1.11

Exhibit 14.13 shows the allocation of unknowns (orders that cannot be tracked to a specific order) to the list segments. The method of allocation used is to distribute the unknowns in the same ratio as the known orders and dollars. This may be changed in the event a match-back is used.

If the house file data has been loaded in the order entry computer, the unknowns may be allocated to only the outside list segments.

If there are more unknowns than desired, this can indicate that the call center is not sufficiently collecting codes or that the coding methods used are flawed.

Exhibit 14.14 Basic List Segment Analysis Explanation

⇨ *Raw Data*

- Code—The numbers and/or letters that are assigned to each list and list segment.

- List Segment Description—Specifics as to the subsegment, e.g., multi-buyers.

- Selects—The selects within the segments, e.g., 0–6 month multi-buyers.

- Pre-Merge Quantity—The number of names rented prior to being de-duped.

- Mailed Quantity—The actual quantity that is mailed after de-duping, address cleaning, and any correction and/or elimination needs.

- Orders—The number of gross orders generated per this segment and its select.

- Demand—The number of gross dollars generated per this segment and its select.

- Response Rate—The percentage response generated per this segment and its select.

- Average Order—The average dollar per order generated per this segment and its select.

⇨ *Adjusted for Unknowns*

- Orders—The number of gross orders generated per this segment and its select.

- **Demand**—The number of gross dollars generated per this segment and its select.

- **Response Rate**—The percentage response generated per this segment and its select.

- **Average Order**—The average dollar per order generated per this segment and its select.

- **Dollars/Catalog**—The number of dollars per catalog mailed generated per this segment and its select.

Basic list segment analysis allows for determining how well a list or list segment has performed. The form also allows for the allocation of unknowns. The type of allocation shown is allocation in the same ratio as known orders. This will not change the relative ranking but will allow for a higher accuracy of *Response Rate*, *Average Order* and *Dollars/Catalog*.

Exhibit 14.15 List Segment Analysis with Costs and Marketing Margin Form

Code	List Segment Description	Selects	Pre-Merge Quantity	Mailed Quantity	Adjusted for Unknowns					Gross Merch. Margin	Cost of List Segment	CIM incl. List Cost	Marketing Margin
					Orders	Demand	Response Rate	Average Order	$/Catalog				
	Unknowns												
TOTALS													

List segment analysis shows the results in terms of dollars generated for each list or list segment. It provides ratings through the marketing contribution (gross margin less cost in-the-mail for each list or segment).

Exhibit 14.16 List Segment Analysis with Costs and Marketing Margin Explanation

- Code—The numbers and/or letters that are assigned to each list and list segment.
- List Segment Description—Specifics as to the subsegment, e.g., multi-buyers.
- Selects—The selects within the segments, e.g., 0–6 month multi-buyers.
- Pre-Merge Quantity—The number of names rented prior to being de-duped.
- Mailed Quantity—The actual quantity that is mailed after de-duping, address cleaning, and any correction and/or elimination needs.
- Orders—The number of gross orders generated per this segment and its select.
- Demand—The number of gross dollars generated per this segment and its select.
- Response Rate—The percentage response generated per this segment and its select.
- Average Order—The average dollar per order generated per this segment and its select.
- Dollars/Catalog—The dollars per catalog mailed generated per this segment and its select.
- Gross Merchandise Margin—After deducting cost of goods, The number of dollars netted per this segment and its select.
- Cost of List Segment—The list cost; this cost is based on the pre-merge quantity.
- CIM (Cost-in-the-Mail) including List Cost—Cost of this quantity of catalogs, at this list price.
- Marketing Margin—The number of dollars were generated for this segment and its select after deducting CIM.

Exhibit 14.17 List Segment Analysis with Costs and Marketing Margin Example

Code	List Segment Description	Selects	Pre-Merge Quantity	Mailed Quantity	Orders	Demand	Response Rate	Average Order	$/Catalog	Gross Merch. Margin	Cost of List Segment	CIM incl. List Cost	Marketing Margin
								Adjusted for Unknowns					
100	Catalog Multi-Buyers	0 to 36 months	7000	7000	387	$77,906	5.52%	$202	$11.13	$44,796	210	$6,160	$38,636
101	Catalog Single Buyers	0 to 18 months	20000	19700	870	$153,475	4.42%	$176	$7.79	$88,248	600	$17,600	$70,648
102	Internet Buyers	0 to 12 months	5000	4800	212	$29,916	4.42%	$141	$6.23	$17,202	150	$4,400	$12,802
103	Requesters	0 to 12 months	3000	2700	75	$11,269	2.76%	$151	$4.17	$6,479	90	$2,640	$3,839
104	Gift Recipients	0 to 12 months	3000	2500	41	$5,217	1.66%	$126	$2.09	$3,000	90	$2,640	$360
200	Rental A	0 to 6 Mo., $100+	20000	18000	249	$31,301	1.38%	$126	$1.74	$17,998	2500	$19,500	($1,502)
201	Rental B	0 to 6 Mo., $100+	20000	18000	249	$31,301	1.38%	$126	$1.74	$17,998	2500	$19,500	($1,502)
202	Rental C	0 to 6 Mo., $100+	20000	18000	159	$14,424	0.88%	$91	$0.80	$8,294	2500	$19,500	($11,206)
203	Rental D	0 to 6 Mo., $100+	20000	18000	398	$52,086	2.21%	$131	$2.89	$29,949	2500	$19,500	$10,449
204	Rental D2	7 to 12 Mo., $100+	10000	9000	169	$17,028	1.88%	$101	$1.89	$9,791	950	$9,450	$341
300	Model A	Insert Type of Models	25000	21250	704	$95,783	3.31%	$136	$4.51	$55,075	1625	$22,875	$32,200
301	Model B	Insert Type of Models	25000	21250	469	$59,125	2.21%	$126	$2.78	$33,997	1625	$22,875	$11,122
302	Model C	Insert Type of Models	25000	21250	352	$44,344	1.66%	$126	$2.09	$25,498	1625	$22,875	$2,623
303	Model D	Insert Type of Models	25000	21250	235	$23,650	1.10%	$101	$1.11	$13,599	1625	$22,875	($9,276)
304	Model E	Insert Type of Models	25000	21250	235	$33,110	1.10%	$141	$1.56	$19,038	1625	$22,875	($3,837)
999	Unknowns							$141	$1.56	$0			
TOTALS			253000	223950	4,803	$679,934	1.10%					$229,105	$155,697

In this example, the unknowns have already been allocated and only the adjusted data is shown. The cost to cover running charges for the list file is $0.03 per name, $0.125 per name for the rental lists except for the 7–12 month segment, which costs $0.095 per name. The running charges for the model are $0.065 per name. The CIM (Cost-in-the-mail), minus the list costs, is $0.85 per piece.

Seasonality

Seasonality analysis is dependent on the circulation plan for the catalog. A catalog that mails monthly would have a different analysis than a catalog that mails once a season.

Seasonality applies to both merchandise and overall catalog performance. An example is Christmas merchandise: sales in November would be much higher than in May.

For catalogs mailing only seasonally, the method is straightforward. Simply compare the dollars per catalog mailed for overall seasonality. For merchandise analysis, use the marketing contribution as a measure of the effect of seasonality.

For merchandise, be sure to normalize so as to avoid results due to circulation differences. Significant mailing segments should be examined separately.

At the other extreme are catalogs that mail monthly. Depending on the accuracy desired, and the actual mailing cycles, a three-month average is used. For "best month," use the monthly Dollars/Catalog but adjusted for actual mailing dates and "spillover" from one month to the next. Again, mailing segments should be examined separately.

Lifetime Value (LTV)

This analysis gives a comparative dollar value over time for list segments or type of segments. Lifetime value can be used to determine the value of multi-buyers versus single buyers, values of types of lists or models, various segmentations (such as value of customer in versus out of a trading area), and, and the value of names from different sources (such as lists versus space advertisements versus Internet-generated).

There are two basic types of LTV:

1. Based on sales with an average number for net profit.

2. Based on net profit per segment.

The first type has the advantage of being relatively simple but is not quite as accurate as the second method. The examples shown here are for the simpler method.

Exhibit 14.18 LTV Form

	Time Period in Months				
	0-6	7-12	13-18	19-24	25-30
	Original Customers				
Revenue:					
Customers					
Original Customer Retention Rate					
Orders					
Spending Rate (Avg. Ord. for period)					
Dollars					

	Spending	Gross Margin	Net Profit
# of singles			
# of multis			
Singles spent overall			
Multis spent overall			
Multis spent after 1st order			
Per single			
Per multi			

Exhibit 14.19 LTV Explanation

⇨ Customers—Number of customers within a particular time frame (time frame shown in examples is in months).

⇨ Original customer retention rate—The percentage of customers that ordered again in the time period indicated.

⇨ Orders—The number of orders from the retained customers in the time period indicated.

⇨ Spending rate—The average amount the retained customer spent.

⇨ Dollars—The amount of dollars from the retained customers in the time period indicated.

⇨ Number of singles—The number who purchased one time in the time period indicated.

⇨ Number of multis—The number who purchased multiple times in the time period indicated.

⇨ Singles spent overall—The amount of money the one timeone-time buyers spend in the time period indicated.

⇨ Multis spent overall—The amount of money the multiple buyers spend in the time period indicated.

⇨ Multis spent after first order—The amount multiple buyers spent after their initial order.

Exhibit 14.20 LTV Example

	Time Period in Months				
	0-6 Original Customers	7-12	13-18	19-24	25-30
Revenue:					
Customers	4,925	815	563	437	374
Original Customer Retention Rate		17%	69%	78%	86%
Orders	5,621	1,057	696	546	514
Spending Rate (Avg. Ord. for period)	$66	$38	$74	$73	$70
Dollars	$373,440	$39,993	$51,182	$39,685	$35,932

	Spending	Gross Margin	Net Profit
# of singles	3,548		
# of multis	1,377		
Singles spent overall	$234,168	$152,209	$23,417
Multis spent overall	$306,065	$198,942	$30,606
Multis spent after 1st order	$213,269		
Per single	$66	$43	$6.60
Per multi	$222	$144	$22.23

The example shown calculates the long-term value of single buyers versus multi-buyers. It could just as easily be used to compare apparel lists versus gift lists or other types of individual sets of lists.

The example is based on a 65 percent margin and an average profit of 10 percent. It is no surprise the multi-buyers are much more profitable than single buyers. This would indicate an increased budget for conversion of single buyers to multi-buyers.

For each group being analyzed, using actual margins and nets could increase the accuracy.

Offer Testing

Offer Testing is simply comparing the results of two or more offers and their associated costs. If the offer is contingent on a dollar amount for the order (e.g., free gift with purchase of $25 or more), be sure to include in the cost all customers who are already at the level needed. In order to assure true randomness, an A/B split of the segments to be mailed is necessary. In addition, in order to maintain statistical validity, attention must be given to sample sizes, response rates, and desired degree of confidence.

Exhibit 14.21 Offer Testing Form

Offer Description: _____

	Test		Control
Circulation (A/B split)			
Response Rate			
Average Order			
$/Catalog			
Demand			
Gross Margin @			
Cost in Mail @			
Cost of Offer			
Customers Already at the Level			
Estimate of New Customers at the Level			
Total Costs			
Estimated Marketing Margin			

Exhibit 14.22 Offer Testing Example

Offer Description: _____
Free S&H with Orders Over $75

	Test	Control
Ciculation (A/B split)	35,000	35,000
Response Rate	2.00%	1.50%
Average Order	$65	$55
Demand	$45,500	$28,875
$/Catalog	1.3	0.825
Gross Margin @ 60%	$27,300	$17,325
Cost in Mail @ $0.40	$14,000	$14,000
Cost of Offer	2.00	
Customers Already at the Level	2000	2000
Estimate of New Customers at the Level	2000	N/A
Costs of Offer	$8,000	
Total Costs	$22,000	$14,000
Estimated Marketing Margin	$5,300	$3,325

In Exhibit 14.22, the test outperformed the control, suggesting that the test should become the control against which further tests will be measured.

Web Site

While most agree that the goal is integration of systems, you still need to assess different selling methods individually. There are a host of companies and software programs that offer web site analysis. Before determining what is right for your company's needs, you should sit back and understand what it is that will give the most useful information. By far, the three most important areas are traffic, quantity and quality. But be aware of other key measurements and opportunities and incorporate them when you can.

Benchmarks in this area of marketing are changing every day; stay abreast of what you should expect from your web site through industry publications and events.

Exhibit 14.23 Web Site Analysis Checklist

- ☐ How many people visited the site is not as important as it used to be, but still can be an indicator if there are many visits and few conversions.

- ☐ How many people actually purchased and how much did they spend? Just like in printed direct marketing, the key to success is the ratio of purchases to contacts, often called browse-to-buy ratio.

- ☐ Browse-to-buy ratio of individual products—Unlike printed catalogs, here you can quickly replace a frequently viewed, but slow moving product.

- ☐ Where did they come from? Also like printed direct marketing, you need to understand the sales per the source of the buyers so you can tap into it increasingly, e.g., did they spend more when they came from one of your affiliate relationships?

- ☐ When did they buy—What day or time of day is best? Once you know this, you can increase your communications at the key times.

- ☐ What path did they take to purchase (most often called path to purchase report)?
    - ___ How did they get to the point of purchase and how can you leverage or improve on this process?
    - ___ Did your editorial or some other non-sales content influence the sale?

☐ Using the *Daily*, *Weekly*, and *Monthly Sales Report* forms and info in Chapter 13, you can create a version separately for web sales or divide the sales in the report by the avenue in which they originated.

___ In addition, you will want reports that provide sales on individual products, product categories and price ranges, including sales per square inch on the home page.

___ Further, roll-up Source to different levels of aggregation. Examples: MSN Holiday Promo (most detailed), then to MSN (one level up), then Portal Deals (next level up), then All Web Paid Advertising (another level up) then Web Sales (the top level).

☐ What percentage gets to the shopping cart and then abandons it? The abandoned cart ratio alerts you how often potential buyers stop at the point of purchase and allows you to take action that saves the sale. Note that Rimm-Kaufman has concluded that some consumers load the cart just to determine the shipping and tax cost; if you provide the shipping and tax costs up front, the abandon rate has more meaning.

☐ What techniques and offers are working best?

___ Is your cross-sell and up-sell creating add-on sales? In what ratio of click-through versus conversion? This is an excellent area for split tests where some users receive an offer and others do not.

___ Use a hyperlink with a source code to track e-mail campaigns as well as the user so that pass-alongs can be tracked for opens, click thru, sales, and delayed sales.

☐ Search function—How often does your search function find the product? How often does it convert into a sale?

Other Forms of Analysis

Many of the analyses listed in this section have been the subject of speeches at the Direct Marketing Association's events, articles in direct marketing academic journals, as well as books on data and its uses in direct marketing.

In all testing, certain test design principles can be used to minimize quantity requirements and/or test multiple effects and/or interrelation effects for the same sample size.

Although well beyond the scope of this chapter, the requisite information can be found in *System of Experimental Design* by Genichi Taguchi.

RFM

The acronym RFM stands for Recency, Frequency, and Monetary. It tells you how recent the last purchase was, how frequently the customers purchase, and is the dollar amount of the purchases.

The RFM segmentation allows the cataloger to decide how often and how many to mail in certain segments as well as when to stop mailing other segments. The segmentation of RFM is arrived at by providing weighting factors for each of the elements within RFM. Although RFM rates can be obtained as a first approximation by inspection, these factors are most often determined by regression. Generally, recency is accepted as the controlling factor for RFM analysis. In recent years, and with the appropriate budget, some catalogers have changed to a regression or individual scoring system, as this seems to provide better results than RFM.

CHAID

CHI Square Automatic Interaction Detector (CHAID) is a segmentation technique used to determine the significant variables needed to differentiate a group of customers. It does this by building a tree diagram. In each level from the top down, the diagram shows the breakout of homogeneous members of the group contained in the level above. It is often used to determine significant variables for a regression analysis.

Regression and Scoring

If the significant variables from a CHAID analysis (or other method of determining significant variables) are used in a regression analysis, the output will be segmentation that will give more accurate information on which segments (names) to mail. Generally the data consists of a score for each segment equivalent to an expected response rate and a ranking that allows decisions of how deeply to mail. This usually results in the increase of overall response rate, average order and dollars/catalog, while cutting the quantity mailed, thus reducing costs.

Regression analysis is, for smaller catalogs, generally performed externally to minimize costs and hardware/software investment.

There are some situations where regression or RFM models do not work. Although few, they occur when the products sold are largely a commodity and the customer base is homogenous.

Marketing/Merchandising to the Highest Value House File Segments

This type of analysis is, to some extent, an extension of the 80/20 rule that says 80 percent of the sales/profit is due to 20 percent of the house file.

The logic here is that the best segments have higher average orders and buy higher margin merchandise. If more goods of the type purchased by these top scoring segments are included in the merchandise mix, and some of the worst products and/or segments are dropped, the average order and gross margin increase.

Prospect Analysis

Although, more difficult to perform than house file analysis, prospect analysis has become mainstream. Through the use of co-op databases and their associated models, many names expected to perform poorly can be eliminated, thus leading to better response rates and average orders.

The models are based on matching the characteristics and purchasing behavior of names in the buyer file to the much larger set of names provided by the co-op members. The best matches are then segmented (mainly to quintiles or deciles) and mailed. The top segments usually perform as well as or better than the top individual list rental names.

Glossary

A/B tests: Allow the cataloger to test two different versions of an ad in the same issue of the same magazine in order to determine which version generates the highest initial response and the most profitable long-term buyer

Actives: Respondents on a particular list who have taken action in response to a solicitation

Advertising allowance: A percentage off the base price of wholesale merchandise

Affiliates: Most often part of another company's Internet site; they can provide an implied endorsement and, often, access to a new market

Alliances: A close association of two or more companies to advance common interests or causes

Alternate customer acquisition: Methods of obtaining customers other than by renting lists

AOV: Acronym for average order value

B2B: Acronym for business-to-business

B2C: Acronym for business-to-consumer

Back end: Term for the operations/service part of cataloging

Back orders: Products not currently available, usually due to an out-of-stock position

Back-ups: Allowing catalogers to place a small initial order with a guarantee that two to three times that number will be available to the catalog if it is needed

BC: Acronym for back cover

Binding: The fastening of a catalog. Perfect-bound is generally used only for thick catalogs or books; the bindery trims and glues the catalog together to form a stiff backbone. Saddle-stitched is when the bindery gathers the sheets and staples them at the spine

BOM: Acronym for beginning of month inventory

Business plan: A written strategy that details how a company intends reach certain sales goals; sometimes confused with a Financial Plan, which tends to outline only economic goals

Business review: A determination of the accuracy and feasibility of financial and strategic statements made regarding a company; can lead to recommendations for improvement in said company

Buyer: The individual responsible for sourcing, developing, negotiating, and reordering merchandise; can work in conjunction with Merchandiser and Rebuyer

Call-outs: Copy information, usually one or two lines, that is inserted in or connected to a picture; the intent is to call attention to a particular attribute of the product in the photo

CHAID: An acronym for CHI Square Automatic Interaction Detector, a segmentation technique used to determine the significant variables needed to differentiate a group of customers

CIM: Acronym for cost in the mail

Circulation: The number of recipients the catalog goes to

Circulation plan: Details every mailing per year by lists used, quantities, and expected returns

CMYK: Acronym for cyan, magenta, yellow, black; the subtractive primary colors used in printing

Contact strategy: Determination of the number of times and the message content received by a customer from a company; can also apply to frequency of contact and message to prospects

Conversion: When a prospect becomes a buyer

Cookie: A small file placed by a web server on a visitor's computer that can contain just about anything; generally, cookies contain a long random tracking string, used so the server can recognize the same visitor across a session and across visits

CPA: Acronym for cost per action

CPC: Acronym for cost per click

CPM: Acronym for cost per thousand impressions

CPO: Acronym for cost per order

CREF: Acronym for computer ready electronic file

Cross-sell: Suggesting merchandise that goes with or complements the product of original interest, e.g., a belt with slacks

CSR: Acronym for customer service representative

CTP: Acronym for computer-to-plate; going from computer to plate eliminates the need for film

DAM: Acronym for digital asset management; putting digital content in an electronic file cabinet so that content can easily be repurposed

Database: Structured collection of information held in a computer

DCM: Acronym for digital content management; another phrase for digital asset management

Decoys: Uniquely identifiable names that are inserted into list-rental names to alert catalogers to the arrival of mailings; also help prevent list renters from unauthorized list usage

Demand: The number of orders received for products individually or overall

Density: The number of items or photos that appear on a spread or a page in a catalog

Direct to plate digital: The process in which a data file is sent electronically to the printer and turned into plates without the film separation stage

Distribution center: The process of getting an ordered product to the customer via picking, packing and shipping; also called Fulfillment and the Back End

Dot whack: A sticker, usually round, affixed to a catalog cover or printed directly on the cover, which highlights a special offer or message

Drop date: The date that the catalog actually goes in the mail or is desired to go in the mail

Duplicate: Two or more name and address records that are found to be equal under the list user's method of comparison; also referred to as a dupe

EAI: Acronym for Enterprise Application Integration

Extranet: An extension of a company's private Internet network that allows secure sharing of an organization's information or operations with their suppliers, vendors, customers, or other organizations

Eye-flow: The process by which the layout directs the eye across the entire layout, often in a "U" formation

FC: Acronym for front cover

Feasibility study: A determination, based on research of relevant factors such as competition and financial ability, of the viability of a plan

Financial plan: A written plan that concentrates on financial operations, overall sales goals and how they will be achieved; sometimes confused with a Business Plan

FOB: Acronym for freight on board and free on board; the cost to get the product or catalog from one point to another

Folio count: The number of pages

Folio: The page number

Font: The name of a group of letters, numbers, and sizes of type

Front end: The strategy, marketing, merchandising, creative and production part of the catalog process

FSI: Acronym for free standing insert, the advertising flyers inserted in newspapers

Fulfillment: The process of getting an ordered product to the customer via picking, packing and shipping; also called the Distribution Center and the Back End

Hero spreads: Where one product is the main focus on the spread

Hi res: Short for high resolution; high number of dots per inch, making material suitable for reproduction

Hybrid: In catalog marketing, usually refers to a cataloger that serves both B2B and B2C

IBC: Acronym for inside back cover

IFC: Acronym for inside front cover

Inactives: Non-respondents on a particular list who have not reacted to a solicitation

In-home date: The date that the catalog is actually received by the business or consumer; the window of time depends on the quantity being mailed, the volume of mail at the post office and uncontrollable effects, such as weather

Ink- jetting: Computer-controlled printing process that applies ink through small orifices to form characters; often used for personalization

In-mail: The dates that a catalog goes from the post office into the mail stream

Insets: The smaller size photos that show a particular attribute or section of the product; used in conjunction with a larger photo showing the entire product

Intranet: A private communications network contained within an organization. The main functions of an Intranet is to allow the sharing of information and computing resources among an organization's employees and to facilitate group work and teleconferencing

IT: Acronym for information technology; the development, setting up and execution of computer systems and their applications

Joint venture: A partnership or conglomerate often formed to share risk or expertise

Key codes: The codes, usually alpha, that tie the copy block to the photo

Lay-down: A photo of an item that is laid down on a simple, usually white, background

Lifetime value: More commonly called LTV, the calculation that tells the true value of a customer over time

List broker: The person who makes list recommendations and coordinates the necessary details between the list owner/manager and the list renter

List card: The printed data or electronic document containing all information about a list

List exchange: An agreement between two list owners to exchange portions of the lists without a rental fee

List maintenance: The updating of names and addresses in a house list

List manager: The person responsible for encouraging others to rent the lists under their management

Mailing date: The date that the catalog goes in the mail, most often over a small time period, such as 2 to 3 days

Margin: The difference between the cost of a product and its selling price

Merchandiser: The individual responsible for developing the overall strategy for products and their pricing

Merge/Purge: the de-duplication of names on the lists in order to avoid duplicate catalogs going to one person

MIF: Acronym for merchandise information form

MIS: Acronym for management information systems

MTD: Acronym for month to date, a comparison measure

Offer testing: Comparing the results of two or more offers and their associated costs

Package inserts: Advertising flyers or extra copies of catalogs that are inserted into outgoing catalog packages

Pagination: Determination of what products go on what pages, at what price points, groupings and potential locations on the page

Positioning: How the company represents itself to its market

Price points: A range of prices, usually in increments of 10

Product density: The concentration of products on a page or a spread

PU: Acronym for pick up—photos and/or products that are being picked-up from one issue to another

Pull marketing: Techniques that make the customer come to you

Push marketing: Pushing the customer to take action on an offer that was sent to them

Reactivation: Getting a customer who has ceased to purchase to buy again

Rebuyer: Works with buyers to coordinate and traffic the paperwork associated with product reorder

Re-mail: Sending virtually the same catalog to the same group of names more than one time

Re-shoots: A photo that is taken again after the first version was unacceptable or inaccurate

Returns: Merchandise that is sent back to the catalog; the response to a catalog mailing

Rev-share: Short for revenue sharing

RFM: Acronym for recency, frequency, monetary—the most common attributes used to score the value of a customer

RFP: Acronym for request for proposal

RFQ: Acronym for request for quote

RGB: Acronym for red, green, blue, the primary colors in reproduction

ROI: Acronym for return on investment

SEO: Acronym for Search Engine Optimization

Search engine: A software program that searches a database and gathers and reports information that contains or is related to the words for which the program has been told to look

Search engine spiders: A software program that electronically looks through documents for previously specified words called keywords; then provides of list of relevant places where that keyword(s) is found

Seasonality: Effect of time of year on sales

Separations: The process in which digital art is separated into separate films representing the colors being used; the films are then used to create plates that allow the press to print the catalog content

Shadow demand: The number of items that would have been purchased if there was sufficient inventory and/or other problems had not prevented the desired order from actually being placed

Signature: A folded, printed sheet that automatically comes off the press

Silo: Short for silhouette, this is a photo that has no background

Size splits: The breakout of the sale of different sizes

SKU: Stock-keeping unit, the number that is assigned to individual products for reference

Spread record sheet: A log that indicates exactly what products go on what spreads in a catalog; also states details like cost, retail, how item should be shown in the catalog

Square inch analysis: A form of analysis that tell the cataloger how effectively the catalog space was utilized

Style guide: A uniform, written guide for all elements of copy and layout

Tag line: The descriptive line, usually under the logo on the cover, which succinctly explains the catalog's positioning

Trim size: The exact size of a catalog after it is printed and trimmed

Universe: The total number of names on a list

Up-sell: The technique by which a customer service representative encourages a customer to buy a product in addition to the one that they are in the process of purchasing

UPS: Acronym for United Parcel Service

USPS: Acronym for United States Post Office

Viral marketing: Marketing that makes it easy and even promotes the passing along of a marketing message

XML: Acronym for extensible markup language, a verbose and precise data exchange readable by computers and humans

YTD: Acronym for year to date; a comparison measure

Index

A

A/B tests   293
Affiliates   24–29, 289   *See also* Alliances and Joint ventures
Alliances   24–28, 289   *See also* Affiliate and Joint ventures
Amazon   26
Ambrosi   xix, 217, 224, 225–226, 226, 238, 240, 245
Analysis   *See* Data analysis
AOL   6
Apple   25
Application file   209
Artist   221–22
Automated text analysis software   57

B

Back end   12, 15, 22, 24   *See also* Cataloging process and Front end
Back orders   335–336
Banta Corporation   260–1
Bean, Leon Leonwood   5, 19, 39
Benchmarking   54, 56
Betty Crocker Enterprises   157
Bindery   268–69
Boorstin, Daniel J.   290
Bounceback questionnaires   58
Brainstorming   12, 13, 156–69
Brand statement   213–15
Business growth, controlling   25
Business plan   12, 20, 27, 83, 100, 114, 117
Business review   103–07
Business-to-business catalogs   7–9, 40
Business-to-consumer catalogs   7–10
Buyer, compared to merchandiser   184–87

C

Casro.org   70
Catalog   5–22
  defined   7
  key needs of   17–22
  organizing   138–55
  scheduling   83–107
Catalog, types of
  business-to-business   7–9
  business-to-consumer   8–11
  electronic   6
  library   6
  printed   5–6
Catalog Age   205, 266
Catalog launch   108–37
  action plan   109–13
  financial plan   114–117, 126–37
  launch preparation   108–114
  sales plan   120–25
  start-up checklist   119–20
Catalog staff   138–55
Cataloging process   12–16, 22–24
  back end   15–16, 24
  front end   12–15, 23
CHAID   372
Circulation   277, 359–65
  list segment analysis and   359–71
Circulation plan   277–86
Code tracking   319
Competitors   31–52
  determining   30–33
  researching   34–52
Consumer catalogs   8–10
  types of   10
Contact strategy   98, 99, 102, 109, 11, 116, 117, 307–11
Co-op databases   277

Copywriting   219–20
Country Curtains   20
Cover weight   266
Creative agencies   *See* Outside agencies
Creative process   205–73
   accuracy checklists   223–26
   copywriting   219–20
   layout   221–24
   photography   235–47
   process overview   205–10
   request for proposal   248–59
   style guide   227–34
Creative strategy   210–214
Customer profile   212–13
Customers, acquiring   274–306
   circulation plan   277–86
   list rental   275–77
   media planning   293–306
   public relations   290–93
   pull marketing   287–90
Customers, leveraging   307–19
   code tracking   319
   contact strategy   307–11
   e-mail marketing   313–149
   house list   307, 312
   loyalty programs   314–17
   offers   311
   package inserts   318
   reactivation   311
Customer service, importance of   20
Customer service policies   331–35
Customer service representatives   333–35

D

Data analysis   21, 346–73
Data capture   346–49
Delphi   6
Demand   280
Delivery costs   341–42

Digital asset management (DAM)   209, 259–64
Digital content management (DCM)   *See* Digital asset management
Digital photography   241–42
Direct Marketing Association (DMA)   337, 371

E

EDGAR   32, 33
Electronic catalogs   6, 7
E-mail marketing   313–14
Endorsements   290
Estee Marketing Group, Inc.   285, 286
Extranet sites   287

F

Feasibility study   83–103, 108
Federal Trade Commission (FTC)   336–37
Flat photography   233
Focus groups   53 54, 66, 73–82, 108, 113, 117
Franklin, Benjamin   5
Front end   12–15, 23   *See also* Cataloging process and Back end

G

Gift certificates   344–45
Gift-wrap   344–45
Gore, Al   6
Gravure   264
Greenfield Online   66
Grid, of competitiors   34–53
Group shot   234

H

Hand-off meeting   217–18
Hewlett-Packard   25

Hoovers   32
Horchow, Roger   5, 6
House file segments   373
House list   174, 307, 312, 378
Hovan, Bob   266

I

In-depth photography   233
Initial fill rate   335
Insets   223, 234
Internet catalogs   6
Internet Explorer   6
Internet marketing plan   298–306
Internet research   66–70
Internet shopping   6

J

Joint ventures   24–28   *See also* Affiliates and Alliances

L

Lay-down   234
Layout   221–24
Library catalogs   6
Lifestyle databases   277
Lifetime value (LTV)   365–67
List card   275–76
List exchange   378
List rental   275–77, 312, 318, 373, 376
List segments, analyzing   359–67
Location photography   246–48, 251
Loyalty programs   314–17

M

Mail surveys   57–66
Market research   12, 53–82
May, Robert L.   5
Media planning   293–306
Merchandise
  selecting   188–93
  square inch analysis and   346, 352–55
Merchandise criteria   181–83
Merchandise information form   194–97
Merchandiser, compared to buyer   184–86
Merchandising   174–204
  development   174
  distribution channel management   204
  organizational tools   201–03
  procurement   174
  product selection   174, 181–83, 189–94
  product strategy   174–80
  sourcing   174, 177
  vendor contracts   187–88
Morrissey, Dan   241

N

National Wildlife Federation   267
Neiman-Marcus Group   6

O

Offers, testing   318, 368–70
Offset printing   264
One-on-one depth interviews   53
Online research companies   54, 66–70
Operations   320–45
  back orders   335–36
  customer service policies   331–28
  delivery costs   341–43
  forecasting   321, 322–27
  gift-wrap   345
  mail order rule   336–37
  packaging   343
  response curves   327–34
  returns   337–40
  sales reports   329–30

Operations and Fulfillment 320
Outside agencies 249–59

P

Package inserts 344, 379
Packaging 343–44
Pagination 188–91, 199–200
Paper 266–68
Patagonia 7, 19, 31, 32
Percent done 327
Photographer 191, 201, 208, 233, 235–37, 239, 242, 243, 244, 245
Photography 233–47
    digital 241–42
    forms 248–51
    locations 242–44
    preparation 234–37
    releases 244–47
    re-shoots 239–40
    techniques 233–34
    terminology 234
Pick-ups 199
Planning sessions 156–69
Portable document format (PDF) 209
Positioning statement 167–73
Pre-press 259–64
Press release 292–93
Printer, consulting with 215–160
Printing, types of 264
Product forecasting 322–28
Production process 205–73
    bindery 268–69
    paper 266–68
    pre-press 59–63
    printing 264–69
    process overview 205–10
    request for proposal (RFP) 248–58
Product strategy 174–180
Public relations 290–93
Pull marketing 287–90

Push marketing 287

Q

Qualitative research 53
Quantitative research 53

R

Reactivation 311
Recycled paper 267
Request for proposal (RFP) 248–59
Request for quote (RFQ) *See* Request for proposal
Requirements, for catalog success 17–22
    customers 19
    financial backing 18
    mindset 20–21
    positioning 18
    product mix 19–20
    research 21–22
    resources 19
Research, competitive 30–52
    competitor determination 30–33
    competitive grid 34–52
Research, market 21–22, 54–84
    focus groups 53, 73–82
    research rules 54–56
Research forms 57, 59–65, 66–70
    Internet 66–70
    printed 57–65
    telephone surveys 70–72
Research goals 55
Research rules 54–56
Research questions 55
Response curves 327–28
Returns 337–40
RFM 372
Rimm-Kaufman, Alan 333
Rimm-Kaufman Group 297, 298, 302, 327

Road Runner Sports   20
R. R. Donnelley   263
Rudolph the Red-Nosed Reindeer   5
Rules, for mail order   336–38

S

Sales reports   329–30
Schedules   83–107
   business review   103–07
   feasibility study   83, 96–103
Scoring   372, 373
Sears, Richard   5
Seasonality analysis   365
Secondary data, in competitive analysis   30
Securities and Exchange Commission   32
Seta Corporation   25
Shadow demand   336, 380
Sharper Image   19
Sheet-fed printing   264, 267
Shipping charges   341
Shipping costs   341, 342
Signature   267
Silhouette   234
Single item   234
Spread record   204–05
Square inch analysis   346, 352–55
Statistical validity   56
Strategy, developing   156–173

Style guide   227–34
Surveyconsole.com   66, 68
Surveys   53, 57–72
   mail   57–66
   online   66–70
   telephone   53, 66, 70–72
System of Experimental Design   371

T

Taguchi, Genichi   371
Telephone surveys   53, 66, 70–72
Text weight   266
Thalheimer, Richard   19
Tie-ins   159, 163, 288, 289, 291

U

U.S. Postal Service   336

V

Vendor contracts   187–88
Vernon, Lillian   5–6
Viral marketing   288

W

Ward, Aaron Montgomery   5
Web design   269–73
Web offset printing   264
Web site analysis   370–71
Work action timeline   *See* Schedules

About the Author

Katie Muldoon has over 30 years of direct marketing experience, including associations with over 300 companies, many in the Fortune 50. Katie Muldoon founded the New York City-based agency, The Muldoon Agency in 1979. A decade later, the Muldoon Agency was sold to a joint venture of the then largest agencies on three continents: Dentsu (Asia), Young & Rubicam, (North American), and Havas (Europe). After completing her contract with the new venture, she and her husband, Jacob Baer, founded Muldoon & Baer.

Muldoon is a former Adjunct Assistant Professor at New York University Center for Direct Marketing and has taught the Direct Marketing Association's (DMA) Catalog Essentials Seminar for both consumer and B2B for almost two decades. She was a long-time columnist for *DM News* and now writes monthly for *Direct* magazine. Her third book, *How to Profit Through Catalog Marketing*, was published in October 1995 (German edition 1997). *The Catalog Strategist's Toolkit*, published by RACOM Communications and the Direct Marketing Association, is her fourth book.

She has served on the Executive Committee of the DMA's Board, is past Chair of the Ethics, ECHO and Image Committees, and currently is a member of the DMA's Hall of Fame Committee. She has also been a board member for New York City Victim Services and Rockland County's Shelter for Abused Women and Children's enterprise, The Company of Women, and Paragon Holdings, Inc.

Winner of many ECHO and Caples awards, Muldoon has also been awarded the 2004 Edward N. Mayer Educational Leadership Award, given by the Direct Marketing Education Foundation in recognition of extraordinary support of direct marketing education; the 1999 Direct Marketing Club of New York Silver Apple, which recognizes the direct marketing industry's most notable innovators and achievers who have served the New York direct marketing community for 25 years or more; and the WDRG's 1989 Woman of the Year Award (now WDMI). Katie Muldoon is a frequent guest speaker and industry judge, both nationally and internationally.

Making Marketing Matter
More Powerful Creative • More Accurate Measurement • Greater Productivity

The Old Marketing Model Is Broken. Here's How It Will Be Fixed
Coming to Concurrence
J. Walker Smith, Craig Wood, and Ann Clurman
6 x 9, 304 pp., h-c, $34.95

Finally! Branding Myths Exploded
Brand Babble: Sense and Nonsense about Branding
Don E. Schultz and Heidi F. Schultz
6 x 9, 160 pp., h-c, $25.95

The #1 Book on Creative Strategy!
Creative Strategy in Direct and Interactive Marketing, 3d ed.
Susan K. Jones
7 x 9, 440 pp., h-c, $49.95

All the Tools You'll Ever Need to Measure, Evaluate, and Manage Catalog Performance
The Catalog Strategist's Toolkit
Katie Muldoon
8-1/2 x 11, 220 pp., paper, $59.95, Plus Forms on CD

The Models for Measuring Business Performance Effectively
Data-Driven Business Models
Alan Weber
6 x 9, 304 pp., h-c, $49.95, Plus CD

The Keys to Making Marketing Matter Are Here
Accountable Marketing
Peter J. Rosenwald
6 x 9, 320 pp., h-c, $59.95, Plus CD of templates for measuring performance

The MasterWork by the Master Copywriter
On the Art of Writing Copy 3d ed.
Herschell Gordon Lewis
Everything you need to write more powerful, more profitable copy.
8-1/2 x 11, 388 pp., paper, $34.95

The Ideal Resource for Every Program Devoted to Integrated Marketing Communications
Readings & Cases in Integrated Marketing Communications
Susan K. Jones and Steven J. Kelly
6 x 9, 448 pp., paper, $49.95

Trade Show and Event Marketing
Ruth P. Stevens

" . . . practical and nuts-and-bolts approach to maximizing your trade show investment."—Seth Godin, Speaker, Author, *Purple Cow & Free Prize Inside*

6 x 9, 370 pp., h-c, $59.95

Business-to-Business Marketing Research
Martin P. Block and Tamara S. Block

" . . . the new bible for b-to-b market research."
—Gary L. Slack, Chairman & Chief Experience Officer, Slack Barshinger

6 x 9, 288 pp., h-c, CD, $59.95

The New Marketing Conversation
Donna Baier Stein and Alexandra MacAaron

" . . . the definitive primer on direct marketing."
—Denny Hatch, Author, *Million Dollar Mailings* and Contributing Editor to *Target Marketing Magazine*

6 x 9, 288 pp., h-c, $34.95

Allowable Cost Per Order
Peter J. Rosenwald

The essential planning tool for direct and database marketing and CRM

Software package on CD plus Manual (132 pp.), $595.00

Marketing Convergence
Susan K. Jones and Ted Spiegel

" . . . a great look at how companies will succeed with tomorrow's new consumer." —Tom Collinger, Northwestern University

6 x 9, 240 pp., h-c, $39.95

Contemporary Database Marketing
Martin Baier, Kurtis Ruf, and Goutam Chakraborty

"I can't think of a better way to learn the art and science of database marketing. You're taught by the masters. . . . " —Bob Stone

7 x 10, 320 pp., h-c, CD, $89.95

Sales & Marketing 365
James Obermayer

". . . loaded with nuggets of wisdom that can spell the difference betweeen success and failure in sales and marketing." —Dr. Tony Alessandra, Author, *Non-Manipulative Sellling* and *The Platinum Rule*

5-1/2 x 8-1/2, 160 pp., paper, $17.95, includes CD

Asinine Advertising: How stupid and unethical advertising cost you MONEY!
Herschell Gordon Lewis

"It's a must read." —Todd Simon, Senior Vice President, Omaha Steaks

6 x 9, 132 pp., paper, $22.95

Marketing Mayhem
Herschell Gordon Lewis

The answers to making marketing more productive.

6 x 9, 270 pp., h-c, $39.95

Public Relations: The Complete Guide
Joe Marconi

6 x 9, 400 pp., h-c, $59.95

" . . . the most comprehensive guide to PR ever written. . . . " —Thomas L. Harris, Former President, Golin/Harris International, Author, *The Marketer's Guide to Public Relations*

High Perfomance Interactive Marketing
Christopher Ryan

" . . . a marketing compendium for the New Economy."
—Don Schultz, President, Agora, Inc.

6 x 9, 272 pp., h-c, $39.95, includes CD

Racom Communications Book Order Form

Quantity	Author/Title	Price	Amount
_____	_____	_____	_____
_____	_____	_____	_____
_____	_____	_____	_____
_____	_____	_____	_____
_____	_____	_____	_____
_____	_____	_____	_____
_____	_____	_____	_____

Shipping is $7.00 for first copy; $1.00 for each additional copy. For more than 10 copies, call for precise costs.

Sub-Total _____

Shipping _____

TOTAL _____

Name _____

Title _____

Street Address _____

City_____ State _____ ZIP _____

Phone _____

Email _____

Credit Card ❑ Visa ❑ MasterCard ❑ Amex ❑ Discover

Number:_____ Exp. Date _____

Signature:_____

- On line: www.Racombooks.com
- Call 800-247-6553
- For quantity discounts call 847-424-2000

Racom Communications
1604 Chicago Ave., Suite 6, Evanston, IL 60201